Yadaan

Reteaching and Practice

Workbook

Grade 3

Scott Foresman·Addison Wesley

enVisionMATH®

Common Core

PEARSON

Glenview, Illinois • Boston Massachusetts • Chandler, Arizona • Upper Saddle River, New Jersey

ISBN-13: 978-0-328-69760-1

ISBN-10: 0-328-69760-5

7 8 9 10 V016 20 19 18 17 16 15 14 13

Reteaching and Practice Workbook

Contents

Name ___________________________

Reteaching
1-1

Representing Numbers

Here are different ways to show 2,365.

place-value blocks:

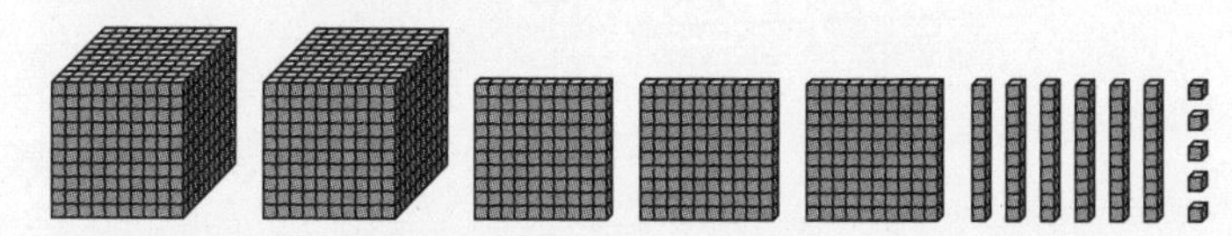

expanded form: 2,000 + 300 + 60 + 5

standard form: 2,365

word form: two thousand, three hundred sixty-five

Write each number in standard form.

1. ______

2. ______

3. 7,000 + 400 + 40 + 8 ______

4. five thousand, seven hundred fifty-five ______

Write each number in expanded form.

5. 1,240 ______

6. 6,381 ______

7. Write a 4-digit number with a 7 in the thousands place and a 6 in the ones place. ______

8. Reason Jason put the digits 4, 7, 2, and 6 in order to make the greatest possible number. What is Jason's number? ______

Name ____________________

Representing Numbers

Write each number in standard form.

1. 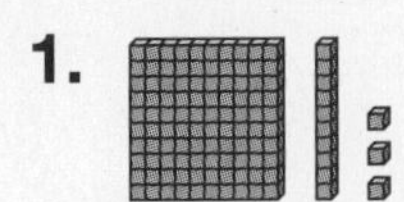

____

2. 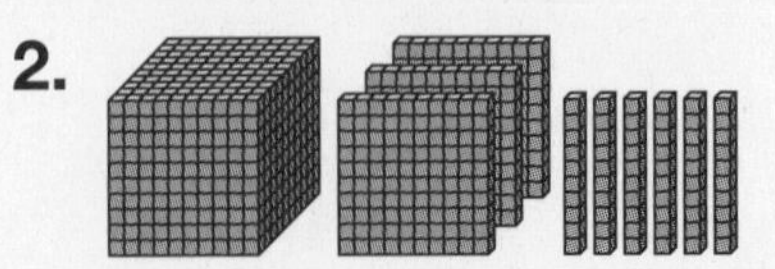

____

3. 900 + 40 + 7

____

4. 6,000 + 70 + 1

____

Write each number in expanded form.

5. 793

____

6. 4,308

____

Write the place of the underlined digit. Then write its value.

7. 5,<u>3</u>42

____

8. <u>7</u>,095

____

9. 6,3<u>9</u>8

____

10. Communicate An arena can seat nine thousand, forty-eight people. How is that number written in standard form? Explain.

____

____

11. Which is the word form of 8,040?

A eight hundred forty

B eight thousand, forty

C eight thousand, four

D eight thousand, four hundred

Name ______________________

Ways to Name Numbers

Reteaching
1-2

You can name the number 1,600 in different ways.

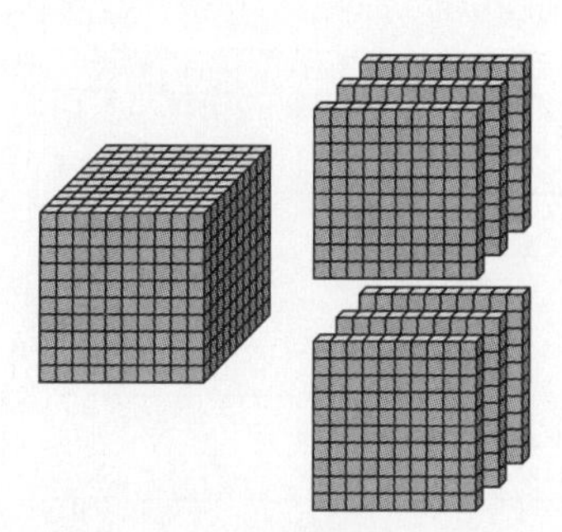

one thousand,
six hundred

Regroup 1 thousand as 10 hundreds.

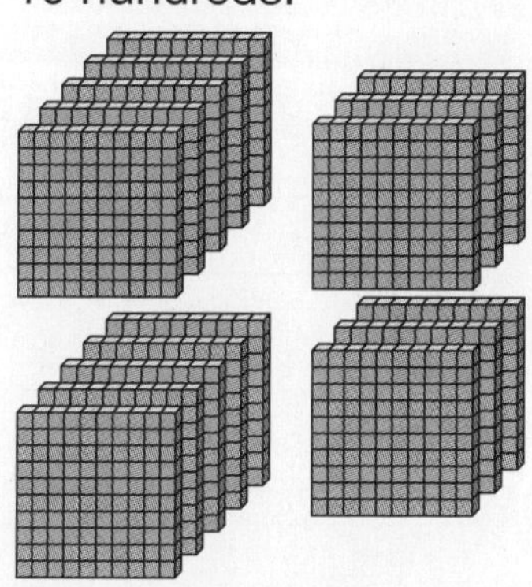

sixteen hundred

Name the number in two ways.

1.

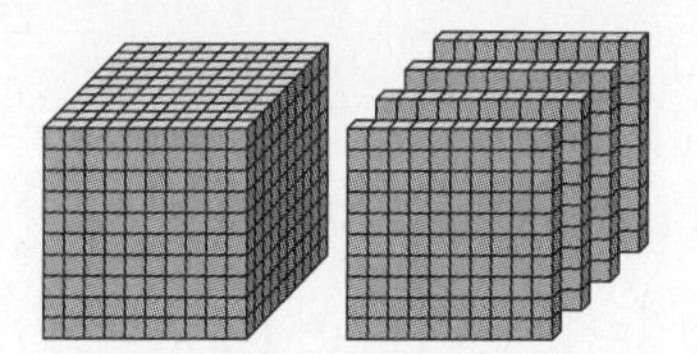

____

____

2.

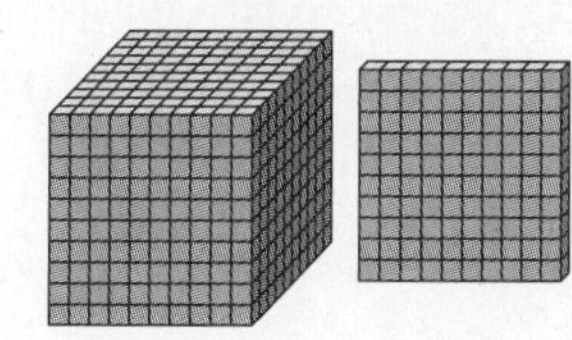

____

____

3. 3,200

____

____

4. 5,700

____

____

5. Reason Martin needs two thousand, five hundred toothpicks for a project. He has twenty-three hundred toothpicks. Does he have enough toothpicks? Explain your reasoning.

____

____

Name ______________________

Ways to Name Numbers

Name the number in two ways.

1. 3,600 ______________________

____

____

2. 8,300 ______________________

____

____

3. 6,900 ______________________

____

____

4. 9,400 ______________________

____

____

5. The Coopers live at one thousand, seven hundred six South Central Avenue. How do you write the number of the Coopers' home?

____

6. What is one way to write the year 1909 in word form?

A nine thousand, nine

B nineteen hundred nine

C nineteen thousand

D nine hundred nine

7. **Communicate** Darcy uses place-value blocks to show a number. She uses 4 thousands blocks and 5 hundreds blocks. What is the number? How can she use place-value blocks to show the number another way? Explain.

____

____

____

Name ____________________

Greater Numbers

A period is a group of three digits in a number, starting from the right. A comma is used to separate two periods.

Thousands Period			Ones Period		
hundred thousands	ten thousands	thousands	hundreds	tens	ones
2	4	7,	0	6	2

Here are different ways to show 247,062.

expanded form: 200,000 + 40,000 + 7,000 + 60 + 2

standard form: 247,062

word form: two hundred forty-seven thousand, sixty-two

Write each number in standard form.

1. 60,000 + 8,000 + 200 + 50 + 1 ____________

2. 30,000 + 600 + 30 + 2 ____________

3. four hundred one thousand, four hundred fifty-four ____________

4. five hundred twenty-nine thousand, three hundred seventy-eight ____________

5. Write 522,438 in expanded form.

____

6. Write 349,281 in expanded form.

____

7. What is the value of the 7 in 86,752? ____________

8. The area of Lake Ontario is 18,960 square kilometers. Write the area of Lake Ontario in expanded form.

____

Name ____________________

Practice
1-3

Greater Numbers

Write each number in standard form.

1. seventy-five thousand, three hundred twelve ________

2. one hundred fourteen thousand, seven ________

3. 100,000 + 40,000 + 2,000 + 500 + 30 + 2 ________

4. 400,000 + 70,000 + 8,000 + 30 + 9 ________

Write each number in expanded form.

5. 73,581 ____________________

6. 390,062 ____________________

Write the place of the underlined digit. Then write its value.

7. 6<u>3</u>,219 ________

8. 3<u>8</u>2,407 ________

9. <u>2</u>34,410 ________

10. Find the missing number.

57,026 = 50,000 + ■ + 20 + 6 ________

11. Reason Which is greater, the greatest whole number with 5 digits or the least whole number with 6 digits?

____

____

____

12. Which is the word form for 280,309?

A two hundred eight thousand, three hundred ninety

B two hundred eighty thousand, thirty-nine

C two hundred eighty thousand, three hundred nine

D two hundred eighty thousand, three hundred ninety

Name ________________________________

Understanding Number Lines

The distance between any two numbers on a number line is exactly the same.

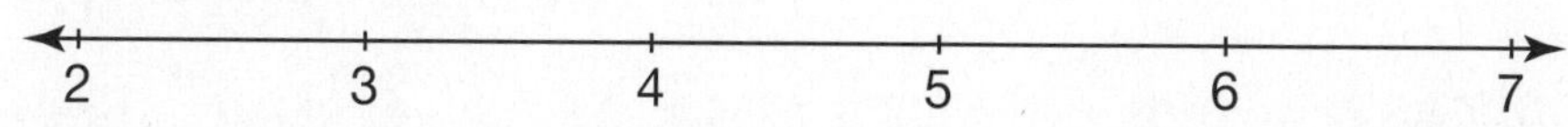

You can make the numbers closer together or farther apart. The numbers in the number line below are closer together than the numbers in the number line above.

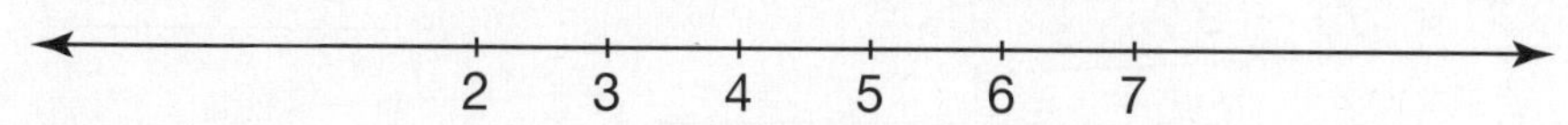

Both number lines show the same numbers.

Write the value of *A* and *B* for each number line.

1.

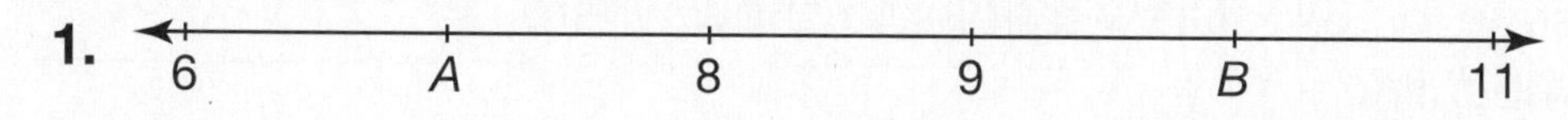

____

2.

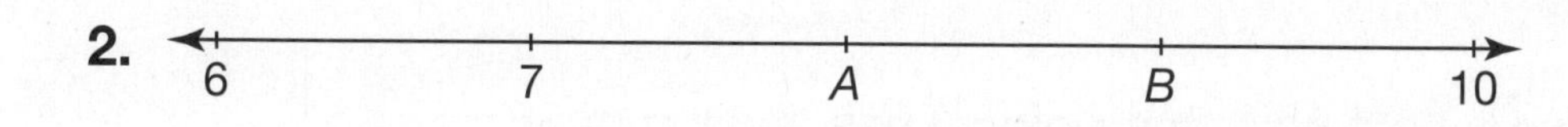

____

3. Reason Which letter on this number line has the greater value: *A* or *B*? Explain your answer.

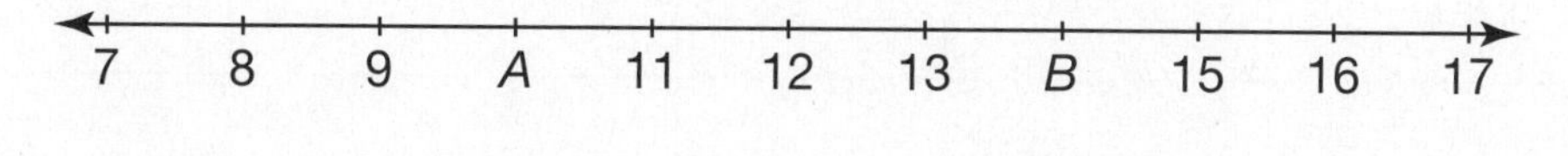

____

____

____

Name ______________________________

Understanding Number Lines

Practice
1-4

Write the value of *A*, *B*, and *C* on each number line.

1. 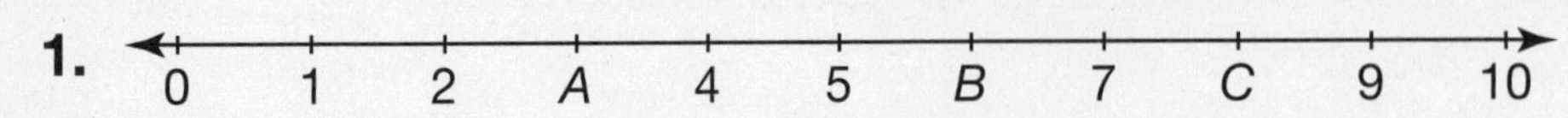

2. 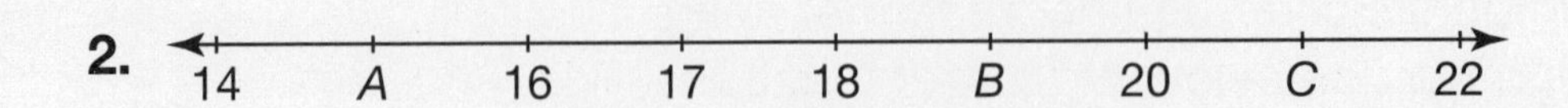

3. 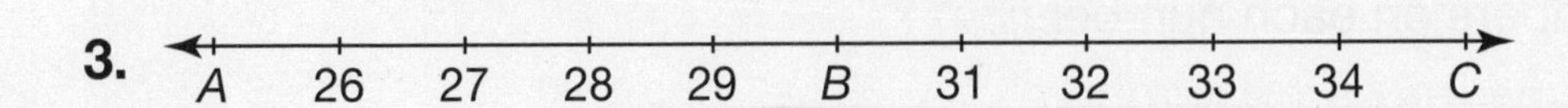

4. Texas became a state in 1845. Draw a point to show where 1845 is on the number line.

1800 1810 1820 1830 1840 1850 1860 1870 1880 1890 1900

5. **Critique Reasoning** Lara said that point *D* has a value of 38. Is her statement reasonable? Explain your answer.

D

0 5 10 15 20 25 30 35 40 45 50

____

____

6. Which letter represents 57 on this number line?

50 *E* *F* *G* *H* 60

A *E* **B** *F* **C** *G* **D** *H*

Name ____________________

Counting on the Number Line

A number line can be used to show a pattern. No matter what the pattern is, the numbers are the same distance apart.

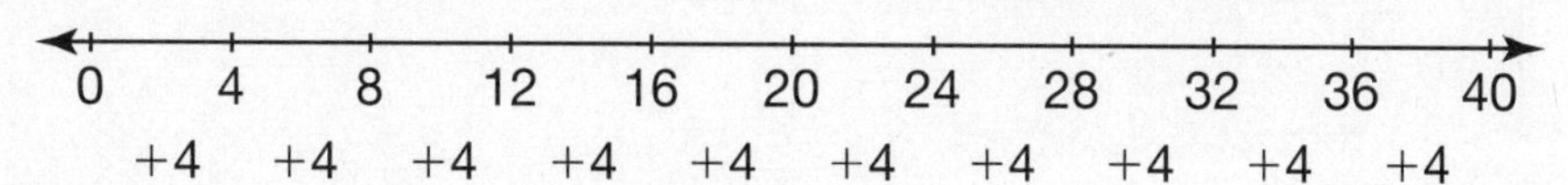

The pattern is to add 4 to the previous number.

Write the missing numbers on each number line.

1.

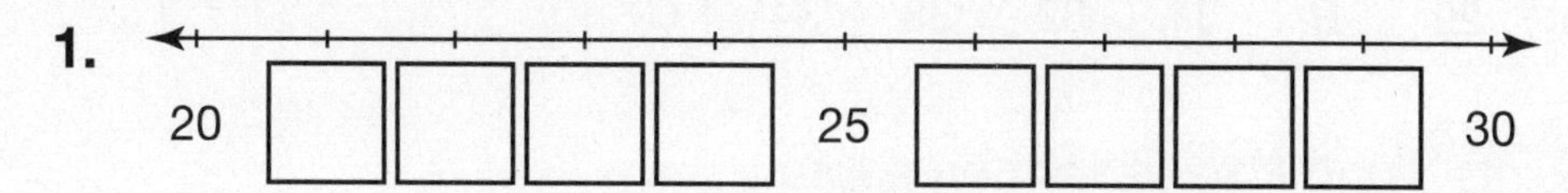

2.

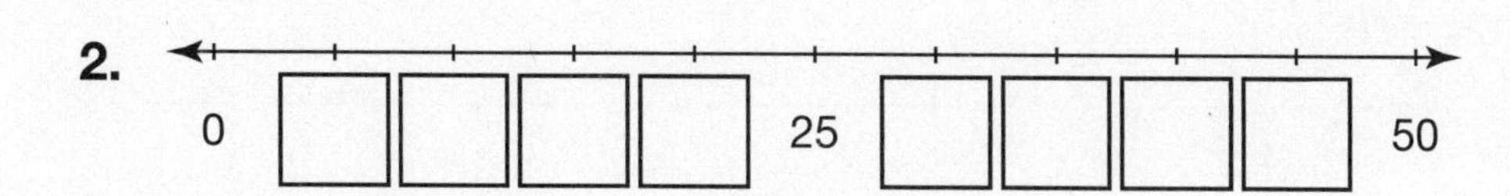

3.

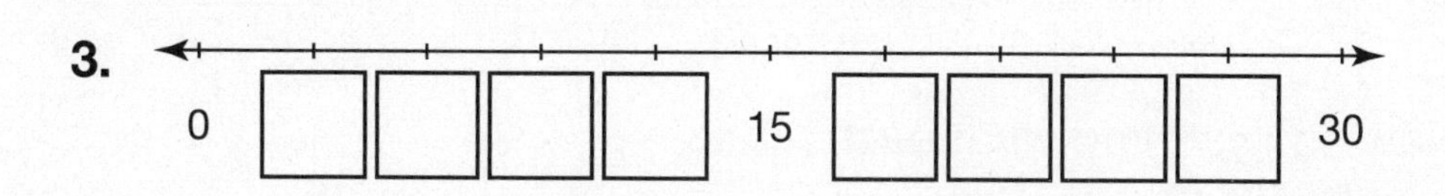

4. Use Structure Make a number line from 0 to 60 counting by sixes.

Name ______________________________

Practice
1-5

Counting on the Number Line

Write the missing numbers for each number line.

1.

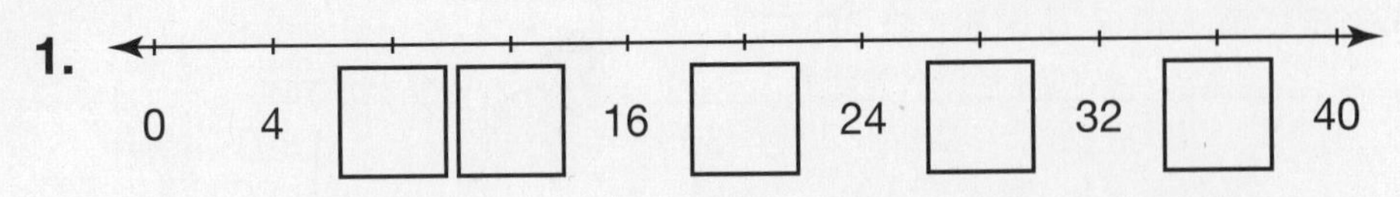

2.

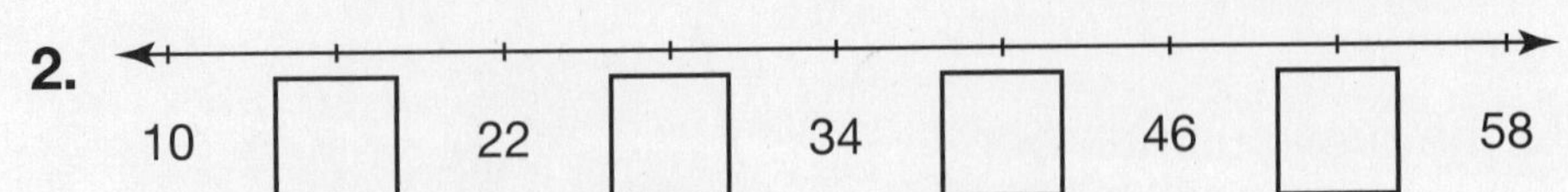

3.

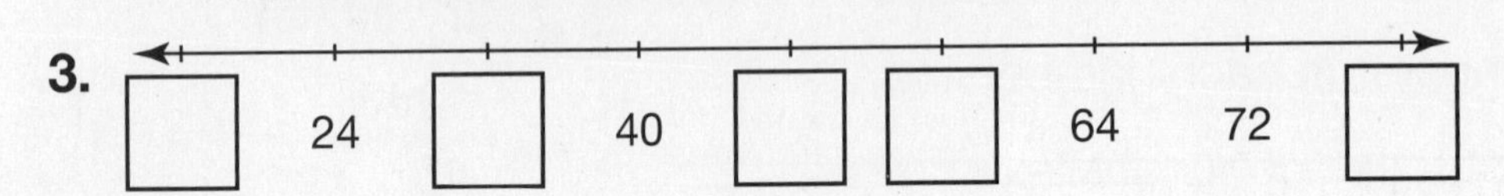

Write the number that points *J* and *K* represent on each number line.

4.

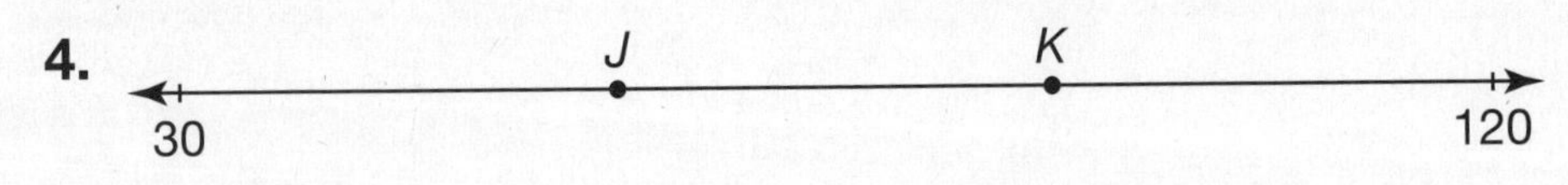

____

5.

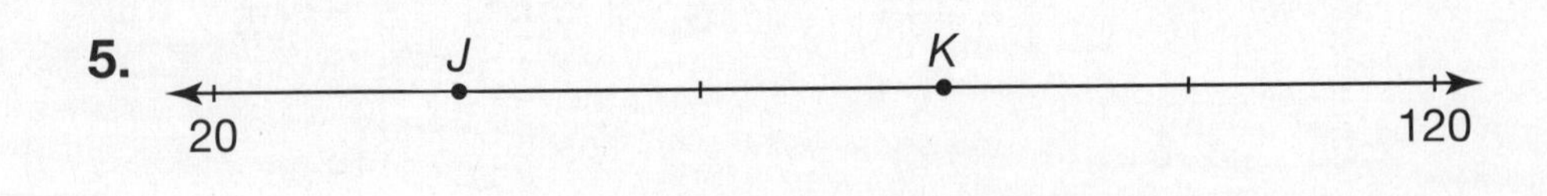

____

6. Communicate How can you find what each mark represents on a number line?

____

____

7. Which point on the number line represents 18?

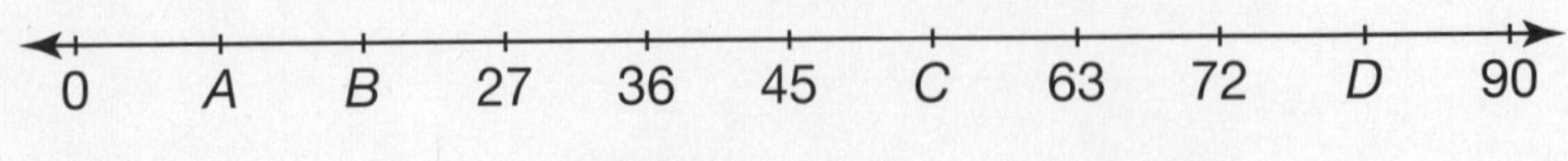

A *A* **B** *B* **C** *C* **D** *D*

Name ______________________________

Reteaching
1-6

Comparing Numbers

Use these symbols to compare numbers.

< is less than **> is greater than** **= is equal to**

Compare 375 and 353.

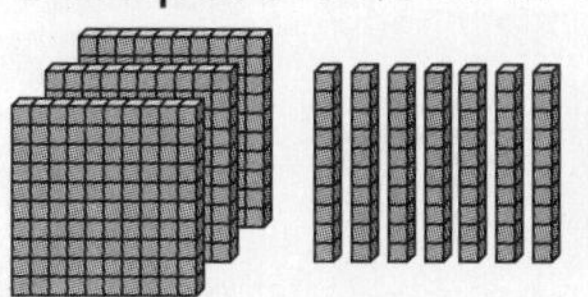

375

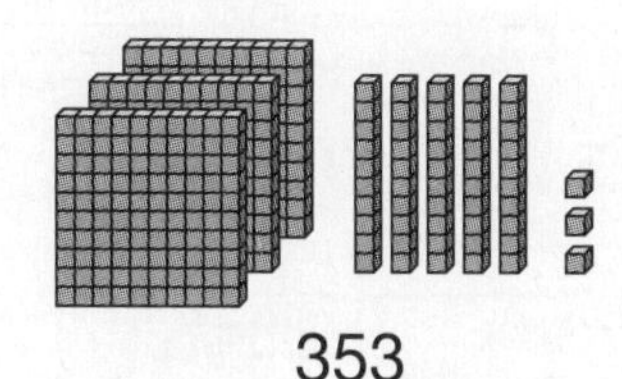

353

Both have the same number of hundreds.
Compare the tens. 375 has more tens.

375 is greater than 353. $375 > 353$

Compare the numbers. Use $<$, $>$, or $=$.

1. 36 ◯ 27 **2.** 278 ◯ 285 **3.** 692 ◯ 690

4. 842 ◯ 824 **5.** 4,669 ◯ 4,705 **6.** 7,305 ◯ 7,305

7. 1,100 ◯ 998 **8.** 5,436 ◯ 5,436 **9.** 323 ◯ 333

10. Reason Write a 3-digit number greater than 699.

____

11. Write a 2-digit number less than 40.

____

12. Communicate Every digit in 798 is greater than any digit in 4,325. Explain why 4,325 is greater than 798.

____

____

____

Name ______________________

Comparing Numbers

Compare the numbers. Use <, >, or =.

1. 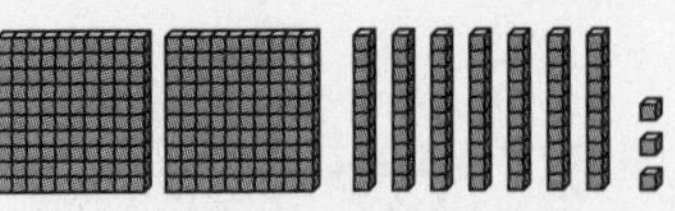

237 _____ 273

2.

130 _____ 113

3. 725 ◯ 739

4. 831 ◯ 813

5. 926 ◯ 926

6. 2,734 ◯ 2,347

7. 4,827 ◯ 583

8. 5,327 ◯ 5,372

Use the table for **9** and **10**.

9. Between which pair of cities is the distance the greatest? See table.

____

____

Distance in Miles

New York, NY, to Rapid City, SD	1,701
Rapid City, SD, to Miami, FL	2,167
Miami, FL, to Seattle, WA	3,334
Portland, OR, to Little Rock, AR	2,217

10. Communicate Which has a greater distance, Rapid City to Miami or Portland to Little Rock? Which digits did you use to compare? See table.

____

____

Reason Write the missing digits to make each number sentence true.

11. 7☐7 < 713

12. 8☐5 > 889

13. 3,☐64 = 3,2☐4

14. Which sentence is true?

A 4,375 > 4,722

B 6,372 > 6,327

C 5,106 = 5,160

D 7,095 < 795

15. Which number is greater than 8,264?

A 8,246 **B** 8,275 **C** 6,842 **D** 8,195

Name ____________________

Ordering Numbers

Reteaching
1-7

You can use place value to order numbers.
Order these from least to greatest.

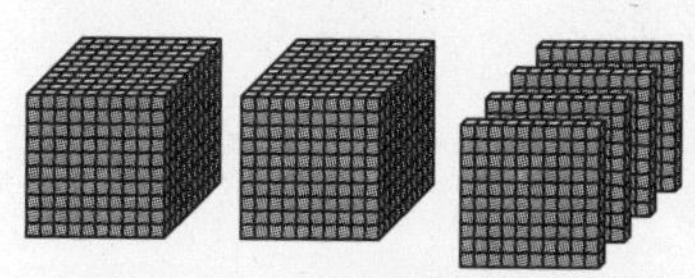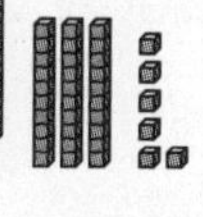

2,436

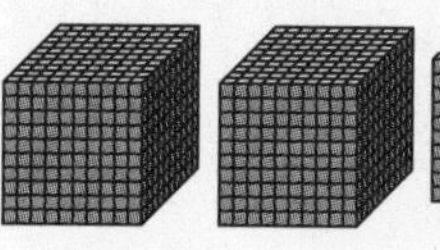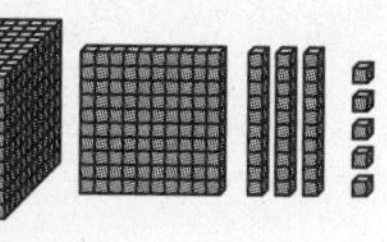

2,135

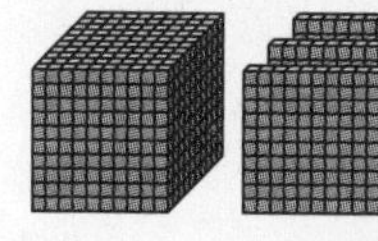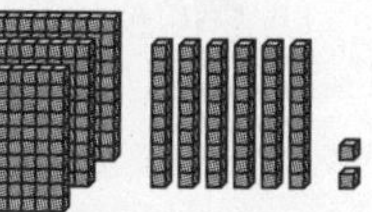

1,362

Compare the thousands.
1 thousand < 2 thousands, so 1,362 is the least number.

Compare the hundreds in the remaining two numbers.
4 hundreds > 1 hundred, so 2,436 is the greatest number.

From least to greatest, the order is: **1,362** (least) **2,135** **2,436** (greatest)

Order the numbers from least to greatest.

1. 560 583 552 ____________

2. 583 575 590 ____________

3. 576 580 557 ____________

Order the numbers from greatest to least.

4. 973 1,007 996 ____________

5. 5,626 5,636 5,716 ____________

6. Reason Use the table. Put the roller coasters in order from shortest to longest.

____

____

____

Roller Coaster	Length
Boss Eureka, Missouri	5,051 feet
Chang Louisville, Kentucky	4,155 feet
Titan Arlington, Texas	5,312 feet

Name ____________________

Practice 1-7

Ordering Numbers

Order the numbers from least to greatest.

1. 216 208 222

____

2. 3,795 3,659 3,747

____

Order the numbers from greatest to least.

3. 633 336 363

____

4. 5,017 5,352 5,193

____

Use the table for **5** through **6**.

5. Reason New Hampshire has a land area of 8,968 square miles. Which states in the table have a greater land area than New Hampshire?

____

____

Land Areas (in square miles)

State	Land Area
Maryland	9,774
Massachusetts	7,840
New Jersey	7,417
Vermont	9,250

6. Order the states in the table from greatest to least land area.

____

7. Reason The Amazon River is 4,000 miles long. The Yangtze River is 3,964 miles long and the Nile River is 4,145 miles long. Write the steps you would use to order the lengths of the rivers from greatest to least.

____

____

8. Which number is between 6,532 and 6,600?

A 6,570 **B** 6,523 **C** 6,325 **D** 5,623

9. Which number makes this sentence true?

$4{,}735 < \_\_\_\_\_ < 4{,}820$

A 4,396 **B** 4,758 **C** 4,832 **D** 4,915

Name ______________________

Problem Solving: Make an Organized List

Todd has given Maclan the information below to guess one or more 3-digit numbers that fit the clues.

- The ones digit is odd.
- The tens digit is greater than 8.
- The hundreds digit is less than 2.

Use the clues for each digit to make an organized list.

The ones digit is odd.

The odd numbers are 1, 3, 5, 7, and 9.

The tens digit is greater than 8.

The only digit greater than 8 is 9. The tens digit is 9.

The hundreds digit is less than 2.

The digit in the greatest place of a whole number cannot be 0. The hundreds digit is 1.

So, the numbers that fit the clues are 191, 193, 195, 197, and 199.

Make an organized list to solve.

1. Barbara, Lisa, and Maria are having their picture taken for the yearbook. List the ways that they can stand in a straight line for the picture. You can use their initials.

____

____

2. List all the 3-digit numbers that fit these clues.
   - The hundreds digit is greater than 7.
   - The tens digit is less than 2.
   - The ones digit is the same as the hundreds digit.

____

____

3. **Reason** In how many ways can you make 10 cents using dimes, nickels, and pennies? List all the ways.

____

____

Name ______________________

Practice
1-8

Problem Solving: Make an Organized List

Make an organized list to solve.

1. List all the 3-digit numbers that fit these clues.

- The hundreds digit is less than 3.
- The tens digit is less than 2.
- The ones digit is greater than 7.

____

____

2. List all the 4-digit numbers that fit these clues.

- The thousands digit is greater than 8.
- The hundreds digit is less than 4.
- The tens and ones digits are the same as the thousands digit.

____

____

3. Jim and Sarah are running for class president. Cayla and Daniel are running for vice president. What combinations of president and vice president could there be?

____

____

____

4. List all the ways that you can arrange the letters A, B, and C.

____

____

____

5. **Persevere** What is this 3-digit number?

- The hundreds digit is 4 greater than 3.
- The tens digit is 1 more than the hundreds digit.
- The ones digit is 3 less than the tens digit.

____

6. In how many ways can you make 30 cents using quarters, dimes, and nickels?

A 4

B 5

C 6

D 8

Name ____________________

Reteaching

2-1

Addition Meaning and Properties

The Commutative (Order) Property

You can add numbers in any order, and the sum will be the same.

$6 + 2 = 8$

$2 + 6 = 8$

The Associative (Grouping) Property

You can group addends in any way, and the sum will be the same.

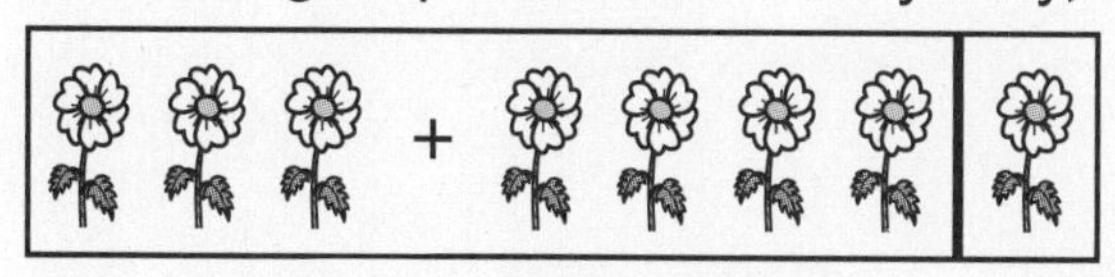

$(3 + 4) + 1 = 8$

$3 + (4 + 1) = 8$

The Identity (Zero) Property

The sum of any number and zero equals that same number.

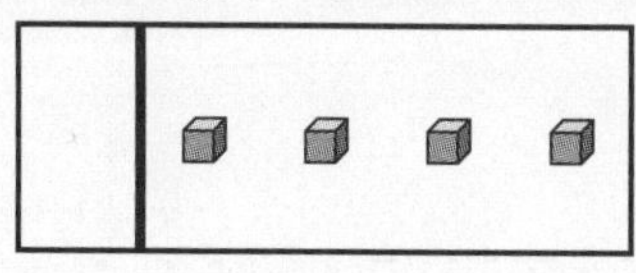

$0 + 4 = 4$

Find each sum.

1. $3 + (2 + 4) =$ ______

2. $(0 + 5) + 2 =$ ______

3. $(8 + 3) + 4 =$ ______

4. $9 + 2 + 6 =$ ______

Write each missing number.

5. $3 + 4 = 4 +$ ______

6. ______ $+ 7 = 7$

7. $(2 + 3) + 4 =$ ______ $+ (3 + 4)$

8. $9 + (2 + 7) = (9 + 2) +$ ______

9. Reason Does $(4 + 5) + 2 = 9 + 2$? Explain.

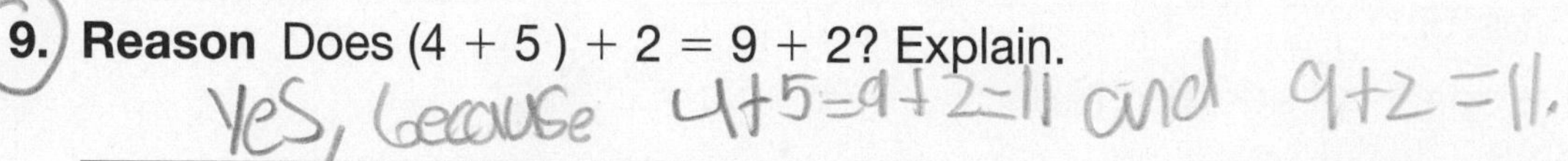

____

Name ____________________

Addition Meaning and Properties

Write each missing number.

1. $7 + 2 = 2 + \blacksquare$ ______

2. $3 + \blacksquare = 3$ ______

3. $(2 + 4) + 5 = 2 + (\blacksquare + 5)$ ______

4. $3 + \blacksquare = 5 + 3$ ______

5. $\blacksquare + 0 = 6$ ______

6. $(5 + 3) + 9 = 8 + \blacksquare$ ______

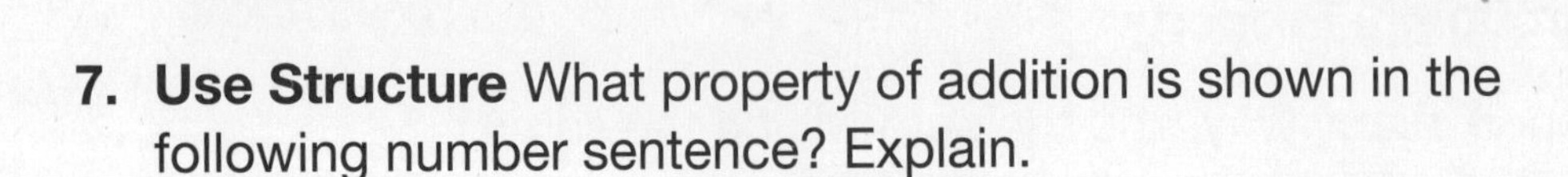

7. Use Structure What property of addition is shown in the following number sentence? Explain.

$7 + (3 + 5) = (7 + 3) + 5$

____

____

8. Minnie has 6 country CDs and 5 rock CDs. Amanda has 5 rock CDs and 6 country CDs. Who has more CDs? Explain.

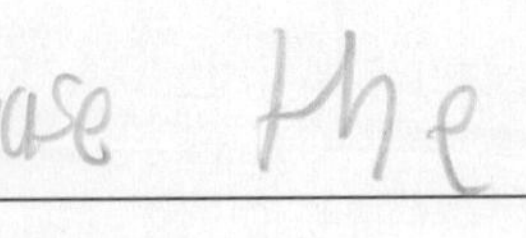

____

____

9. Show how the Commutative Property of Addition works using the numbers 2, 3, and 5.

____

10. Critique Reasoning Jake says that adding 0 does not change a sum. Is he correct? Explain.

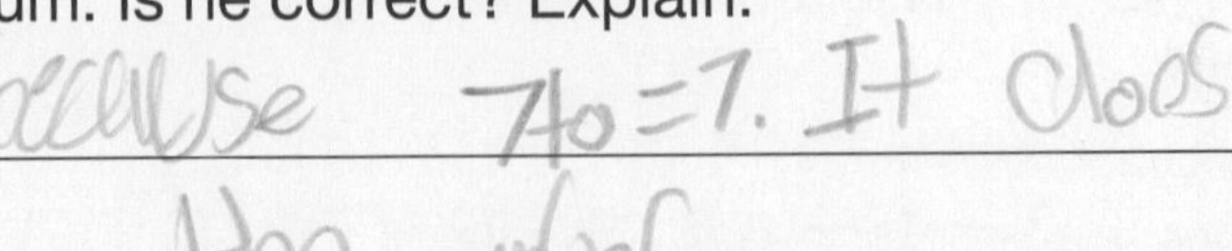

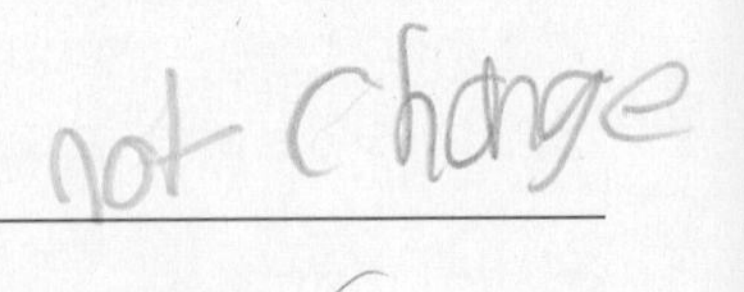

____

____

11. Which property of addition is shown by $5 + 2 = 2 + 5$?

A Associative Property

B Distributive Property

C Commutative Property

D Identity Property

Name ______________

Subtraction Meanings

Dawn received a total of 12 stars on Monday and Tuesday. She received 7 of the stars on Monday. How many stars did she receive on Tuesday?

You can draw a picture to find how many stars Dawn received on Tuesday.

First, draw 12 stars.

Next, put a line through the 7 stars that Dawn received Monday.

Count the number of stars that are not crossed off.
There are 5.
So, $12 - 7 = 5$.

You can add to check subtraction: $7 + 5 = 12$, so $12 - 7 = 5$.

Dawn received 5 stars on Tuesday.

Find each difference. Make a drawing to help you.

1. $13 - 4 =$ 9
2. $16 - 9 =$ ______
3. $15 - 7 =$ ______
4. $11 - 6 =$ ______
5. $12 - 8 =$ 4
6. $14 - 5 =$ 9
7. **Estimation** There are 21 players on the Titans baseball team. Only 9 players can play at any one time. About how many players are not playing? ______
8. An octagon has 8 sides. A pentagon has 5 sides. How many more sides does an octagon have than a pentagon? 3 more sides

Name

Subtraction Meanings

Write a number sentence for each situation. Solve.

1. Terrance has 14 CDs. Robyn has 9 CDs. How many more CDs does Terrance have than Robyn?

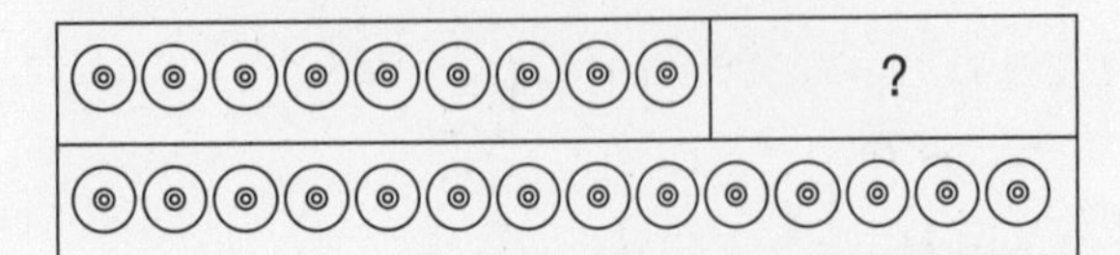

14 − 9 = 5

2. How many more black stars are there than white stars?

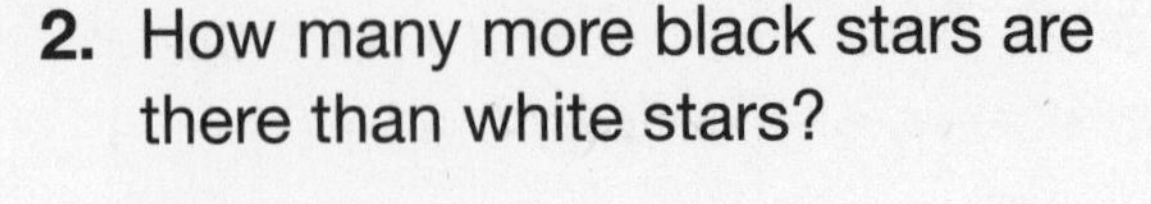

3. Arizona has 15 counties. Connecticut has 8 counties. How many more counties does Arizona have than Connecticut?

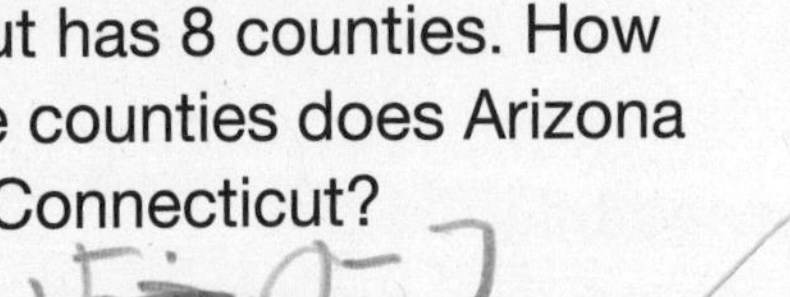

4. A baseball hat costs $12. Nancy has a coupon for $4 off. How much money will Nancy spend on the baseball hat?

5. Carrie invited 13 girls to a party. Five of the girls have already arrived. How many girls have yet to arrive? Draw a picture to show the problem.

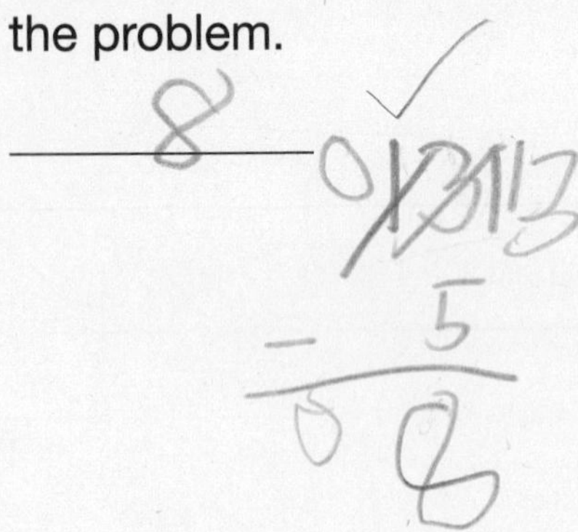

6. **Use Structure** Write the fact family for 3, 9, and 12.

9 + 3 = 12, 3 + 9 = 12, 12 − 9 = 3, 12 − 3 = 9

7. LaToya has 12 postcards and 4 photographs on a bulletin board. How many more postcards does LaToya have than photographs?

A 7 **B** 8 **C** 9 **D** 16

Name ______________________

Using Mental Math to Add

Reteaching
2-3

You can break apart numbers to make them easier to add mentally.

Add 31 + 45 by breaking apart numbers.

Break the numbers into tens and ones.

	tens		ones
31 =	30	+	1
45 =	40	+	5

Add the tens: 30 + 40 = 70.

Add the ones: 1 + 5 = 6.

Add the sums: 70 + 6 = 76.

So, 31 + 45 = 76.

Add 26 + 17 by breaking apart numbers to make a ten.

Use a number that adds with the 6 in 26 to make a 10. Since 6 + 4 = 10, use 4.

Think: 17 = 4 + 13.

Add 26 + 4 = 30.

Add 30 + 13 = 43.

So, 26 + 17 = 43.

Find each sum using mental math.

1. 24 + 71 = ______ **2.** 36 + 43 = ______ **3.** 54 + 23 = ______

4. 25 + 49 = ______ **5.** 37 + 56 = ______ **6.** 77 + 13 = ______

7. Communicate To add 32 + 56, Juanita first added 30 + 50. What two steps does she still need to do to find the sum? What is Juanita's sum?

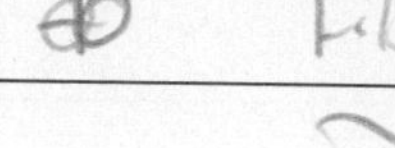

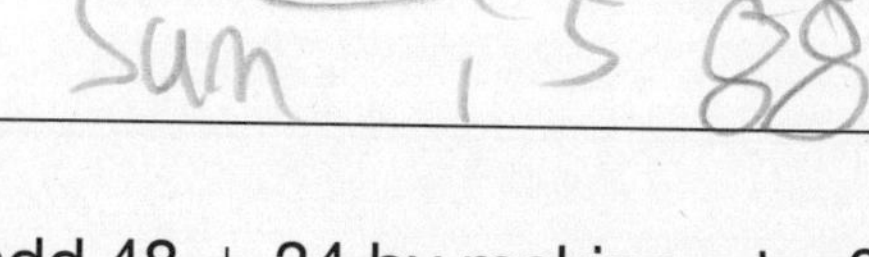

____

____

8. Reason How can Steve add 48 + 34 by making a ten? What is the sum?

____

____

____

Name ____________________

Practice
2-3

Using Mental Math to Add

Use breaking apart to add mentally.

1. 53 + 34

34 = 30 + □

53 + □ = 83

83 + □ = 87

So, 53 + 34 = □

2. 42 + 29

29 = 20 + □

42 + □ = 62

□ + 9 = 71

So, 42 + 29 = □

3. 47 + 41

41 = □ + 1

47 + □ = 87

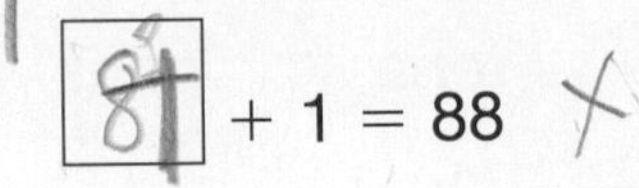

□ + 1 = 88

So, 47 + 41 = □

Make a ten to add mentally.

4. 27 + 24

24 = 3 + □

27 + □ = 30

□ + 21 = 51

So, 27 + 24 = □

5. 54 + 19

19 = □ + 6

□ + 6 = 60

60 + □ = 73

So, 54 + 19 = □

6. 38 + 27

27 = □ + 25

38 + □ = 40

40 + □ = 65

So, 38 + 27 = □

Find each sum using mental math.

7. 52 + 26 ______

8. 47 + 8 ______

9. 32 + 17 ______

10. 28 + 31 ______

11. 43 + 38 ______

12. 72 + 7 ______

13. 42 + 33 ______

14. 36 + 14 ______

15. Generalize Ashton broke apart a number into 30 + 7. What number did he start with? ______

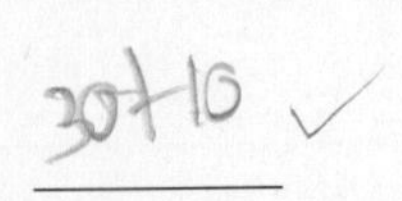

16. What is the sum of 27 + 42 using mental math?

A 68 **B** 69 **C** 78 **D** 79

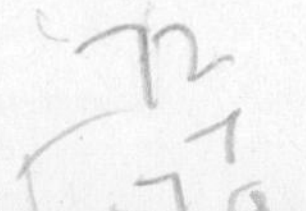

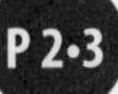

Name ____________________

Using Mental Math to Add

You can break apart numbers to make them easier to add mentally.

Add 31 + 45 by breaking apart numbers.

Break the numbers into tens and ones.

	tens		ones
31 =	30	+	1
45 =	40	+	5

Add the tens: 30 + 40 = 70.

Add the ones: 1 + 5 = 6.

Add the sums: 70 + 6 = 76.

So, 31 + 45 = 76.

Add 26 + 17 by breaking apart numbers to make a ten.

Use a number that adds with the 6 in 26 to make a 10. Since 6 + 4 = 10, use 4.

Think: 17 = 4 + 13.

Add 26 + 4 = 30.

Add 30 + 13 = 43.

So, 26 + 17 = 43.

Find each sum using mental math.

1. 24 + 71 = ______
2. 36 + 43 = ______
3. 54 + 23 = ______
4. 25 + 49 = ______
5. 37 + 56 = ______
6. 77 + 13 = ______

7. **Communicate** To add 32 + 56, Juanita first added 30 + 50. What two steps does she still need to do to find the sum? What is Juanita's sum?

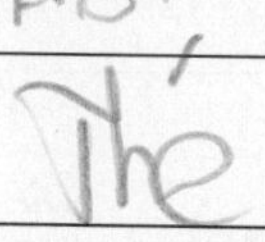

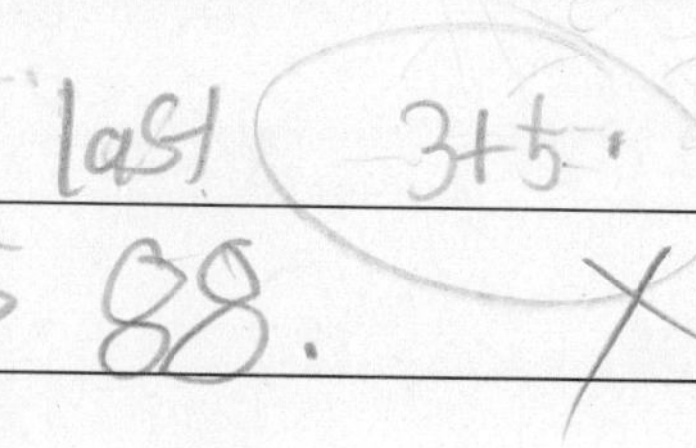

____

____

8. **Reason** How can Steve add 48 + 34 by making a ten? What is the sum?

____

____

____

Name ______________________

Practice
2-3

Using Mental Math to Add

Use breaking apart to add mentally.

1. 53 + 34

34 = 30 + ☐

53 + ☐ = 83

83 + ☐ = 87

So, 53 + 34 = ☐

2. 42 + 29

29 = 20 + ☐

42 + ☐ = 62

☐ + 9 = 71

So, 42 + 29 = ☐

3. 47 + 41

41 = ☐ + 1

47 + ☐ = 87

☐ + 1 = 88

So, 47 + 41 = ☐

Make a ten to add mentally.

4. 27 + 24

24 = 3 + ☐

27 + ☐ = 30

☐ + 21 = 51

So, 27 + 24 = ☐

5. 54 + 19

19 = ☐ + 6

☐ + 6 = 60

60 + ☐ = 73

So, 54 + 19 = ☐

6. 38 + 27

27 = ☐ + 25

38 + ☐ = 40

40 + ☐ = 65

So, 38 + 27 = ☐

Find each sum using mental math.

7. 52 + 26 ______

8. 47 + 8 ______

9. 32 + 17 ______

10. 28 + 31 ______

11. 43 + 38 ______

12. 72 + 7 ______

13. 42 + 33 ______

14. 36 + 14 ______

15. Generalize Ashton broke apart a number into 30 + 7. What number did he start with? ______

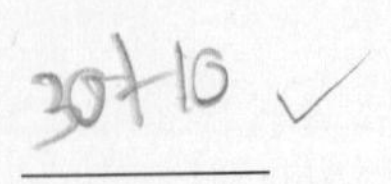

16. What is the sum of 27 + 42 using mental math?

A 68 **B** 69 **C** 78 **D** 79

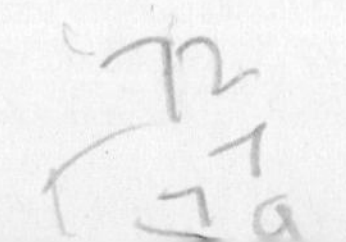

Name ______________________

Reteaching
2-4

Using Mental Math to Subtract

You can change numbers to make subtraction problems easier.

There are two ways to subtract 42 − 28.

One way is to add 2 to 28.

$$\begin{array}{rr} 42 & \rightarrow 42 \\ -\ 28 + 2 & \rightarrow 30 \\ \hline & 12 \end{array}$$

Because you added 2 to 28, add 2 to the difference.

12 + 2 = 14

So, 42 − 28 = 14.

Another way is to add 2 to both 42 and 28.

$$\begin{array}{rr} 42 + 2 & \rightarrow 44 \\ -\ 28 + 2 & \rightarrow 30 \\ \hline & 14 \end{array}$$

What you do to the bottom number, also do to the top number.

So, 42 − 28 = 14.

Find each difference using mental math.

1. 32 − 17 = ______
2. 51 − 46 = ______
3. 42 − 18 = ______
4. 36 − 19 = ______
5. 63 − 56 = ______
6. 78 − 16 = ______
7. 94 − 18 = ______
8. 55 − 33 = ______
9. 81 − 13 = ______

10. **Model** Rob had $60 when he went to the mall. He bought a DVD for $15. How much money does he have left? Write the number sentence you used to solve the problem.

____

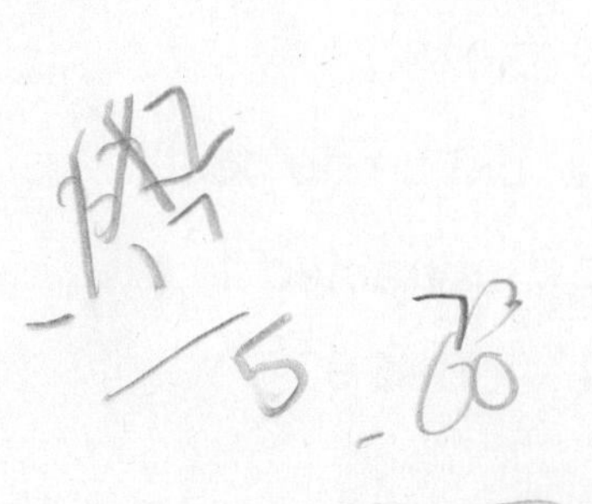

Name ______________________

Practice
2-4

Using Mental Math to Subtract

Find each difference using mental math.

1. 38 − 14

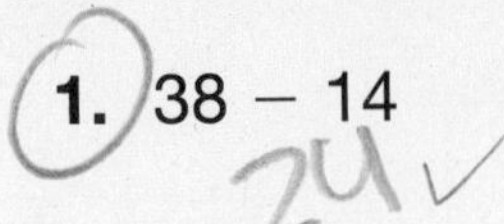

2. 42 − 13 ______

3. 55 − 12 ______

4. 62 − 17 ______

5. 72 − 19 ______

6. 94 − 11 ______

7. 32 − 15 ______

8. 85 − 18 ______

9. 43 − 16 ______

10. 66 − 15 ______

11. 53 − 19 ______

12. 72 − 16 ______

13. Reason Gillian started solving 88 − 29.
This is what she did.

88 − 29 = ?
88 − 30 = 58

What should Gillian do next? ______________________

14. Communicate Tell how to find 81 − 16 using mental math.

____

____

____

15. Tiffany will use a total of 63 tiles for her art project. She only needs 17 more tiles. Use mental math to find how many tiles she has already.

____

16. To solve 35 − 19, Jack used 35 − 20. What did he do next?

A Added 1
B Subtracted 9
C Subtracted 1
D Added 9

Name ______________________

Rounding

Reteaching
2-5

You can use place value to round to the nearest ten or hundred.

Find the rounding place. If the digit in the ones or the tens place is 5, 6, 7, 8, or 9, then round to the next greater number. If the digit is less than 5, do not change the digit in the rounding place.

Round 17 to the nearest ten: 20

Explain. 7 is in the ones place. Round to the next greater ten.

Round 153 to the nearest ten. 150

Explain. Because 3 is in the ones place and 3 is less than 5, the digit in the tens place does not change.

Round 575 to the nearest hundred. 600

Explain. Because the 7 in the tens place is 5 or greater, round to the next greater hundred.

1. Round 63 to the nearest ten: 60

Explain. It is 60 because the ones digit's 3.

Round each number to the nearest ten.

2. 58 — 60

3. 71 — 70

4. 927 — 930

5. 3,121 — 3,120

Round each number to the nearest hundred.

6. 577 — 580

7. 820 — 820

8. 2,345 — 2,350

9. 8,750 — 8,750

10. **Reasonableness** If you live 71 miles from a river, does it make sense to say you live about 80 miles from the river? Explain.

No because 71 is rounded to 70 not 80.

Name ______________________

Practice

2-5

Rounding

Round to the nearest ten.

1. 37 **2.** 93 **3.** 78 **4.** 82 **5.** 24

6. 426 **7.** 329 **8.** 815 **9.** 163 **10.** 896

Round to the nearest hundred.

11. 395 **12.** 638 **13.** 782 **14.** 246 **15.** 453

16. 529 **17.** 877 **18.** 634 **19.** 329 **20.** 587

21. Critique Reasoning Tyrell says 753 rounds to 800. Sara says 753 rounds to 750. Who is correct? Explain.

22. Communicate How would you use a number line to round 148 to the nearest ten? Explain.

23. There are 254 counties in Texas. What is that number rounded to the nearest ten? What is that number rounded to the nearest hundred?

24. Reason Which number does not round to 400?

A 347 **B** 369 **C** 413 **D** 448

Name ______________________________

Estimating Sums

The students at your school are saving cereal box tops.

136
box tops

152
box tops

About how many box tops have the students saved?

When you find about how many, you estimate.

Estimate by rounding each addend. Then add the rounded numbers.

Round to the nearest ten.

$$\begin{array}{rcr} 136 & \rightarrow & 140 \\ +\ 152 & \rightarrow & 150 \\ \hline & & 290 \end{array}$$

The students have saved about 290 box tops.

Round to the nearest hundred.

$$\begin{array}{rcr} 136 & \rightarrow & 100 \\ +\ 152 & \rightarrow & 200 \\ \hline & & 300 \end{array}$$

The students have saved about 300 box tops.

Round to the nearest ten to estimate each sum.

1. 42 + 98 = _____ **2.** 36 + 59 = _____ **3.** 288 + 475 = _____

Round to the nearest hundred to estimate each sum.

4. 378 + 136 = _____ **5.** 436 + 309 = _____ **6.** 76 + 487 = _____

7. Critique Reasoning Sun-Yi estimated 270 + 146 and got 300. Is her estimate reasonable? Explain.

____

____

____

Name ______________________

Practice 2-6

Estimating Sums

Round to the nearest ten to estimate.

1. 58 + 43   91

2. 87 + 69   ______

3. 37 + 141   310

4. 422 + 296   ______

Round to the nearest hundred to estimate.

5. 536 + 393

6. 242 + 359   ______

7. 713 + 82

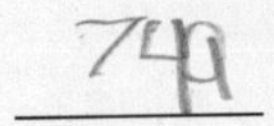

8. 313 + 405   ______

Use compatible numbers to estimate.

9. 83 + 34   ______

10. 329 + 64   ______

11. 212 + 347   ______

12. 537 + 244   ______

13. Reasonableness Miguel has 325 baseball cards and 272 football cards. He said that he has 597 cards in all. Is his answer reasonable? Explain using estimation.

hIS Answer is resnoble because 325 is rounded 200 and 272 is rounded to 300 So 200 + 300 = 500.

14. Write a Problem Natalie has 138 DVDs and 419 CDs. Write a number sentence that you could use to estimate the sum of the DVDs and CDs. Then find your estimated sum.

____

15. Which of the following shows estimating 287 + 491 by using compatible numbers?

A 100 + 500   **B** 300 + 400   **C** 280 + 400   **D** 280 + 500

Name ____________________

Reteaching
2-7

Estimating Differences

Members of the Biology Club caught 288 butterflies and 136 grasshoppers in their nets. About how many more butterflies than grasshoppers did the club catch?

You can estimate by rounding. To round to a certain place, look at the digit to the right of that place. If the digit is 5 or greater, round up. If the digit is less than 5, round down.

Round to the nearest hundred.
Look at the digits in the tens place.

$$\begin{array}{rcr} 288 & \rightarrow & 300 \\ -\ 136 & \rightarrow & 100 \\ \hline & & 200 \end{array}$$

There were about 200 more butterflies than grasshoppers caught.

Round to the nearest ten.
Look at the digits in the ones place.

$$\begin{array}{rcr} 288 & \rightarrow & 290 \\ -\ 136 & \rightarrow & 140 \\ \hline & & 150 \end{array}$$

There were about 150 more butterflies than grasshoppers caught.

Estimate by rounding to the nearest hundred.

1. $\begin{array}{r} 442 \\ -\ 112 \\ \hline \end{array}$

2. $\begin{array}{r} 725 \\ -\ 278 \\ \hline \end{array}$

3. $\begin{array}{r} 363 \\ -\ 187 \\ \hline \end{array}$

Estimate by rounding to the nearest ten.

4. 68 − 42 = ______

5. 88 − 17 = ______

6. 231 − 109 = ______

7. Critique Reasoning Charlie estimated 293 − 44 and got a difference of about 250. Is this a reasonable estimate? Explain.

____

____

____

Name ______________________

Practice **2-7**

Estimating Differences

Round to the nearest hundred to estimate each difference.

1. 478 − 267 ______ **2.** 236 − 119 ______ **3.** 588 − 321 ______

Round to the nearest ten to estimate each difference.

4. 677 − 421 ______ **5.** 296 − 97 ______ **6.** 312 − 157 ______

Use compatible numbers to estimate each difference.

7. 84 − 36 ______ **8.** 427 − 163 ______ **9.** 609 − 243 ______

10. Critique Reasoning Fern rounded to the nearest ten to estimate 548 − 132. She subtracted 540 − 130 and got 410. Is Fern's estimate correct? Explain.

____

____

11. On Friday, 537 people attended a play. For Saturday's matinee, there were 812 people. About how many more people attended the play on Saturday than on Friday? ______________

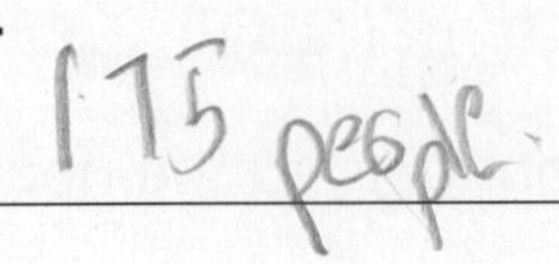

12. A football team scored 529 points one season and then 376 points the next. About how many points less did the team score in the second season? Round to the nearest ten. ______________

13. Waco, TX, has an elevation of 405 feet. Dallas, TX, has an elevation of 463 feet. About how many feet greater is Dallas's elevation than Waco's elevation?

A 470 − 400 = 70

B 460 − 410 = 50

C 450 + 400 = 850

D 460 + 400 = 860

Name ______________________

Reteaching
2-8

Making Sense of Addition and Subtraction Equations

An **equation** is a number sentence that uses an equal sign (=) to show that the value to its left is the same as the value to its right.

$12 + 4 = 16$ is an example of an equation.

Some equations have letters in them or *unknowns*.

$$9 = n + 2$$

This equation means: 9 is equal to some number + 2

You can find the value of n that makes the equation true or equal on each side by thinking of addition or subtraction facts.

Think: You know that $7 + 2 = 9$, so $n = 7$.

In **1–8,** write a basic fact that is related to each equation. Then find the value for n that makes the equation true.

1. $18 = 9 + n$ ______ ______

2. $n - 4 = 2$ ______ ______

3. $12 = 7 + n$ ______ ______

4. $3 - n = 3$ ______ ______

5. $14 = 6 + n$ ______ ______

6. $n - 5 = 6$ ______ ______

7. $6 = 7 - n$ ______ ______

8. $10 + n = 17$ ______ ______

9. Critique Reasoning Fred decides that $12 + 40 = 62$ is NOT a true equation. Is Fred correct? Explain.

____

Name ______________________

Practice **2-8**

Making Sense of Addition and Subtraction Equations

In **1–8,** decide if the two sides are equal. If *yes*, write $=$. If *no*, write $\neq$ (not equal).

1. $9 \bigcirc 5 + 4$ ______

2. $10 - 4 \bigcirc 5$ ______

3. $23 + 6 \bigcirc 29$ ______

4. $12 \bigcirc 14 - 1$ ______

5. $9 + 2 \bigcirc 7$ ______

6. $14 \bigcirc 5 + 9$ ______

7. $33 \bigcirc 44 - 11$ ______

8. $27 - 9 \bigcirc 18$ ______

In **9–16,** find the value for *n* that makes the equation true.

9. $16 = 7 + n$ ______

10. $12 = n - 3$ ______

11. $8 = 5 + n$ ______

12. $n - 6 = 3$ ______

13. $7 + n = 7$ ______

14. $24 - n = 14$ ______

15. $n = 45 + 6$ ______

16. $8 = 10 - n$ ______

For **17** and **18,** use the given equation to solve the problem.

17. Dina has 5 orchids. Mae has 13 orchids. How many more orchids does Mae have than Dina?

$5 + n = 13$

____

18. Juan collected 7 fewer stamps than Jenn. Juan collected 24 stamps. How many stamps did Jenn collect?

$n - 7 = 24$

____

19. Model Derrick has 7 marbles. Roger has *n* marbles. Together they have 14 marbles. Write an equation to model the problem. How many marbles does Roger have?

____

20. Which value for *n* makes the equation $n + 8 = 45$ true?

A $n = 37$

B $n = 38$

C $n = 41$

D $n = 53$

Name ______________________

Reteaching
2-9

Problem Solving: Reasonableness

The island of Elba has an area of 86 square miles. The island of St. Helena has an area of 47 square miles. How many square miles larger is Elba than St. Helena?

You can subtract to find how many square miles larger Elba is than St. Helena. Use mental math or a hundred chart to subtract.

86 in all

47	?

86 square miles in all

$86 - 47 = 39$

Elba is 39 square miles larger than St. Helena.

Make sure you answered the correct question.

The question asked how many square miles larger Elba is than St. Helena. The correct question was answered.

Make sure that your answer is reasonable.

Since $47 + 39 = 86$, the answer is reasonable.

1. The JP Morgan Chase Tower in Houston has 75 stories. The Renaissance Tower in Dallas has 56 stories. How many more stories does the JP Morgan Chase Tower have than the Renaissance Tower?

75 stories in all

56	

2. The Bulldogs scored 49 points in last week's game. This week, they scored 62 points. How many points did the Bulldogs score in all in the two games?

__________ points in all

49	62

3. Write a Problem Write a problem about something you did that can be solved using addition or subtraction. Then solve the problem and check that your answer is reasonable.

____

____

____

Name ______________________

Practice 2-9

Problem Solving: Reasonableness

Solve. Then check that your answer is reasonable.

1. The Aggies scored 59 points in the first half and 56 points in the second half. How many points did the Aggies score altogether?

   _______ points in all

59	56

2. Ms. Rice is driving 92 miles to a meeting. After driving 54 miles, she stops to buy gasoline. How many more miles does she have left?

   92 miles in all

54	

3. There are 45 students going on a field trip. Of those students, 27 are from Mrs. Unser's class. The rest are from Mr. King's class. How many students are from Mr. King's class?

   45 students in all

27	

4. **Estimation** In the 2004 Summer Olympics, the United States won 36 gold, 39 silver, and 27 bronze medals. About how many medals did the United States win?

   _______ medals in all

40	40	30

5. Christine is reading a short story that is 76 pages long. She just finished reading page 47. How many more pages does she have left to read?

   76 pages in all

47	

6. Wyoming has 23 counties. Wisconsin has 49 more counties than Wyoming. How many counties does Wisconsin have?

   A 26
   B 62
   C 72
   D 82

Name

Adding with an Expanded Algorithm

Find 234 + 451.

You can use place-value blocks to show each number.

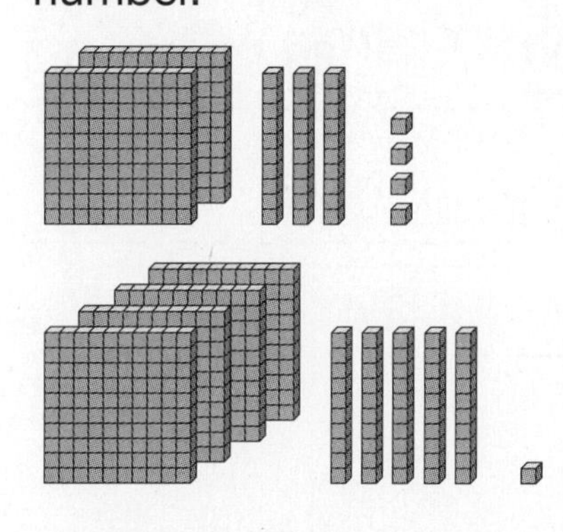

Step 1
Break the problem into smaller problems.

	H	T	O
234 =	200	30	4
451 =	400	50	1
Sums →	600	80	5

Step 2
Add the sums.

Hundreds → 600
Tens → 80
Ones → + 5
234 + 451 = 685

1. 211 + 334.

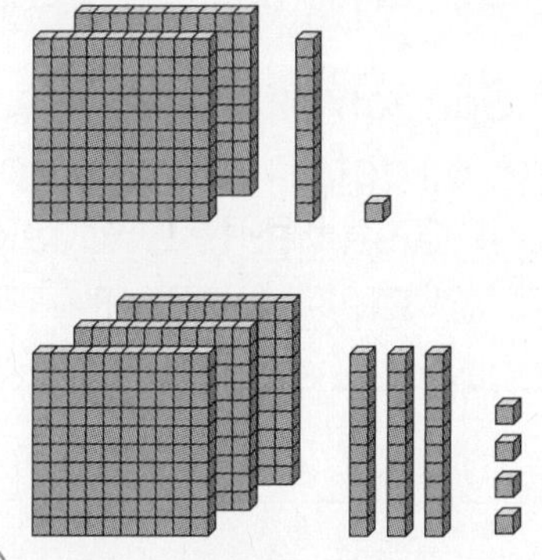

Hundreds	Tens	Ones	Total
200	10	1	____
+ 300	+ 30	+ 4	____
			+ ____

2. 516 + 140.

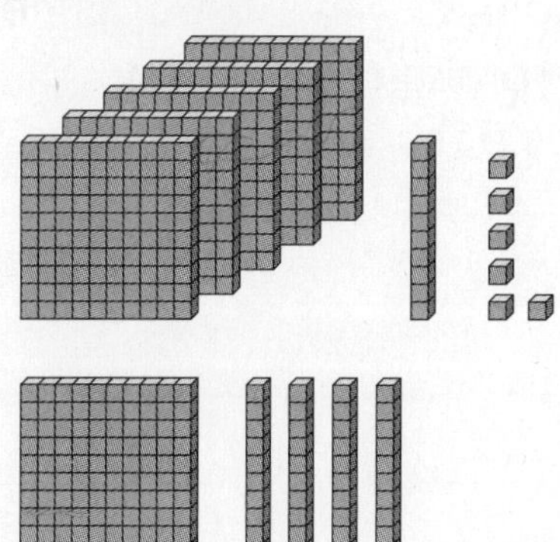

Hundreds	Tens	Ones	Total
500	10	6	____
+ 100	+ 40	+ 0	____
			+ ____

3. 439 + 520. ____

4. 731 + 176 ____

5. 156 + 432. ____

Name ______________________

Practice 3-1

Adding with an Expanded Algorithm

In **1–4** find each sum.

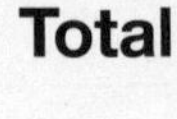

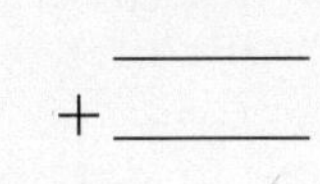

1. 134 + 221.

Hundreds	Tens	Ones
100	30	4
+ 200	+ 20	+ 1
____	____	____

Total

____

____

+ ____

2. 226 + 423.

Hundreds	Tens	Ones
200	20	6
+ 400	+ 20	+ 3
____	____	____

Total

____

____

+ ____

3. 344 + 421.

____

4. 575 + 342.

____

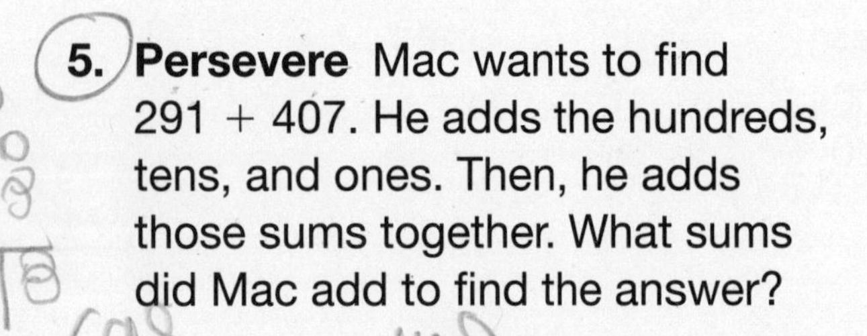

5. Persevere Mac wants to find 291 + 407. He adds the hundreds, tens, and ones. Then, he adds those sums together. What sums did Mac add to find the answer?

____

6. At Green School, 325 students walk, bike, or get a ride to school. There are 413 students who take the bus to school. How many students go to Green School?

____

7. Generalize Lauren is trying to find how far her family traveled on a road trip. On the first day, they drove 436 miles. On the second day, they drove 342 miles. How many miles did Lauren's family drive in all? Explain how you found the answer.

____

____

____

____

____

8. Which of the following shows the sums of the hundreds, tens, and ones for 627 + 361?

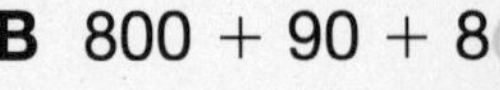

A 800 + 80 + 9 **B** 800 + 90 + 8 **C** 900 + 80 + 8 **D** 900 + 90 + 8

Name ______________________

Models for Adding 3-Digit Numbers

Find 152 + 329.

Step 1: Show each number with place-value blocks.

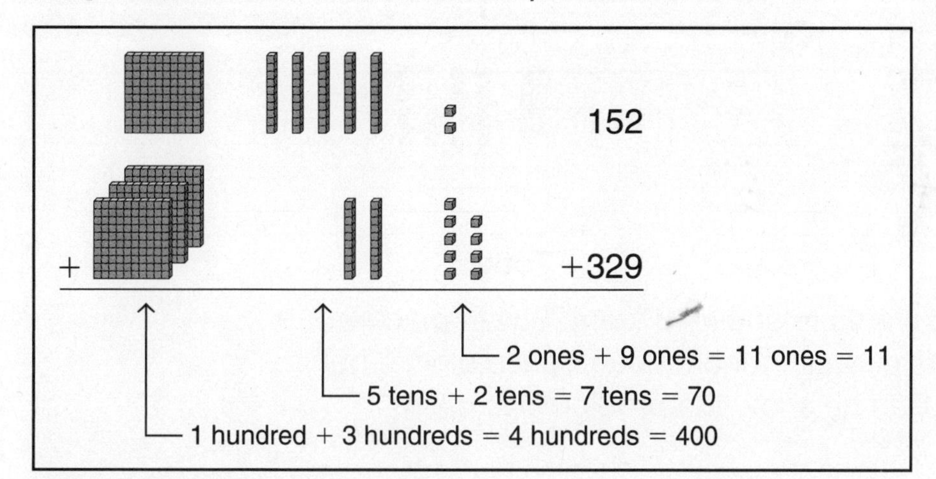

Step 2: Combine the ones. $2 + 9 = 11$

Step 3: Combine the tens. $50 + 20 = 70$

Step 4: Combine the hundreds. $100 + 300 = 400$

Step 5: Add. $400 + 70 + 11 = 481$

Write each problem and find the sum.

1. 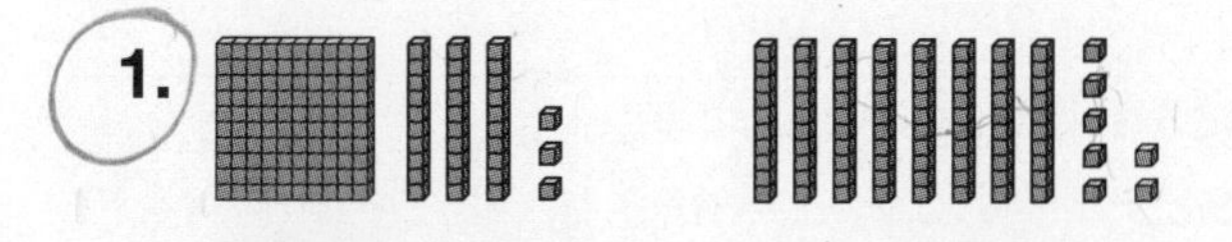 ______________________

2. 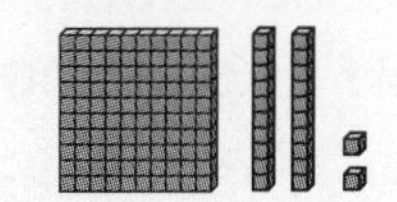 ______________________

3. 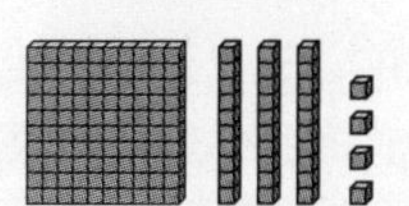 ______________________

4. 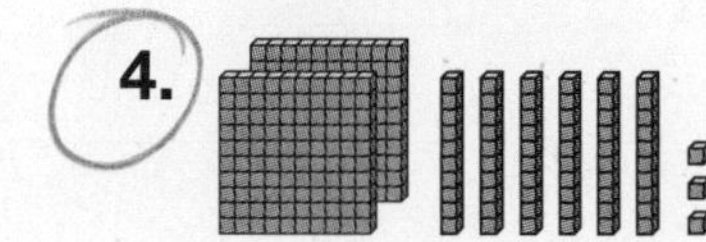 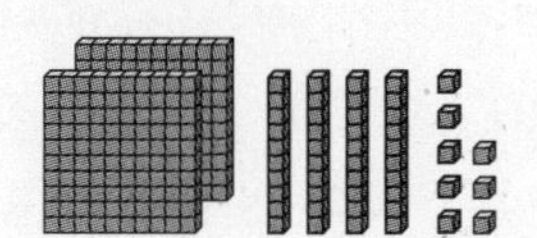 ______________________

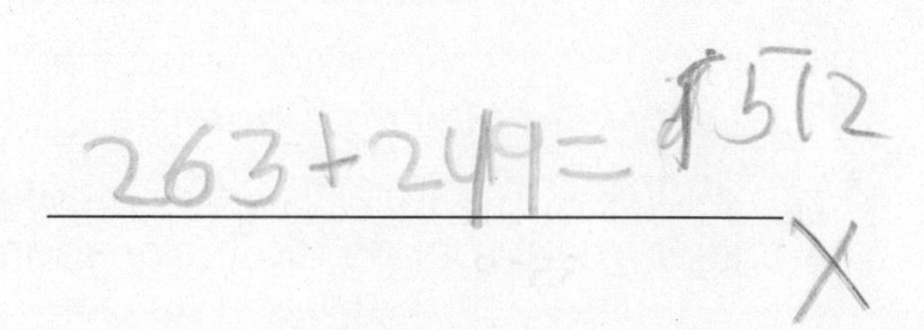

Name ____________________

Practice
3-2

Models for Adding 3-Digit Numbers

Write each problem and find the sum.

1. **2.**

______________________ ______________________

3. Number Sense Ed wants to show 137 + 429 with place-value blocks. He has enough hundreds and ones blocks but only 4 tens blocks. Can he show the problem? Explain.

____

____

4. Museum A has 127 steps. Museum B has 194 steps. How many steps do the museums have all together? Place-value blocks may help.

____

5. The country of Malta has an area of 316 square miles. The country of Saint Kitts and Nevis has an area of 261 square miles. What is the area of the two countries all together?

__________ square miles

6. The longest vertical lift drawbridge in the United States is the Arthur Kill Bridge at 558 feet. The longest steel truss bridge in the United States is the Glade Creek Bridge. The Glade Creek Bridge is 226 feet longer than the Arthur Kill Bridge. How many feet long is the Glade Creek Bridge? __________ feet

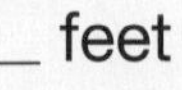

7. Larry was playing a board game. Larry scored 273 points on the first game and 248 points on the second game. How many points did Larry score in all?

A 411 **B** 421 **C** 511 **D** 521

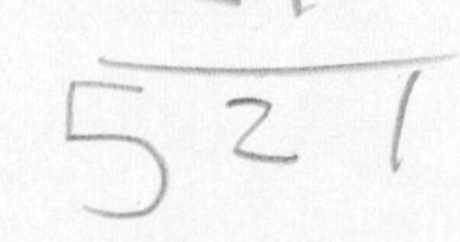

Name ______________________

Reteaching
3-3

Adding 3-Digit Numbers

Find 237 + 186.

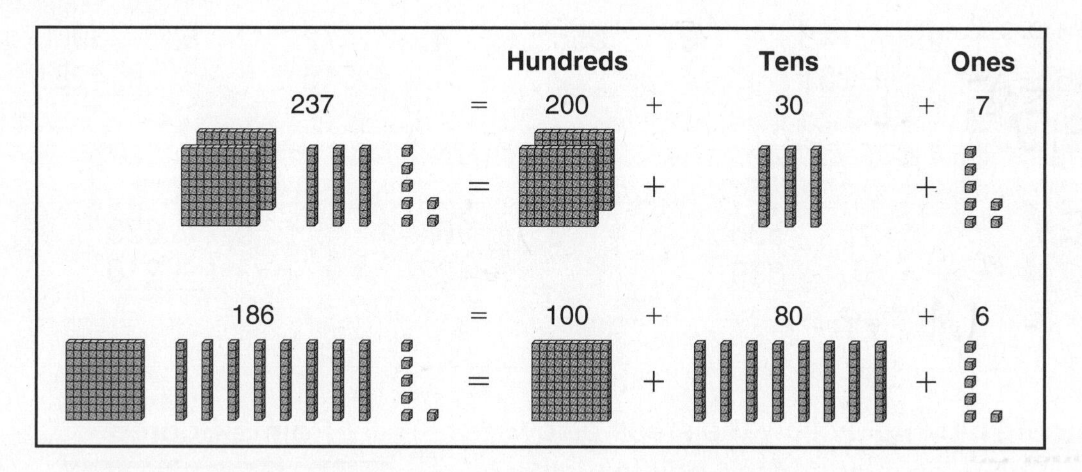

Step 1: Add the ones. 7 ones + 6 ones = 13 ones

Regroup. 13 ones = 1 ten, 3 ones

Step 2: Add the tens. 1 ten + 3 tens + 8 tens = 12 tens

Regroup. 12 tens = 1 hundred, 2 tens

Step 3: Add the hundreds.

1 hundred + 2 hundreds + 1 hundred = 4 hundreds

Add together the hundreds, tens, and ones.

400 + 20 + 3 = 423

Estimate by rounding to the nearest hundred. Then find each sum.

1. 118 + 146

2. 283 + 147

3. 542 + 109

4. 220 + 479

5. Find the sum of 456 and 238. ______________

6. Add 109 and 656. ______________

7. Estimation Estimate to decide which sum is less than 600: 356 + 292 or 214 + 356. ______________

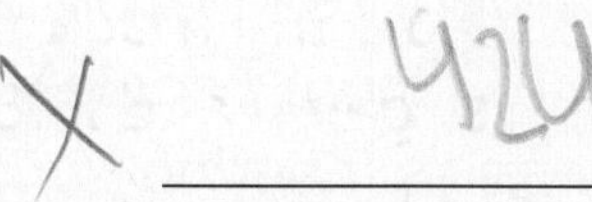

Name ______________________

Adding 3-Digit Numbers

Estimate. Then find each sum.

1. 329 + 468

2. 148 + 231

3. 555 + 222

4. 472 + 515

5. 396 + 428

6. 645 + 79

7. 536 + 399

8. 268 + 422

9. 633 + 210

10. **Critical Thinking** Follow the steps below to find how many combined points were scored by Howie and Theo.

Points Scored

Player	Points
Howie	272
Theo	325
Isabel	288

a. Write a number sentence to show how to solve the problem.

____

b. Estimate the total points scored by Howie and Theo.

____

c. Find the actual total. ______________________

11. **Explain It** Write an addition story for two 3-digit numbers. Write the answer to your story.

____

12. Sharon can run 278 yards in one minute. Pete can run 145 more yards than Sharon in one minute. How many yards can Pete run in one minute?

____

13. There were 752 people at a town meeting last week. There were 163 more people this week. How many people attended this week's meeting?

A 815 **B** 825 **C** 915 **D** 925

Name ______________________________

Adding 3 or More Numbers

Find 137 + 201 + 109.

To add three numbers, you can add two numbers first. Then add the sum of the first two numbers and the third number.

Step 1	Step 2
Add 137 + 201.	Add 338 + 109.
137 + 201 338	1 338 + 109 447

So, 137 + 201 + 109 = 447.

Find each sum.

1. 32
64
+ 71

2. 127
39
+ 87

3. 293
312
+ 78

4. 358
427
+ 127

5. 382 + 45 + 181 = ______________

6. 52 + 238 + 76 = ______________

7. **Number Sense** Ranier has 37 baseball cards, 65 football cards, and 151 hockey cards. How many sports cards does he have in all? Explain how you found your answer.

____

____

Name ________________________

Practice
3-4

Adding 3 or More Numbers

1. $75 + 36 + 58$

2. $142 + 297 + 116$

3. $524 + 97 + 176$

4. $273 + 187 + 64 + 249$

5. $319 + 48 + 136 + 347$

6. 237 + 75 + 49 ________

7. 49 + 7 + 63 + 8 ________

8. 143 + 47 + 219 + 136 ________

9. Estimation Estimate the sum of 327 + 419 + 173.

____

10. Number Sense Justine has 162 red buttons, 98 blue buttons, and 284 green buttons. She says she knows she has more than 500 buttons without adding. Do you agree? Explain.

____

____

11. Carlos ate or drank everything that is listed in the table. How many calories did Carlos consume?

____

Food	Amount	Calories
Bran flakes	1 ounce	90
Banana	1	105
Orange juice	1 cup	110
Milk	1 cup	150

12. In winning the 1884 U.S. presidential election, Grover Cleveland received 219 electoral votes. He received 168 electoral votes in 1888, and lost. Then he received 277 electoral votes and won in 1892. How many electoral votes did Cleveland receive in all?

____

13. Kyle has 378 pennies, 192 nickels, and 117 dimes. How many coins does he have all together?

A 495 **B** 570 **C** 677 **D** 687

Name ____________________

Problem Solving: Draw a Picture

Don sold 18 watermelons in the morning and 14 in the afternoon. How many watermelons did he sell in all?

You can draw a rectangle to show addition.

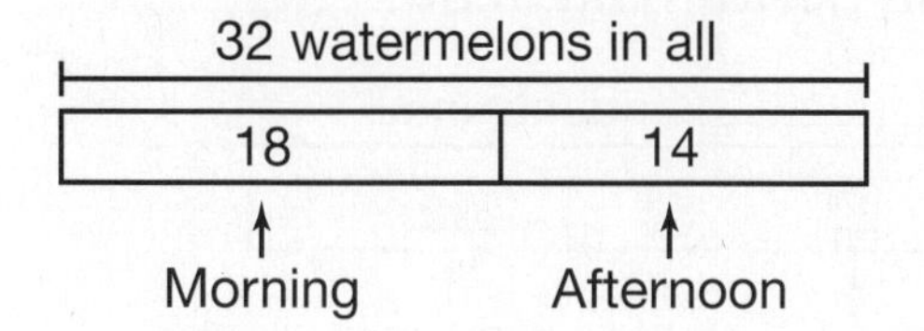

Each part of the rectangle represents one of the addends. Add the parts to show how many in all.

Don sold 32 watermelons in all.

1. Two buses are carrying students to a field trip. There are 36 students on one bus and 30 students on the other. How many students are on the buses in all?

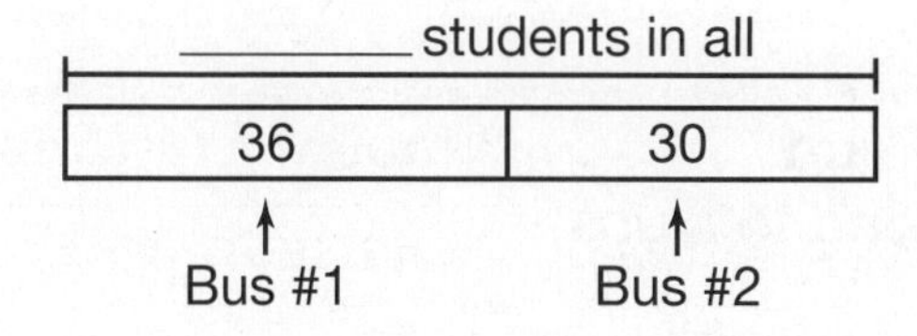

2. **Estimation** Vanessa bought a sweater for $27 and a skirt for $22. About how much money did Vanessa spend in all?

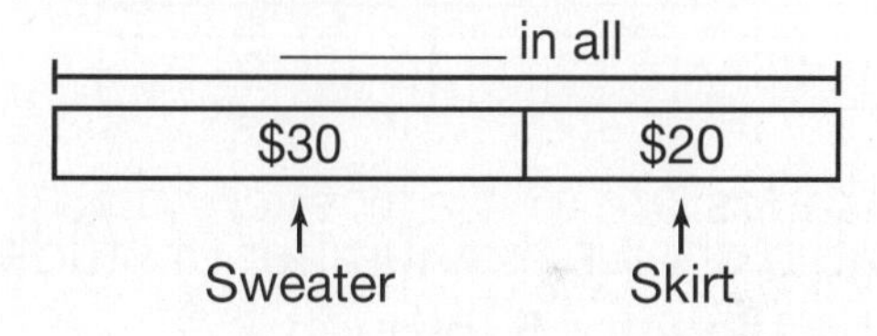

3. A pet store sold 26 puppies and 14 kittens last month. How many animals were sold in all?

______ animals in all

26	14

4. Ken has 15 rap CDs, 20 country CDs, and 30 rock CDs. How many CDs does Ken have in all?

______ CDs in all

15	20	30

Name ______________________

Practice
3-5

Problem Solving: Draw a Picture

1. Kelly bought a CD for $15 and a book for $13. How much money did Kelly spend in all?

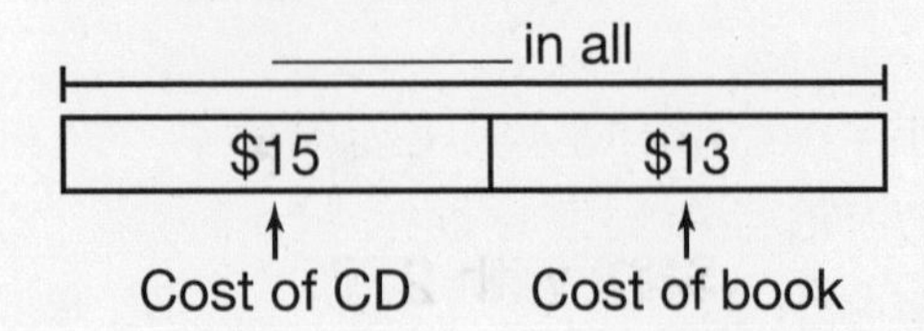

2. **Estimation** There are 28 students in the chorus and 31 students in the band. All will be performing tonight. About how many students will be performing in all?

_______ students in all

30	30

Chorus — Band

3. Jane sold 25 raffle tickets Monday, 30 raffle tickets Tuesday, and 40 raffle tickets Wednesday. How many raffle tickets did Jane sell all together?

_______ tickets in all

25	30	40

4. Dan cycled 12 miles Saturday and 18 miles Sunday. How many miles did he cycle all together?

_______ miles in all

12	18

The table shows the number of students who belong to clubs. Use the table for **5** through **7**.

Club Membership

Club	Members
Math	24
Spanish	18
Running	15
Science	6

5. How many students belong to the Spanish and Science clubs?

_______ members in all

6. About how many students belong to the Math and Spanish clubs?

_______ members in all

7. How many students belong to the Math, Running, and Science clubs?

_______ members in all

Name ______ (W)

Reteaching
3-6

Subtracting with an Expanded Algorithm

Apple Hill is 568 feet high. Banana Hill is 293 feet high. How many feet higher is Apple Hill than Banana Hill?

Find 568 − 293.

"I need to find 568 − 293."

Step 1

568 − 293 = ?

Start with 568.

Subtract the **2 hundreds** in 293.

568 − 200 = 368

So far, 200 has been subtracted.

Step 2

Now, start with 368.

Subtract the **9 tens** in 293.

There are not enough tens. So, subtract the **6 tens** that are there.

368 − 60 = 308

Then, subtract the tens that are left.

9 tens − 6 tens = 3 tens

308 − 30 = 278

So far, 200 + 60 + 30 = 290 has been subtracted.

Step 3

Start with 278.

Subtract the **3 ones** in 293.

278 − 3 = 275

In all 200 + 60 + 30 + 3 = 293 has been subtracted.

Apple Hill is 275 feet higher than Banana Hill.

1. Follow these steps to find 576 − 471.
   First subtract 400.
   Then, subtract 70.
   Then, subtract 1.
   105 ✓

2. Follow these steps to find 365 − 138.
   First subtract 100.
   Then, subtract 30.
   Then, subtract 5.
   Then, subtract 3.
   ______

3. Find 756 − 602. ______

4. Find 848 − 276. ______

5. Find 641 − 139. 502 ✓

6. Sue's story is 367 words long. Rob's story is 296 words long. How many more words does Sue's story have than Rob's?
   ______

7. **Reason** Find 496 − 217. Were there enough ones to subtract? How did you know?
   496−217=279. The ones are 7 because the last digit is the ones.

Name ______________________

Practice

3-6

Subtracting with an Expanded Algorithm

1. Follow these steps to find 879 − 659.
First subtract 600.
Then, subtract 50.
Then, subtract 9.

220 ✓

2. Follow these steps to find 775 − 431.
First subtract 400.
Then, subtract 30.
Then, subtract 1.

____

3. Follow these steps to find 564 − 117.
First subtract 100.
Then, subtract 10.
Then, subtract 4.
Then, subtract 3.

____

4. Follow these steps to find 428 − 275.
First subtract 200.
Then, subtract 20.
Then, subtract 50.
Then, subtract 5.

153 ✓

5. Find 684 − 362.

____

6. Find 208 − 135.

____

7. Find 479 − 283.

196 ✓

8. Find 614 − 153.

461 ✓

9. Eric and Kim are on a game show. Eric has 583 points. Kim has 349 points. How many more points does Eric have than Kim?

534 234 more points than Kim.

10. **Reason** Malcolm is trying to find 775 − 342. He subtracts hundreds first, then tens, then ones. What three numbers did Malcolm subtract to find the answer?

____

11. **Communicate** Kyle is making a building out of blocks. So far his building is made up of 129 blocks. When his building is finished, it will have 275 blocks. How many more blocks does Kyle need to finish his building? Explain how you found your answer.

Kyle need 145 more blocks. First, subtract 100. Then, 20. last, subtract 9.

disgusting handwriting

12. Which of the following shows the numbers that can be subtracted to find 395 − 129?

A 300, 90, 5 **B** 900, 20, 1 **C** 100, 20, 9, 5 **D** 100, 20, 5, 4

Name ______________________________

Models for Subtracting 3-Digit Numbers

You can use place-value blocks to subtract.

Find 234 − 192.

Estimate: 230 − 190 = 40, so the answer should be about 40.

	What You Show	What You Write
Step 1 Show 234 with place-value blocks.		234 −192
Step 2 Subtract the ones. 4 > 2. No regrouping is needed.	4 ones − 2 ones = 2 ones	234 −192 2
Step 3 Subtract the tens. 3 tens < 9 tens, so regroup 1 hundred for 10 tens.	13 tens − 9 tens = 4 tens	1 13 234 −192 42
Step 4 Subtract the hundreds.	1 hundred − 1 hundred = 0 hundreds	1 13 234 −192 42

Find the value of the remaining blocks:

4 tens + 2 ones = 40 + 2 = 42

So, 234 − 192 = 42.

Use place-value blocks or draw pictures to subtract.

1. 156 − 28

2. 261 − 122

3. 321 − 76

4. 446 − 257

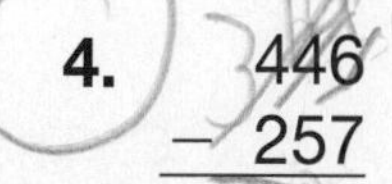

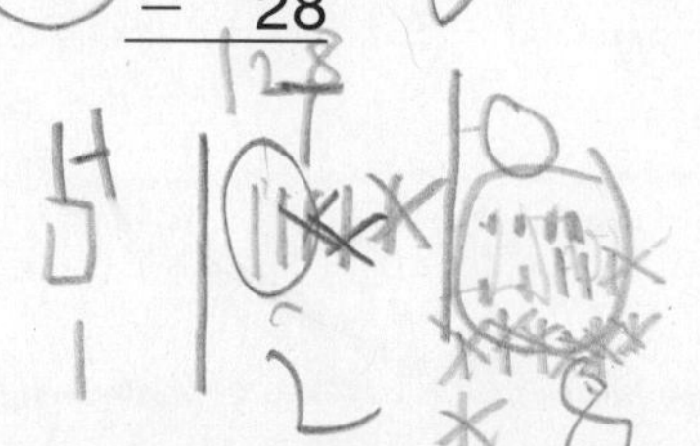

Name ______________________________

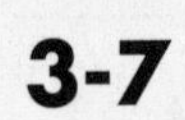
Practice
3-7

Models for Subtracting 3-Digit Numbers

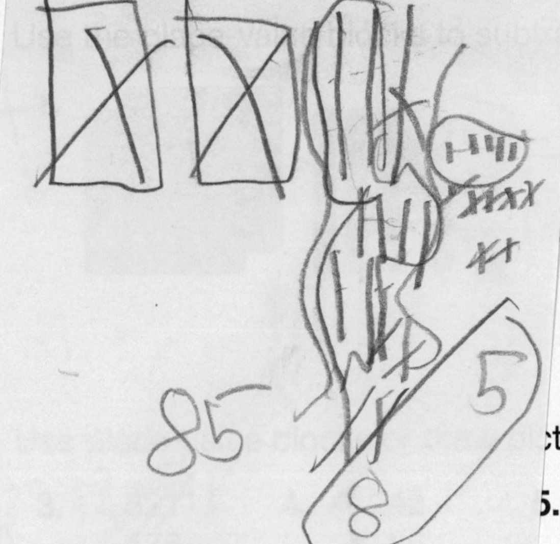

...ct.

232
− 147

2. 324 − 156

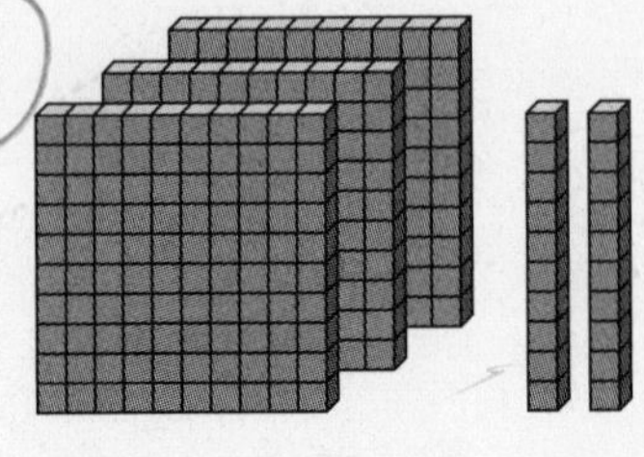

...tures to subtract.

5. 332 − 117 **6.** 267 − 149 **7.** 413 − 237

8. 165 − 137 **9.** 251 − 137 **10.** 372 − 283 **11.** 511 − 324 **12.** 346 − 138

For **13** and **14**, use the table at the right.

Pages Read

Name	Pages Read
Lance	322
Annie	263
Brad	415

13. What is the difference between the greatest and least number of pages read? __________

14. How many more pages did Lance read than Annie? __________

15. Number Sense Edie wanted to subtract 273 − 188. She began by finding 2 − 1. What did Edie do wrong?

____

____

16. Alice defeated Ralph 313 to 188 in a board game. By how many points did Alice win?

A 115 **B** 125 **C** 215 **D** 225

Name ____________________

Reteaching
3-8

Subtracting 3-Digit Numbers

Find 726 − 238.

Estimate: 700 − 200 = 500, so the answer should be about 500.

Step 1

First subtract the ones.
Regroup 1 ten into 10 ones.

```
  1 16
  726
 −238
    8
```

Step 2

Subtract the tens.
Regroup 1 hundred into 10 tens.

```
   11
 6 1 16
  726
 −238
   88
```

Step 3

Subtract the hundreds.

```
   11
 6 1 16
  726
 −238
  488
```

Is your answer correct?
Check by adding:
488 + 238 = 726.
It checks.

Find each difference. Estimate and check answers for reasonableness.

1. 318 − 123 = 196

2. 441 − 187

3. 334 − 275

4. 512 − 299 = 213

5. 423 − 156 = ______

6. 327 − 159 = 268

7. The town library had 634 CDs for rent. During one week, 288 of them were rented. How many CDs were left? ______

8. **Number Sense** If you had to subtract 426 from 913, how many times would you need to regroup? How can you tell?

____

____

____

____

Name ______________________

Subtracting 3-Digit Numbers

Practice
3-8

Find each difference. Estimate and check answers for reasonableness.

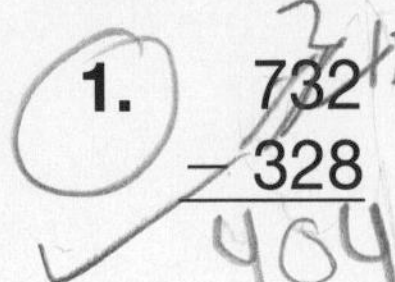
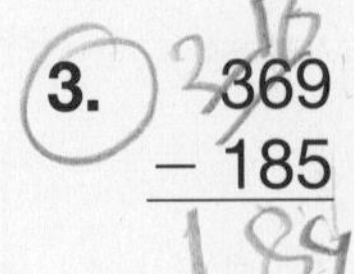

1. 732 − 328	**2.** 621 − 153	**3.** 369 − 185	**4.** 267 − 78	**5.** 527 − 279
6. 917 − 436	**7.** 555 − 189	**8.** 422 − 244	**9.** 853 − 456	**10.** 451 − 363

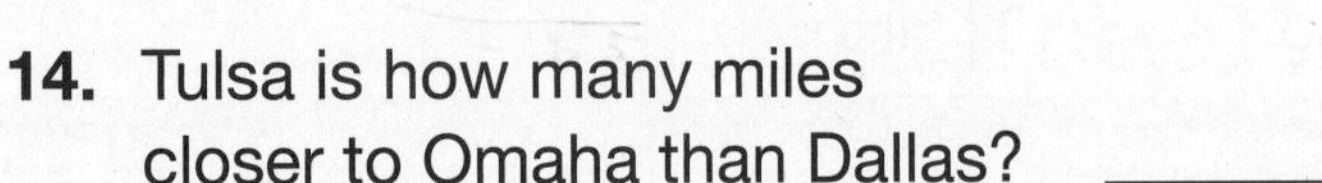

11. 527 − 242 = ______ **12.** 746 − 437 = ______ **13.** 941 − 267 = ______

All Roads Lead to Omaha

Start	Finish	Miles
Dallas	Omaha	644
Chicago	Omaha	459
Tulsa	Omaha	387

14. Tulsa is how many miles closer to Omaha than Dallas? ______

15. Tulsa is how many miles closer to Omaha than Chicago? ______

16. Strategy Practice Jill is going on a trip from Chicago to Omaha to Tulsa. Bill will travel from Dallas to Omaha. How much farther will Jill travel than Bill?

a. What do you need to do first?

____

____

b. What is the next step?

____

c. Solve the problem.

______ miles

17. Texas has 254 counties. California has 58 counties and Florida has 67 counties. How many more counties does Texas have than California and Florida combined?

A 125 **B** 129 **C** 139 **D** 196

Name ______

Subtracting Across Zero

Reteaching
3-9

To subtract from a number with 0 in the tens place, you need to regroup one hundred into 10 tens.

Find 207 − 98.

Step 1	Step 2	Step 3
Subtract the ones. Since there are 0 tens, you must first regroup the hundreds.	Regroup the hundreds. 2 hundreds and 0 tens = 1 hundred and 10 tens.	Regroup the tens. 10 tens and 7 ones = 9 tens and 17 ones. Subtract.
207 − 98	207 − 98 (regrouped: 1 10)	207 − 98 = 109 (regrouped: 1 9 17)

Is your answer correct? Check by adding: 109 + 98 = 207.

Find each difference.

1. 301 − 72 (229)
2. 205 − 36
3. 400 − 228 (172)
4. 502 − 225
5. 603 − 215 (388)

6. 307 − 149 = 158
7. 702 − 259 = ______
8. 504 − 397 = ______

9. **Number Sense** Waco has an elevation of 405 feet above sea level. Texarkana has an elevation of 324 feet above sea level. How many feet greater is Waco's elevation than Texarkana's? Show your work. 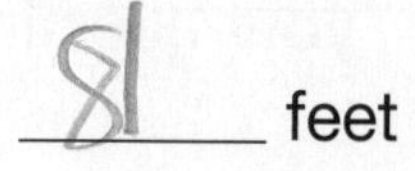 feet

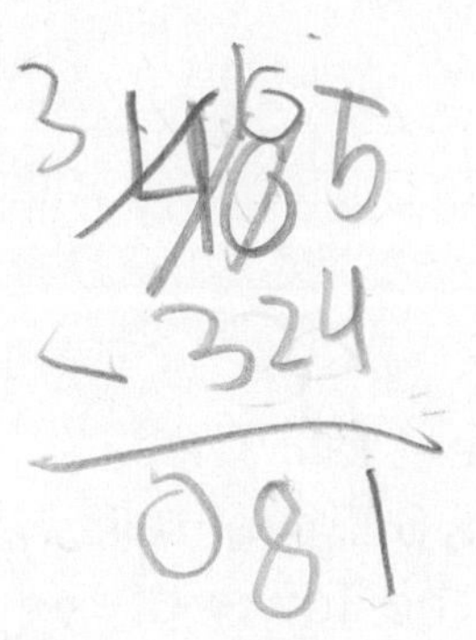

Name ______________________________

Subtracting Across Zero

Find each difference.

1. $406 - 28$

2. $300 - 211$

3. $501 - 268$

4. $705 - 347$

5. $605 - 219$

6. $800 - 579$

7. $907 - 728$

8. $603 - 347$

9. $507 - 388$

10. $706 - 497$

11. $404 - 305 =$ ______

12. $501 - 223 =$ ______

13. $302 - 166 =$ ______

14. There were 600 ears of corn for sale at the produce market. At the end of the day, there were 212 ears left. How many ears of corn were sold? ______

15. Darrin has 702 CDs in his collection. Dana has 357 CDs in her collection. How many more CDs does Darrin have than Dana? ______

16. **Strategy Practice** Party Palace has an order for 505 party favors. It packaged 218 favors on Saturday and 180 favors on Sunday. How many more party favors does it still need to package? ______

17. **Write a Problem** Write a subtraction problem involving regrouping that has Ted reading 304 pages. Answer your question.

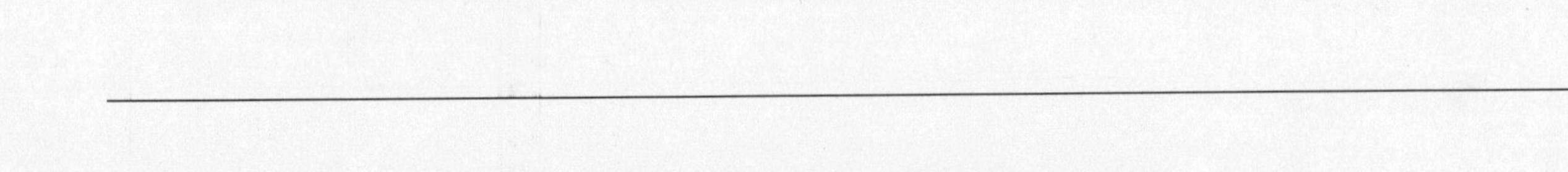

18. The Williams Tower in Houston, TX, is 901 feet tall. The Tower of the Americas in San Antonio, TX, is 622 feet tall. How much taller is the Williams Tower than the Tower of the Americas?

A 279 feet **B** 289 feet **C** 379 feet **D** 389 feet

Name ______________________

Reteaching **3-10**

Problem Solving: Draw a Picture and Write a Number Sentence

The distance from Cleveland, OH, to Pittsburgh, PA, is 129 miles. Detroit, MI, is 170 miles away from Cleveland. How much closer is Cleveland to Pittsburgh than to Detroit?

You can subtract to find how many miles closer Cleveland is to Pittsburgh than to Detroit.

170 miles

129	?

$$\begin{array}{r} 170 \\ -\ 129 \\ \hline 41 \end{array}$$

Cleveland is 41 miles closer to Pittsburgh than to Detroit.

You can estimate $170 - 130 = 40$ to show that the answer is reasonable.

Solve.

1. Honolulu, HI, has an area of 86 square miles. Corpus Christi, TX, has an area that is 69 square miles greater than the area of Honolulu. How many square miles is Corpus Christi?

______ square miles

86	69

2. Bakersfield, CA, has an area of 113 square miles. Its area is 64 square miles greater than the area of Anaheim, CA. What is the area, in square miles, of Anaheim?

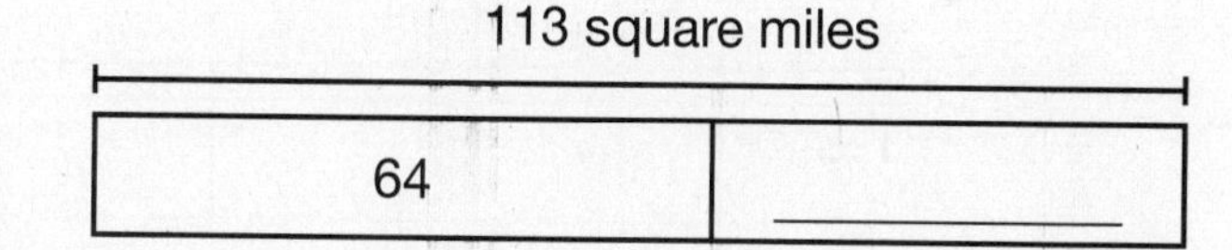

3. Writing to Explain How did you know which operation to use to solve Problem 2?

____

____

____

Name ____________________

Practice
3-10

Problem Solving: Draw a Picture and Write a Number Sentence

The table below shows the areas of some of the smallest countries in the world. Use the table for **1–3.**

Area of Countries

Country	Area (in sq mi)
San Marino	24
Liechtenstein	62
Maldives	116
Palau	177

1. How many square miles greater is Maldives than San Marino?

116 square miles

24	____

2. Draw a Picture Draw a diagram to show how to find the difference between the areas of Liechtenstein and San Marino. Use your diagram to solve the problem.

3. Grenada is 15 square miles greater than Maldives. What is the area of Grenada?

____ square miles

116	15

4. There are 237 students at Johnson Elementary School. There are 188 students at Hoover Elementary School. How many more students are at Johnson than at Hoover?

237 students

188	____

5. Write a Problem Write a real-world problem that you can solve by adding or subtracting. Then give your problem to a classmate to solve.

____

____

____

Name ____________________

Reteaching

4-1

Multiplication as Repeated Addition

Each group below has the same number of squares. There are 5 groups of 4 squares. There are a total of 20 squares.

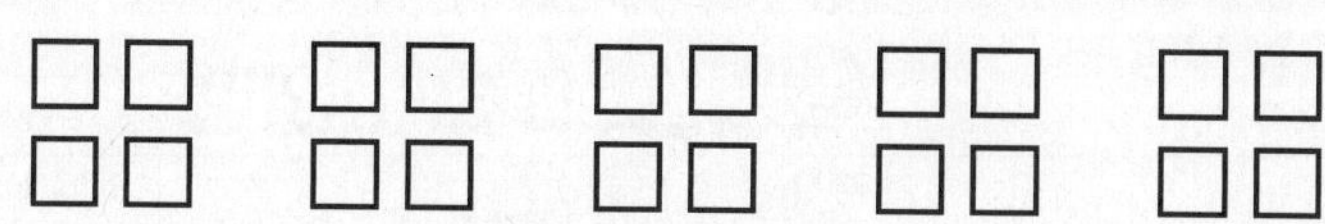

Here is the addition sentence for this problem: $4 + 4 + 4 + 4 + 4 = 20$

Here is the multiplication sentence for this problem: $5 \times 4 = 20$

Complete the addition and multiplication sentences.

1. 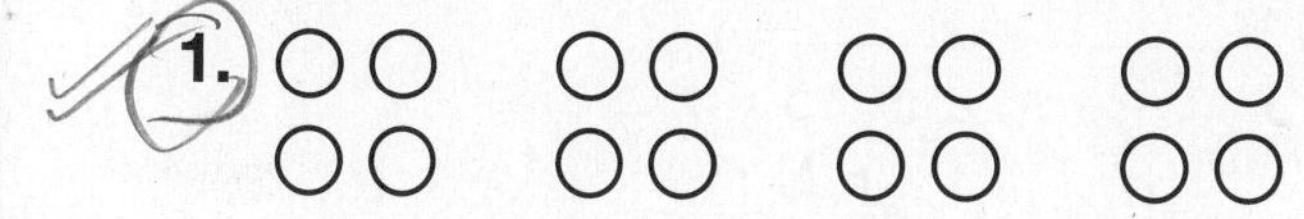

4 groups of 4 $4 + 4 + 4 + 4 =$ 16 $4 \times$ 4 $= 16$

2. ○○○○ ○○○○ ○○○○ ○○○○
○○○ ○○○ ○○○ ○○○

4 groups of 7 7 + 7 + 7 + 7 $= 28$

4 $\times 7 =$ 28

Write each addition sentence as a multiplication sentence.

3. $1 + 1 + 1 + 1 + 1 = 5$ 5x1=5

4. $8 + 8 + 8 = 24$ 8x3=24

Write each multiplication sentence as an addition sentence.

5. $5 \times 5 = 25$ 5+5+5+5+5=25

6. $6 \times 2 = 12$ 

7. Communicate Juan says, "When you put together unequal groups, you can only add." Is he correct? Explain.

____

Name ____________________

Practice

4-1

Multiplication as Repeated Addition

Complete.

1. 

2 groups of ____

5 + ____ = ____

2 × ____ = ____

2.

3 groups of ____

4 + ____ + ____ = ____

3 × ____ = ____

3. 4 + 4 + 4 + 4 + 4 = 5 × ____

4. ____ + ____ + ____ = 3 × 8

5. 9 + ____ + ____ = ____ × 9

6. 7 + 7 + 7 + 7 = ____ × ____

Write +, −, or × for each ☐.

7. 5 ☐ 4 = 9 **8.** 6 ☐ 2 = 12 **9.** 7 ☐ 3 = 4

10. 3 ☐ 3 = 9 **11.** 8 ☐ 6 = 2 **12.** 3 ☐ 3 = 6

13. Reason Marlon has 4 cards, Jake has 4 cards, and Sam has 3 cards. Can you write a multiplication sentence to find how many cards they have in all? Explain.

14. Write a Problem Draw a picture that shows equal groups. Then write an addition sentence and a multiplication sentence for your picture.

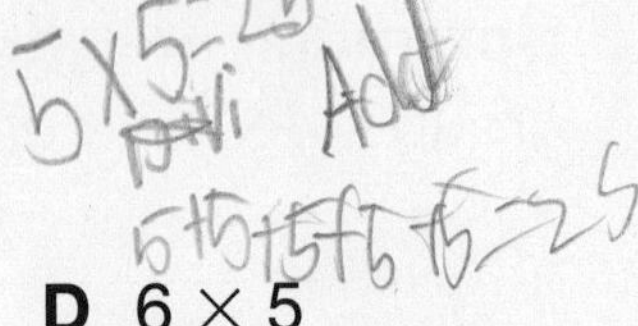

15. Which is equal to 6 + 6 + 6 + 6?

A 6 × 3 **B** 3 × 6 **C** 4 × 6 **D** 6 × 5

Name ______________________

Reteaching
4-2

Arrays and Multiplication

Multiplication can be used to find the total in an array.

Scott arranged some apples in an array. He made 4 rows with 3 apples in each row. How many apples does Scott have?

Draw Scott's array.

The array shows 4 rows of 3 apples.

$3 + 3 + 3 + 3 = 12$

Say, 4 times 3 equals 12

Write, $4 \times 3 = 12$

Scott has 12 apples.

Write a multiplication sentence for each array.

1.

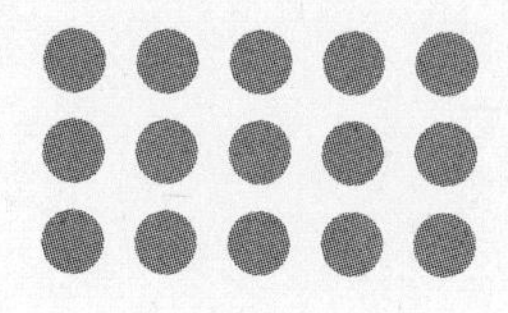

____

2.

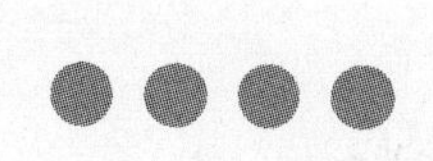

____

3.

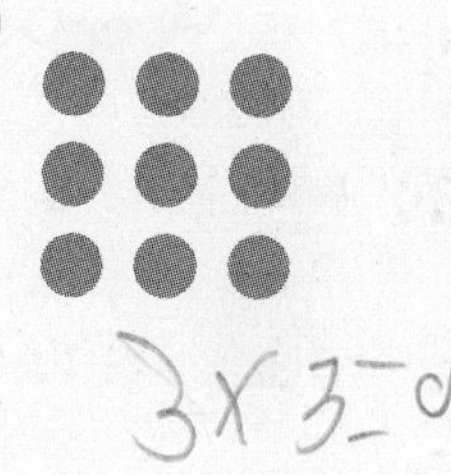

____

4. Draw an array to show the fact 3×4.

5. Model Priya is arranging 28 chairs with 7 chairs in each row. How many rows will there be? You can use an array to help.

____

Name ____________

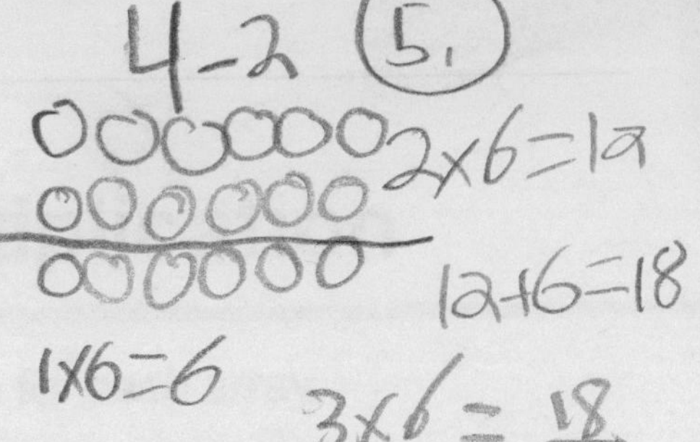

Arrays and Mu

Write a multiplication sente

1.  

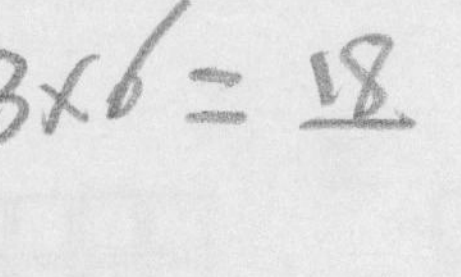

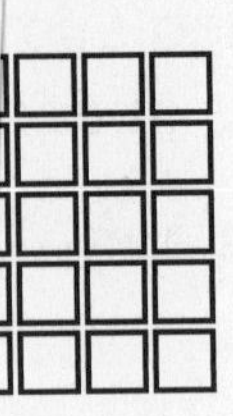

____ × ____ = ____   9 × 3 = 27   ____ × ____ = ____

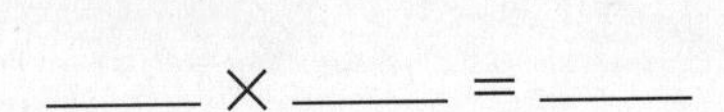

Draw an array to show each multiplication fact. Write the product.

4. $2 \times 8 =$ ______

5. $3 \times 6 =$ 18

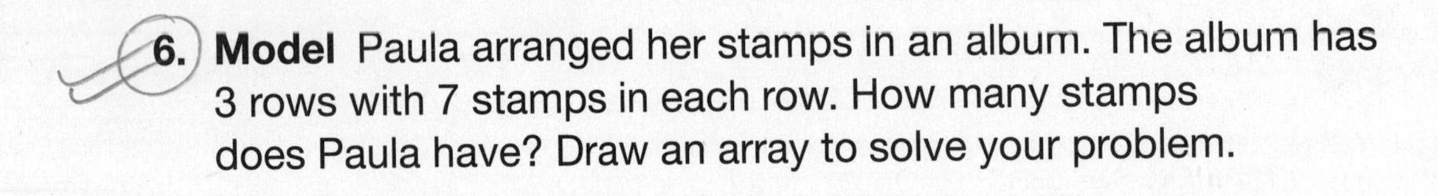

6. **Model** Paula arranged her stamps in an album. The album has 3 rows with 7 stamps in each row. How many stamps does Paula have? Draw an array to solve your problem.

____

7. Jonathan is arranging 36 pictures, with 9 pictures in each row. How many rows will there be?

A 9   **B** 5   **C** 4   **D** 2

Name ______________________________

The Commutative Property

Reteaching
4-3

An array shows objects in equal rows.
This array shows 3 rows of 6 pennies.

The multiplication sentence for this array is
$3 \times 6 = 18$.

You can use the Commutative (Order) Property of Multiplication to multiply the numbers in any order:
$3 \times 6 = 18$ and $6 \times 3 = 18$.

Write a multiplication sentence for each array.

1. 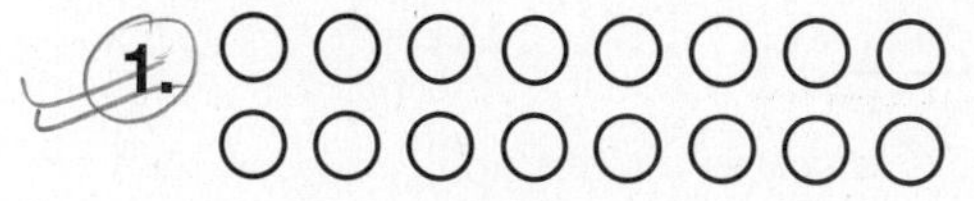

____

2.

____

Complete each multiplication sentence. You may use counters or draw a picture to help.

3. $3 \times 4 = 12$ ______ $\times 3 = 12$

4. $5 \times 2 = 10$ $2 \times$ ______ $= 10$

5. Number Sense How can you use the Commutative Property to know that

is equal to ?

____

____

____

Name ______________________

Practice

4-3

The Commutative Property

Write a multiplication sentence for each array.

1. (array of 3 rows of 5) ______________
2. (array of 2 rows of 10) ______________
3. (array of 4 rows of 6) ______________

Draw an array to find each multiplication fact. Write the product.

4. $3 \times 6 =$ ______
5. $4 \times 7 =$ 28

Complete each multiplication sentence.
Use counters or draw an array to help.

6. $3 \times$ 7 $= 21$

   $7 \times$ ____ $= 21$

7. $4 \times 9 =$ ____

   $9 \times 4 =$ ____

8. $5 \times 6 =$ ____

   $6 \times 5 =$ ____

9. $4 \times 7 =$ ____

   $7 \times 4 =$ ____

10. $6 \times 8 =$ ____

    $8 \times 6 =$ ____

11. $9 \times 5 =$ 45

    $5 \times 9 =$ ____

12. **Explain It** If you know that $7 \times 8 = 56$, how can you use the Commutative (Order) Property of Multiplication to find the product of 8×7?

You can swich the factors and the Product will Stay the Same. The commurative Proerty Says You can multiply the factors in any order and the Product will stay the same.

13. Which of the following is equal to 8×4?

A 4×8 **B** $4 + 8$ **C** $8 - 4$ **D** $8 + 4$

Name Done

Reteaching 4-4

Writing Multiplication Stories

When you write a multiplication story you should:

- Always end the story with a question.
- Draw a picture to show the main idea.

Example:
Write a multiplication story for 5 × 9.

Josephine has 5 friends over for a snack. She gives each friend 9 grapes. How many grapes did Josephine give all together?

Josephine gave 45 grapes all together.

Write a multiplication story for each exercise. Draw a picture to find each product.

1. 4 × 3

____

____

2. 5 × 2

I have 5 belts in each baseket. There are 2 baskets. How many belts are there in all? There are 10 belts in all

=10

3. 4 × 6

____

____

4. **Model** Leshon has seven $5 bills. How much money does Leshon have? Write a multiplication sentence to show the answer.

5+5+5+5+5=25 or
5x5=25

Name ______________________

Writing Multiplication Stories

Write a multiplication story for each.

Draw a picture to find each product.

1. 3×6

2. 2×8

3. 4×3

Write a multiplication story for each picture.

4. 

5. 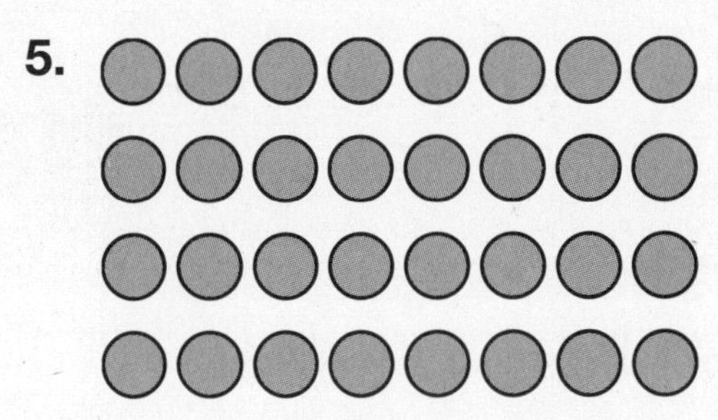

6. **Model** Hot dog buns come in packages of 8. Mrs. Wilson has a total of 40 hot dog buns. Draw a picture to find how many packages of hot dog buns Mrs. Wilson has.

7. There are 9 players on a baseball team. At the park, 4 teams are playing. How many baseball players are playing at the park?

A 27 **B** 32 **C** 36 **D** 40

Name ______________________

Reteaching
4-5

Problem Solving: Writing to Explain

David is making 3 pancakes for each person in his family. Today, there are 6 family members at breakfast. How many pancakes does he need to make? Explain how you can solve this problem.

You can make a table to solve this problem.

As the number of people increases by 1, the number of pancakes David needs to make increases by 3.

People	1	2	3	4	5	6
Pancakes	3	6	9	12	15	18
		3 + 3 = 6	6 + 3 = 9	9 + 3 = 12	12 + 3 = 15	15 + 3 = 18

David needs to make 18 pancakes.

1. Marcia got on an elevator on the fourth floor. She went down 2 floors. Then she went up 6 floors. Then she went down 3 floors. What floor is Marcia on now?

______

2. **Explain It** How did you find your answer to Exercise 1?

____

____

____

3. Look at the numbers below.
75, 74, 72, 69, 65, ...

a. Describe the pattern.

____

____

____

b. What are the next two numbers in the pattern?

______

4. Ms. Skidmore is setting up basketball teams. There are 5 players on each team.

a. Complete the table below.

Teams	1	2	3	4	5
Players	5	10	15		

b. Describe the pattern by how the number of teams and players change.

____

____

Name ______________________

Problem Solving: Writing to Explain

1. Look at the numbers below.
13, 15, 19, 25, ...

a. Describe the pattern.

____

____

____

b. Explain how you can find the next two numbers. What are the next two numbers?

____

____

2. Mr. Wilson is setting up volleyball teams. There are 6 players on a team.

a. Complete the table below.

Teams	1	2	3	4	5
Players	6	12	18		

b. Explain how the number of players changes as the number of teams changes.

____

____

____

3. **Look for Patterns** The table below shows the amount of money that Louise earns in allowance each week.

a. Complete the table.

Louise's Allowance

Number of Weeks	Allowance
1	$8
2	$16
3	$24
4	
5	

b. How did the table help you to find the pattern?

____

____

4. Diana is training to run a race.

a. Complete the table for Diana's first week of training.

Diana's Training Schedule

Day	Minutes
Monday	15
Tuesday	20
Wednesday	25
Thursday	
Friday	

b. If she continues the pattern, for how many minutes will Diana run on Saturday?

____

Name ____________________

Reteaching
5-1

2 and 5 as Factors

Done

When you multiply by 2, you can use a doubles fact.
For example, 2×3 is the same as adding $3 + 3$.

You can use a pattern to multiply by 5.

2s Facts		5s Facts	
$2 \times 0 = 0$	$2 \times 5 = 10$	$5 \times 0 = 0$	$5 \times 5 = 25$
$2 \times 1 = 2$	$2 \times 6 = 12$	$5 \times 1 = 5$	$5 \times 6 = 30$
$2 \times 2 = 4$	$2 \times 7 = 14$	$5 \times 2 = 10$	$5 \times 7 = 35$
$2 \times 3 = 6$	$2 \times 8 = 16$	$5 \times 3 = 15$	$5 \times 8 = 40$
$2 \times 4 = 8$	$2 \times 9 = 18$	$5 \times 4 = 20$	$5 \times 9 = 45$

Each multiple of 2 ends in 0, 2, 4, 6, or 8. All multiples of 2 are even.

Each multiple of 5 ends in 0 or 5.

Find each product.

1. $3 \times 2 =$ ______ **2.** $4 \times 2 =$ ______ **3.** $6 \times 2 =$ ______

4. $4 \times 5 =$ ______ **5.** $3 \times 5 =$ 15 **6.** $7 \times 5 =$ ______

7. $5 \times 2 =$ ______ **8.** $6 \times 5 =$ ______ **9.** $8 \times 2 =$ 16

10. 9×5 **11.** 2×7 **12.** 2×2 **13.** 5×5 **14.** 0×2

15. What is 9 times 2? ______

16. What is 5 times 8?

17. Communicate Is 25 a multiple of 2 or 5? How do you know?

____

____

Name ______________________

Practice
5-1

2 and 5 as Factors

Find each product.

1. 2×5 ______ **2.** 4×5 ______ **3.** 3×2 ______ **4.** 8×5 ______ **5.** 7×2 ______

6. $\begin{array}{r} 9 \\ \times 2 \\ \hline \end{array}$ **7.** $\begin{array}{r} 6 \\ \times 5 \\ \hline \end{array}$ **8.** $\begin{array}{r} 5 \\ \times 9 \\ \hline \end{array}$ **9.** $\begin{array}{r} 2 \\ \times 6 \\ \hline \end{array}$ **10.** $\begin{array}{r} 5 \\ \times 5 \\ \hline \end{array}$

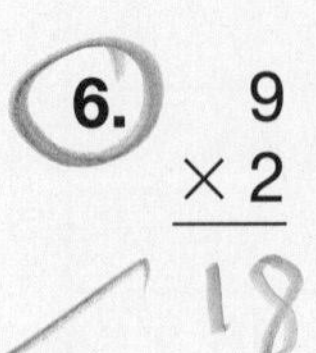

11. Multiply 7 and 5. ______

12. Find 8 times 2. ______

Compare. Use $<$, $>$, or $=$.

13. $3 \times 5 \bigcirc 4 \times 5$ **14.** $6 \times 3 \bigcirc 6 \times 2$ **15.** $8 \times 2 \bigcirc 2 \times 8$

16. $6 \times 5 \bigcirc 5 \times 6$ **17.** $4 \times 2 \bigcirc 5 \times 2$ **18.** $7 \times 5 \bigcirc 5 \times 6$

19. Tara walks 2 miles each day. How many miles does she walk in a week?

______

20. There are 5 days in each school week. How many school days are there in 9 weeks?

______

21. Writing to Explain How can adding doubles help you to multiply by 2? Give an example.

______

______

______

______

22. If the ones digit of a number greater than 1 is 0, what factor or factors must that number have?

A 2 only **B** 5 only **C** 2 and 5 **D** Neither 2 nor 5

Name ______________________________

Reteaching
5-2

9 as a Factor

You can use two patterns to help you remember 9s facts.

9s Facts
$9 \times 0 = 0$
$9 \times 1 = 9$
$9 \times 2 = 18$
$9 \times 3 = 27$
$9 \times 4 = 36$
$9 \times 5 = 45$
$9 \times 6 = 54$
$9 \times 7 = 63$
$9 \times 8 = 72$
$9 \times 9 = 81$

1. The tens digit will be 1 less than the factor being multiplied by 9.

2. The sum of the digits of the product will always be 9, unless the other factor is 0.

Find 9×7.

The tens digit must be 1 less than 7.
The tens digit is 6.

The sum of the digits must be 9.
$9 - 6 = 3$, so the ones digit is 3.

The product is 63.

Find each product.

1. $9 \times 3 =$ ______ **2.** $2 \times 9 =$ ______ **3.** $1 \times 9 =$ ______

4. $5 \times 9 =$ ______ **5.** $5 \times 8 =$ ______ **6.** $6 \times 9 =$ ______

7. $2 \times 7 =$ ______ **8.** $0 \times 9 =$ ______ **9.** $4 \times 9 =$ ______

10. 9×9 **11.** 9×5 **12.** 8×9 **13.** 7×9 **14.** 9×2

15. Multiply 6 and 9. ______ **16.** Multiply 0 and 9. ______

17. **Communicate** Look at the table of 9s facts. Do you see another number pattern in the multiples of 9? Explain.

____

____

Name ______________________

9 as a Factor

Practice **5-2**

Find each product.

1. 9×4 ______ **2.** 7×9 ______ **3.** 9×9 ______ **4.** 9×8 ______ **5.** 5×3 ______

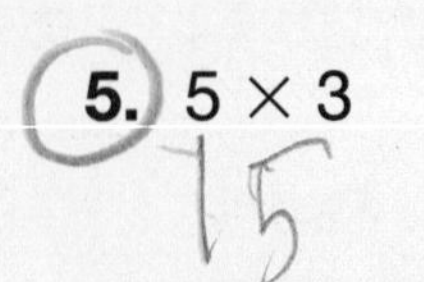

6. 9×5 **7.** 2×9 **8.** 6×9 **9.** 2×7 **10.** 8×9

11. Multiply 4 and 9. ______

12. Find 3 times 9. ______

Complete. Use $+$, $-$, or $\times$.

13. $2 \times 9 = 10 \square 8$

14. $20 + 16 = 9 \square 4$

15. $9 \times 5 = 50 \square 5$

16. $9 \times 8 = 70 \square 2$

17. $10 \square 1 = 1 \times 9$

18. $9 \square 3 = 20 + 7$

19. Paula's hair was put into 9 braids. Each braid used 3 beads. How many beads were used in all?

____

20. A baseball game has 9 innings. A doubleheader is 2 games in the same day. How many innings are there in a doubleheader?

____

21. **Write a Problem** Write a multiplication story for 9×8. Include the product in your story.

____

____

22. Which number below is a multiple of 9?

A 35 **B** 46 **C** 54 **D** 65

Name ______________________________

Multiplying with 0 and 1

Zero and one have special multiplication properties.

The Identity (One) Property of Multiplication	The Zero Property of Multiplication
When you multiply a number and 1, the product is that number.	When you multiply a number and 0, the product is 0.
Examples:	Examples:
$4 \times 1 = 4$ $16 \times 1 = 16$	$5 \times 0 = 0$ $123 \times 0 = 0$
$1 \times 9 = 9$ $13 \times 1 = 13$	$17 \times 0 = 0$ $0 \times 58 = 0$
$251 \times 1 = 251$ $1 \times 48 = 48$	$0 \times 51 = 0$ $74 \times 0 = 0$

1. $1 \times 2 =$ ______ **2.** $0 \times 3 =$ ______ **3.** $4 \times 1 =$ ______

4. $8 \times 0 =$ ______ **5.** $6 \times 1 =$ ______ **6.** $1 \times 7 =$ ______

7. $\begin{array}{r} 1 \\ \times\ 7 \\ \hline \end{array}$ **8.** $\begin{array}{r} 6 \\ \times\ 0 \\ \hline \end{array}$ **9.** $\begin{array}{r} 8 \\ \times\ 1 \\ \hline \end{array}$

10. $\begin{array}{r} 10 \\ \times\ \ 0 \\ \hline \end{array}$ **11.** $\begin{array}{r} 1 \\ \times\ 2 \\ \hline \end{array}$ **12.** $\begin{array}{r} 0 \\ \times\ 9 \\ \hline \end{array}$

Complete each number sentence. Write <, >, or = for each ◯.

13. 8×2 ◯ 4×4 **14.** 19×1 ◯ 37×0 **15.** 7×2 ◯ $13 + 1$

Complete each number sentence. Write × or + for each ◯.

16. 5 ◯ 0 = 5 **17.** 5 ◯ 1 = 6 **18.** 1 ◯ 5 = 5

19. **Write a Problem** Write a multiplication sentence that shows the Zero Property of Multiplication. Explain why it shows this property.

____

Name ______________________

Practice
5-3

Multiplying with 0 and 1

Find each product.

1. 1×4 ______ **2.** 0×5 ______ **3.** 6×1 ______ **4.** 0×3 ______ **5.** 5×1 ______

6. $\begin{array}{r} 1 \\ \times 1 \\ \hline \end{array}$ **7.** $\begin{array}{r} 0 \\ \times 9 \\ \hline \end{array}$ **8.** $\begin{array}{r} 1 \\ \times 8 \\ \hline \end{array}$ **9.** $\begin{array}{r} 6 \\ \times 1 \\ \hline \end{array}$ **10.** $\begin{array}{r} 7 \\ \times 0 \\ \hline \end{array}$

11. Multiply 1 and 7. ______

12. Find 0 times 8. ______

Complete. Write $<$, $>$, or $=$ for each ◯.

13. 1×6 ◯ 3×0 **14.** 5×0 ◯ 1×7 **15.** 1×3 ◯ 3×1

Complete. Write $\times$, $+$, or $-$ for each ☐.

16. 1 ☐ $7 = 7$ **17.** 8 ☐ $0 = 8$ **18.** 6 ☐ $1 = 5$

19. Sara keeps 4 boxes under her bed. Each box is for holding a different type of seashell. There are 0 shells in each box. Write a multiplication sentence to show how many shells Sara has in all.

4x0=0 ✓

20. **Communicate** Is the product of 0×0 the same as the sum of $0 + 0$? Explain.

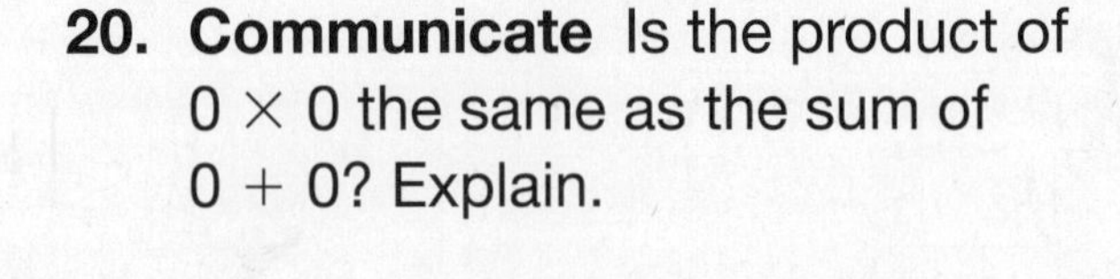

____

____

21. A pentagon has 5 sides. Lonnie has a table shaped like a pentagon. How many chairs does Lonnie need if he wants 1 chair on each side?

______

22. Which multiplication problem below has the greatest product?

A 5×1 **B** 6×0 **C** 0×7 **D** 8×0

Name ______________________

Patterns for Facts

Pattern	Example
All multiples of 2 are even numbers.	2, 8, 16
All multiples of 5 end in 0 or 5.	5, 10, 15
For all multiples of 9, the sum of the digits is always a multiple of 9.	27 $2 + 7 = 9$ 63 $6 + 3 = 9$

1. 9×5

2. 2×8

3. 5×8

4. 9×4

5. 9×3

6. 2×7

7. 5×3

8. 5×6

9. 9×2

10. 5×7

11. 9×6

12. 2×6

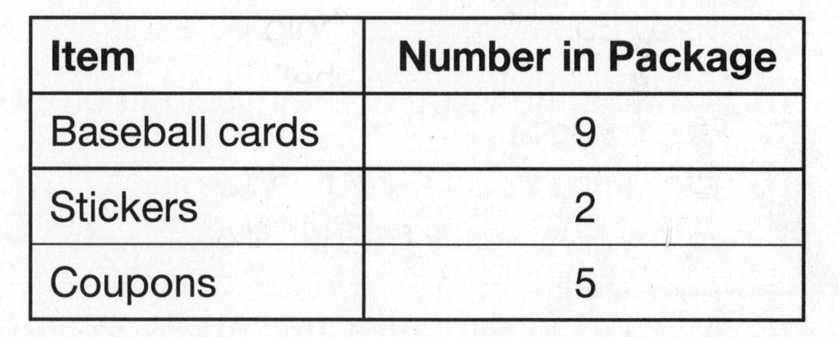

Item	Number in Package
Baseball cards	9
Stickers	2
Coupons	5

13. How many baseball cards are in 3 packages?

14. How many stickers do you get if you buy 7 packages?

14

15. How many coupons do you get if you buy 7 packages?

35

Name ______________________

Practice 5-4

Patterns for Facts

1. $\begin{array}{r} 5 \\ \times\ 4 \\ \hline \end{array}$

2. $\begin{array}{r} 2 \\ \times\ 3 \\ \hline \end{array}$

3. $\begin{array}{r} 9 \\ \times\ 5 \\ \hline \end{array}$

4. $\begin{array}{r} 5 \\ \times\ 8 \\ \hline \end{array}$

5. $\begin{array}{r} 7 \\ \times\ 2 \\ \hline \end{array}$

6. $\begin{array}{r} 5 \\ \times\ 3 \\ \hline \end{array}$

7. $\begin{array}{r} 9 \\ \times\ 3 \\ \hline \end{array}$

8. $\begin{array}{r} 5 \\ \times\ 7 \\ \hline \end{array}$

9. $9 \times 6 =$ ______

10. $2 \times 6 =$ ______

11. $5 \times 5 =$ ______

Find the missing number.

12. ______ $\times 9 = 63$

13. $2 \times$ ______ $= 16$

14. A package of baseball cards includes 5 cards. How many baseball cards are in 6 packages?

____

15. What is the value of the missing number?
$9 \times \square = 36$

A 6 **B** 4 **C** 3 **D** 2

16. **Writing to Explain** Chris needs to find the product of two numbers. One of the numbers is 6. The answer also needs to be 6. How will he solve this problem? Explain.

____

____

____

Name ______________________________

Reteaching **5-5**

10 as a Factor

The table shows the multiplication facts for 10.

10s Facts	
$10 \times 0 = 0$	$10 \times 5 = 50$
$10 \times 1 = 10$	$10 \times 6 = 60$
$10 \times 2 = 20$	$10 \times 7 = 70$
$10 \times 3 = 30$	$10 \times 8 = 80$
$10 \times 4 = 40$	$10 \times 9 = 90$

All multiples of 10 end with zero.

Find 10×5.

To find the answer, you can skip count or you can write a zero after the 5.

1 2 3 4 5

0 10 20 30 40 50

or

Tens	Ones
	5

$\times 10 =$

Tens	Ones
5	0

$5 \times 10 = 50$

1. $10 \times 2 =$ ______ **2.** $5 \times 10 =$ ______ **3.** $10 \times 8 =$ ______

4. $2 \times 8 =$ ______ **5.** $\$10 \times 6 =$ ______ **6.** $7 \times 5 =$ ______

7. $\$10 \times 4 =$ ______ **8.** $9 \times 2 =$ ______ **9.** $8 \times 9 =$ ______

10. 10×3

11. $\$4 \times 5$

12. 2×2

13. $\$10 \times 5$

14. $\$8 \times 5$

15. 10×4

16. Reason When you multiply a whole number by 10, what is always true about the ones place in the product?

____

Name ______________________

Practice
5-5

10 as a Factor

Find each product.

1. 3×10 ______

2. 7×10 ______

3. 10×5 ______

4. 7×5 ______

5. 10×8 ______

6. 9×10 ______

7. 6×1 ______

8. 10×2 ______

9. 9×7 ______

10. 4×10 ______

11. 1×10 ______

12. 6×10 ______

13. 5×4 ______

14. 10×10 ______

15. 10×3 ______

16. 8×5

17. 10×9

18. 10×8

19. 10×4

20. 10×7

21. 10×6

22. 5×2

23. 10×1

24. 10×5

25. 9×0

26. Mary Ann earns $10 each day walking the neighborhood dogs. How much will she earn in 7 days?

______

27. A game of basketball requires 10 players. At the park, there are 5 games being played. How many total players are at the park?

______

28.

29. Which is **NOT** a multiple of 10?

A 30

B 55

C 70

D 90

Name ________________

Multiplying by Multiples of 10

Reteaching
5-6

You can use basic facts to help you multiply by numbers that are multiples of 10.

$2 \times 7 = 14$ $3 \times 9 = 27$ $5 \times 6 = 30$

$2 \times 7\mathbf{0} = 14\mathbf{0}$ $3 \times 9\mathbf{0} = 27\mathbf{0}$ $5 \times 6\mathbf{0} = 30\mathbf{0}$

To find each of the products above, first complete the basic multiplication fact, then write one zero after the product.
For example:

$9 \times 60 = 540$

First find 9×6. **9 × 6 = 54**

Then, write one zero after the product. **540**

Find each product.

1. $2 \times 60 =$ ______
2. $9 \times 20 =$ ______
3. $5 \times 80 =$ ______
4. $2 \times 20 =$ ______
5. $70 \times 3 =$ 210
6. $50 \times 6 =$ 300
7. $30 \times 5 =$ ______
8. $9 \times 50 =$ ______
9. $7 \times 90 =$ ______
10. $7 \times 50 =$ ______

11. **Generalize** To find 5×40, multiply 5 and 4, then write ______ zero to form the product.

Name ______________________

Practice
5-6

Multiplying by Multiples of 10

Find each product. Use mental math.

1. $5 \times 70 =$ ______
2. $80 \times 5 =$ ______
3. $40 \times 9 =$ ______
4. $20 \times 7 =$ ______
5. $2 \times 60 =$ ______
6. $9 \times 70 =$ ______
7. $8 \times 90 =$ 720
8. $60 \times 9 =$ ______
9. $50 \times 7 =$ ______
10. $80 \times 2 =$ ______
11. How many zeros will the product of 5×60 have?

    2 Zeros

Mr. Garcia has 30 times as many pencils as Emma. The whole third grade class has 50 times as many pencils as Emma. Emma has 5 pencils. Use this information for **12** and **13**.

12. How many pencils does Mr. Garcia have?

    150

13. How many pencils does the whole third grade class have?

    250

14. Find 3×60.

    A 18 **B** 90 **C** 180 **D** 1800

15. **Writing to Explain** Amanda says that the product of 5×40 will have 1 zero. Is she correct? Explain.

____

____

____

Name ______________________

Reteaching
5-7

Problem Solving: Two-Question Problems

Sometimes you need the answer to one question to help you answer another question.

Ms. Williams bought 3 pizzas for $8 each. She gave the cashier $30. How much change did she receive?

First, find the cost of the pizzas.

_____ in all

$8	$8	$8

$\$8 \times 3 = \$24$

The pizzas cost $24.

Next, find the change.

$30 in all

$24	___

$\$30 - \$24 = \$6$

Ms. Williams received $6 in change.

1a. Ray bought a pair of sunglasses for $22 and a hat for $19. How much money did the items cost?

$41 in all

$22	$19

1b. Ray gave the cashier a $50 bill. How much change should Ray receive?

$50 in all

$41	$9

2. Communicate Cindy bought 4 lunch specials for $7 each. She gave the cashier $40. How much change should Cindy receive? Explain how you found your answer.

____

____

____

____

Name ______________________

Practice
5-7

Problem Solving: Two-Question Problems

Use the answer from the first problem to solve the second problem.

1a. Lynette bought a book for $13 and a DVD for $22. How much money did the items cost?

______ in all

$22	$13

1b. Suppose Lynette paid the cashier with a $50 bill. How much change should Lynette get?

$50 in all

$35	______

2a. Melissa bought 2 T-shirts for $9 each. How much money did Melissa spend on T-shirts?

______

2b. Melissa had $32 in her purse. How much money does she have left?

______

3a. Curt bought 3 tickets to the movies for $8 each. How much money did Curt spend on movie tickets?

$24

3b. Curt also bought a large popcorn for $5. How much money did Curt spend altogether?

$29

4. Lenny bought 4 packs of baseball cards for $3 each. He paid the cashier with a $20 bill. How much change will Lenny receive?

A $7 **C** $12

B $8 **D** $13

5. Write a Problem Write two problems that can be solved by using the answer from the first problem to solve the second problem.

____

____

____

Name ______________________________

The Distributive Property

Reteaching
6-1

With the Distributive Property, you can break apart a multiplication fact into the sum of two other facts.

The array below shows 6×4 or 6 rows of 4 circles.

6×4

You can draw a line to break apart **6** rows of 4 circles into **2** rows of 4 circles *and* **4** rows of 4 circles.

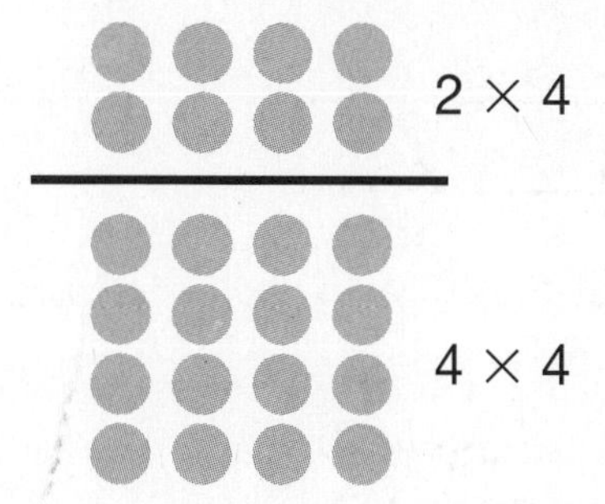

2×4

4×4

The new facts that stand for the two smaller arrays are (2×4) and (4×4).

You can write a number sentence to show this relationship:
$6 \times 4 = (2 \times 4) + (4 \times 4)$.

Draw a line to separate each array into two smaller arrays. Write the new facts.

1.

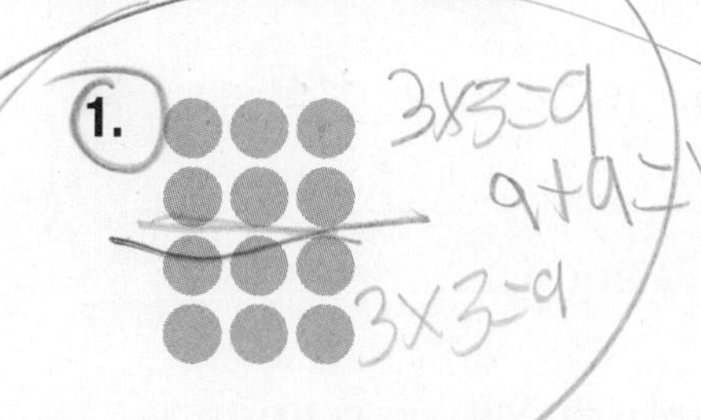

(3 × 3) and (3 × 3)

2.

3x6=18
18+12=30
2x6=12

(3 × 6) and (2 × 6)

3. Model Don breaks a 4×7 array into a 2×7 array and another array. What is the fact for Don's second array? Write a number sentence that models the relationship of the 4×7 array to the other two arrays.

____

____

Name ____________________

Practice
6-1

The Distributive Property

Draw a line to separate each array into two smaller arrays. Write the new facts.

1.

6x4=24
24+24=48
6x4=24

(6 × 4) and (6 × 4)

2.

(4 × 4) and (5 × 5)

Use the smaller arrays and the Distributive Property to find each missing factor. You may use counters to help.

3.

$8 \times 3 =$

$(2 \times \_\_\_\_) + (\_\_\_\_ \times 3)$

4.

$7 \times \_\_\_\_ =$

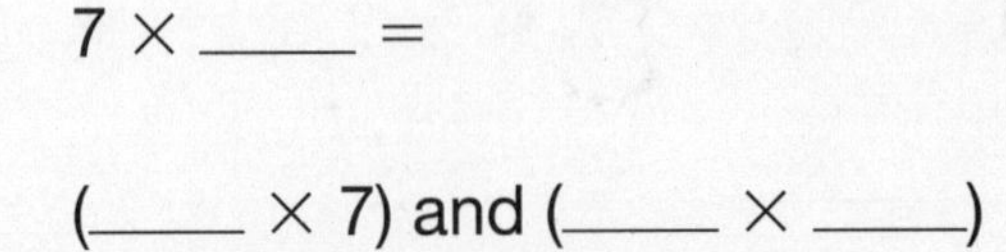

$(\_\_\_\_ \times 7)$ and $(\_\_\_\_ \times \_\_\_\_)$

5. Tony broke a larger array into a 2×9 array and a 4×9 array. What did the larger array look like? Draw a picture. Write a number sentence to show the relationship between the larger array and the two smaller arrays.

6. Use Structure Which number makes this number sentence true?

$7 \times 5 = (\blacksquare \times 5) + (2 \times 5)$

A 2

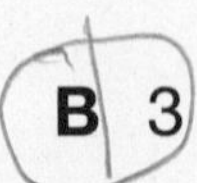

B 3

C 4

D 5

Name ______________________________

3 as a Factor

Reteaching 6-2

You can use an array to show 3s facts.

3s Facts

$3 \times 0 = 0$	$3 \times 5 = 15$
$3 \times 1 = 3$	$3 \times 6 = 18$
$3 \times 2 = 6$	$3 \times 7 = 21$
$3 \times 3 = 9$	$3 \times 8 = 24$
$3 \times 4 = 12$	$3 \times 9 = 27$

Multiply 2×3 using arrays.

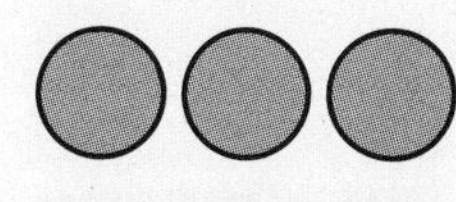

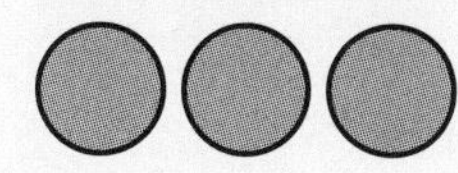

$2 \times 3 = 6$

You can also use a 2s and a 1s fact to find a 3s fact.

Find 7×3.

a. Find a 2s fact with 7: $2 \times 7 = 14$

b. Find a 1s fact with 7: $1 \times 7 = 7$

c. Add the facts: $14 + 7 = 21$

Find each product.

1. 3×2 ______ **2.** 3×4 ______ **3.** 3×5 ______ **4.** 3×1 ______ **5.** 3×9 ______

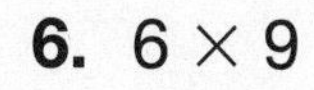

6. 6×9 ______ 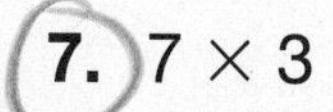 **7.** 7×3 ______ **8.** 0×3 ______ **9.** 8×5 ______ **10.** 3×3 ______

11. Reason How can you use a 2s fact and a 1s fact to find 3×8?

____

____

Name ___________________

Practice **6-2**

3 as a Factor

Find the product.

1. 1×3 ______ **2.** 3×7 ______ **3.** 6×3 ______ **4.** 8×3 ______ **5.** 10×5 ______

6. 3×2 ______ **7.** 4×3 ______ **8.** 3×0 ______ **9.** 2×7 ______ **10.** 3×3 ______

11. 5×3 **12.** 10×3 **13.** 2×3 **14.** 3×9 **15.** 9×3

16. A bicycle store also sells tricycles. It has 6 tricycles in stock. How many wheels do the tricycles have in all?

______

17. There were 5 people who bought tickets to a football game. They bought 3 tickets each. How many tickets were bought all together?

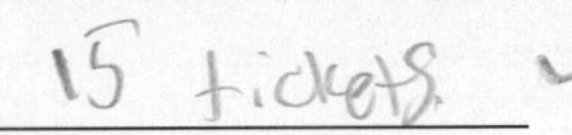

18. **Model** What addition sentence is equal to 4×3? ______

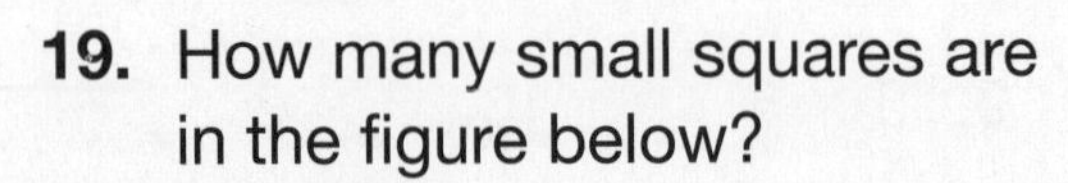

19. How many small squares are in the figure below? ______

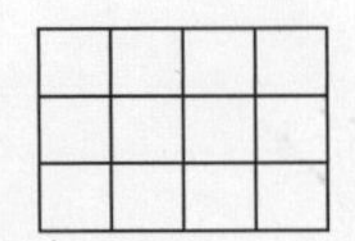

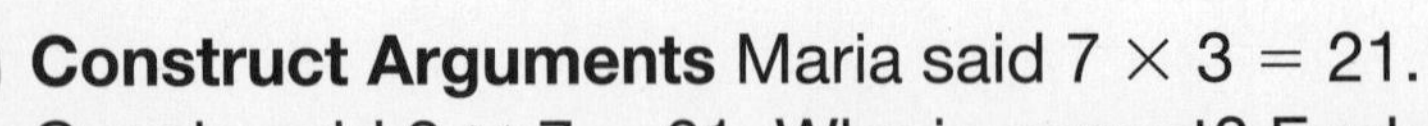

20. **Construct Arguments** Maria said $7 \times 3 = 21$. Connie said $3 \times 7 = 21$. Who is correct? Explain.

______

______

______

21. Which number is a multiple of 3?

A 16 **B** 20 **C** 24 **D** 28

Name ____________________

4 as a Factor

If you know a 2s multiplication fact, you can find a 4s multiplication fact.

4s Facts

$4 \times 0 = 0$	$4 \times 5 = 20$
$4 \times 1 = 4$	$4 \times 6 = 24$
$4 \times 2 = 8$	$4 \times 7 = 28$
$4 \times 3 = 12$	$4 \times 8 = 32$
$4 \times 4 = 16$	$4 \times 9 = 36$

You can double a 2s fact or add a 2s fact by itself to find a 4s fact.

When you double an array of 2×1, you get an array of 4×1.

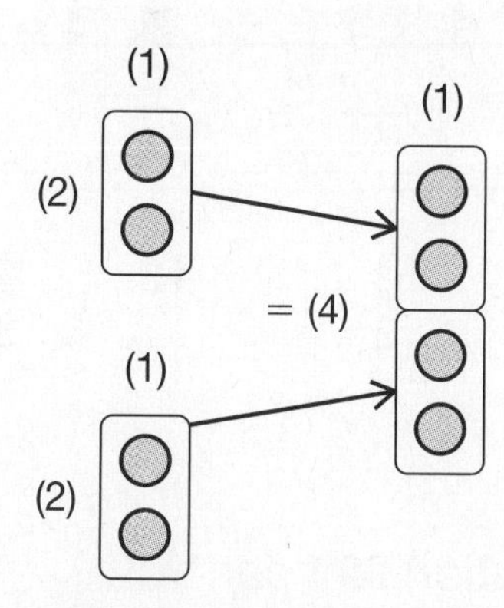

Find 4×3 by doubling a 2s fact.

a. Find a 2s fact with 3 as a factor.

$2 \times 3 = 6$

b. Double it.

$2 \times 6 = 12$

Find 4×3 by adding a 2s fact by itself.

a. Find a 2s fact with 3 as a factor.

$2 \times 3 = 6$

b. Add the fact to itself.

$6 + 6 = 12$

Find each product.

1. 4×6 ________ **2.** 8×4 ________ **3.** 4×5 ________ **4.** 9×4 ________ **5.** 4×1 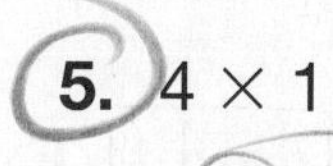

6. 4×3 ________ **7.** 4×7 28 **8.** 12×2 ________ **9.** 0×4 0 **10.** 4×4 ________

11. Reason How can you use 2×8 to find 4×8?

____

____

Name ______________________

4 as a Factor

Practice 6-3

Find the product.

1. 2×4 ______ **2.** 4×5 ______ **3.** 3×4 ______ **4.** 4×4 ______ **5.** 5×8 ______

6. 4×6 ______ **7.** 1×4 ______ **8.** 4×3 ______ **9.** 0×4 ______ **10.** 4×7 ______

11. 10×4 **12.** 1×4 **13.** 2×4 **14.** 4×9 **15.** 8×4

16. What multiplication fact can you double to find 4×7?

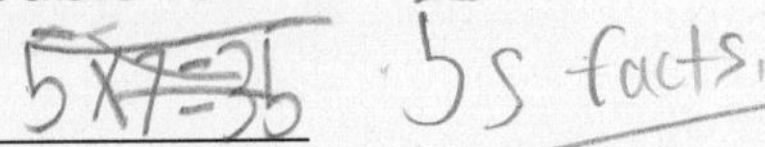

17. Each square table can seat 4 people. How many people can be seated at 8 square tables?

______

18. Jillian sold 4 books of raffle tickets. Each book had 9 tickets. How many tickets did Jillian sell all together?

______

19. The soccer team has practice 4 times each week during the season. If the season is 10 weeks long, how many practices does the team have?

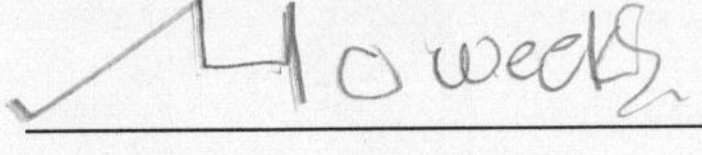

20. Writing to Explain If you know that $4 \times 5 = 20$, how can you use the Commutative (Order) Property of Multiplication to find 5×4?

______

______

______

21. Aaron changed the tires on 5 cars. Each car had 4 tires. How many tires did Aaron change?

A 12 **B** 16 **C** 20 **D** 24

Name ____________________

Reteaching **6-4**

6 and 7 as Factors

You can use multiplication facts that you already know to find other multiplication facts.

You can use a 3s fact to find a 6s fact. Find the 3s fact and then add the product to itself.

Find 6×9.

a. Find the 3s fact with 9: $3 \times 9 = 27$.

b. Add the product to itself: $27 + 27 = 54$.

You can use a 2s and a 5s fact to find a 7s fact.

Find 7×5.

a. Find the 2s fact with 5: $2 \times 5 = 10$.

b. Find the 5s fact with 5: $5 \times 5 = 25$.

c. Add the products: $10 + 25 = 35$.

Find each product.

1. 2×7 14 **2.** 6×7 ____ **3.** 7×9 ____ **4.** 6×4 ____ **5.** 6×8 ____

6. 7×7 ____ **7.** 6×2 ____ **8.** 8×7 ____ **9.** 3×7 21 **10.** 6×6 ____

11. 5×6 **12.** 7×4 28 **13.** 6×9 **14.** 7×3 **15.** 7×6

16. **Construct Arguments** Harold says, "To find 6×8, I can use the facts for 5×4 and 1×4." Do you agree? Explain.

____

____

Name ____________________

Practice
6-4

6 and 7 as Factors

Find the product. You may draw pictures to help.

1. 5×6 ______ **2.** 6×3 ______ **3.** 6×8 ______ **4.** 3×7 ______ **5.** 7×10 ______

6. 7×4 ______ **7.** 6×4 ______ **8.** 5×7 ______ **9.** 7×8 ______ **10.** 6×6 ______

11. 7×6 **12.** 10×6 **13.** 10×7 **14.** 7×7 **15.** 2×6

16. **Reason** What multiplication fact can be found by using the arrays for 2×9 and 5×9?

______

17. The chicken eggs that Raul's science class is watching take 3 weeks to hatch. There are 7 days in each week. How many days will it be until the eggs hatch?

21 days.

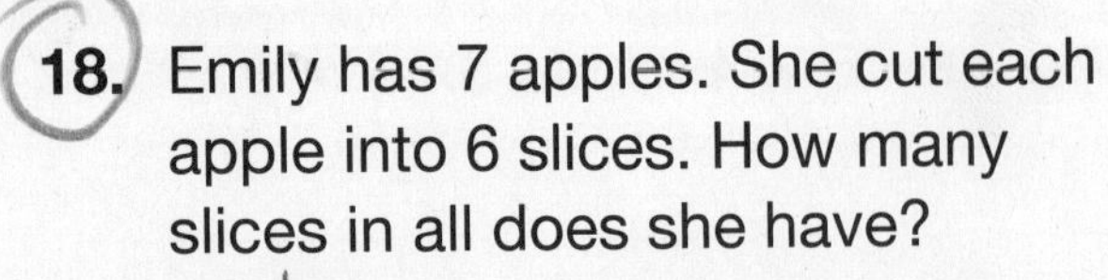

18. Emily has 7 apples. She cut each apple into 6 slices. How many slices in all does she have?

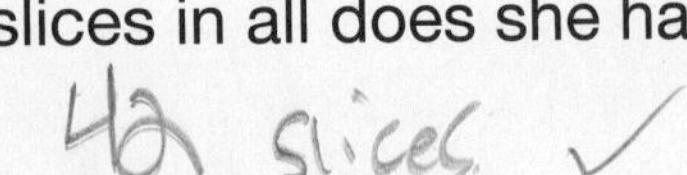

19. At a picnic there are 6 tables set up. Each table can seat 8 people. How many people can be seated at the tables all together?

______

20. How could you use $5 \times 6 = 30$ to find the product 6×6?

______

______

______

21. Barry takes 7 minutes to ride his bicycle one mile. At this rate, how long would Barry take to ride his bicycle 4 miles?

A 21 minutes **B** 24 minutes **C** 27 minutes **D** 28 minutes

Name ______________________

8 as a Factor

Reteaching 6-5

You can double a 4s fact to multiply with 8.

8s Facts

$8 \times 0 = 0$	$8 \times 5 = 40$
$8 \times 1 = 8$	$8 \times 6 = 48$
$8 \times 2 = 16$	$8 \times 7 = 56$
$8 \times 3 = 24$	$8 \times 8 = 64$
$8 \times 4 = 32$	$8 \times 9 = 72$

Find 8×6.

a. Find $4 \times 6 = 24$.

b. Add the product to itself: $24 + 24 = 48$

$4 \times 6 = 24$

$24 + 24 = 48$

$4 \times 6 = 24$

So, $8 \times 6 = 48$.

Find each product.

1. 2×8 16

2. 4×8 32

3. 8×5 40

4. 7×8 56

5. 8×8 64

6. 0×8 0

7. 6×7 42

8. 9×8 72

9. 1×8 8

10. 6×8 48

11. A gallon is equal to 8 pints. How many pints are in 5 gallons?

40

12. Writing to Explain How can you use 4s facts to find 7×8? Give the product in your explanation.

First find 7x4=28. Then add the product 2 times, 28+28=56, So, 7x8=56

Name ______________________

8 as a Factor

Practice 6-5

Find the product.

1. 1×8 ______ **2.** 8×0 ______ **3.** 4×6 ______ **4.** 2×8 ______ **5.** 8×7 ______

6. 8×3 ______ **7.** 4×8 ______ **8.** 8×9 ______ **9.** 8×5 ______ **10.** 8×8 ______

11. 10×8 **12.** 7×8 **13.** 7×6 **14.** 8×3 **15.** 9×8

16. An octopus has 8 arms. At the zoo, there are 3 octopuses in one tank. How many arms do the octopuses have all together? ______

17. Reason How can you use 4×7 to find 8×7? Find the product.

____

____

18. Construct Arguments Jose said all of the multiples of 8 are also multiples of 2. Jamila said that all of the multiples of 8 are also multiples of 4. Who is correct? Explain.

____

____

19. A package of fruit juice contains 8 boxes. How many boxes are there in 5 packages? ______

20. What is the next number in the pattern below?
16, 24, 32, 40, 48

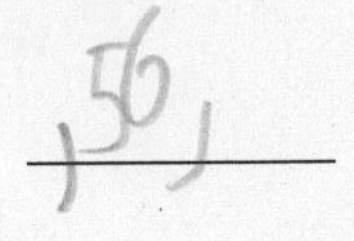

21. Each package of rolls contains 8 rolls. Ted bought 6 packages. How many rolls did he buy in all?

A 42 **B** 48 **C** 49 **D** 54

Name ____________________

Multiplying with 3 Factors

You can use the Associative Property of Multiplication to multiply three factors. The Associative Property states that the way the factors are grouped does not change the product.

The Associative Property of Multiplication is applied like the Associative Property of Addition.

Addition	Multiplication
$4 + 3 + 3 = 4 + (3 + 3)$	$4 \times 3 \times 3 = 4 \times (3 \times 3)$
$= 4 + 6$	$= 4 \times 9$
$= 10$	$= 36$

Find the product that is easy to find. Then multiply by the third number.

Find each product. You may draw a picture to help.

1. $3 \times 2 \times 1$ ______

2. $2 \times 3 \times 5$ ______

3. $3 \times 3 \times 2$ 18

4. $7 \times 3 \times 2$ ______

5. $4 \times 2 \times 7$ ______

6. $3 \times 4 \times 5$ 60

7. $2 \times 2 \times 6$ ______

8. $2 \times 5 \times 7$ ______

9. Each package of fruit juice has 2 rows. There are 6 boxes in each row. Mrs. Stokes bought 3 packages. How many boxes of fruit juice did Mrs. Stokes buy? Write a number sentence with your answer.

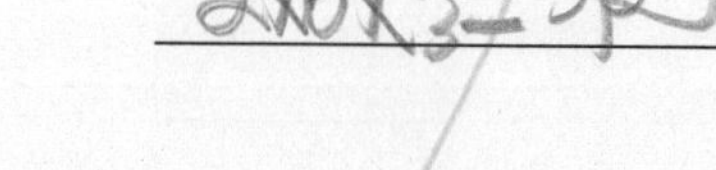

10. Communicate How do you know that $4 \times 2 \times 2$ is the same as 4×4? Explain.

Name ______________________

Practice
6-6

Multiplying with 3 Factors

Find the product. You may draw a picture to help.

1. $2 \times 3 \times 3$ ______

2. $2 \times 2 \times 4$ ______

3. $8 \times 2 \times 2$ ______

4. $6 \times 2 \times 3$ ______

5. $3 \times 3 \times 4$ ______

6. $5 \times 2 \times 5$ ______

7. $5 \times 4 \times 2$ ______

8. $4 \times 2 \times 3$ ______

Find the missing number.

9. $4 \times 4 \times 3 = 48$, so $4 \times (4 \times 3) = \square$ 48

10. $(5 \times 2) \times 8 = \square$

11. Sarah and Amanda each have 2 bags with 4 marbles in each. How many marbles do they have altogether?

8 marbles altogether.

12. Jesse bought 2 sheets of stamps. On each sheet there are 5 rows of stamps with 6 stamps in each row. How many stamps did Jesse buy?

______

13. Reason Is the product of $6 \times 2 \times 4$ less than 50? Explain.

______

______

14. Which number makes this number sentence true?

$8 \times 2 \times 4 = 8 \times (\blacksquare \times 4)$

A 2 **B** 4 **C** 8 **D** 64

15. Write three ways to find $3 \times 2 \times 4$.

______

______

Name ______________________

Multiplication Facts

You can use different strategies to multiply.

Find 6×4.

One Way

Use a pattern.

6×4 means 6 groups of 4.

So, you can count by 4s.

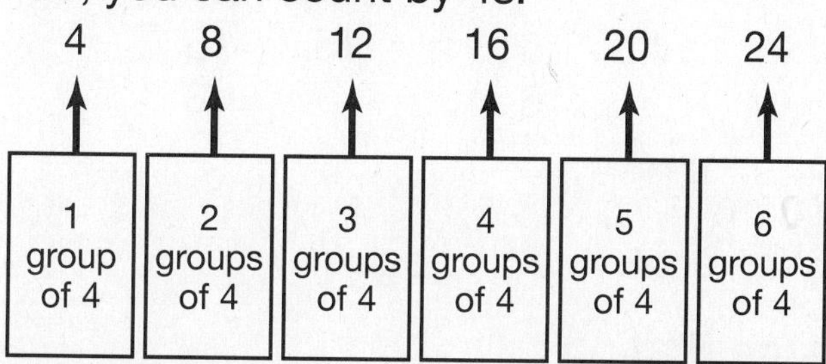

$6 \times 4 = 24$

Another Way

Use facts you already know.

Use 3s facts to help.

$$6 \times 4 \begin{cases} 3 \times 4 & 3 \times 4 = 12 \\ 3 \times 4 & 3 \times 4 = 12 \end{cases}$$

Add the products.

$12 + 12 = 24$

$6 \times 4 = 24$

In **1** and **2,** use a pattern to find the product.

1. $7 \times 2 =$ ________

Write the numbers you count.

____, ____, ____, ____,

____, ____, ____

2. $8 \times 5 =$ ________

Write the numbers you count.

____ ____ ____ ____

____ ____ ____ ____

In **3–5,** use known facts to find the product. List the facts you used.

3. $6 \times 8 =$ ________

____

____

4. $9 \times 5 =$ ________

____

____

5. $7 \times 6 =$ ________

____

____

6. Writing to Explain Show how to use known facts to find 6×9. Explain how you chose the facts you did.

____

____

Name ______________________

Practice 6-7

Multiplication Facts

Find the product.

1. 8×2 ______
2. 5×4 ______
3. 4×9 ______
4. 7×7 ______
5. 9×8 ______
6. 2×6 ______
7. 1×3 ______
8. 5×7 ______
9. 4×8 ______
10. 6×9 ______
11. 5×4
12. 1×0
13. 9×9
14. 6×6
15. 10×8

In **16** and**17**, use the table. Write a multiplication sentence and solve.

International Space Station

Expedition Number	Number of Crew Members	Expedition Number	Number of Crew Members	Expedition Number	Number of Crew Members
1	3	5	3	9	2
2	3	6	3	10	2
3	3	7	2	11	2
4	3	8	2	12	2

16. How many crew members in all were in Expeditions 1 through 6?

____

17. How many crew members in all were in Expeditions 7 through 12?

____

18. Tia counted the campers in 7 cabins. There were 9 campers in each cabin. How many campers were in the 7 cabins?

A 81 **B** 79 **C** 72 **D** 63

19. Construct Arguments Rick says to find 2×5, he can use counting by 5s: 5, 10, 15, 20, 25. Explain what he did wrong.

____

____

Name ______________________________

Multiplying to Find Combinations

You can use pictures, arrays, and multiplication to help find the number of possible combinations.

Choose one piece of fruit and one kind of toast from the menu. How many different combinations are there?

Fruit	Apple	Banana	Orange
Toast	Wheat	White	

Draw all the combinations of each piece of fruit with wheat toast and each piece of fruit with white toast.

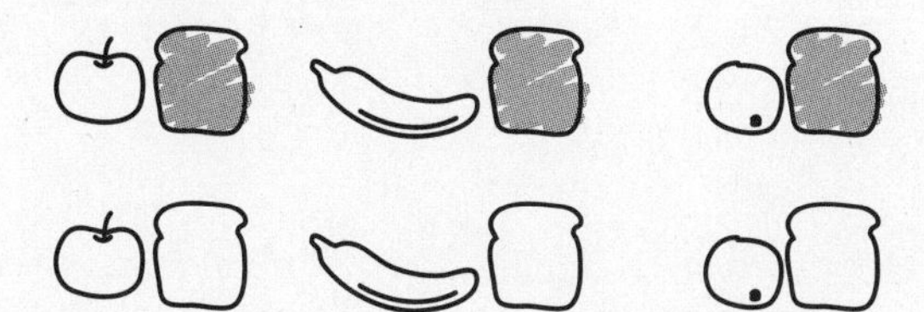

There are 2 rows with 3 combinations in each row. There are 6 combinations.

You can multiply.
Write a multiplication sentence.

$2 \times 3 = 6$

In **1** and **2**, find the number of possible combinations. Use objects, pictures, or multiplication.

1. Choose one letter: A, B, or C and one number: 1, 2, or 3.

   ____

2. Choose one tile color: black or white and one paint color: blue, gray, green, or yellow.

   ____

3. **Communicate** Gina wants one kind of yogurt and one kind of topping. She can choose lemon, lime, or vanilla yogurt. For the topping, she can choose berries, granola, nuts, or peaches. Explain how Gina can find the number of possible combinations.

   ____

   ____

Name ______________________

Practice
6-8

Multiplying to Find Combinations

Roy needs to choose one mark and one shape to make a sign. Show the possible combinations by filling in the array.

1. 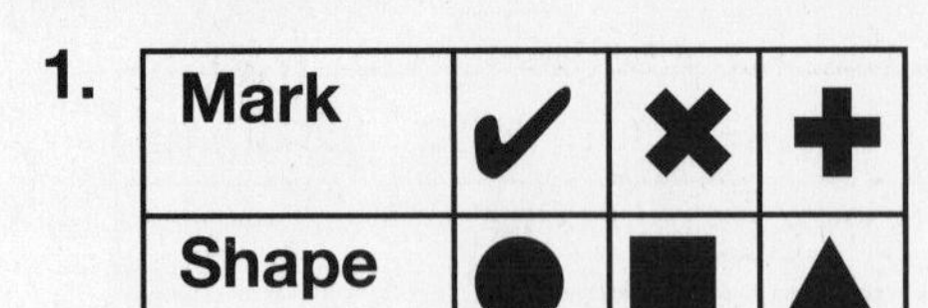

✔, ___	✖, ___	___, ●
___, ■	✖, ___	✚, ___
✔, ___	___, ▲	✚, ___

How many different combinations of one mark and one shape are there?

____

For **2** and **3**, find the number of possible combinations. Use objects, pictures, or multiplication.

2. Choose one of 5 kinds of juice and one of 3 glass sizes. ______________

3. Choose one of 7 shirts and one of 3 pairs of pants. ______________

4. **Reason** June has 1 coat and 7 scarves. How many combinations of a coat and a scarf does she have? ______________

5. Ross has 3 ties and 4 shirts. How many possible combinations of a tie and a shirt does he have?

A 3 **B** 4 **C** 12 **D** 21

6. Carl has one kind of bread, crunchy peanut butter and smooth peanut butter, and different flavors of jelly. What information do you need to find the number of possible combinations of peanut butter and jelly sandwiches he can make?

____

Name ____________________

Reteaching
6-9

Problem Solving: Multiple-Step Problems

Enzo's puts 3 meatballs in each of its meatball subs. Carlos's uses 2 times as many meatballs for its meatball subs. Mr. Kerwin orders 4 meatball subs from Carlos's. How many meatballs will be in his subs?

Find and solve the hidden question.

How many meatballs does Carlos's put in each meatball sub?

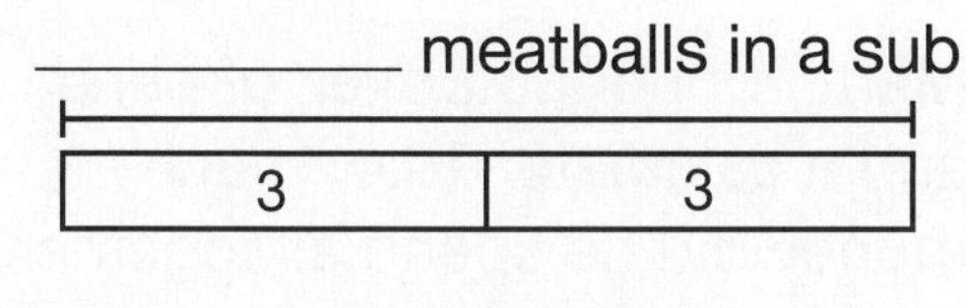

$3 \times 2 = 6$

Carlos's puts 6 meatballs in each of its meatball subs.

Use the answer to the hidden question to solve the problem.

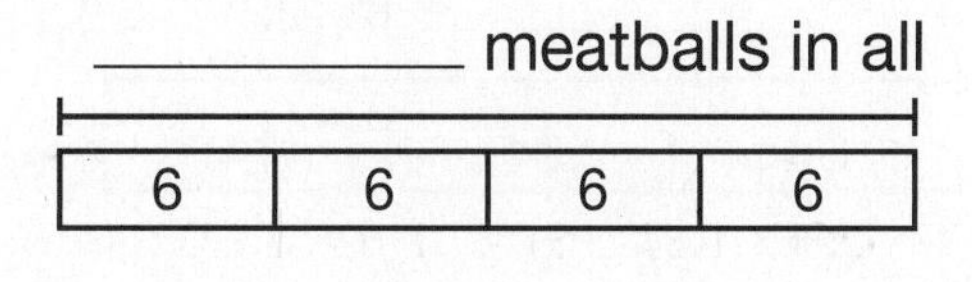

$6 \times 4 = 24$

Mr. Kerwin will have 24 meatballs altogether in his 4 meatball subs.

1. Meredith bought a book for \$8, a magazine for \$5, and bottled water for \$2. She paid with a \$20 bill. How much change should she get?

   Tip: Find the total cost of the three items.

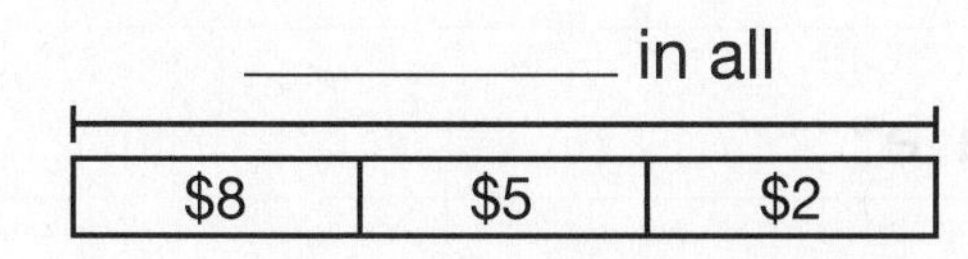

\$20 in all

\$15	?

____

2. Sue bought 3 T-shirts for \$8 each. She paid with a \$50 bill. How much change should she get?

   ____

3. **Writing to Explain** What steps did you take to answer Exercise 2?

   ____

   ____

   ____

   ____

   ____

Name ______________________

Problem Solving: Multiple-Step Problems

For **1** through **4**, use the pictures.

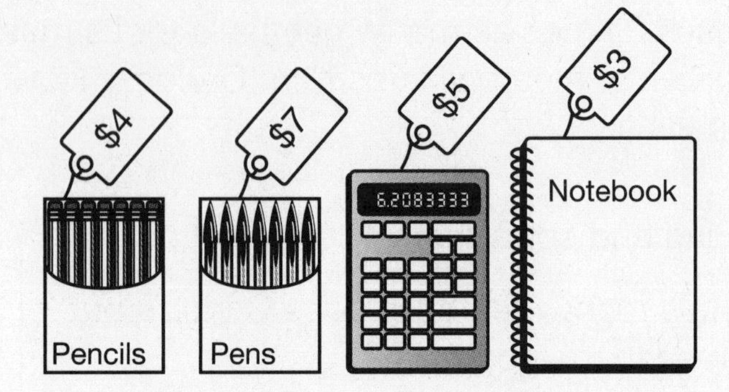

1. Teri bought 3 boxes of pencils. She paid with a $20 bill. How much change did she receive?

Tip First find the cost of the pencils.

__________ in all

$4	$4	$4

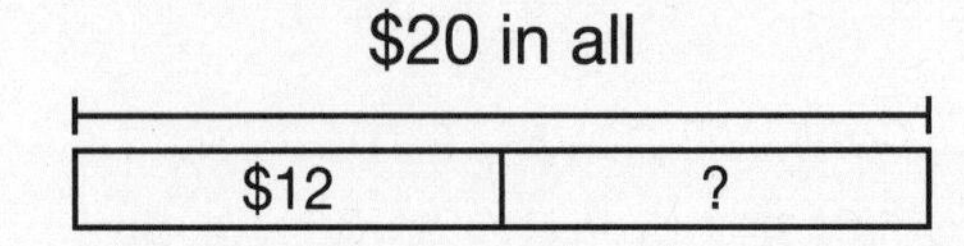

____

2. Martin bought 3 boxes of pens and a calculator. How much money did he spend all together?

Tip First find the cost of the pens.

____

3. Joey bought 2 notebooks and 2 boxes of pencils. How much money did he spend all together?

____

4. Allie bought 3 notebooks and 2 boxes of pens. She paid with $40. How much change did she receive?

____

5. Write a Problem Write a real-world problem involving multiple steps. Then solve your problem.

____

____

____

____

6. Bert has $50 in his wallet. Then he buys 2 CDs for $13 each. How much money does he have left?

A $12 **B** $24 **C** $26 **D** $37

Name ______________________________ Today ① ✗

Division as Sharing

Division shows how many items are in each group or how many equal groups there are.

There are 15 counters that are going to be put into 5 groups. How many counters will be in each group?

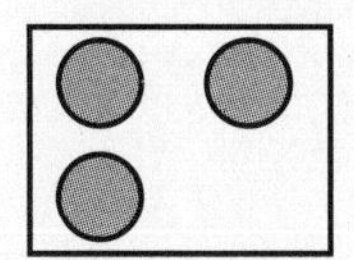 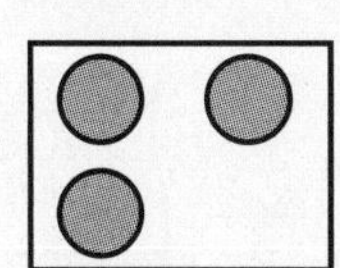 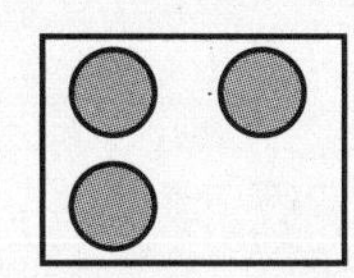 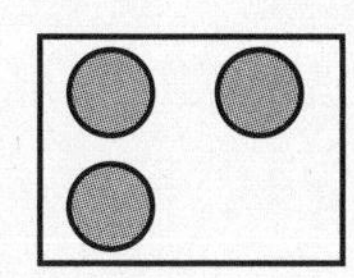 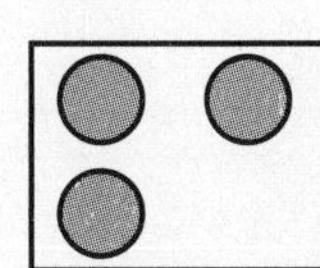

There are 15 counters. There are 5 groups.
There are 3 counters in each group.
So, $15 \div 5 = 3$.

Use counters or draw a picture to solve.

1. 12 tennis balls, 4 cans
   How many tennis balls in each can?
   ____

2. 20 cookies, 5 bags ✓
   How many cookies in each bag?
   4

3. 16 apples, 2 baskets
   How many apples in each basket?
   ____

4. 20 fingers, 4 hands
   How many fingers on each hand?
   ____

5. One box contains 12 granola bars. Two bars are in each package. How many packages are in each box of granola bars?
   ____

6. **Reason** Could you divide 14 shirts into two equal groups? Why or why not?
   ____
   ____

Name ______________________

Division as Sharing

Use counters or draw a picture to solve.

1. 24 people, 4 rows
How many people in each row?

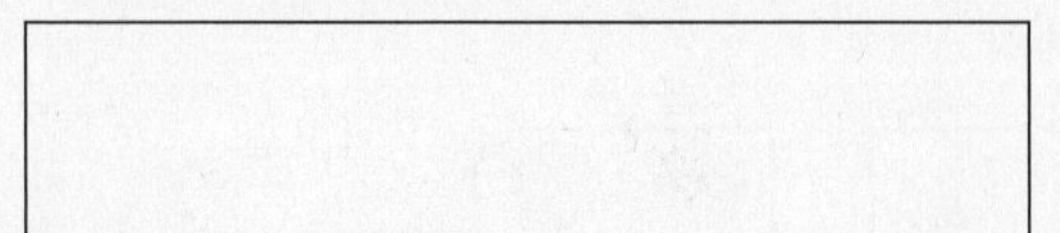

____

2. 18 marbles, 2 people
How many marbles for each person?

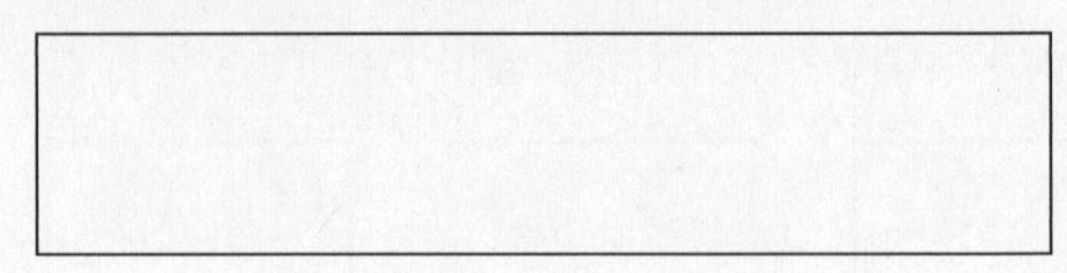

____

3. 25 apples, 5 trees
How many apples on each tree?

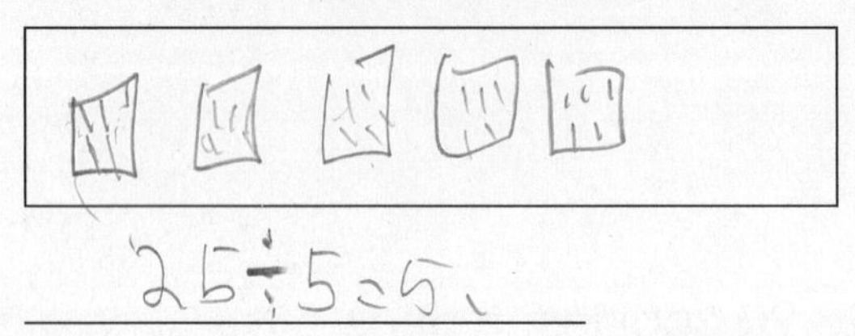

____

4. 21 books, 3 shelves
How many books on each shelf?

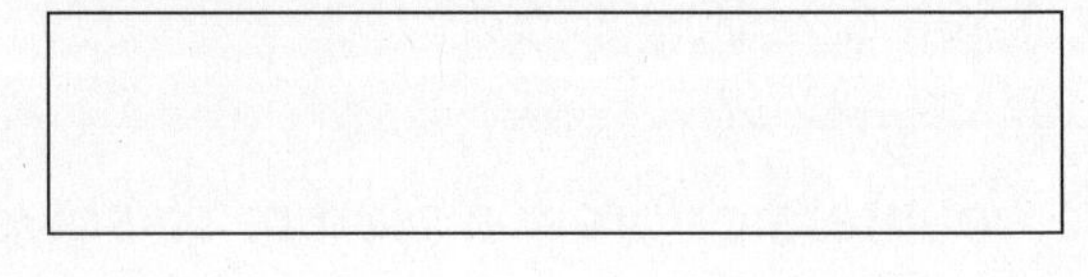

____

Complete each division sentence.

5.

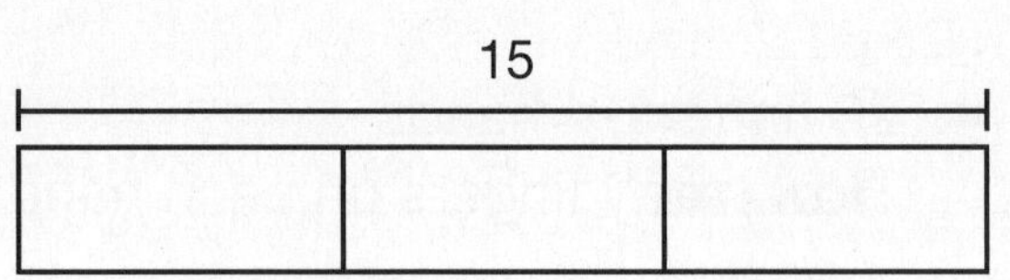

$15 \div 3 = \square$

6.

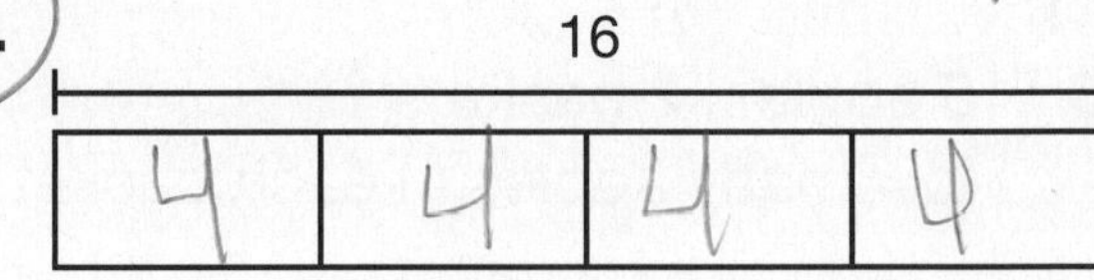

$16 \div 4 = \square$

7. Explain It Ron and Pam each have 20 pennies. Ron will put his pennies into 4 groups. Pam will put her pennies into 5 groups. Who will have more pennies in each group? Explain.

____

____

8. There are 28 days in February. There are 7 days in a week. How many weeks are there in February?

A 3 **B** 4 **C** 5 **D** 6

Name ______________________ (3) X

Reteaching
7-2

Division as Repeated Subtraction

You can think of division as repeated subtraction.

Emily has 20 raffle tickets. There are 5 tickets in each book.
How many books of raffle tickets does Emily have?

Start with 20 tickets. Subtract 5.	$20 - 5 = 15$
Subtract 5 more tickets.	$15 - 5 = 10$
Subtract 5 more tickets.	$10 - 5 = 5$
Subtract 5 more tickets.	$5 - 5 = 0$
You have reached 0.	

You
So, 2

Emily

Use c

1.

2. 8 hamsters
2 hamsters in each cage
How many cages?

____

3. 1
4 books on each shelf
How many shelves?

____

4. 18 players
3 players on each team
How many teams?

____

5. Annie had 16 balloons. She shares them equally with Connie.
How many balloons does each girl have now?

____

6. Communicate Show how you can use repeated subtraction to find how many groups of 7 are in 28.
Then write the division sentence for the problem.

You walld repetad subtraction for 7 and 28. You would start from 28 and subtract 7 every time until you get to 0. You cant how many times you subtracted. That is your

Name ______

Practice 7-2

Division as Repeated Subtraction

Use counters or draw a picture to solve.

1. 18 pens
3 pens in each box
How many boxes?

18 ÷ 3 = 6.

2. 24 students
3 students on each team
How many teams?

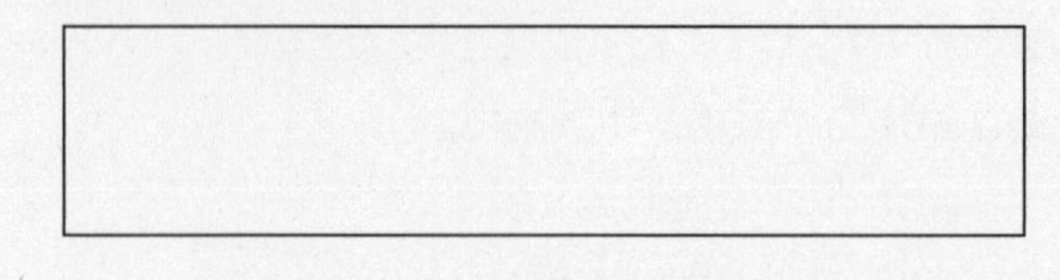

______

3. 35 stickers
5 stickers on each sheet
How many sheets?

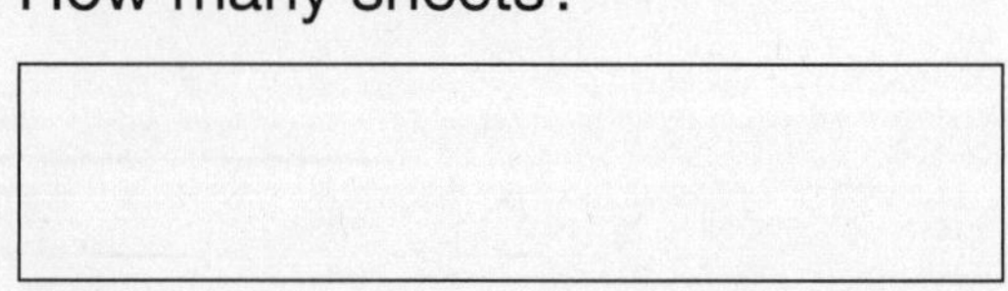

______

4. 30 leaves
6 leaves painted on each vase
How many vases?

______

5. **Number Sense** What division sentence means the same as the following subtraction sentences?

$12 - 4 = 8$

$8 - 4 = 4$

$4 - 4 = 0$

12 ÷ 4 = 3.

6. Tandem bicycles are ridden by 2 people. If 14 people rented tandem bicycles, how many bicycles were rented?

______

7. **Explain It** Tamara says that $15 \div 3 = 5$. Is she correct? Explain.

______

______

______

8. Keisha has to carry 32 boxes to her room. She can carry 4 boxes on each trip. How many trips will she take?

A 6 **B** 7 **C** 8 **D** 9

Name ____________________

Reteaching

7-3

Finding Missing Numbers in a Multiplication Table

Find $24 \div 6$.

You can think of a division problem as a multiplication fact with a missing factor.

Write a missing factor equation.

$24 \div 6 = n$ $\quad\quad$ $6 \times n = 24$

6 times what number equals 24?

Use a multiplication table. Follow the steps.

1. Find the factor you know, 6, in the first column of the table.

2. Go across the row to the product, 24.

3. Go straight to the top of that column. The number at the top of the column is 4. The missing factor is 4.

$24 \div 6 = 4 \quad n = 4$

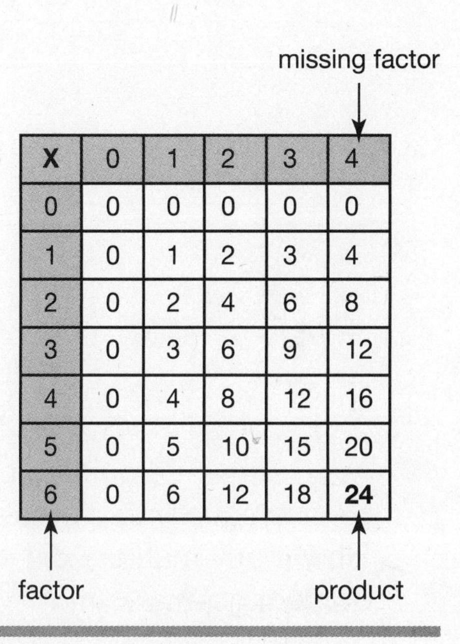

X	0	1	2	3	4
0	0	0	0	0	0
1	0	1	2	3	4
2	0	2	4	6	8
3	0	3	6	9	12
4	0	4	8	12	16
5	0	5	10	15	20
6	0	6	12	18	**24**

Use a multiplication table to find the value for n that makes the equation true.

1. $8 \div 2 = n$ ______ $\quad$ **2.** $12 \div 4 = n$ ______ $\quad$ **3.** $15 \div 5 = n$ ______

4. $10 \div 5 = n$ ______ $\quad$ **5.** $20 \div 4 = n$ ______ $\quad$ **6.** $30 \div 5 = n$ ______

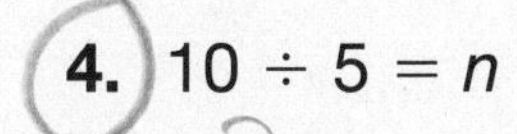

7. Communicate How can you use a multiplication table to find $16 \div 4$?

____

____

____

____

Name ______________________________

Practice
7-3

Finding Missing Numbers in a Multiplication Table

Find the value for *n* that makes the equation true.
Use a multiplication table.

1. $21 \div 7 = n$ ________
2. $12 \div 2 = n$ ________
3. $10 \div 5 = n$ ________
4. $48 \div 6 = n$ ________
5. $16 \div 4 = n$ ________
6. $27 \div 3 = n$ ________
7. $72 \div 8 = n$ 9 ✓
8. $63 \div 9 = n$ ________
9. $35 \div 7 = n$ ________

10. Mr. Bell had 24 colored markers to give equally to 6 students. How many markers did each student get?

____

11. A pet shop has 54 fish in 6 tanks. If there are an equal number of fish in each tank, how many fish are in each tank?

____

12. James has 36 tomato plants. If he plants 6 plants in a row, how many rows will he plant?

13. **Critique Reasoning** Hana uses a multiplication table to find the value of *n* in $49 \div 7 = n$. She says the answer is 6. Is she correct? Why or why not?

____

____

____

____

14. Enrico put 54 photographs into a scrapbook. He put 6 photographs on each page. How many pages did he fill?

A 6 **B** 7 **C** 8 **D** 9

Name ______________________

Reteaching

7-4

Problem Solving: Choose an Appropriate Equation

Nora has 10 marbles. She puts the marbles into 2 bags. How many marbles does she put in each bag?

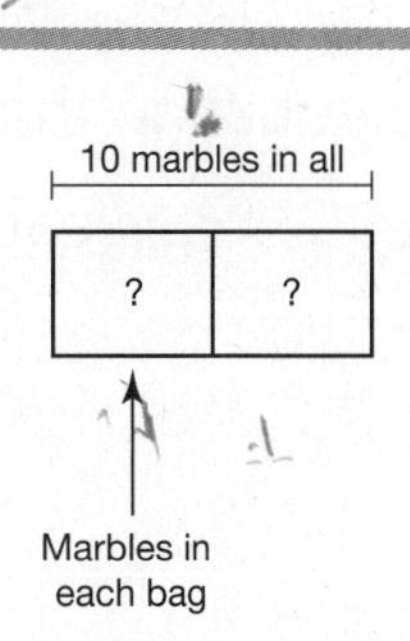

First, draw a picture to show what you know.

You know the total, 10 marbles.

You know how many groups, 2.

You need to find out how many in each group.

Which equation shows the problem?

A $2 + n = 10$ No, this equation shows putting together groups that are different sizes.

B $n = 2 \times 10$ No, this shows 2 groups of 10 marbles.

C $10 \div 2 = n$ Yes, this shows the total number of marbles divided, or separated into 2 equal groups.

D $10 - 2 = n$ No, this shows taking away from the total number of marbles.

Choose the equation that shows the problem.

1. Kali has 15 cards. She makes 3 stacks of cards. How many cards are in each stack?

A $15 \div 3 = n$

B $n \div 3 = 15$

C $15 - 3 = n$

D $3 + n = 15$

2. The pet shop has 5 fish tanks. There are 8 fish in each tank. How many fish are there in all?

A $8 + 5 = n$

B $n = 8 \times 5$

C $8 \div n = 5$

D $5 + n = 8$

Name ____________________

Practice
7-4

Problem Solving: Choose an Appropriate Equation

Choose the equation that shows the problem.

1. Abby runs 3 miles 4 times a week. How many miles does she run in a week?

A $3 + 4 = n$

B $3 \times 4 = n$

C $n \div 4 = 4$

D $4 \div 3 = n$

2. The school received a shipment of 45 newspapers. The newspapers will be shared equally by 5 classes. How many newspapers will each class get?

A $45 - 5 = n$

B $5 \times n = 45$

C $n \div 4 = 45$

D $n + 5 = 45$

3. Marco collects stamps in a scrapbook. So far, he has 36 stamps. He puts 9 stamps on a page. How many pages has he used?

A $n \div 9 = 36$

B $36 - 4 = n$

C $9 \times n = 36$

D $n + 9 = 36$

Write a different equation that could be used to show each problem.

4. Problem 1: ____________________

5. Problem 2: ____________________

6. Problem 3: ____________________

7. Model Mrs. Wu makes blueberry pancakes for the school breakfast. She makes 2 batches of pancakes. Mrs. Wu makes 24 pancakes in all. Write an equation to find how many blueberry pancakes are in each batch.

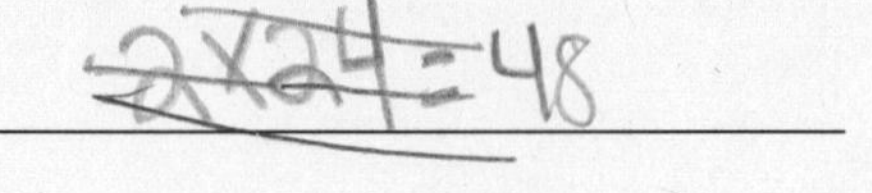

Name ______________________________

Reteaching
7-5

Writing Division Stories

Eddie was asked to write a division story using 12 ÷ 4.

Eddie wrote his story this way.

Cami has 12 crayons and some cans.
She puts 4 crayons into each can.

H

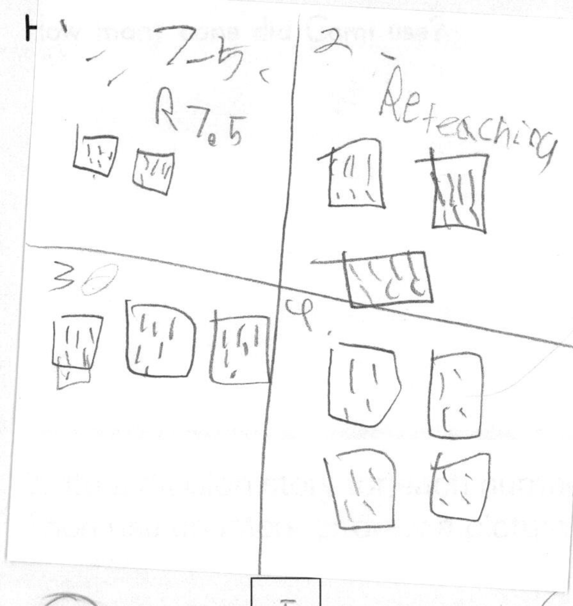

Think of a situation where the larger number can be put into groups.

Write your question.

You can show Eddie's story this way.

 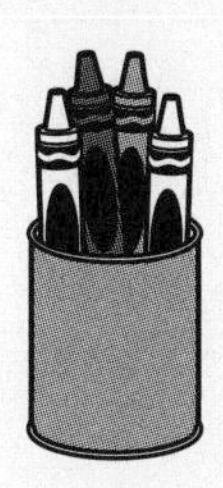 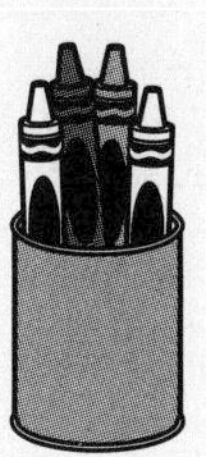

Cami used 3 cans.

…er sentence.
…to solve.

1. 10 ÷ 2 = ☐

____

____

____

2. 21 ÷ 3 = ☐

____

____

____

3. 18 ÷ 3 = ☐

____

____

____

4. 16 ÷ 4 = ☐

____

____

____

5. Explain It Sheila wrote a division story. She asked how many equal groups 24 flowers could be put into. What information must she give about the groups?

____

____

Name ____________________

Practice
7-5

Writing Division Stories

Write a division story for each number sentence.
Then use counters or draw a picture to solve.

1. $54 \div 6 = \square$

2. $36 \div 9 = \square$

3. $42 \div 7 = \square$

4. $25 \div 5 = $ 5

Pebbles has 25 dimes. He puts some dimes in 5 wallets. How many dimes are in each wallet?

There are 5 dimes in each wallet.

5. There are 40 relatives at a party. There are 5 tables that each seat the same number of people. How many people can sit at each table?

6. A softball pitcher needs to get 3 outs in an inning. If a pitcher gets 21 outs, how many innings did she pitch?

7. Explain It There are 16 people at a party. They want to set up relay teams with exactly 3 people each. Will each person be on a team? Explain.

Name ___________________________________

Reteaching
7-6

Problem Solving: Use Objects and Draw a Picture

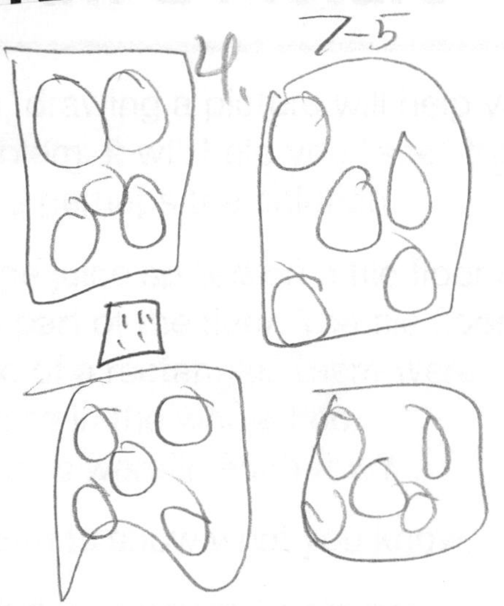

Sometin
solve a p
problem

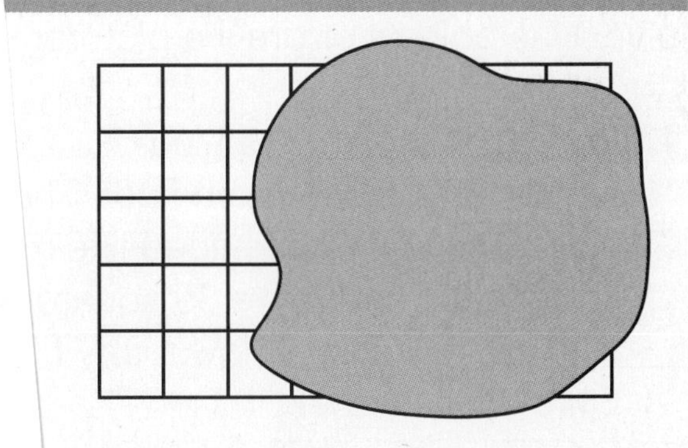

Some ora
covered u
in the sha
40 square
How many

Draw a pic … sh the picture to solve the problem.

You can se … There should be 40 tiles in all.
covered by juice on the floor.

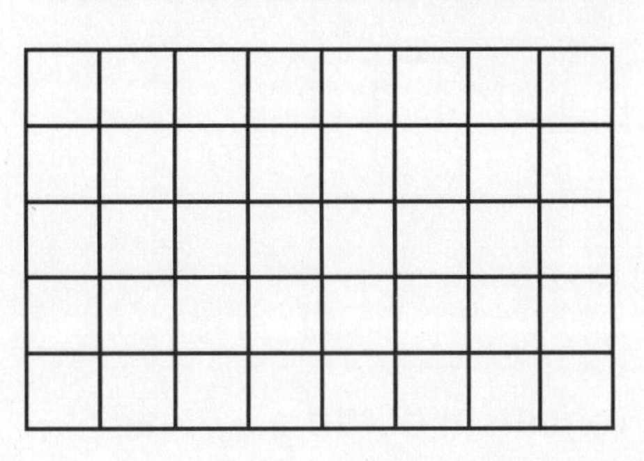

So there are 8 tiles in each row.

Solve. Use objects or draw a picture.

1. Mr. Robbins spilled stain on part of a tiled floor. The whole section of floor was shaped like a rectangle. There were 45 squares in the section. How many squares were in each row?

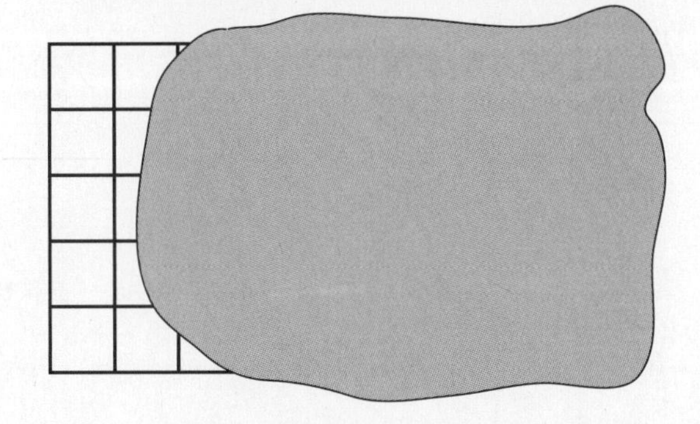

____

2. Kate is painting a wall. She painted over part of a section of 30 square tiles. The whole section of tiles was shaped like a rectangle. How many rows of tiles were in the whole section?

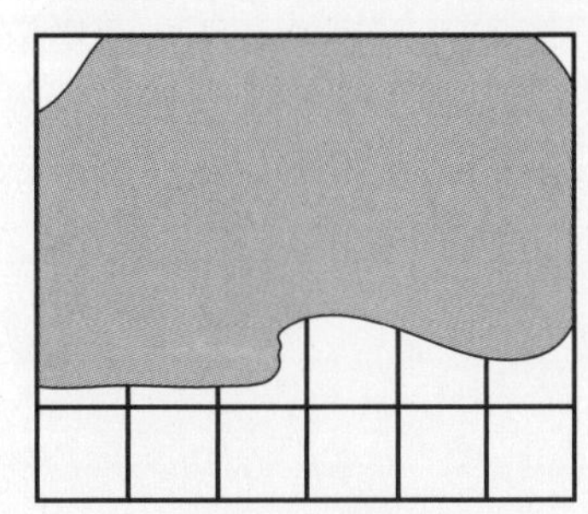

____

Name ______________________________

Practice
7-6

Problem Solving: Use Objects and Draw a Picture

Solve. Use objects or draw a picture.

1. Ron painted part of a tiled section of his bathroom floor. The whole section was shaped like a rectangle. There were 35 square tiles in the section. How many tiles were in each row?

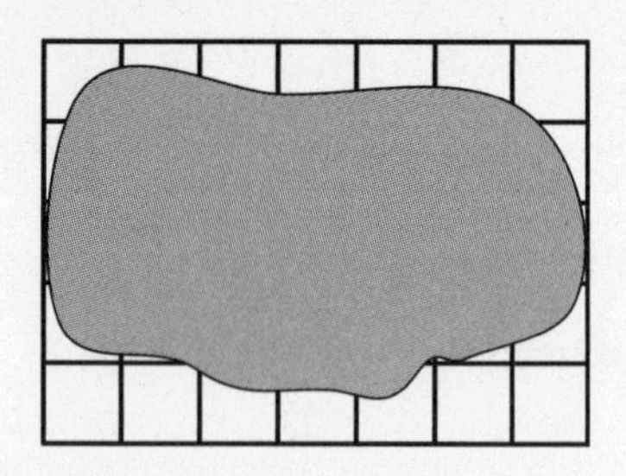

____

2. Some syrup spilled on a checkerboard-style table. The syrup covered some of the tiles. There were 36 squares on the table. How many of the squares had syrup on them?

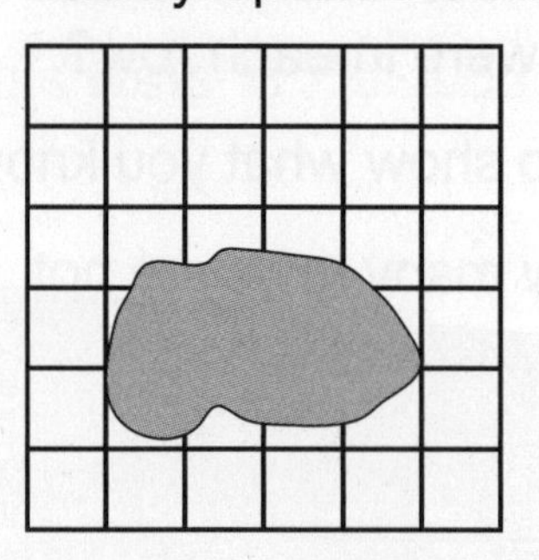

____

3. Dress rehearsal of the play was attended by 142 people. Opening night was attended by 238 people. How many people saw the two shows in all?

______ people in all	
142	238

4. Carol and Deanna drove 320 miles altogether this weekend. They drove 196 miles on Sunday. How many miles did they drive on Saturday?

320 miles in all	
	196

5. **Write a Problem** Write and solve a real-world problem that you can solve by using objects or drawing a picture.

____

____

Name ______________________

Reteaching
8-1

Relating Multiplication and Division

You can use multiplication facts to understand division.
Fact families show how multiplication and division are related.

Here is the fact family for 3, 8, and 24:

$3 \times 8 = 24$ $24 \div 3 = 8$

$8 \times 3 = 24$ $24 \div 8 = 3$

Complete. Use counters or draw a picture to solve.

1. $3 \times \square = 6$

   $6 \div 3 = \square$

2. $7 \times \square = 14$

   $14 \div 7 = \square$

3. $5 \times$ 4 $= 20$

   $20 \div 5 =$ 4

4. $4 \times \square = 24$

   $24 \div 4 = \square$

5. **Reason** What other number is a part of this fact family? 3, 4, ______

6. There are 28 days in 4 weeks. What fact family would you use to find the number of days in 1 week?

____

7. There are 12 inches in 1 foot. What fact family would you use to find the number of inches in 2 feet?

12x2=24, 2x12=24, 24÷12=2 and 24÷2=12.

Name ______________________

Relating Multiplication and Division

Complete. Use counters or draw a picture to help.

1. $5 \times \square = 15$

$15 \div 5 = \square$

2. $6 \times \square = 24$

$24 \div 6 = \square$

3. $7 \times \square = 35$

$35 \div 7 = \square$

4. $5 \times \square = 25$

$25 \div 5 = \square$

5. $3 \times \square = 12$

$12 \div 3 = \square$

6. $3 \times \square = 27$

$27 \div 3 = \square$

7. Write a fact family for 3, 6, and 18.

____

____

8. Patrick purchased 12 books. He needed 4 books for each of his projects at school. How many projects did he have?

____

9. **Model** Draw an array. Then write a fact family to describe your array.

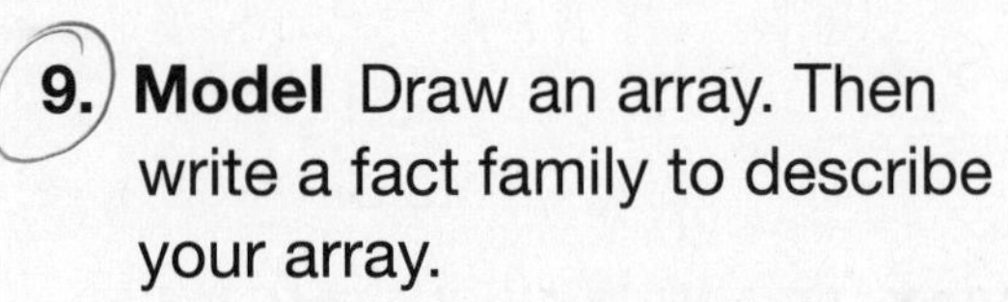

____

____

10. **Critique Reasoning** Evan told his class that the people in his family have 14 legs altogether. Quinton said that there must be 7 people in Evan's family. Is Quinton correct? Explain.

____

____

11. Which number makes this number sentence true? $\blacksquare \div 6 = 8$

A 2 **B** 14 **C** 24 **D** 48

Name ______________________________

Fact Families with 2, 3, 4, and 5

You can use multiplication facts to help you find quotients.

Example 1
Darren and Molly have 16 sheets of paper to share. Each will get the same number of sheets of paper. How many sheets will each get?

What You Think	What You Write
2 times what number equals 16? $2 \times \mathbf{8} = 16$	$16 \div 2 = \mathbf{8}$ Darren and Molly will each get 8 sheets of paper.

Example 2
Peter has 24 pennies. He puts the pennies into 4 equal rows. How many pennies are in each row?

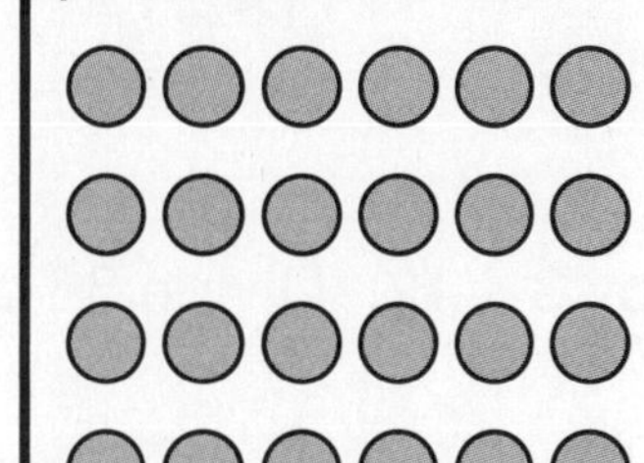

What You Think	What You Write
4 times what number equals 24? $4 \times \mathbf{6} = 24$	$24 \div 4 = \mathbf{6}$ Peter has 6 pennies in each row.

Find each quotient.

1. $14 \div 2$ ______

2. $35 \div 5$ ______

3. $15 \div 3$ ______

4. $32 \div 4$ ______

5. $24 \div 3$ ______

6. $2\overline{)12}$

7. $3\overline{)27}$

8. $5\overline{)25}$

9. $4\overline{)20}$

10. $4\overline{)36}$

11. Write a fact family using the numbers 5, 6, and 30.

____

____

Name ______________________________

Practice 8-2

Fact Families with 2, 3, 4, and 5

Find each quotient.

1. $14 \div 2$ ______ **2.** $12 \div 3$ ______ **3.** $16 \div 4$ ______ **4.** $30 \div 5$ ______ **5.** $20 \div 2$ ______

6. $3\overline{)21}$ **7.** $4\overline{)32}$ **8.** $5\overline{)40}$ **9.** $3\overline{)18}$ **10.** $5\overline{)45}$

11. Find 18 divided by 3. ______ **12.** Divide 36 by 4. ______ **13.** Find 35 divided by 5. ______

Find each missing number.

14. $27 \div \square = 3$ **15.** $30 \div 3 = \square$ **16.** $\square \div 2 = 7$

Reason Write < or > to compare.

17. $5 \times 2 \bigcirc 8 \div 2$ **18.** $3 \times 6 \bigcirc 6 \div 3$ **19.** $4 + 8 \bigcirc 4 \times 8$

20. Gabriella and 3 friends shared a pack of 12 stickers equally. How many stickers did each person get?

____

21. Erica counted 45 fingers when the students were asked who wants to play kickball. How many hands went up?

____

22. Franklin says that if he divides 40 by 5, he will get 8. Jeff says he should get 9. Who is correct? Explain.

____

____

23. Which fact does NOT belong in the same fact family as $24 \div 4 = 6$?

A $4 \times 6 = 24$ **B** $6 + 4 = 10$ **C** $24 \div 6 = 4$ **D** $6 \times 4 = 24$

Name ____________________

Fact Families with 6 and 7

Multiplication facts can help you to find division facts when 6 or 7 is the divisor.

Find $35 \div 7$.

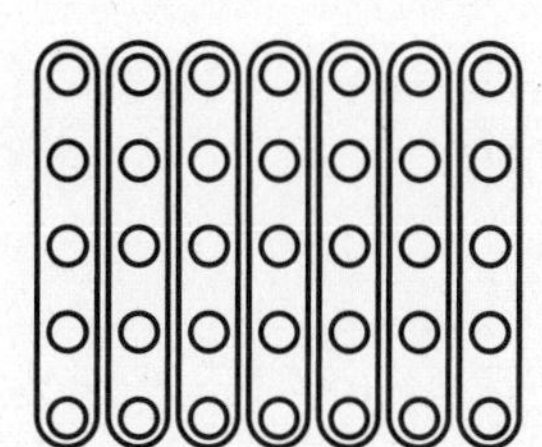

There are 48 marbles. They come in packages of 6. How many packages of marbles are there?

Find $48 \div 6$.

What You Think	What You Write	What You Think	What You Write
What number times 7 equals 35? $7 \times \mathbf{5} = 35$	$35 \div 7 = \mathbf{5}$	What number times 6 equals 48? $6 \times \mathbf{8} = 48$	$48 \div 6 = \mathbf{8}$ There are 8 packages of marbles.

Find each quotient.

1. $30 \div 6$ ______ **2.** $28 \div 7$ ______ **3.** $36 \div 6$ ______ **4.** $21 \div 7$ ______ **5.** $42 \div 6$ ______

6. $7\overline{)49}$ **7.** $6\overline{)54}$ **8.** $7\overline{)70}$ **9.** $6\overline{)48}$ **10.** $7\overline{)56}$

11. Reason Name a number that can be evenly divided by 6 and by 7.

____

12. Reason Using 6 as one of the numbers, write a fact family with only two facts.

____

Name ______________________________

Practice
8-3

Fact Families with 6 and 7

Find each quotient.

1. $24 \div 6$ ____ **2.** $42 \div 7$ ____ **3.** $36 \div 4$ ____ **4.** $63 \div 7$ ____ **5.** $40 \div 5$ ____

6. $6\overline{)48}$ **7.** $7\overline{)49}$ **8.** $2\overline{)12}$ **9.** $6\overline{)36}$ **10.** $3\overline{)27}$

11. Find 70 divided by 7. ____ **12.** Divide 66 by 6. ____ **13.** Find 48 divided by 6. ____

14. Communicate How can you use a multiplication fact to find a division fact?

____

____

15. Sierra's karate class lasts 56 days.
How many weeks does the class last? ______________

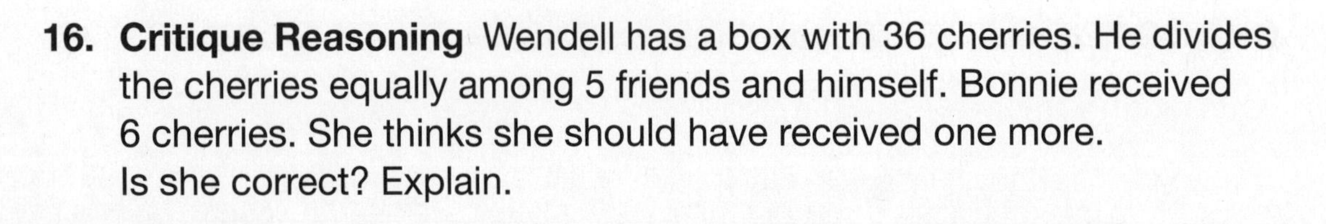

16. Critique Reasoning Wendell has a box with 36 cherries. He divides the cherries equally among 5 friends and himself. Bonnie received 6 cherries. She thinks she should have received one more.
Is she correct? Explain.

____

____

____

17. Mr. Kline brought 30 boxes of fruit juice to a soccer game. Fruit juice comes in packages of 6. How many packages did Mr. Kline bring? ______________

18. Katie bought 42 baseball cards. The cards come in packs of 7. How many packs of cards did Katie buy?

A 5 **B** 6 **C** 7 **D** 8

Name ______________________

Reteaching
8-4

Fact Families with 8 and 9

Multiplication facts can help you to find division facts when 8 or 9 is the divisor.

There are 32 counters. There are 8 counters in each row. How many rows are there?		There are 45 counters. There are 9 rows. How many counters are in each row?	
What You Think	**What You Write**	**What You Think**	**What You Write**
8 times what number equals 32? $8 \times \mathbf{4} = 32$	$32 \div 8 = \mathbf{4}$ There are 4 rows of counters.	9 times what number equals 45? $9 \times \mathbf{5} = 45$	$45 \div 9 = \mathbf{5}$ There are 5 counters in each row.

Find each quotient.

1. $54 \div 9$ ____ **2.** $24 \div 8$ ____ **3.** $56 \div 8$ ____ **4.** $36 \div 9$ ____ **5.** $63 \div 9$ ____

6. $9\overline{)72}$ **7.** $8\overline{)48}$ **8.** $8\overline{)40}$ **9.** $8\overline{)80}$ **10.** $9\overline{)81}$

11. Reason What multiplication fact could you use to find a number that can be divided evenly by 8 and by 9?

____

Name ______________________________

Practice
8-4

Fact Families with 8 and 9

Find each quotient.

1. 48 ÷ 8 ______ **2.** 18 ÷ 9 ______ **3.** 49 ÷ 7 ______ **4.** 64 ÷ 8 ______ **5.** 45 ÷ 9 ______

6. $6\overline{)42}$ **7.** $8\overline{)72}$ **8.** $9\overline{)36}$ **9.** $5\overline{)15}$ **10.** $8\overline{)56}$

11. Find 81 divided by 9. ______

12. Divide 40 by 8. ______

13. Find 90 divided by 9. ______

Write < or > to compare.

14. 63 ÷ 9 ◯ 8 **15.** 32 ÷ 8 ◯ 8 **16.** 54 ÷ 9 ◯ 5

17. **Reason** It costs $7 for a matinee and $8 for an evening movie. With $56, would you be able to buy more matinee tickets or evening tickets? Explain.

____

____

18. Teri scored 64 points in the first 8 basketball games she played in. She scored the same number of points in each game. How many points did she score in each game? ______

19. **Communicate** Adam made 19 paper cranes Monday and 8 more Tuesday. He gave 9 friends an equal number of cranes. How many cranes did each friend receive? Explain how you found your answer.

____

____

____

20. A short story consists of 81 pages. Andrea will read 9 pages each day. How many days will it take Andrea to finish the story?

A 6 **B** 7 **C** 8 **D** 9

Name ______________________________

Problem Solving: Multiple-Step Problems

To solve a multiple-step problem, you may need to find the answer to a hidden question first. Then you can use that answer to solve the problem.

Sandra has $22 to spend on school supplies. She buys a backpack and spends the rest of her money on notebooks. How many notebooks does she buy?

What do you know?		What do you need to do?
• Sandra has $22 and spends $10 on a backpack.	→	Subtract 10 from 22. $22 - 10 = 12$
• Sandra has $12 left to spend on notebooks that cost $3 each.	→	Divide 12 by 3. $12 \div 3 = 4$

Sandra buys 4 notebooks.

Solve.

1. There are 5 players on a basketball team. All but 2 players scored 6 points each. The other two players scored the same number of points. The team scored a total of 34 points. How many points did the other two players each score?

HINT: Hidden Question—How many points were scored in all by the players who scored 6 points each?

Each of the two plays scored 9 goals.

2. There are 45 students taking a trip to the museum. They form 3 groups with 7 students each. The rest of the groups have 6 students each. How many groups of 6 are there?

____

3. Juan has $20 to spend. He wants to spend $3 each day for 5 days and $4 on the weekend. Does he have enough money? If so, how much will he have left?

____

Name ______________________ (9)

Practice
8-5

Problem Solving: Multiple-Step Problems

Solve. Answer the hidden question first.

1. Marcus counted a total of 40 wheels from bicycles and tricycles while sitting on a park bench. Marcus counted 8 bicycles. How many tricycles did Marcus count?

____

HINT: Hidden Question—How many wheels did the bicycles have?

2. Julie bought 3 baseballs and some softballs. The total cost of the balls was $45. Each ball costs $5. How many softballs did Julie buy?

____

HINT: How much money did Julie spend on baseballs?

3. Bert bought 4 books for $7 each and a magazine for $5. He paid with a $50 bill. How much money did Bert receive back from the cashier?

____

HINT: Hidden Question—How much money did Bert spend?

4. A community group bought 9 student tickets and 3 adult tickets to the movies. The total cost of the tickets was $78. Student tickets cost $6. How much money does an adult ticket cost?

$8 for 1 adult ticket

HINT: How much money did the group spend on student tickets?

5. There are 48 students in the band. The boys and girls are in separate rows. There are 6 students in each row. There are 3 rows of boys. How many rows of girls are there? Explain your work.

____

____

____

6. Write a Problem Write a problem that can be solved by finding and answering a hidden question.

____

____

____

Name ____________________

Reteaching
8-6

Making Sense of Multiplication and Division Equations

Remember that an equation is a number sentence that uses an equal sign (=) to show that the value to its left is the same as the value to its right.

$2 \times 3 = 6$ is an example of a multiplication equation.

Some equations have letters in them or *unknowns*.

$$10 = 40 \div n$$

This equation means: 10 is equal to 40 divided by some number.

You can find the value of n that makes the equation true or equal on each side by thinking of multiplication or division facts.

Think: You know that $40 \div 10 = 4$, so $n = 4$.

In **1–8**, write a basic fact that is related to each equation. Then find the value for n that makes the equation true.

1. $81 = 9 \times n$ ____________ ____________

2. $n \times 4 = 0$ ____________ ____________

3. $7 = 49 \div n$ ____________ ____________

4. $16 \div n = 4$ 16÷4=4 n=4

5. $8 = 56 \div n$ ____________ ____________

6. $n \times 5 = 15$ ____________ ____________

7. $6 = 48 \div n$ ____________ ____________

8. $5 \times n = 40$ ____________ ____________

9. Critique Reasoning Alex decides that $21 \div 3 = 7$ is NOT a true equation. Is Alex correct? Explain.

____

____

Name ______________________________

Practice
8-6

Making Sense of Multiplication and Division Equations

In **1–8**, decide if the two sides are equal. If yes, write =. If no, write ≠ (not equal).

1. $54 \bigcirc 9 \times 6$ ______

2. $10 \div 5 \bigcirc 2$ ______

3. $25 \div 5 \bigcirc 7$ ______

4. $16 \bigcirc 4 \times 5$ ______

5. $9 \div 1 \bigcirc 1$ ______

6. $45 \bigcirc 5 \times 9$ ______

7. $14 \bigcirc 2 \times 7$ ______

8. $81 \div 9 \bigcirc 8$ ______

In **9–16**, find the value for n that makes the equation true.

9. $30 = 6 \times n$ ______

10. $3 = n \div 7$ ______

11. $80 = 10 \times n$ ______

12. $n \div 6 = 7$ ______

13. $20 \div n = 5$ ______

14. $36 \div n = 6$ ______

15. $n = 9 \times 2$ ______

16. $56 = 8 \times n$ ______

For **17** and **18**, use the given equation to solve the problem.

17. Together Karen and Mary have n bouquets of roses in their window display. There are 9 roses in each bouquet and 36 roses in all. How many bouquets are in the display?

$n \times 9 = 36$

____

18. Hector found an equal number of shells at the beach on 7 different days. If Hector found 63 shells in all, how many shells did he find each day?

$63 \div n = 7$

____

19. **Model** Bruce has 35 pencils on his desk arranged in groups with 7 pencils in each group. How many groups of pencils are on his desk? Write an equation using n for the unknown value. Solve for n.

____

20. Which value for n makes the equation $n \div 8 = 1$ true?

A $n = 1$

B $n = 4$

C $n = 2$

D $n = 8$

Name ______________________

Dividing with 0 and 1

There are special rules to follow when dividing by 1 or 0.

Rule	Example	What You **Think**	What You **Write**
When any number is divided by 1, the quotient is that number.	$7 \div 1 = ?$	1 times what number = 7? $1 \times 7 = 7$ So, $7 \div 1 = 7$	$7 \div 1 = 7$ or $1\overline{)7}$ with quotient 7
When any number (except 0) is divided by itself, the quotient is 1.	$8 \div 8 = ?$	8 times what number = 8? $8 \times 1 = 8$ So, $8 \div 8 = 1$	$8 \div 8 = 1$ or $8\overline{)8}$ with quotient 1
When zero is divided by a number (except 0), the quotient is 0.	$0 \div 5 = ?$	5 times what number = 0? $5 \times 0 = 0$ So, $0 \div 5 = 0$	$0 \div 5 = 0$ or $5\overline{)0}$ with quotient 0
You cannot divide a number by 0.	$9 \div 0 = ?$	0 times what number = 9? There is no number that works, so $9 \div 0$ cannot be done.	$9 \div 0$ cannot be done

Find each quotient.

1. $25 \div 1$ ______
2. $9 \div 9$ ______
3. $0 \div 8$ ______
4. $6 \div 6$ ______
5. $4 \div 1$ ______

6. $1\overline{)7}$
7. $12\overline{)12}$
8. $17\overline{)0}$
9. $5\overline{)5}$
10. $1\overline{)9}$

Compare. Use <, >, or =.

11. $15 \div 1$ ◯ $15 \div 15$
12. $0 \div 12$ ◯ $12 \div 12$

Name ____________________

Dividing with 0 and 1

Find each quotient.

1. $0 \div 6$ ______ **2.** $8 \div 8$ ______ **3.** $6 \div 1$ ______ **4.** $0 \div 5$ ______ **5.** $9 \div 9$ ______

6. $1\overline{)5}$ **7.** $4\overline{)0}$ **8.** $6\overline{)6}$ **9.** $1\overline{)8}$ **10.** $1\overline{)3}$

11. $3\overline{)24}$ **12.** $6\overline{)42}$ **13.** $8\overline{)72}$ **14.** $5\overline{)30}$ **15.** $7\overline{)63}$

16. Find 0 divided by 2. ______ **17.** Divide 7 by 1. ______ **18.** Find 4 divided by 4. ______

Write <, >, or = to compare.

19. $6 \div 6$ ◯ $8 \div 8$ **20.** $0 \div 5$ ◯ $5 \div 5$ **21.** $9 \div 1$ ◯ $7 \div 1$

22. Tickets for rides cost \$1 each at the fair. Bob has \$6 to buy tickets. How many tickets can Bob buy? ______

23. **Reason** Nikki is the goalie on her soccer team. She has allowed 0 goals in 8 games. How many goals has she allowed in each game? ______

24. **Communicate** Why is $10 - 0 = 10$, but $0 \div 10 = 0$? Explain.

______

______

______

25. Which has the greatest quotient?

A $6 \div 6$ **B** $5 \div 1$ **C** $0 \div 3$ **D** $8 \div 8$

Name ______________________________

Reteaching
8-8

Multiplication and Division Facts

A class is making popcorn for a carnival. Each batch makes 30 cups. They put the popcorn in bags that hold 6 cups each. How many bags of popcorn does one batch make?

You can solve the problem using division or multiplication.

Division

How many groups of 6 are in 30?

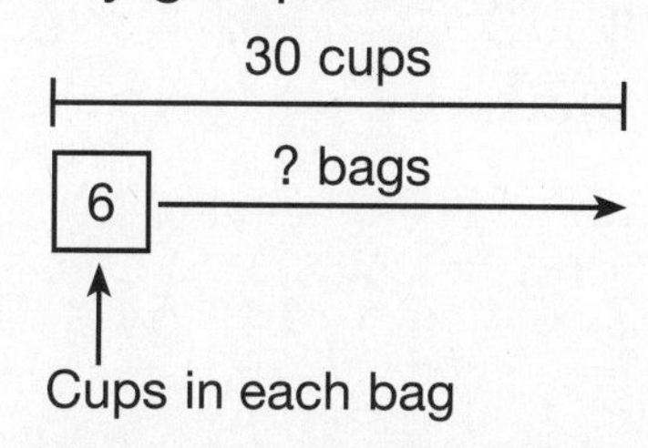

Divide the total number of cups by the number of cups in each bag:
$30 \div 6 = \mathbf{5}$ ← Number of bags

Multiplication

What number times 6 equals 30?

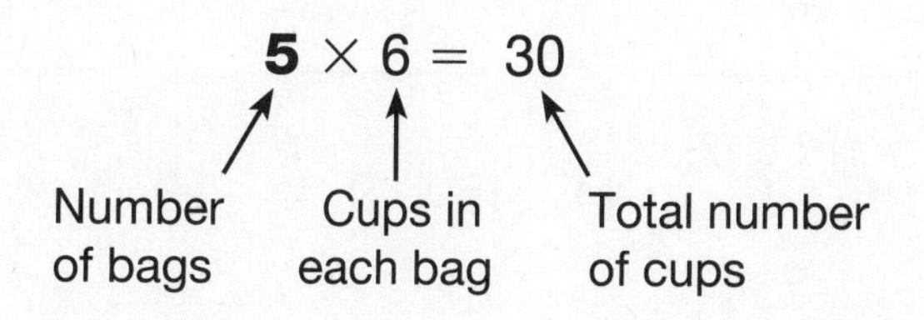

Each batch of popcorn makes 5 bags.

Complete the equations.

1. $21 \div 3 = \square$
$3 \times \square = 21$

2. $36 \div 6 = \square$
$6 \times \square = 36$

3. $18 \div 9 = \square$
$9 \times \square = 18$

4. $54 \div 9 = \square$
$9 \times \square = 54$

5. There are 24 students running in a relay race. Each relay team needs 4 students. How many teams will they make? Write a division sentence and a multiplication sentence.

______________________________ ______________________________

6. Writing to Explain The same number makes both of these equations true. What number is it? Explain.

$56 \div 8 = \blacksquare$ $8 \times \blacksquare = 56$

____

____

Name ___________________________________

Multiplication and Division Facts

Practice
8-8

Complete the number sentences.

1. $35 \div 5 = \square$

$\square \times 5 = 35$

2. $27 \div \square = 3$

$3 \times \square = 27$

3. $42 \div 7 = \square$

$\square \times 7 = 42$

4. $32 \div \square = 4$

$4 \times \square = 32$

Find each product or quotient.

5. $16 \div 4$ ______

6. 9×7 ______

7. $30 \div 5$ ______

8. 8×3 ______

9. 4×9 ______

10. $25 \div 5$ ______

11. $45 \div 9$ ______

12. 8×8 ______

13. 7×4 ______

14. $54 \div 6$ ______

15. Find 36 divided by 6. ______

16. Multiply 8 and 9. ______

17. Divide 48 by 8. ______

18. A music store has 5 guitars for sale. Each guitar has 6 strings. The manager wants to replace all the strings. How many new strings does he need?

A 6

B 18

C 24

D 30

19. Tolen has 18 dog treats. He gives the same number of treats to the 6 dogs at the pet store where he works. Which equation can be used to find the number of treats each dog gets?

A $18 + 6 = 24$

B $18 \div 6 = 3$

C $18 - 6 = 12$

D $18 \div 18 = 1$

20. **Communicate** Jason has 3 bags with 5 mangos in each bag. Maria has 5 bags with 4 mangos in each bag. Explain how you can tell who has more without finding the total number of mangos each person has.

____

____

Name ______________________________

Problem Solving: Draw a Picture and Write a Number Sentence

You can draw a picture to help you divide.

Neil has 54 CDs. He has the CDs equally placed among 6 shelves. How many CDs can go on each shelf?

Draw a diagram to show the problem. Make 6 rows with the same number of CDs until you reach 54.

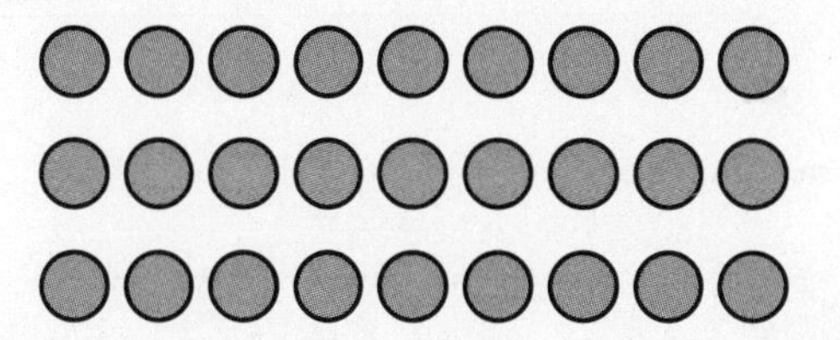

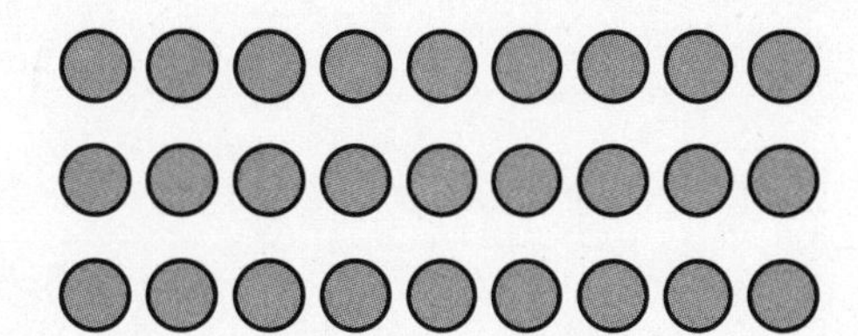

Write a number sentence: $54 \div 6 = 9$.

Check your answer by using multiplication: $6 \times 9 = 54$.

Neil can put 9 CDs on each shelf.

Draw a diagram to show what you know.
Then write a number sentence and solve.

1. There are 5 cars taking students to a museum. Each car can seat 4 students. How many students can go to the museum?

   ____

2. There are 16 players competing in the beach volleyball tournament. There are 8 teams competing. How many players are on each team?

   ____

3. **Communicate** Sandy said she could use addition to answer question 1. How could this be done?

   ____

   ____

Name ____________________

Practice
8-9

Problem Solving: Draw a Picture and Write a Number Sentence

In **1** and **2**, draw a diagram to show what you know. Then write a number sentence and solve.

1. Maria bought 5 cans of tennis balls. Each can contained 3 tennis balls. How many tennis balls did Maria buy altogether?

____

2. In Ms. Ramirez's class, there are 28 students. They sit in 4 equal rows. How many students are in each row?

____

In **3** and **4**, use the chart.

Players on Team	
Sport	**Players**
Tennis	2
Basketball	5
Softball	10

3. A community center has 3 tennis teams and 5 basketball teams. No one is on both teams. How many athletes are there?

____

4. Critique Reasoning Fabio said that there are 3 times as many people on a basketball team as on a tennis team. Is he correct? Explain.

____

____

____

Write a number sentence and solve. Use this information for **5** and **6**.

Marshall sleeps 8 hours each day.

5. How many hours does Marshall sleep in one week? ____________________

6. How many hours is Marshall awake each day? ____________________

7. Tricia spent $12 to rent ice skates. She rented them for 4 hours. Which number sentence can you write to find how much it costs to rent skates for one hour?

A $12 − 4 = ■ **B** $12 + 4 = ■ **C** $12 × 4 = ■ **D** $12 ÷ 4 = ■

Name ____________________

Dividing Regions into Equal Parts

A whole can be divided into equal parts in different ways.

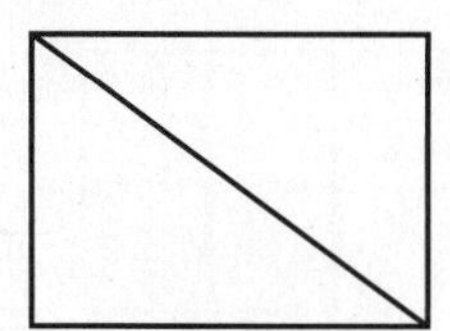
2 equal parts
halves

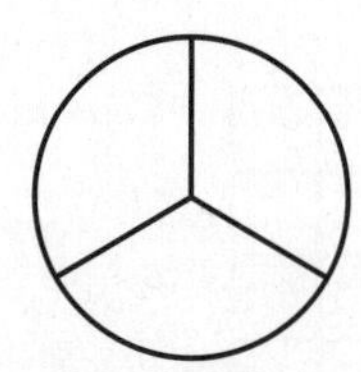
3 equal parts
thirds

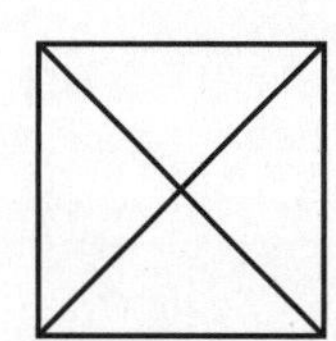
4 equal parts
fourths

5 equal parts
fifths

6 equal parts
sixths

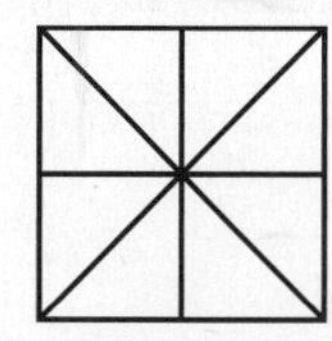
8 equal parts
eighths

10 equal parts
tenths

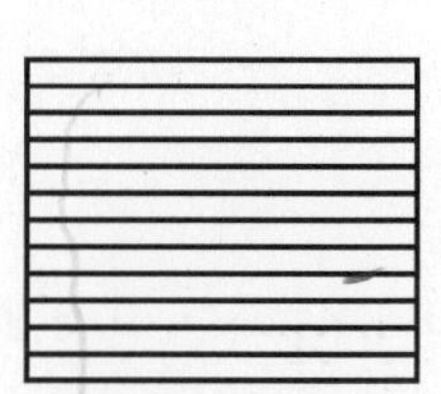
12 equal parts
twelfths

Tell if each shows equal parts or unequal parts.
If the parts are equal, name them.

1. fourths

2. Unequal

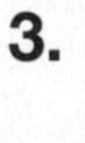

3. 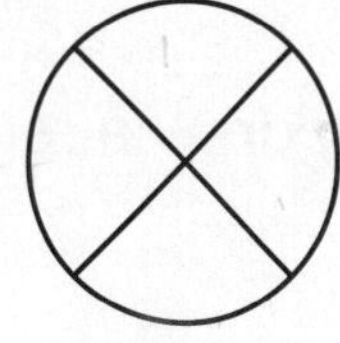

fourths

Name the equal parts of the whole.

4. 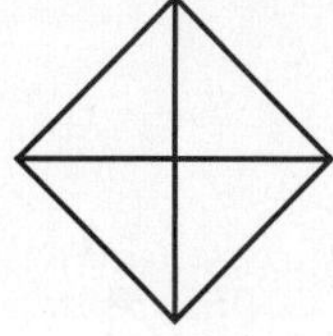

fourths

5. 

twelfths

6. 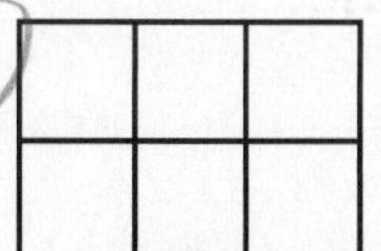

Sixths.

7. Using grid paper, draw a picture of a whole that is divided into thirds.

8. Reason How many equal parts are there when you divide a figure into fifths? 5 equal parts

Name ____________________

Dividing Regions into Equal Parts

Tell if each shows equal or unequal parts.
If the parts are equal, name them.

1. 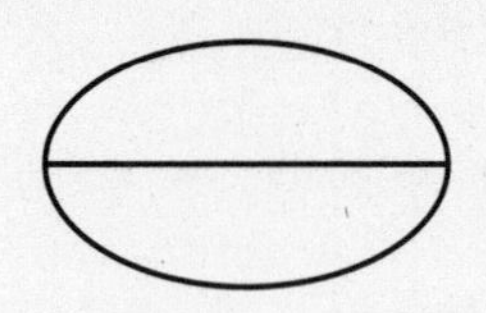

halv-es

2. 

unequal

3. 

eighths

4. 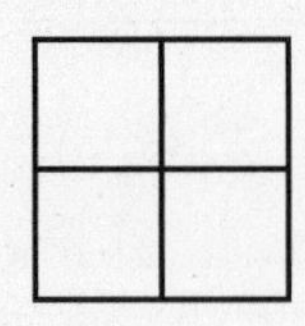

fourths

Name the equal parts of the whole.

5. 

eights

6. 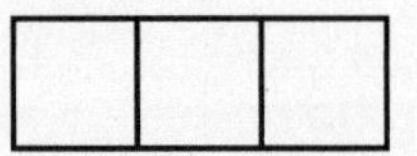

thirds

7. 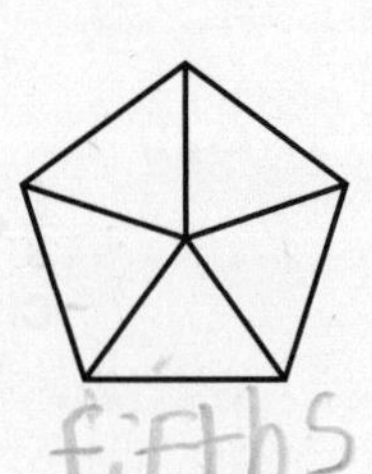

fifths

8. 

sixths

Use the grid to draw a region showing the number of equal parts named.

9. eighths

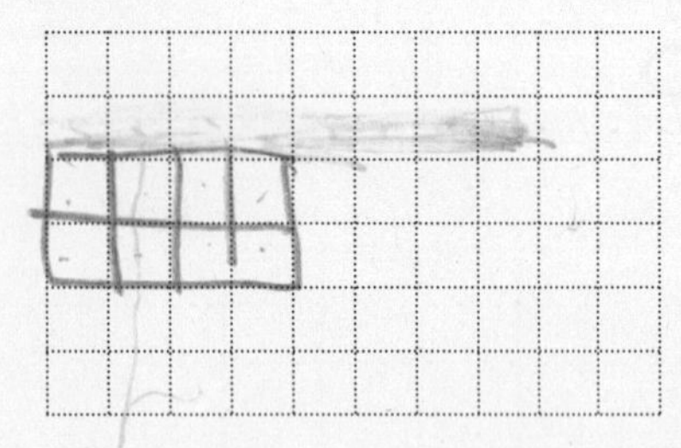

10. sixths

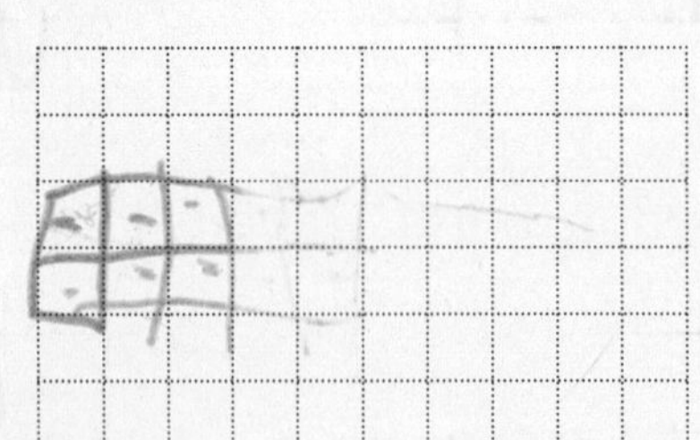

11. How many equal parts does this figure have?

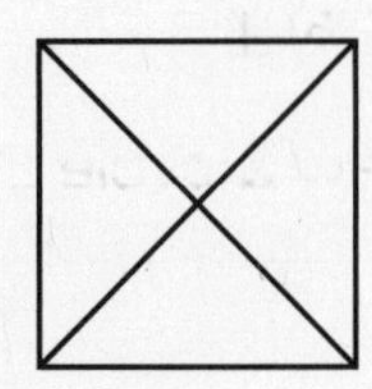

12. Which is the name of 12 equal parts of a whole?

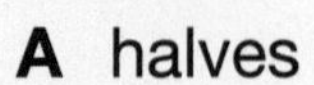

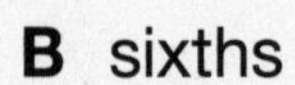

A halves **B** sixths **C** tenths **D** twelfths

Name ____________________

Fractions and Regions

A fraction can be used to name part of a whole.

A unit fraction is a fraction with a numerator of 1.

The denominator shows the total number of equal parts in a whole.

The numerator shows how many equal parts are described.

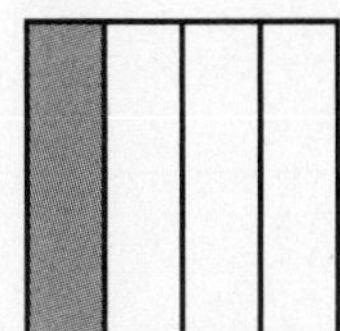

number of parts shaded ⟶ 1 ⟵ Numerator

number of equal parts ⟶ 4 ⟵ Denominator

One fourth of the rectangle is shaded.

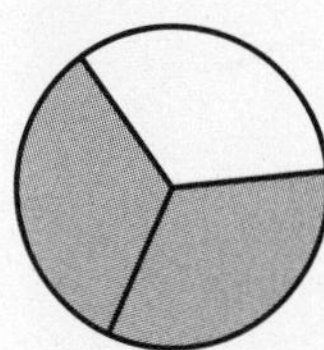

Each part of the circle is $\frac{1}{3}$. There are 2 parts shaded. $\frac{2}{3}$ of the whole circle is shaded.

In **1–4,** write the unit fraction that represents each part of the whole. Write the number of shaded parts and the fraction of the whole that is shaded.

1. 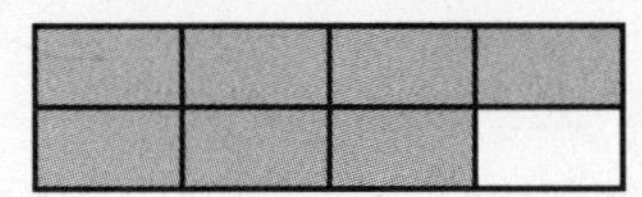

7/8

2. 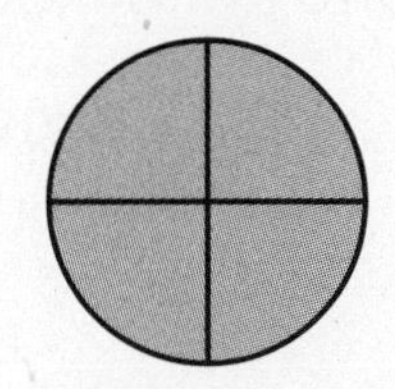

4/4

3. 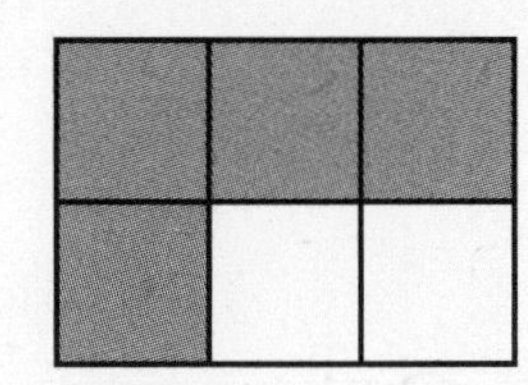

4/6

4. 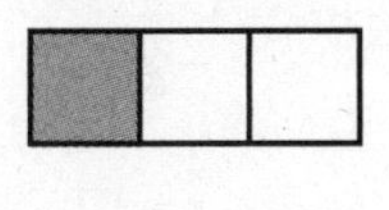

1/3

5. Draw a rectangle that shows 2 equal parts. Shade $\frac{1}{2}$ of the rectangle.

6. Draw a circle that shows 4 equal parts. Shade $\frac{3}{4}$ of the circle.

Rectangle

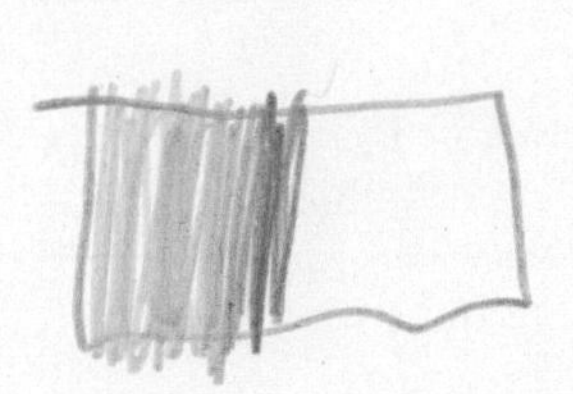

Circle

Name ______________________

Fractions and Regions

In 1–4, write the unit fraction that represents each part of the whole. Write the number of shaded parts and the fraction of the whole that is shaded.

1. 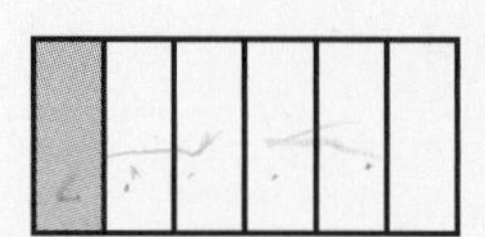

2. 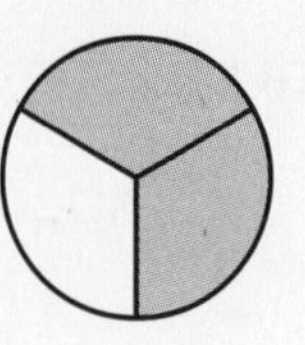

3. 

4. 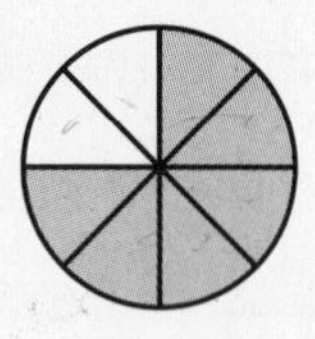

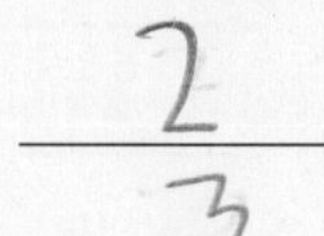

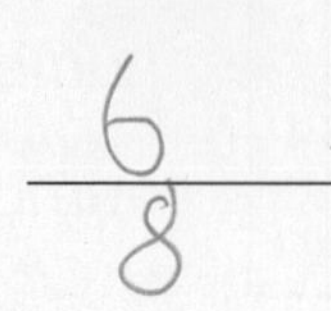

5. Draw a circle that shows 4 equal parts. Shade $\frac{2}{4}$ of the circle.

6. Draw a hexagon that shows 6 equal parts. Shade $\frac{4}{6}$ of the hexagon.

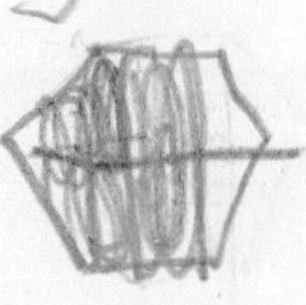

In 7 and 8, use the information below.

Three parts of a rectangle are red. Two parts are blue.

7. What fraction of the rectangle is red?

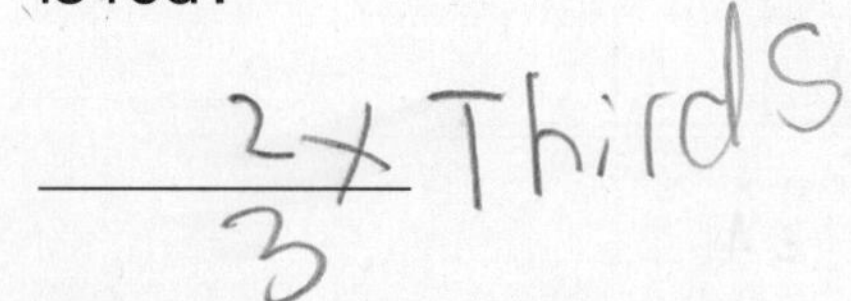

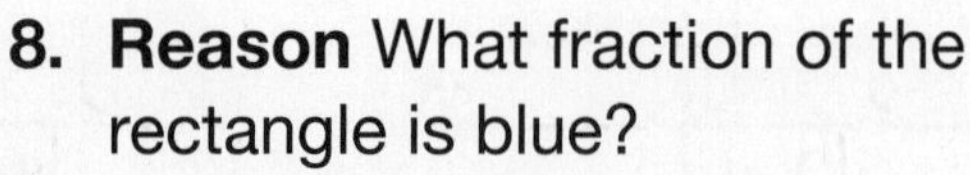

8. **Reason** What fraction of the rectangle is blue?

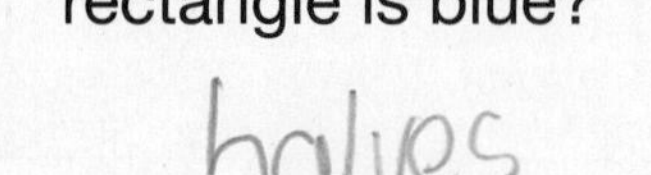

9. **Model** A banner is made of 8 equal parts. Five of the parts contain stars. Three of the parts contain hearts. Draw the banner.

10. How can you write the fraction $\frac{4}{6}$ in word form?

A fourth sixth **B** four sixes **C** four sixths **D** fourth six

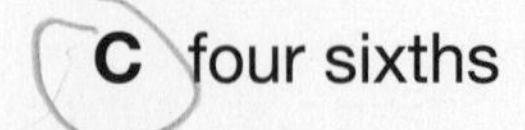

Name ____________________

Fractions and Sets

A fraction can name part of a group.

What fraction of the marbles are black?

3 ⟵ Number of black marbles
8 ⟵ Total number of marbles

$\frac{3}{8}$ of the marbles are black.

1. What fraction of the toys are balls? ________

2. What fraction of the fruits are oranges? ________

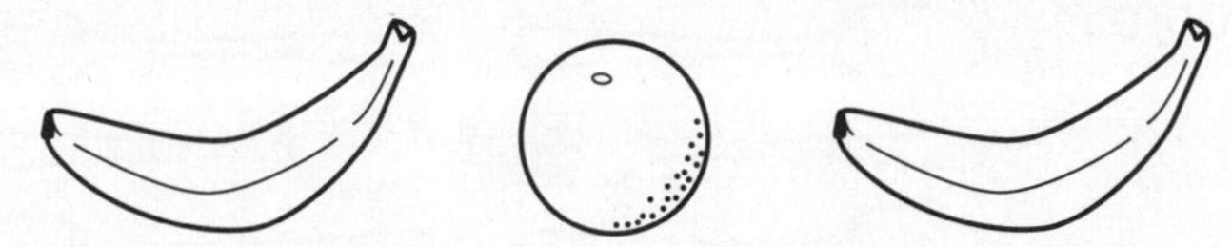

3. What fraction of the blocks have letters on them? ________

4. What fraction of the letters in the word Monday is *M*? ________

For **5** and **6** draw a picture to show each fraction of a set.

5. $\frac{3}{6}$ of the squares are shaded.

6. $\frac{2}{3}$ of the balls are footballs.

7. **Reason** Out of 6 cats, 2 are tan. What fraction of cats are **NOT** tan? ________

Name ____________________

Practice
9-3

Fractions and Sets

In **1** through **3**, write the fraction of the counters that are shaded.

1. 

____

2. 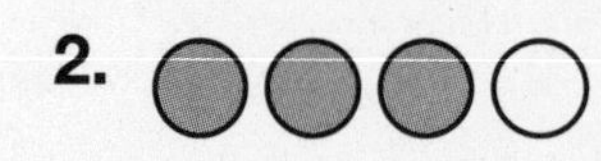

____

3. 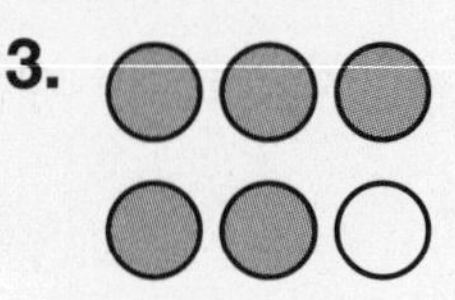

____

Draw a picture of the set described.

4. 4 shapes, $\frac{3}{4}$ of the shapes are squares

5. 6 shapes, $\frac{1}{6}$ of the shapes are circles

6. 8 shapes, $\frac{7}{8}$ of the shapes are triangles

In **7** and **8**, use the utensils to answer the questions.

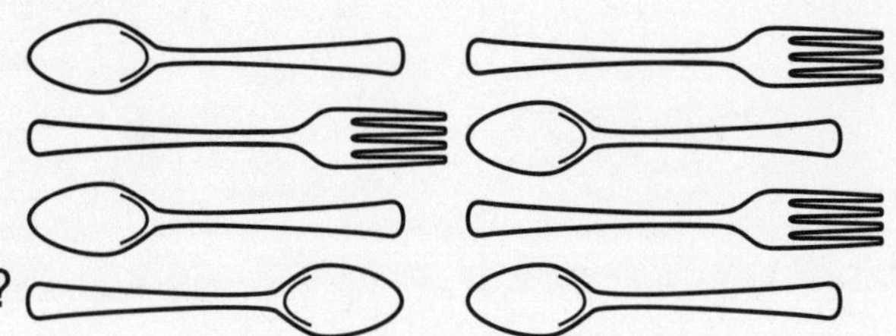

7. What fraction of the utensils are forks?

____

8. What fraction of the utensils are spoons?

____

9. Persevere Johnny bought 6 movie tickets and spent $54. Of the tickets he bought, $\frac{3}{6}$ were children's tickets that cost $8 each. The other tickets were adult tickets. How much does one adult ticket cost?

____

10. Pamela has 4 pink ribbons, 3 green ribbons, and 1 blue ribbon. What fraction of Pamela's ribbons are green?

A $\frac{1}{3}$ **B** $\frac{3}{8}$ **C** $\frac{2}{3}$ **D** $\frac{3}{4}$

Name ______________________

Reteaching
9-4

Fractional Parts of a Set

You can find how many there are in a fraction of a set.

Find $\frac{1}{3}$ of 15 triangles.

First look at the denominator of the fraction.

$\frac{1}{3} \leftarrow$ 3 equal parts in all

So, put 15 triangles into **3** equal groups.

Next, look at the numerator of the fraction.

$\frac{1}{3} \leftarrow$ 1 of the equal parts

So, find how many triangles are in 1 of the equal parts.

There are 5 triangles.
$\frac{1}{3}$ of 15 = 5

1. Use the drawing at the right. Morris used $\frac{1}{4}$ of 12 squares to make a picture. Find $\frac{1}{4}$ of 12 squares.

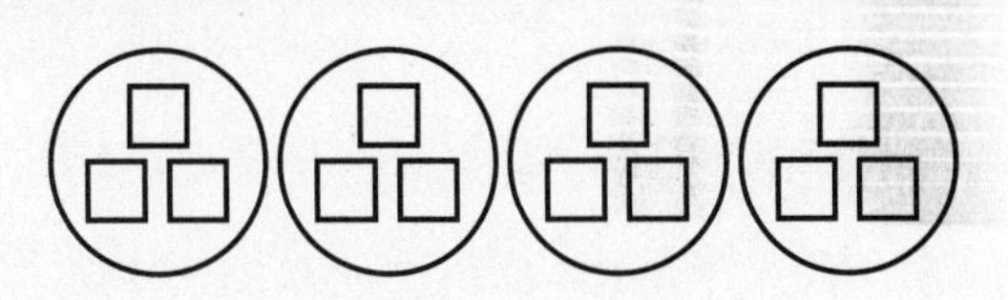

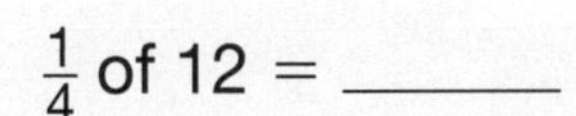
$\frac{1}{4}$ of 12 = ______

Morris used ______ squares.

In **2** and **3,** draw a picture to help.

2. Thea used $\frac{1}{2}$ of 10 blocks to build a house. Find $\frac{1}{2}$ of 10 blocks.

$\frac{1}{2}$ of 10 = ______

Thea used ______ blocks.

3. Nate used $\frac{1}{8}$ of 24 crayons to draw a picture. Find $\frac{1}{8}$ of 24.

$\frac{1}{8}$ of 24 = ______

Nate used ______ crayons.

4. **Writing to Explain** When you divide 24 by 6, what fraction of 24 are you finding? Find the answer.

____

____

Name ___________________________

Fractional Parts of a Set

1. Luann read $\frac{1}{3}$ of 18 books on her reading list. How many books did Luann read? Find $\frac{1}{3}$ of 18 books.

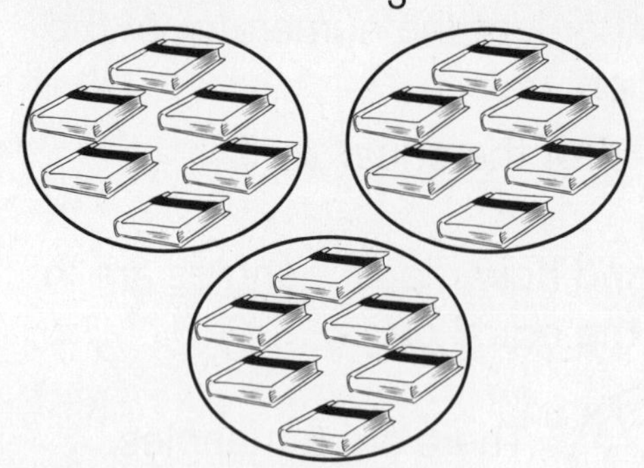

$\frac{1}{3}$ of 18 = ______

Luann read ______ books.

2. Jake used $\frac{1}{6}$ of 30 pencils in a pack. How many pencils did Jake use? Find $\frac{1}{6}$ of 30 pencils.

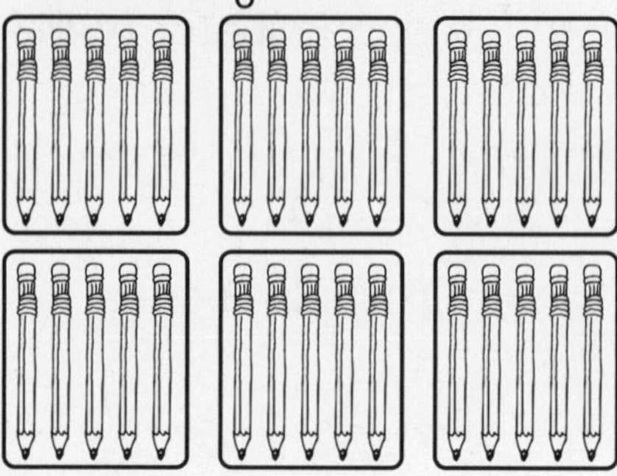

$\frac{1}{6}$ of 30 = ______

Jake used ______ pencils.

3. There are 12 eggs in a carton. Kim used $\frac{1}{3}$ of a carton of eggs to make muffins. How many eggs did she use? Explain how you found your answer.

____

____

____

____

4. **Model** Draw a picture in the space at the right to show how you would find $\frac{1}{2}$ of 8 marbles.

5. What number represents $\frac{1}{8}$ of 24 students?

A 2 **B** 3 **C** 4 **D** 8

Name ____________________

Locating Fractions on the Number Line

Number lines can be used to show fractions. In the number lines below, the denominator shows the number of equally sized sections between 0 and 1.

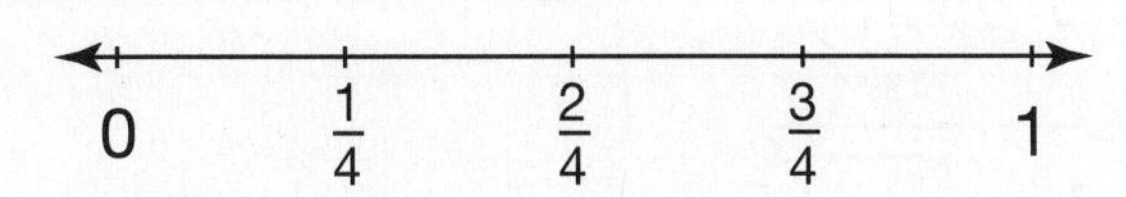

This number line is divided into fourths.

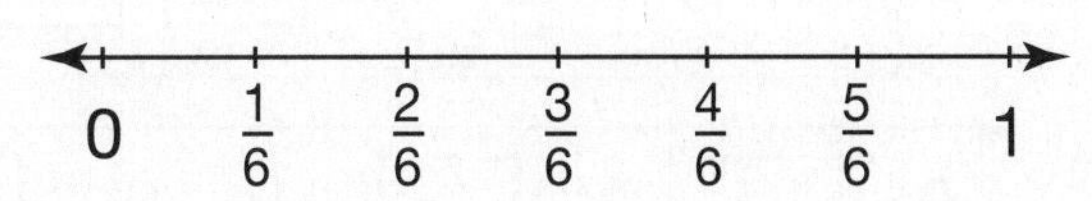

This number line is divided into sixths.

Number lines can also represent mixed numbers.

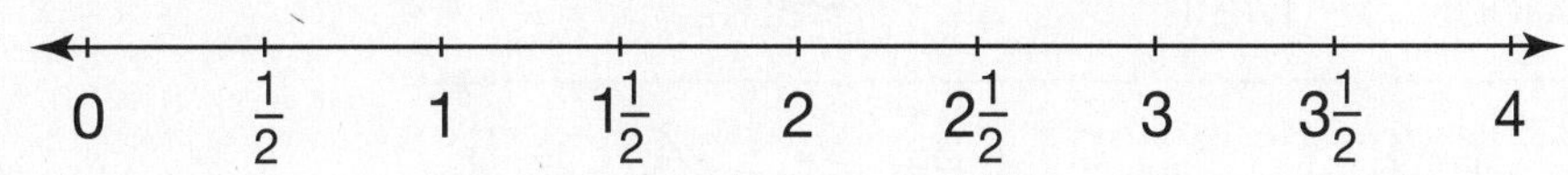

This number line is divided into halves.

Write the missing fraction or mixed number for each number line.

1. 0, $\frac{1}{8}$, $\frac{2}{8}$, $\frac{3}{8}$, ☐, ☐, ☐, ☐, 1

2. 0, $\frac{1}{3}$, $\frac{2}{3}$, 1, $1\frac{1}{3}$, ☐, 2, $2\frac{1}{3}$, $2\frac{2}{3}$, 3

3. 0, ☐, $\frac{2}{4}$, ☐, 1, ☐, $1\frac{2}{4}$, ☐, 2, $2\frac{1}{4}$, ☐, ☐, 3

4. Construct Arguments Erica said that $1\frac{3}{4}$ is between 2 and 3 on a number line. Do you agree? Why or why not?

____

____

Name ______________________________

Locating Fractions on the Number Line

Write the missing fraction or mixed number for each number line.

1.

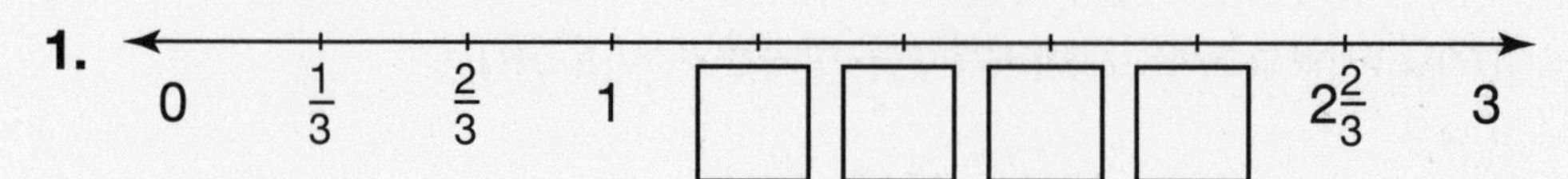

2.

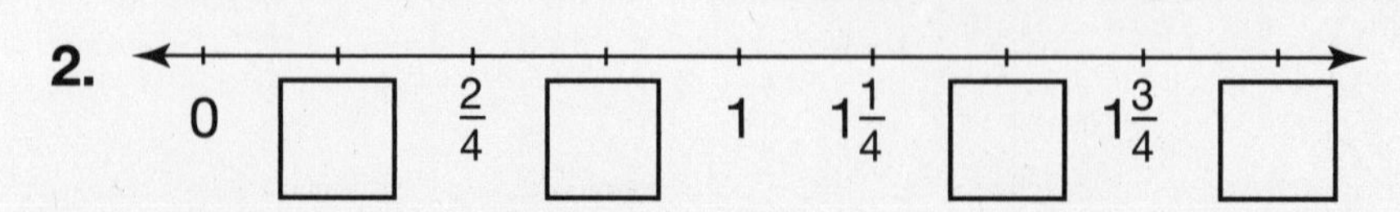

The number line below shows how many miles different places are from the pet shop. Use the number line for **3–5**.

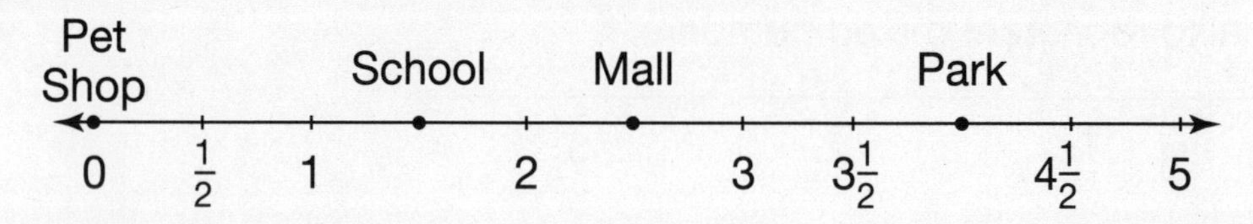

3. The park is 4 miles from the pet shop. How far is the mall from the pet shop?

____

4. **Reason** Ken lives halfway between the pet shop and the park. How far does Ken live from school?

____

5. The movie theater is twice as far from the school as the mall. If the movie theater is to the right of the school, at which location is the movie theater?

____

6. Roberta is going to make a number line from 0 to 4 by $\frac{1}{4}$s. Not including the mark for 0, how many marks should she draw?

A 8 **B** 12 **C** 16 **D** 20

Name ______________________

Benchmark Fractions

You can use benchmark fractions to help you estimate parts.
Benchmark fractions are $\frac{1}{4}$, $\frac{1}{3}$, $\frac{1}{2}$, $\frac{2}{3}$, and $\frac{3}{4}$.

One way to think of benchmark fractions is to think of part of a clock.

$\frac{1}{2}$ shaded

$\frac{1}{3}$ shaded

$\frac{2}{3}$ shaded

$\frac{1}{4}$ shaded

$\frac{3}{4}$ shaded

Estimate the fractional part that is shaded.

1. ______________________

2. ______________________

3. ______________________

4. ______________________

5. **Number Sense** About how much of the casserole is left over?

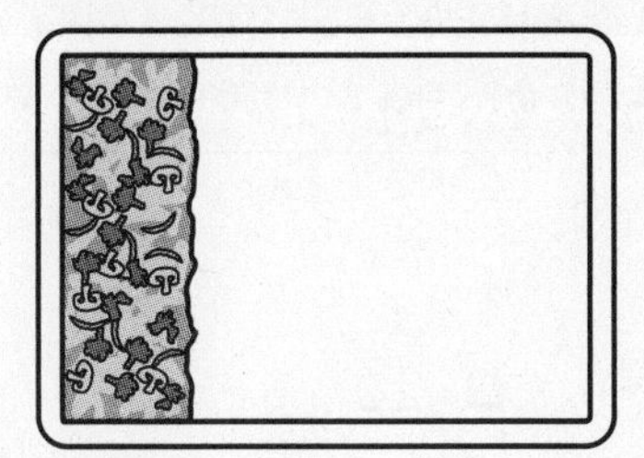

____

Name ____________________

Practice 9-6

Benchmark Fractions

Estimate the fractional part of each strip that is shaded.

1. 

2. 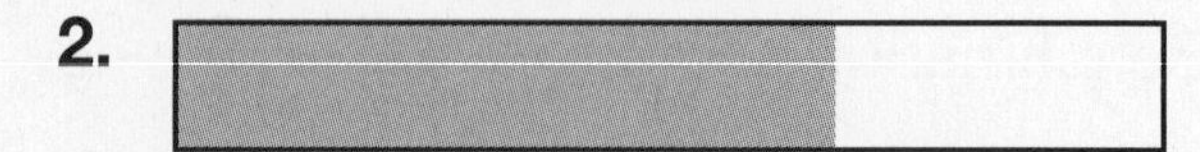

3. 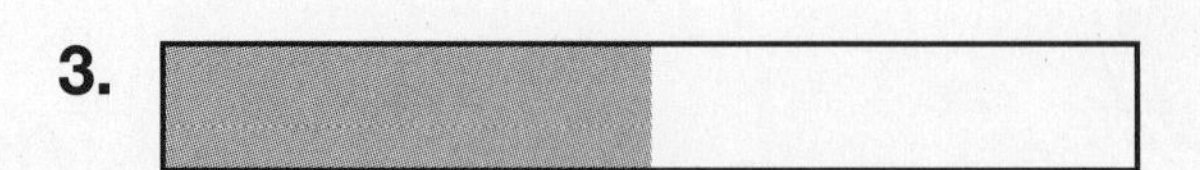

4.

What benchmark fraction is closest to each point? Choose from the benchmark fractions $\frac{1}{2}$, $\frac{1}{3}$, $\frac{2}{3}$, $\frac{1}{4}$, and $\frac{3}{4}$.

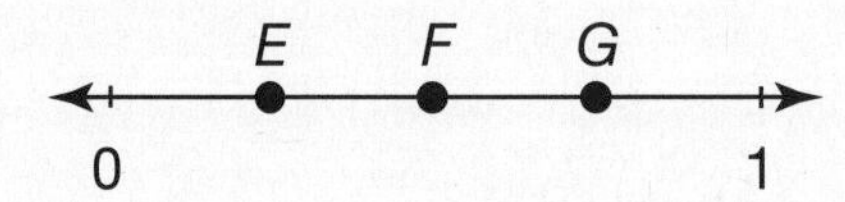

5. *E* __________ 6. *F* __________ 7. *G* __________

Estimate the amount that is left.

8. 

9. 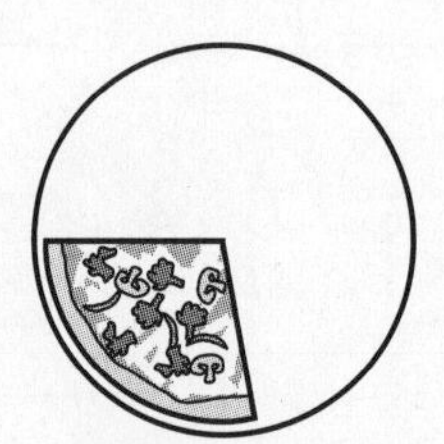

10. 

11. **Model** Draw a circle and shade it to show about $\frac{1}{3}$ shaded.

12. Which is the best estimate for the amount of the square that is shaded?

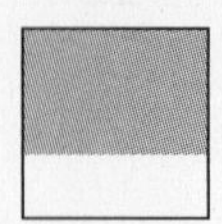

A $\frac{1}{4}$ **C** $\frac{1}{2}$

B $\frac{1}{3}$ **D** $\frac{2}{3}$

Name ______________________

Fractions and Length

A fraction can name part of the length of an object.

What part of this line segment is black?

You can use fraction strips to find the part of the whole.

$\frac{1}{4}$	$\frac{1}{4}$	$\frac{1}{4}$	$\frac{1}{4}$

The line segment is $\frac{3}{4}$ black. The line segment is $\frac{1}{4}$ gray.

What fraction of the length of the 1 strip do the other strips show?

1. 1

$\frac{1}{4}$

______

2. 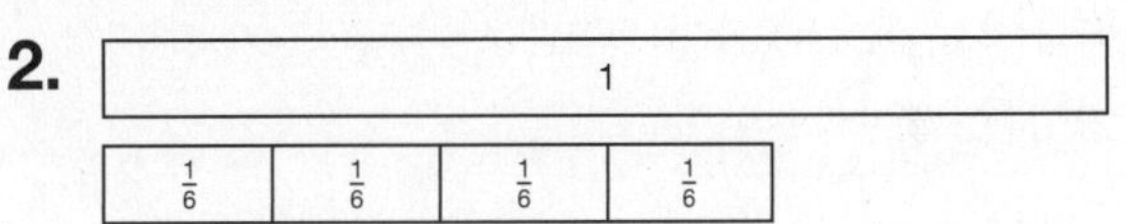

______

3. 1

$\frac{1}{8}$ $\frac{1}{8}$

______

4. 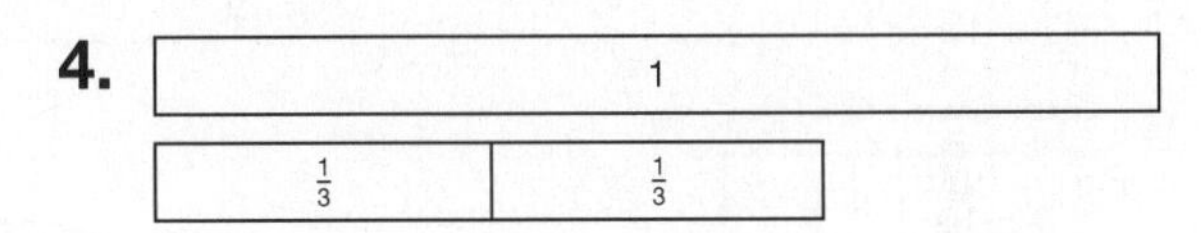

______

5. What fraction of the line segment is black? ______

$\frac{1}{8}$	$\frac{1}{8}$	$\frac{1}{8}$	$\frac{1}{8}$	$\frac{1}{8}$	$\frac{1}{8}$	$\frac{1}{8}$	$\frac{1}{8}$

6. Reason A figure is part blue and part red.

It is $\frac{5}{8}$ red. What part of the figure is blue? ______

Name ______________________________

Practice
9-7

Fractions and Length

What fraction of the length of the 1 strip do the other strips show?

1.

1
$\frac{1}{3}$

______

2.

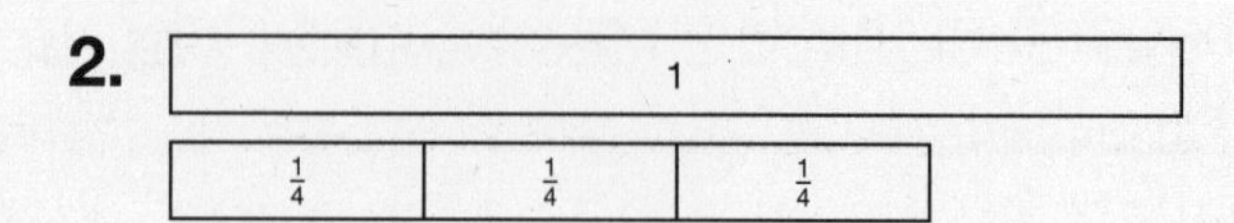

______

3.

1				
$\frac{1}{8}$	$\frac{1}{8}$	$\frac{1}{8}$	$\frac{1}{8}$	$\frac{1}{8}$

______

4.

1			
$\frac{1}{6}$	$\frac{1}{6}$	$\frac{1}{6}$	$\frac{1}{6}$

______

In **5** and **6**, what fraction of each length of yarn is black?

5.

$\frac{1}{3}$	$\frac{1}{3}$	$\frac{1}{3}$

______

6.

$\frac{1}{2}$	$\frac{1}{2}$

______

7. Writing to Explain What is the purpose of using fraction strips and a 1 strip?

____

____

____

____

____

8. About $\frac{6}{8}$ of Earth's surface is covered by water. About what fraction of Earth's surface is not covered by water?

A $\frac{5}{8}$

B $\frac{1}{2}$

C $\frac{3}{8}$

D $\frac{2}{8}$

Name ______________________

Problem Solving: Make a Table and Look for a Pattern

Unger Soda hired 20 testers to try their new celery soda. Seven of the testers did not like the taste of the new soda. Suppose that pattern continues. If 100 people were hired in all, how many would **NOT** like the taste of the soda?

Make a table. Then write the information that you know. Find a pattern to extend the table until you find the results for 100 testers.

Doesn't Like	7	14	21	28	35	Increases by 7.
Total Testers	20	40	60	80	100	Increases by 20.

So, 35 people out of 100 will not like the taste of the Unger's celery soda.

Complete each table to solve.

1. Ms. Lee is buying bags of mixed dumplings. There are 40 dumplings in each bag. In each bag are 10 pork dumplings. If Ms. Lee buys 200 dumplings, how many will be pork dumplings?

Pork Dumplings	10				
Total Dumplings	40				

2. Packages of mixed socks contain 8 pairs of socks. In each package, there are 5 pairs of white socks. How many pairs of white socks would there be in 40 pairs of socks?

Pairs of White Socks	5				
Total Pairs of Socks	8				

3. **Look for a Pattern** Look back at Exercise 2. What pattern do you see?

____

____

____

____

4. **Write a Problem** Write a problem that can be solved by making a table and using a pattern. Then solve the problem.

____

____

____

Name ______________________________

Practice
9-8

Problem Solving: Make a Table and Look for a Pattern

Complete each table to solve.

1. Roses at a flower shop are sold in packages of 6. Each package contains 4 red roses. How many red roses will you get if you buy 30 roses?

Red Roses	4				
Total Roses	6				

2. There are 20 lollipops in each package of Yum's Lollipops. Each package contains 4 grape lollipops. How many grape lollipops will you get if you buy 100 lollipops?

Grape Lollipops	4				
Total Lollipops	20				

3. There are 9 bottles of salsa in a gift pack of Pedro's Salsa. In each gift pack, 2 of the bottles are extra spicy. Suppose someone buys 45 bottles. How many of the bottles will be extra spicy?

Extra Spicy Bottles	2				
Total Bottles	9				

4. Reason Look back at Exercise 3. Suppose Jackie bought 27 bottles.

a. How many of the bottles would NOT be extra spicy?

____

b. How many more bottles are not extra spicy than are extra spicy?

____

5. In a package of 25 colored pencils, 8 are red. If you bought 125 pencils, how many would be red?

Red Pencils	8				
Total Pencils	25				

6. Write a Problem Write a problem that can be solved by making a table and using a pattern. Then solve the problem.

____

____

____

Name ____________________

Reteaching
10-1

Using Models to Compare Fractions: Same Denominator

You can use fraction strips to compare fractions with the same denominator.

Compare $\frac{2}{4}$ and $\frac{3}{4}$.

1			
$\frac{1}{4}$	$\frac{1}{4}$		
$\frac{1}{4}$	$\frac{1}{4}$	$\frac{1}{4}$	

$\frac{2}{4} \bigcirc \frac{3}{4}$

When fractions have the same denominator, the fraction with the *greater* numerator is greater.

Compare. Write $>$, $<$, or $=$.

1.

1							
$\frac{1}{8}$	$\frac{1}{8}$	$\frac{1}{8}$	$\frac{1}{8}$				
$\frac{1}{8}$	$\frac{1}{8}$	$\frac{1}{8}$	$\frac{1}{8}$	$\frac{1}{8}$			

$\frac{5}{8} \bigcirc \frac{4}{8}$

2.

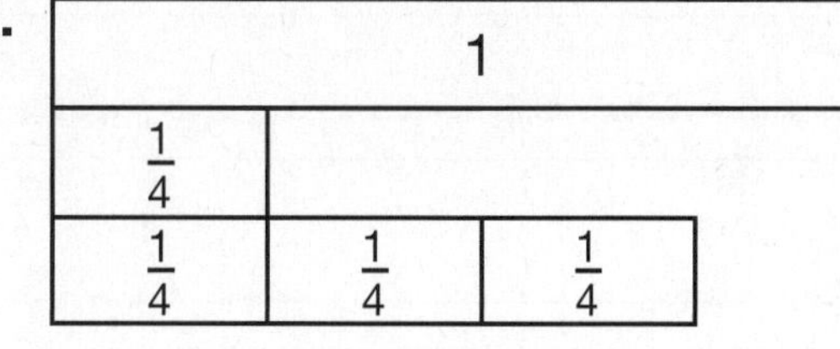

$\frac{1}{4} \bigcirc \frac{3}{4}$

3. $\frac{5}{6} \bigcirc \frac{2}{6}$

4. $\frac{2}{3} \bigcirc \frac{1}{3}$

5. If two fractions have the same denominator but different numerators, which fraction is greater? Give an example.

____

____

____

Name ______________________

Practice
10-1

Using Models to Compare Fractions: Same Denominator

Compare. Write >, <, or =.

1. 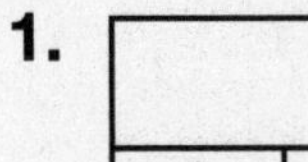

1		
$\frac{1}{6}$	$\frac{1}{6}$	$\frac{1}{6}$
$\frac{1}{6}$	$\frac{1}{6}$	

$\frac{3}{6}$ ◯ $\frac{2}{6}$

2. 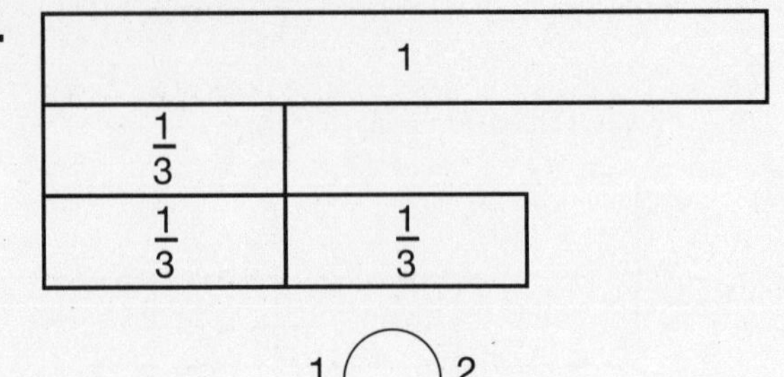

$\frac{1}{3}$ ◯ $\frac{2}{3}$

3. $\frac{2}{4}$ ◯ $\frac{3}{4}$

4. $\frac{5}{6}$ ◯ $\frac{3}{6}$

5. $\frac{4}{6}$ ◯ $\frac{1}{6}$

6. $\frac{3}{8}$ ◯ $\frac{6}{8}$

7. Why is $\frac{6}{8}$ greater than $\frac{5}{8}$ but less than $\frac{7}{8}$?

____

____

____

____

____

8. Reasonableness Marty ate $\frac{4}{6}$ of his pizza and Luis ate $\frac{5}{6}$ of his pizza. Marty ate more pizza than Luis. How is that possible?

____

____

____

____

9. Two fractions have the same denominator. Which is the greater fraction: the fraction with the greater numerator or the lesser numerator?

____

____

10. Which is the greatest fraction?

A $\frac{0}{4}$ **B** $\frac{1}{4}$ **C** $\frac{3}{4}$ **D** $\frac{2}{4}$

Name ______________________

Using Models to Compare Fractions: Same Numerator

You can compare fractions with the same numerator using fraction strips.

Compare $\frac{1}{3}$ and $\frac{1}{4}$.

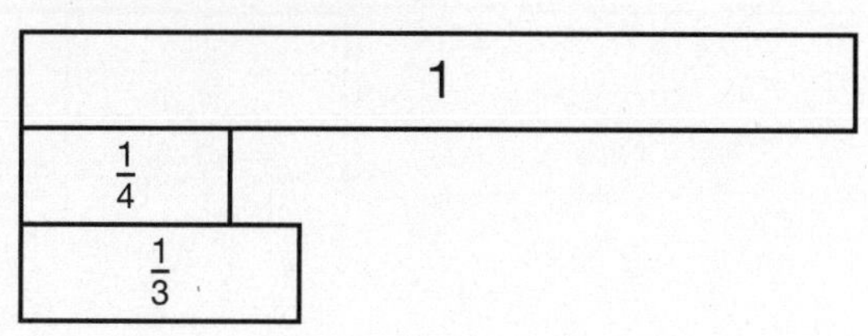

$\frac{1}{3}$ ◯ $\frac{1}{4}$

When fractions have the same numerator, the fraction with the *lesser* denominator is greater.

Compare. Write $<$, $>$, or $=$.

1.

1			
$\frac{1}{8}$	$\frac{1}{8}$		
$\frac{1}{6}$	$\frac{1}{6}$		

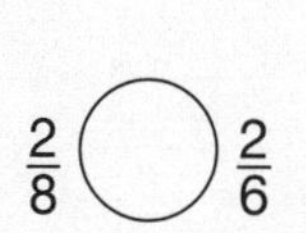

2.

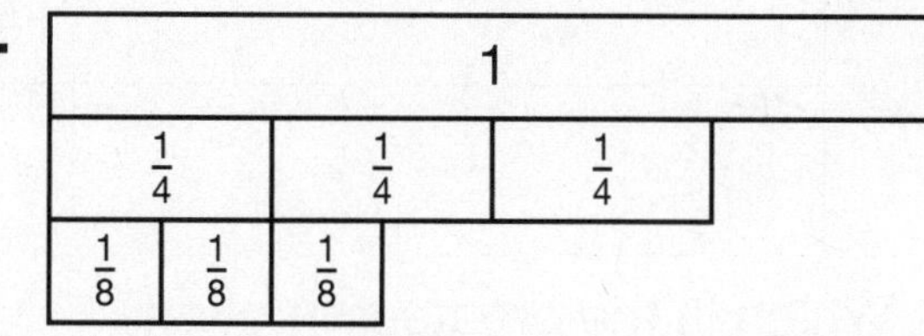

$\frac{3}{4}$ ◯ $\frac{3}{8}$

3. $\frac{2}{3}$ ◯ $\frac{2}{3}$

4. $\frac{3}{4}$ ◯ $\frac{3}{6}$

5. Reason If two fractions have the same numerator but different denominators, which fraction is greater? Give an example.

____

____

____

Name ______________________________

Using Models to Compare Fractions: Same Numerator

Compare. Write <, >, or = for each .

1.

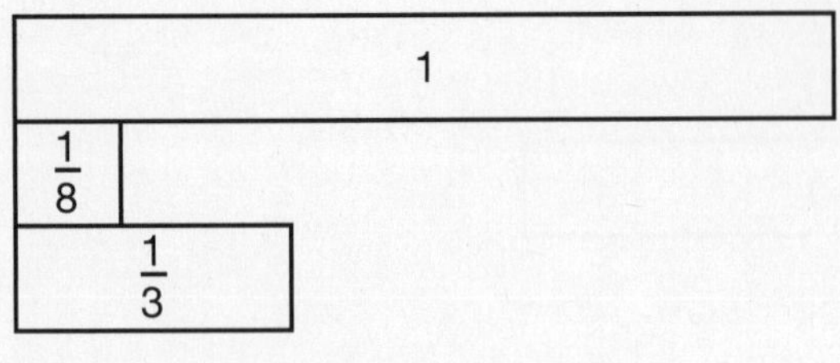

$\frac{1}{8}$ ◯ $\frac{1}{3}$

2.

1		
$\frac{1}{3}$		$\frac{1}{3}$
$\frac{1}{6}$	$\frac{1}{6}$	

$\frac{2}{3}$ ◯ $\frac{2}{6}$

3. 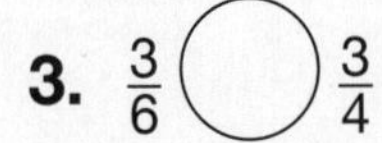 $\frac{3}{6}$ ◯ $\frac{3}{4}$

4. $\frac{1}{2}$ ◯ $\frac{1}{2}$

5. $\frac{2}{8}$ ◯ $\frac{2}{6}$

6. $\frac{3}{8}$ ◯ $\frac{3}{4}$

7. Ricardo has read $\frac{2}{3}$ of a book. Lin had read $\frac{2}{4}$ of the same book. Who has read more of the book?

____

8. Maria and Nina each ordered a small pizza. Maria ate $\frac{3}{8}$ of her pizza. Nina ate $\frac{3}{6}$ of her pizza. Who ate more pizza?

____

9. Which is the greatest fraction?

A $\frac{1}{2}$ **B** $\frac{1}{4}$ **C** $\frac{1}{6}$ **D** $\frac{1}{8}$

10. **Writing to Explain** Why is $\frac{1}{6}$ greater than $\frac{1}{8}$ but less than $\frac{1}{3}$? Explain.

____

____

Name ______________________________

Comparing Fractions Using Benchmarks

In Ms. Adams' class, $\frac{2}{3}$ of students are wearing red and $\frac{2}{8}$ of students are wearing blue. She wants to know if more students are wearing red or blue.

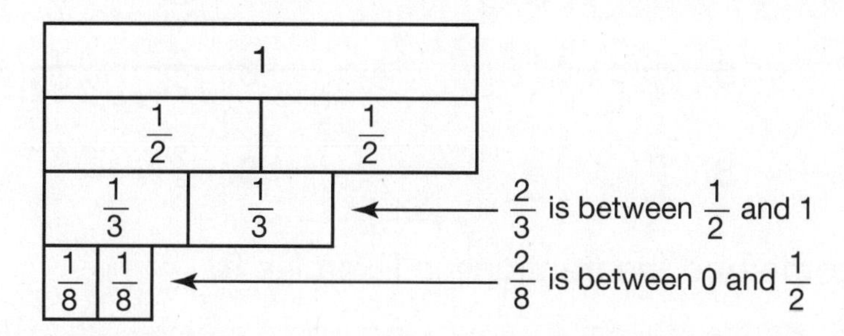

Ms. Adams can compare each fraction to the benchmark numbers 0, $\frac{1}{2}$, and 1.

$\frac{2}{3}$ is between $\frac{1}{2}$ and 1. $\frac{2}{8}$ is between 0 and $\frac{1}{2}$. So, $\frac{2}{8}$ is less than $\frac{2}{3}$.

More students in Ms. Adams' class are wearing red.

Mina, Bobby, and Julia each have the same number of pencils. $\frac{2}{6}$ of Mina's pencils are red, $\frac{2}{3}$ of Bobby's pencils are red, and $\frac{2}{4}$ of Julia's pencils are red.

1
$\frac{1}{2}$ $\frac{1}{2}$
$\frac{1}{3}$ $\frac{1}{3}$
$\frac{1}{4}$ $\frac{1}{4}$
$\frac{1}{6}$ $\frac{1}{6}$

1. Who has more red pencils, Julia or Bobby?

____

2. Who has more red pencils, Mina or Julia?

____

3. **Reason** Which student has the most red pencils? Explain.

____

____

____

Name ____________________

Practice
10-3

Comparing Fractions Using Benchmarks

For **1–9,** use benchmark numbers to compare. Write < or > for each ◯.

1. $\frac{3}{6}$ ◯ $\frac{3}{8}$ **2.** $\frac{2}{3}$ ◯ $\frac{1}{3}$ **3.** $\frac{4}{8}$ ◯ $\frac{6}{8}$

4. $\frac{2}{4}$ ◯ $\frac{2}{6}$ **5.** $\frac{1}{4}$ ◯ $\frac{1}{3}$ **6.** $\frac{3}{4}$ ◯ $\frac{1}{4}$

7. $\frac{3}{3}$ ◯ $\frac{3}{4}$ **8.** $\frac{5}{8}$ ◯ $\frac{5}{6}$ **9.** $\frac{2}{6}$ ◯ $\frac{2}{3}$

10. Explain how you compared the fractions in Exercise 9.

____

____

11. Which fraction is closer to 1 than to 0?

A $\frac{1}{4}$ **B** $\frac{1}{2}$ **C** $\frac{3}{6}$ **D** $\frac{7}{8}$

12. Lucy has a collection of buttons. $\frac{2}{3}$ of her buttons are square and $\frac{2}{8}$ of her buttons are round. Does Lucy have more square buttons or round buttons?

____

13. Reason On Monday, Carlos ran $\frac{1}{8}$ of a mile. On Wednesday, he ran $\frac{5}{6}$ of a mile. Carlos ran $\frac{3}{8}$ of a mile on Friday. Which day did Carlos run the farthest?

____

14. Writing to Explain Sydney says that $\frac{4}{8}$ is closer to 0 than to 1. Is she correct? Explain.

____

____

____

____

Name ___________________________

Reteaching
10-4

Comparing Fractions on the Number Line

Yoko used a number line to compare $\frac{1}{4}$ and $\frac{3}{4}$.

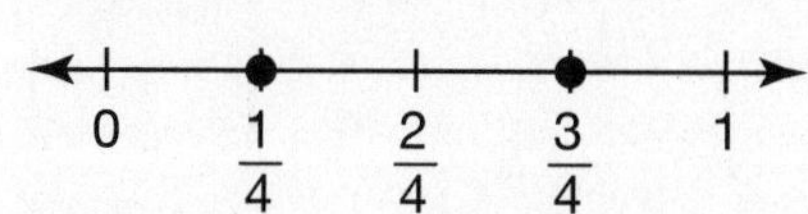

She marked where $\frac{1}{4}$ and $\frac{3}{4}$ are on the number line.
Then she looked for the fraction that was farther to the right.
She wrote > to show which fraction is greater.

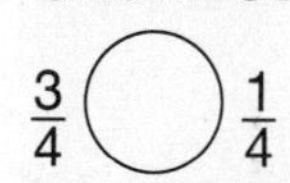

1. Mark $\frac{2}{3}$ and $\frac{1}{3}$ on the number line below.

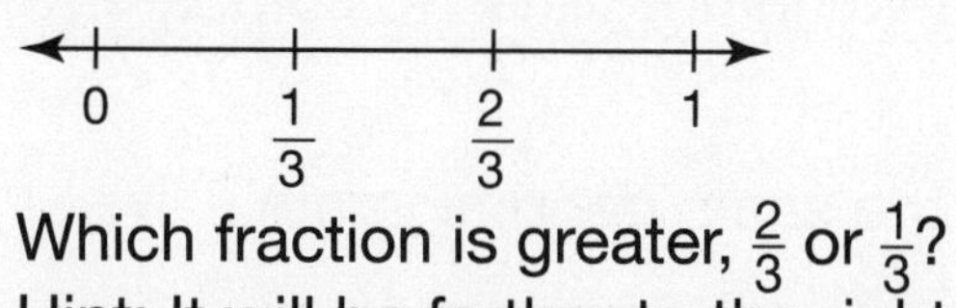

Which fraction is greater, $\frac{2}{3}$ or $\frac{1}{3}$?
Hint: It will be farther to the right.
Write > or <.

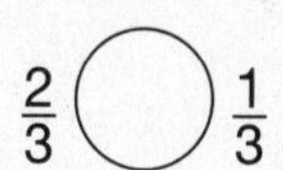

2. Mark $\frac{1}{2}$ and $\frac{1}{6}$ on the number lines below.

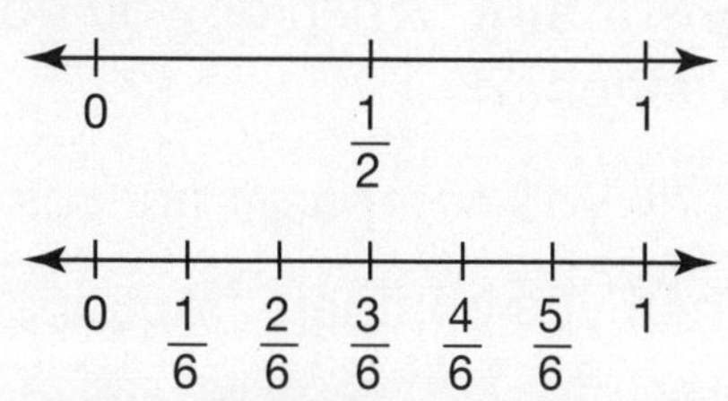

Which fraction is greater, $\frac{1}{2}$ or $\frac{1}{6}$?
Hint: It will be farther to the right.
Write > or <.

$\frac{1}{2}$ ◯ $\frac{1}{6}$

3. Use Structure Simon is comparing $\frac{1}{3}$ yard and $\frac{2}{3}$ yard of rope.
Circle the two denominators.

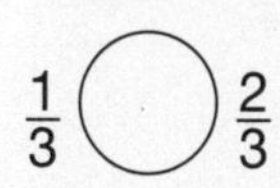

Since the denominators are the same, Simon can compare them on the same number line. Which number line should he use?

A
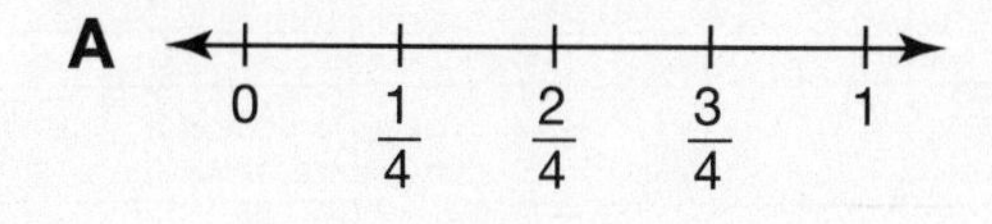

C
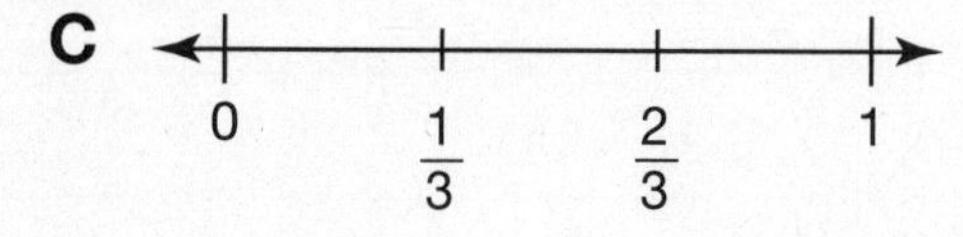

B
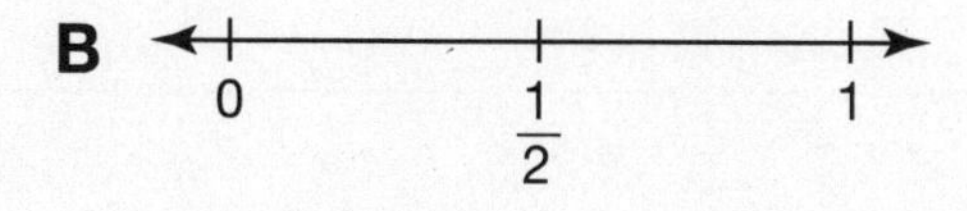

D
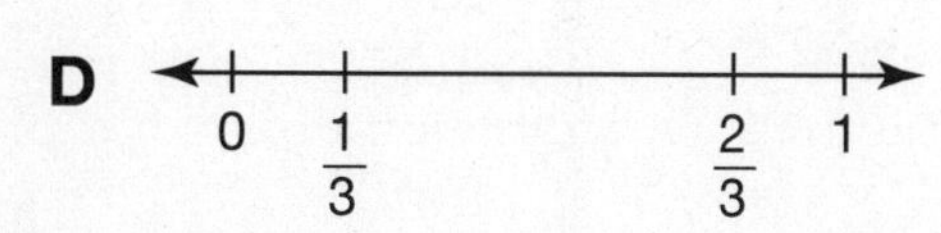

Name ______________________________

Practice
10-4

Comparing Fractions on the Number Line

In **1–3,** compare. Write $<$, $>$, or $=$.
Draw number lines to help.

1. 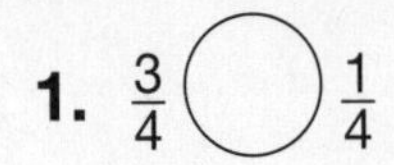

$\frac{3}{4}$ ◯ $\frac{1}{4}$

2. $\frac{2}{3}$ ◯ $\frac{1}{3}$

3. $\frac{6}{8}$ ◯ $\frac{7}{8}$

In **4–6,** compare. Write $<$, $>$, or $=$.
Draw number lines to help.

4. $\frac{1}{2}$ ◯ $\frac{1}{4}$

5. $\frac{2}{3}$ ◯ $\frac{2}{4}$

6. $\frac{1}{4}$ ◯ $\frac{1}{8}$

7. Use Structure When do you need to use two number lines to compare two fractions?

A When you compare fractions that have the same denominators.

B When you compare fractions that have different denominators.

C When you compare fractions that are greater than 1.

D When you compare fractions that refer to different wholes.

8. Reason Explain how you can use a number line to show that $\frac{5}{8}$ is greater than $\frac{3}{8}$.

____

____

____

Name ______________________________

Finding Equivalent Fractions

Reteaching
10-5

Equivalent fractions are fractions that name the same part of a whole. Equivalent fractions have different numerators and denominators, but their values are equal.

You can find equivalent fractions by using fraction strips.

$$\frac{1}{4} = \frac{\square}{8}$$

Find how many $\frac{1}{8}$s are equal to $\frac{1}{4}$. The denominator is 8 so use $\frac{1}{8}$ strips.

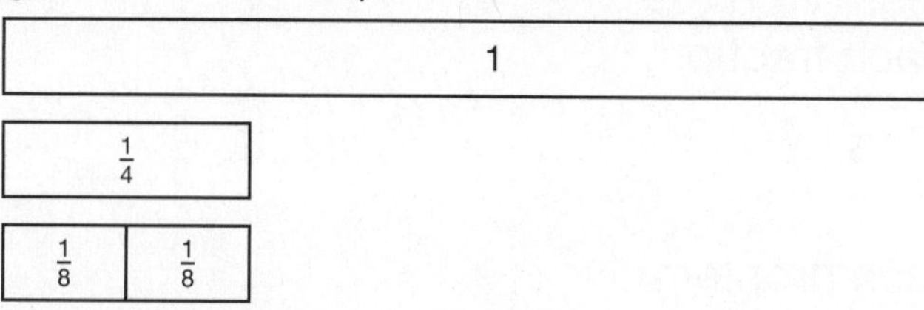

So, two $\frac{1}{8}$ strips are equal to $\frac{1}{4}$.

$$\frac{1}{4} = \frac{2}{8}$$

Another name for $\frac{1}{4}$ is $\frac{2}{8}$.

Complete each number sentence.

1.

1			
$\frac{1}{2}$			
$\frac{1}{8}$	$\frac{1}{8}$	$\frac{1}{8}$	$\frac{1}{8}$

$\frac{1}{2} = \frac{\square}{8}$

2.

1			
$\frac{1}{3}$		$\frac{1}{3}$	
$\frac{1}{6}$	$\frac{1}{6}$	$\frac{1}{6}$	$\frac{1}{6}$

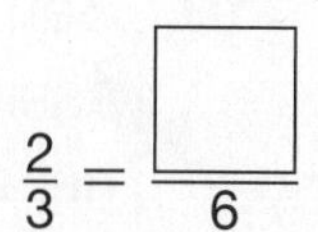

$\frac{2}{3} = \frac{\square}{6}$

3.

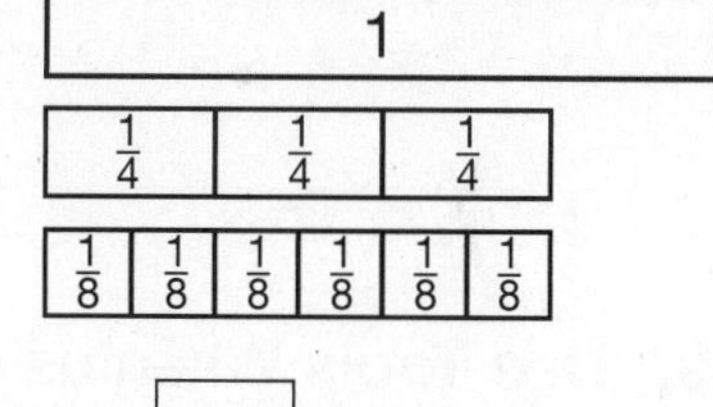

$\frac{3}{4} = \frac{\square}{8}$

4. Name two fractions that are equivalent to $\frac{1}{2}$.

____

5. Reason Larry and Willa are each reading the same book. Larry has read $\frac{2}{3}$ of the book. Willa said that she has read more than Larry because she read $\frac{4}{6}$ of the book. Is Willa correct? Explain.

____

____

____

Name ______________________

Finding Equivalent Fractions

Complete each number sentence.

1.

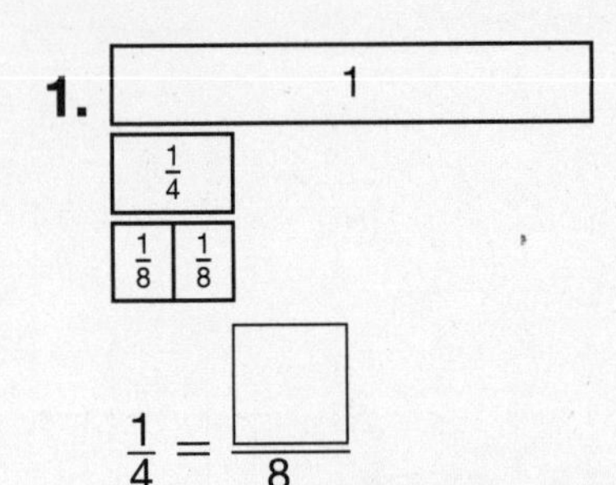

$\frac{1}{4} = \frac{\square}{8}$

2.

1					
$\frac{1}{4}$		$\frac{1}{4}$		$\frac{1}{4}$	
$\frac{1}{8}$	$\frac{1}{8}$	$\frac{1}{8}$	$\frac{1}{8}$	$\frac{1}{8}$	$\frac{1}{8}$

$\frac{3}{4} = \frac{\square}{8}$

3.

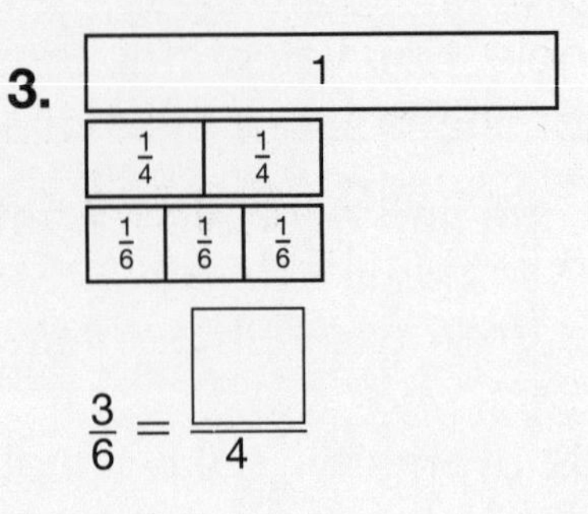

$\frac{3}{6} = \frac{\square}{4}$

Find the simplest form of each fraction.

4. $\frac{3}{6}$ ____________

5. $\frac{4}{6}$ ____________

6. $\frac{3}{8}$ ____________

Name a fraction to solve each problem.

7. Rob colored $\frac{1}{4}$ of a rectangle. What is another way to name $\frac{1}{4}$?

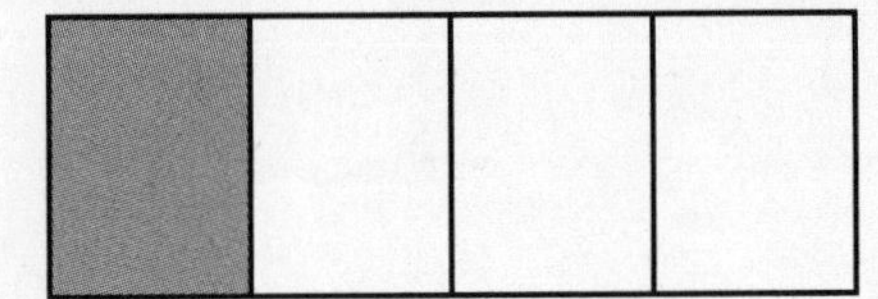

____

8. Three eighths of the cast in a musical have to sing. What fraction of the cast does not have to sing?

____

9. Use Tools When using fraction strips, how do you know that two fractions are equivalent?

____

____

____

____

____

10. Samuel has read $\frac{3}{6}$ of his assignment. Judy has read $\frac{4}{8}$ of her assignment. Their assignments were the same size. Which sentence is true?

A Samuel read more than Judy.

B Judy read more than Samuel.

C They read the same amount.

D They will both finish the assignment at the same time.

Name ___________________

Equivalent Fractions and the Number Line

Anna equally shares a bookshelf with her sister. Her sister says Anna's books use $\frac{2}{4}$ of the shelf. Anna thought her books used $\frac{1}{2}$ of the shelf. Anna drew two number lines to see if the two numbers are equivalent fractions.

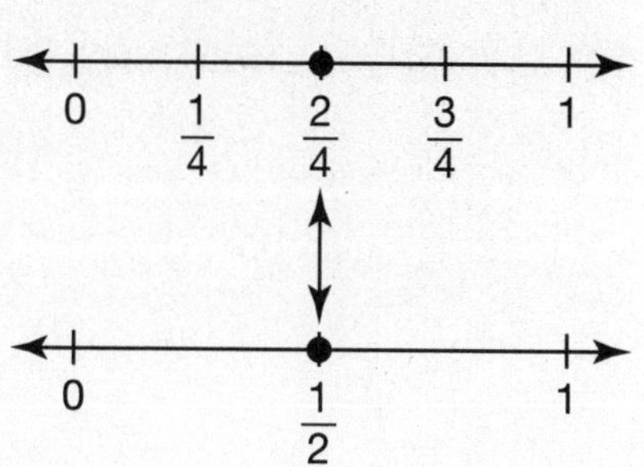

The fractions are at the same location on the number line. The fractions are equivalent. $\frac{2}{4} = \frac{1}{2}$

For **1** and **2,** use the number lines given to complete the number sentence.

1.

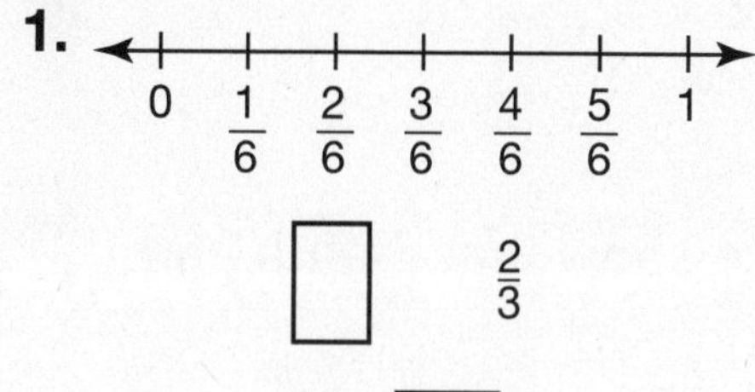

$\frac{2}{6} = \square$

2.

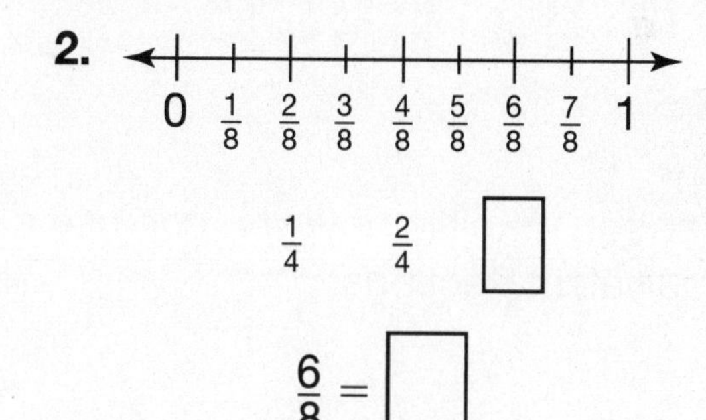

$\frac{6}{8} = \square$

3. Reason Mick uses two pieces of rope to make ties for two cloth sacks. One rope is $\frac{4}{8}$ yard. The other rope is $\frac{1}{2}$ yard. He wants to know if they are the same length. Which number line correctly models the rope lengths?

A

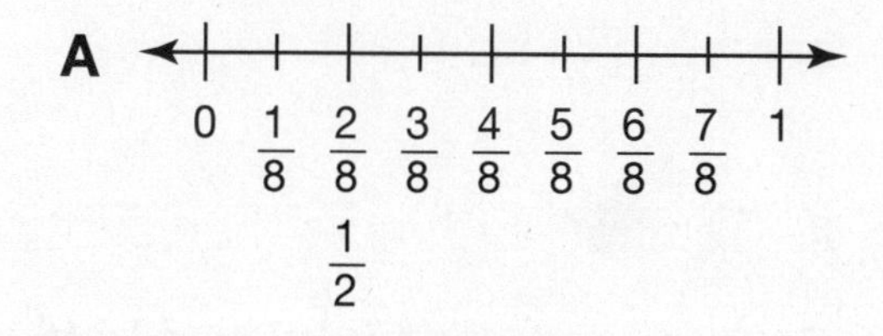

C

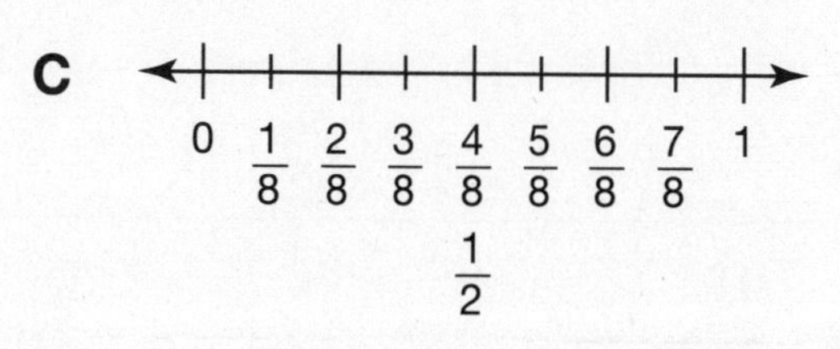

B

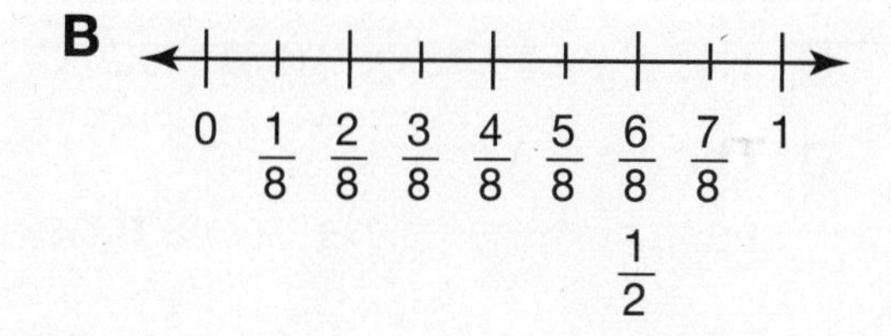

D

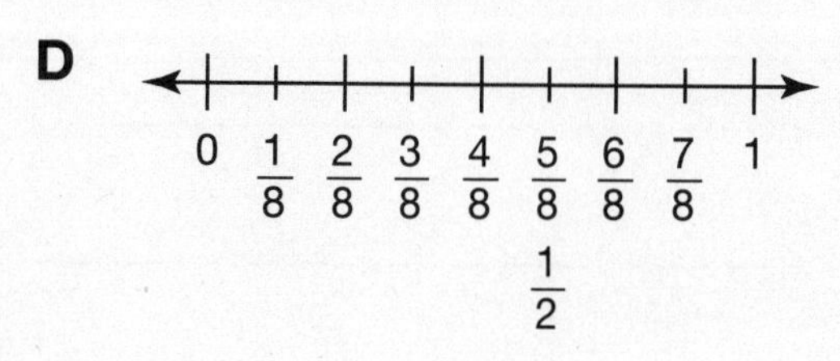

Name ____________________

Equivalent Fractions and the Number Line

1. Write two fractions that name the location on the number line below.

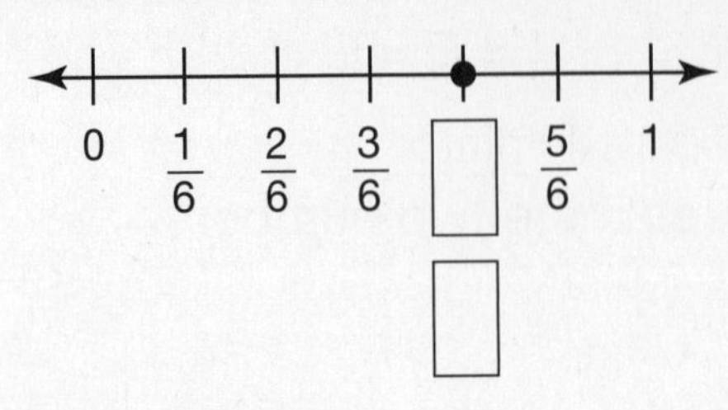

For **2** and **3,** draw a number line to show that the fractions are equivalent.

2. $\frac{3}{4} = \frac{6}{8}$

3. $\frac{1}{4} = \frac{2}{8}$

4. Reason Explain how you can use a number line to show that $\frac{3}{6}$ and $\frac{1}{2}$ are equivalent fractions.

____

____

____

____

____

Name ______________________

Whole Numbers and Fractions

Sal ate $\frac{1}{3}$ of a granola bar at breakfast. He ate another $\frac{1}{3}$ of the bar at lunch. Then he ate $\frac{1}{3}$ of the bar at dinner. How much of the granola bar did he eat in all?

You can use fraction strips to model how much of the granola bar Sal ate.

Count the fraction strips.

Breakfast	Lunch	Dinner
$\frac{1}{3}$	$\frac{1}{3}$	$\frac{1}{3}$

There are three. Sal ate three $\frac{1}{3}$s of a granola bar. You can write this as the fraction $\frac{3}{3}$.

Now, compare the fraction strips to 1 whole.

1		
$\frac{1}{3}$	$\frac{1}{3}$	$\frac{1}{3}$

So, $\frac{3}{3}$ is equal to 1 whole. You can say Sal ate $\frac{3}{3}$ of a granola bar. Or you can say Sal ate 1 granola bar.

For **1** and **2,** count the fraction strips.
Write the fraction name and equivalent whole number name for each.

1.

1			
$\frac{1}{4}$	$\frac{1}{4}$	$\frac{1}{4}$	$\frac{1}{4}$

______

2.

1		1	
$\frac{1}{2}$	$\frac{1}{2}$	$\frac{1}{2}$	$\frac{1}{2}$

______

For **3–6,** write an equivalent fraction for each whole number.

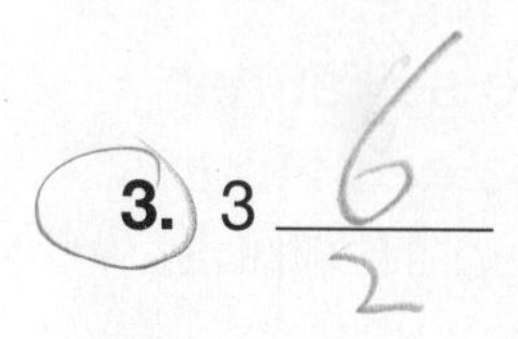

3. 3 ______

4. 2 ______

5. 6 ______

6. 4 ______

7. Persevere Jane gets $\frac{1}{2}$ of a gold star each time she helps her teacher clean up the classroom after art class. How many times would Jane need to help her teacher to earn 3 whole gold stars? Draw fraction strips to help.

______

Name ________________________

Whole Numbers and Fractions

In **1–6**, write an equivalent fraction for each whole number.

1. 6 $\frac{12}{2}$ **2.** 8 **3.** 4 **4.** 3 **5.** 1 $\frac{2}{2}$ **6.** 5

7. Reason Explain how you know $\frac{6}{6}$ and 1 are equivalent.

Because on a fraction strip the vertical line $\frac{6}{6}$ is equal to one whole.

In **8–9**, complete each number line.

8. thirds

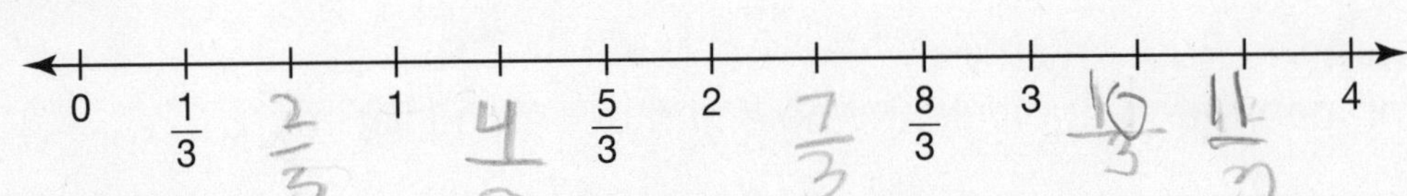

9. fourths

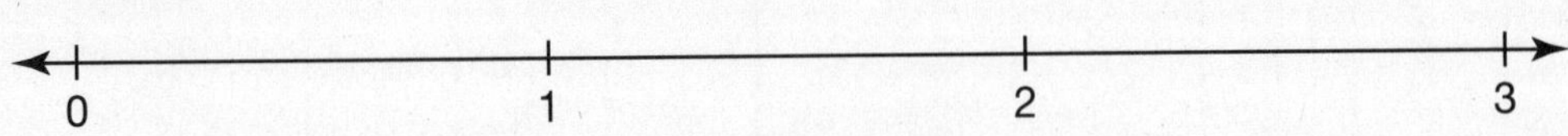

10. Which whole number is equivalent to $\frac{8}{2}$?

A 2 **B** 4 **C** 6 **D** 8

11. Critique Reasoning Molly is wrapping up parts of sandwiches to sell at her sandwich cart. She cuts each sandwich in fourths and then wraps each fourth separately. She says that she wrapped 16 fourths, so she wrapped 16 whole sandwiches. What was Molly's mistake?

Molly's mistake is that she wrapped 16 whole sandwiches when she was supposed to wrape 4 whole sandwiches.

Name ______________________

Using Fractions

You can use fraction strips or a number line to compare and order fractions and mixed numbers.

Compare $\frac{3}{4}$, $\frac{5}{8}$, and $\frac{1}{2}$. Which fraction is the greatest? the least?

Use fraction strips to compare.

$\frac{1}{4}$		$\frac{1}{4}$		$\frac{1}{4}$	
$\frac{1}{8}$	$\frac{1}{8}$	$\frac{1}{8}$	$\frac{1}{8}$	$\frac{1}{8}$	
$\frac{1}{2}$					

$\frac{3}{4} > \frac{5}{8}$ and $\frac{5}{8} > \frac{1}{2}$

$\frac{3}{4}$ is the greatest.

$\frac{1}{2}$ is the least.

Use a number line to compare.

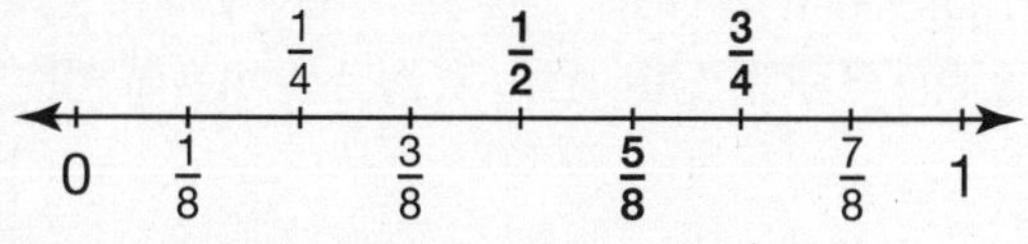

$\frac{3}{4}$ is to the right of $\frac{5}{8}$ so $\frac{3}{4} > \frac{5}{8}$.

$\frac{5}{8}$ is to the right of $\frac{1}{2}$ so $\frac{5}{8} > \frac{1}{2}$.

$\frac{3}{4}$ is the greatest.

$\frac{1}{2}$ is the least.

In **1–4**, write the fractions in order from least to greatest.

1. $\frac{4}{6}, \frac{3}{8}, \frac{1}{2}$ ______________________

2. $\frac{5}{6}, \frac{3}{4}, \frac{4}{8}$ ______________________

3. $\frac{1}{2}, \frac{6}{8}, \frac{2}{6}$ ______________________

4. $\frac{3}{8}, \frac{1}{2}, \frac{1}{4}$ ______________________

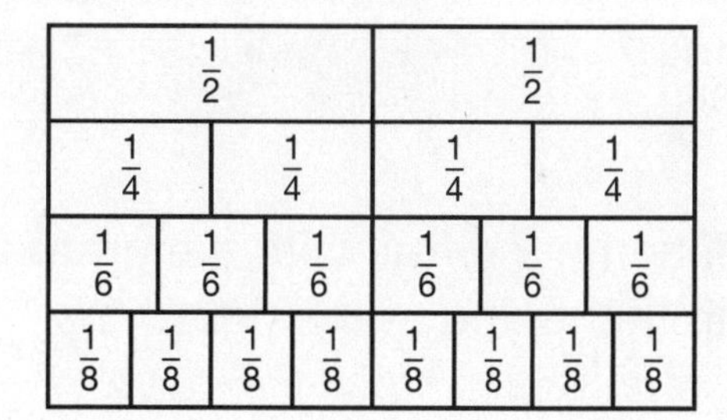

In **5–8**, use the number line to compare. Write <, >, or =.

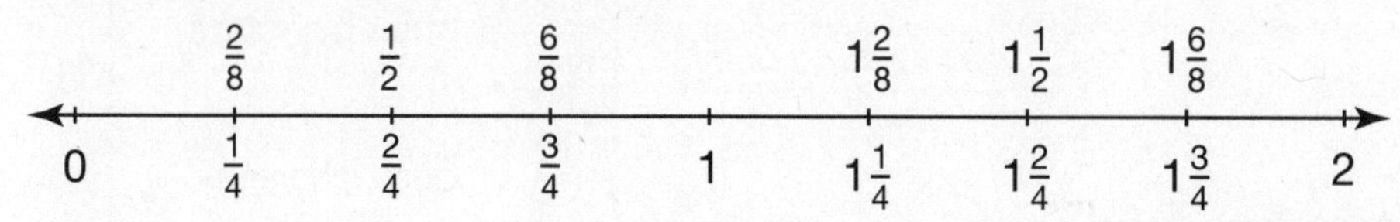

5. $\frac{2}{4}$ ◯ $\frac{1}{2}$ **6.** $1\frac{1}{4}$ ◯ $1\frac{6}{8}$ **7.** $\frac{3}{4}$ ◯ $1\frac{3}{4}$ **8.** $\frac{2}{4}$ ◯ $\frac{2}{8}$

9. Compare $\frac{3}{4}$ and $\frac{3}{6}$. Without using fraction strips or a number line, how can you tell which fraction is greater?

____

____

Name ____________________

Using Fractions

Practice
10-8

In **1–6,** compare. Write <, >, or =.

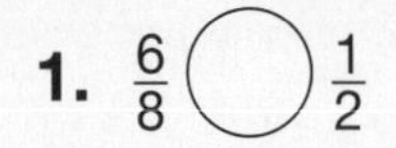

1. $\frac{6}{8}$ ◯ $\frac{1}{2}$ **2.** $\frac{2}{4}$ ◯ $\frac{3}{6}$ **3.** $\frac{2}{8}$ ◯ $\frac{2}{6}$

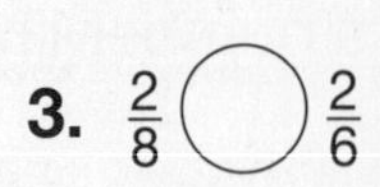

4. $\frac{1}{2}$ ◯ $\frac{2}{6}$ **5.** $\frac{3}{4}$ ◯ $\frac{3}{8}$ **6.** $\frac{1}{4}$ ◯ $\frac{3}{8}$

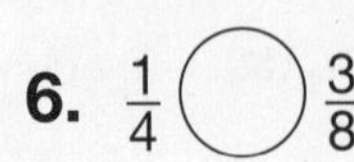

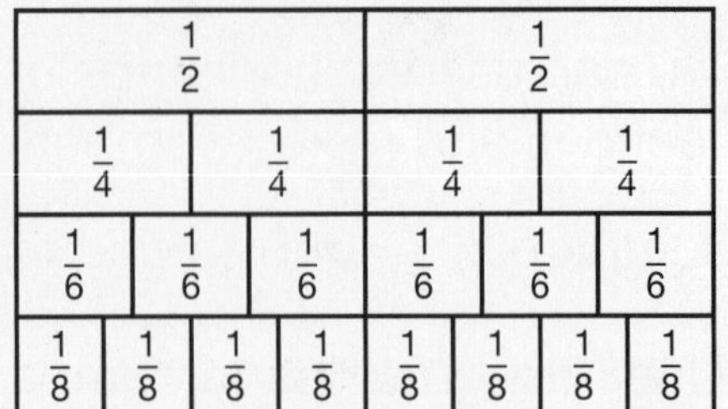

7. Complete the number line by writing the missing fractions and mixed numbers.

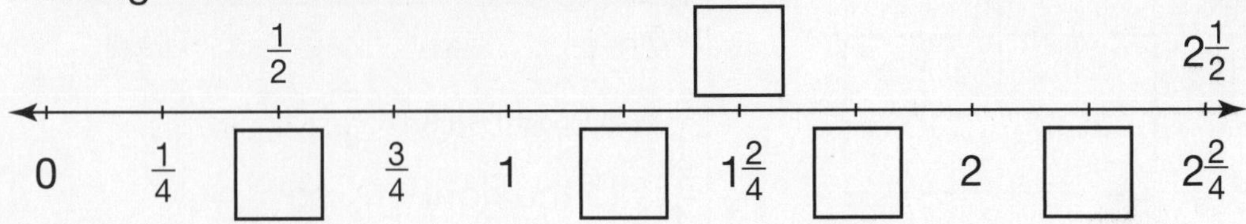

8. About how much of this glass is filled?

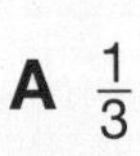

A $\frac{1}{3}$
B $\frac{3}{4}$
C $\frac{1}{2}$
D $\frac{1}{8}$

9. Which fraction describes the part of this blanket that is white?

A $\frac{2}{3}$
B $\frac{1}{2}$
C $\frac{2}{4}$
D $\frac{2}{8}$

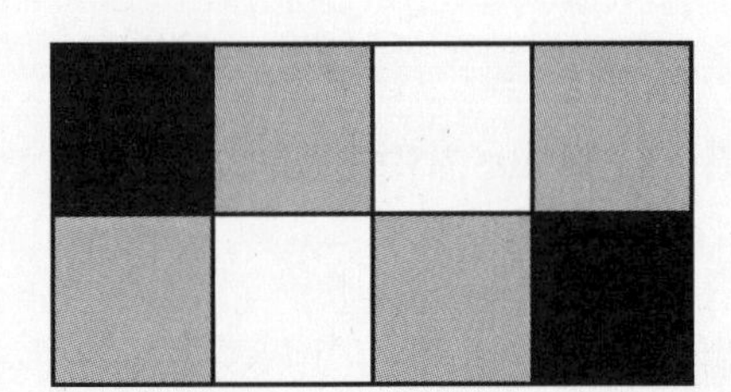

In **10–13,** name the fruit with the greater number of cups in the recipe at the right.

Fruit Salad
1 batch

- $1\frac{1}{2}$ cups apples
- $1\frac{3}{4}$ cups grapes
- $\frac{1}{2}$ cup raisins
- $2\frac{2}{4}$ cups bananas
- $\frac{3}{4}$ cup coconut
- $1\frac{2}{4}$ cups cherries
- $2\frac{1}{4}$ cups pineapple

10. Apples or bananas? ____________________

11. Grapes or coconut? ____________________

12. Raisins or cherries? ____________________

13. Apples or pineapple? ____________________

14. One batch of fruit salad has equal amounts of which kinds of fruit? Explain how you decided.

____

____

Name ____________________

Problem Solving: Draw a Picture

A fence is 20 feet long. It has a post at each end. The fence also has a post every 4 feet between the two ends. How many fence posts are there in all?

Read and Understand

Step 1 What do you know?

The fence is 20 feet long.
A fence post is at each end.
There is a fence post every 4 feet.

Step 2 What are you trying to find?

How many posts the fence has

Plan and Solve

Step 3 What strategy will you use?

Strategy: Draw a picture

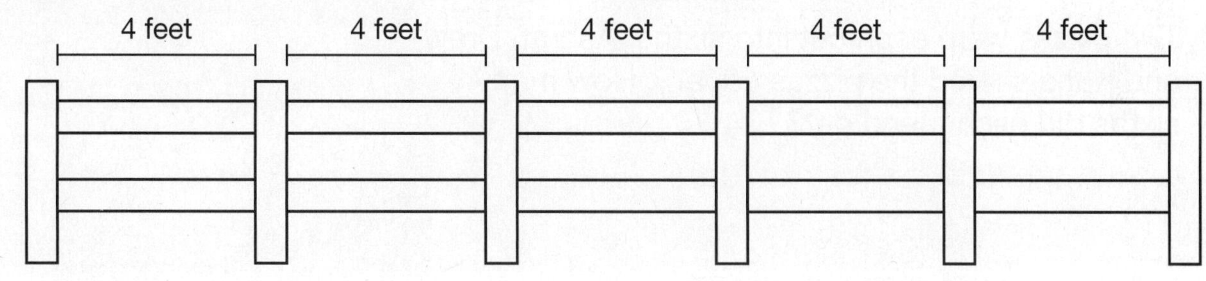

There are 6 fence posts in all.

Look Back and Check

Step 4 Is your work correct?

Yes, the picture shows a fence that is 20 feet long. It has a fence post at each end, and a fence post every 4 feet. There are 6 fence posts.

Solve. Draw a picture.

1. Jamie put 8 squares together to make a rectangle. There are 2 rows of squares. Each row has 4 squares. How many pairs of sides touch each other in the rectangle?

2. Trent, Linda, and Pam will work together to paint a poster that is 4 feet long. Each student will paint an equal length of the poster. How many feet of the poster length will each student paint?

_______________ _______________

Name ____________________

Problem Solving: Draw a Picture

Solve. Draw a picture.

1. Larry used a pattern of colors to make a cube train. He used a red cube, a blue cube, a red cube, and another red cube before he started the pattern again. He used 15 cubes. How many red cubes did Larry use?

____

2. Two pizzas were each cut into sixths. Ashraf, Drew, and Katie shared the pizzas equally. How many sixths did each friend get?

____

3. Eric and Frank want to equally share $\frac{4}{3}$ feet of rope. What length of rope should each friend get? Explain how to use a drawing to help solve the problem.

____

____

____

4. A square garden is 12 feet long on each side. Janet needs to put a post at each corner. She also needs to put a post every 3 feet on each side. How many posts does Janet need?

A 12 **B** 16 **C** 20 **D** 24

Name ______________________________

Reteaching
11-1

Lines and Line Segments

You can find lines and parts of lines in shapes and objects.

			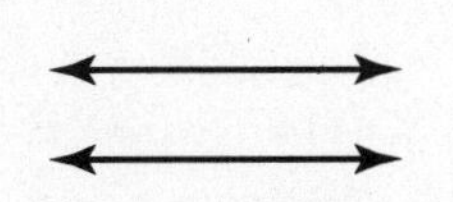	
A point is an exact location in space.	A line is a set of points that goes without end in both directions.	A line segment is part of a line with two endpoints.	Parallel lines never meet or cross. They are always the same distance apart.	Intersecting lines cross at one point.

Write the name for each.

1. 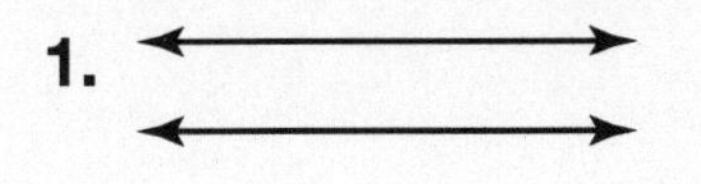
____

2. 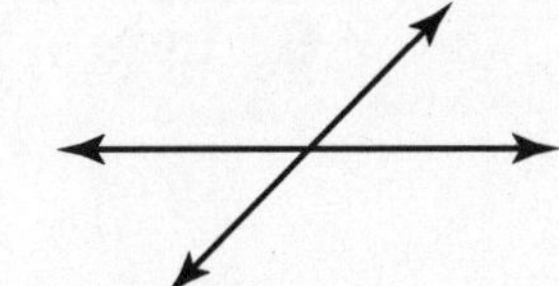
____

3. 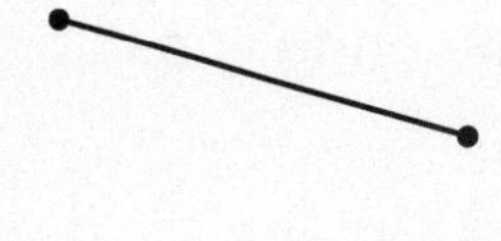
____

4. 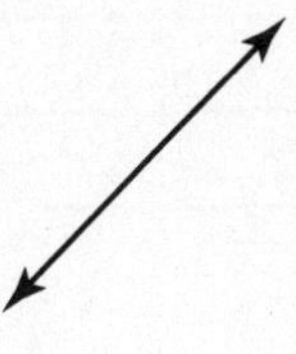
____

5. ______________

6. 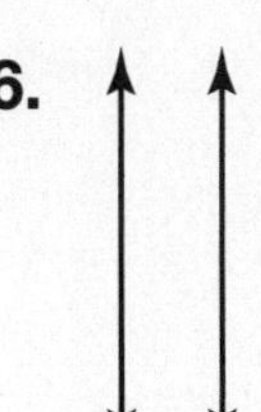
____

7. Name the place where two intersecting lines cross.

____

8. **Reason** Leo said that a line is part of a line segment. Carol said that a line segment is a part of a line. Who is correct? Explain.

____

____

____

Name ___________________________

Practice
11-1

Lines and Line Segments

Write the name for each.

1. 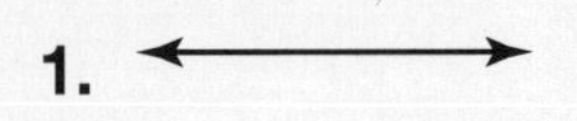 **2.** 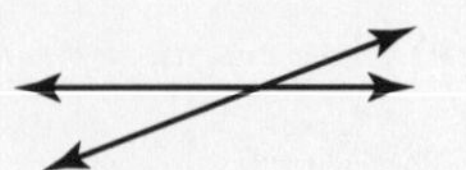 **3.** 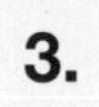 **4.** 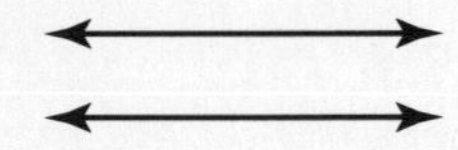

_______ _______ _______ _______

Draw a picture of each.

5. Parallel lines

6. Line segment

7. Intersecting lines

8. Line

For **9** and **10**, use the map at the right. Tell if the trails named look like intersecting lines or parallel lines.

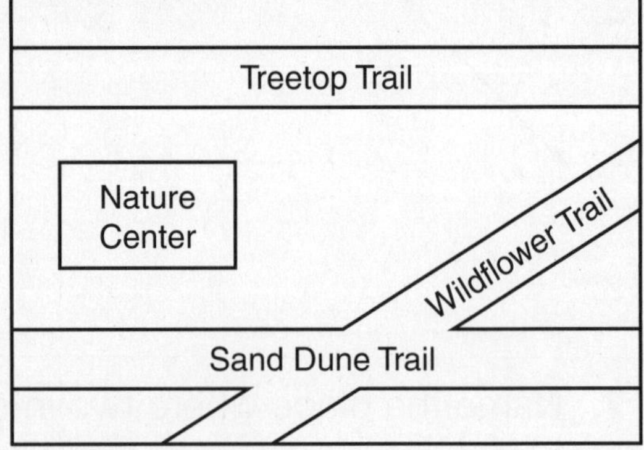

9. Treetop and Sand Dune

____

10. Sand Dune and Wildflower

____

11. What is the difference between a line and a line segment?

____

____

____

12. How many times does a pair of intersecting lines cross?

A Never **B** 1 time **C** 2 times **D** 3 times

Name ______________________________

Reteaching
11-2

Angles

An angle is formed by two rays that have the same endpoint. The endpoint is the vertex of the angle. Three types of angles are right angles, acute angles, and obtuse angles.

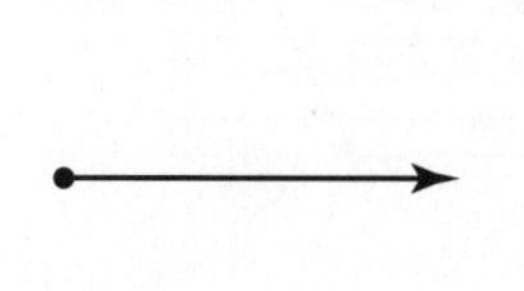

A ray is part of a line that has one endpoint and goes forever in one direction.

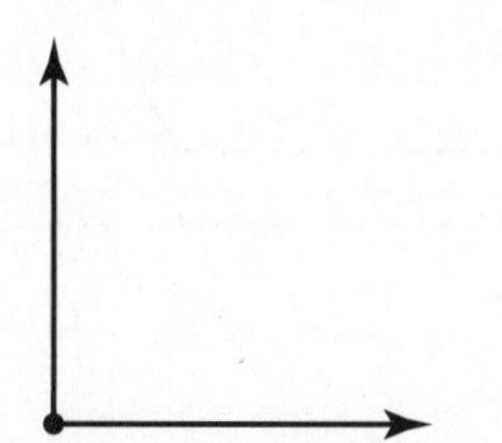

A right angle forms a square corner.

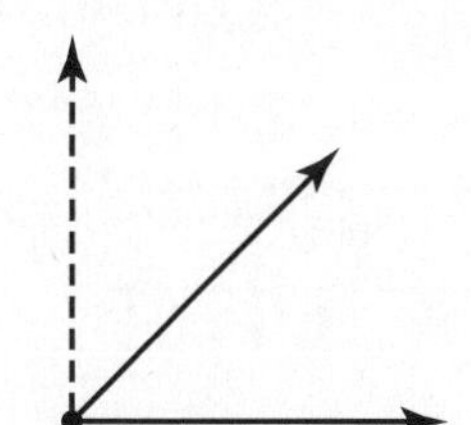

An acute angle is open less than a right angle.

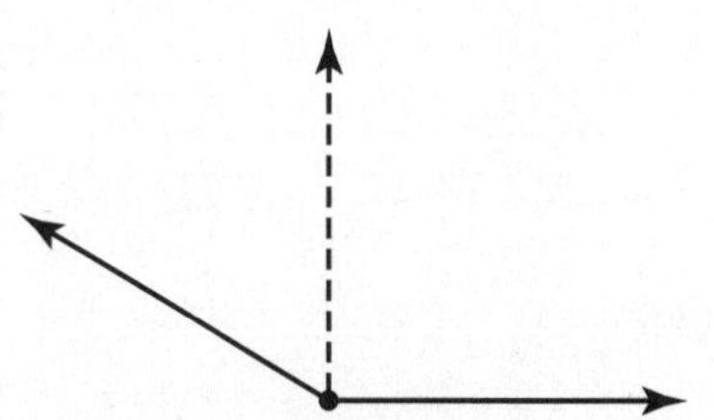

An obtuse angle is open more than a right angle.

Lines, line segments, or rays that meet or cross at a right angle are perpendicular.

Tell if each angle is right, acute, or obtuse.

1.

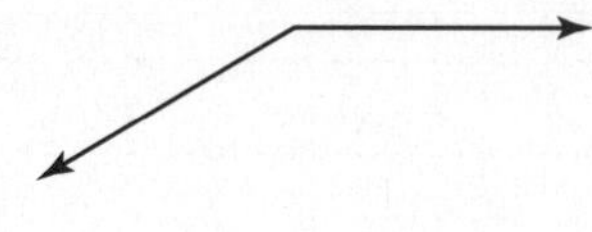

____

2.

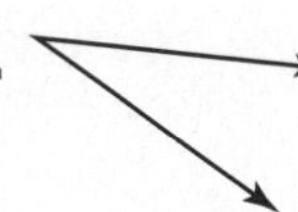

____

3.

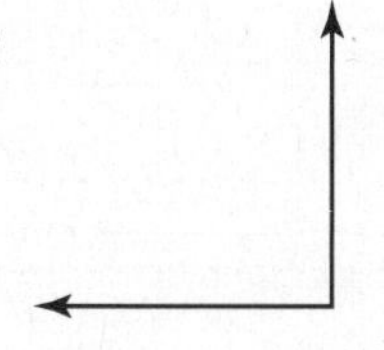

____

4.

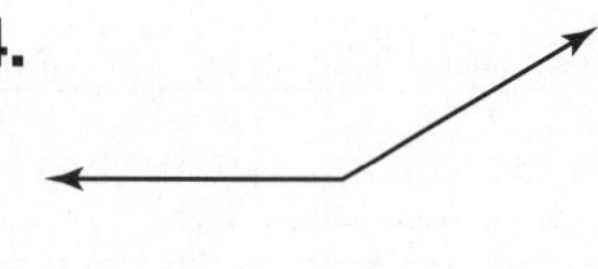

____

5. Writing to Explain How can you use a right angle to decide how to name another angle?

____

____

____

Name ____________________

Practice
11-2

Angles

Tell if each angle is right, acute, or obtuse.

1. **2.**

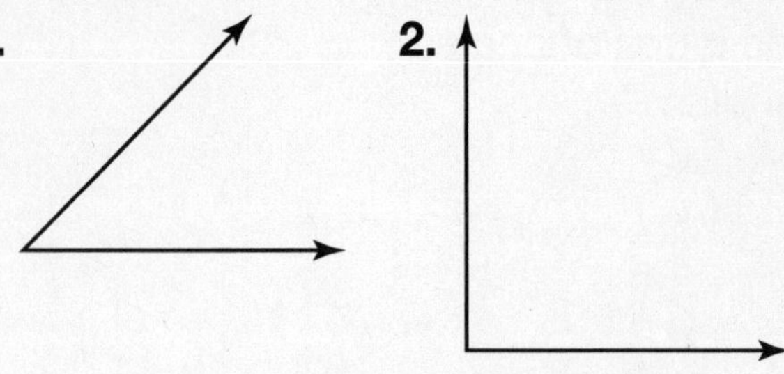

3. **4.**

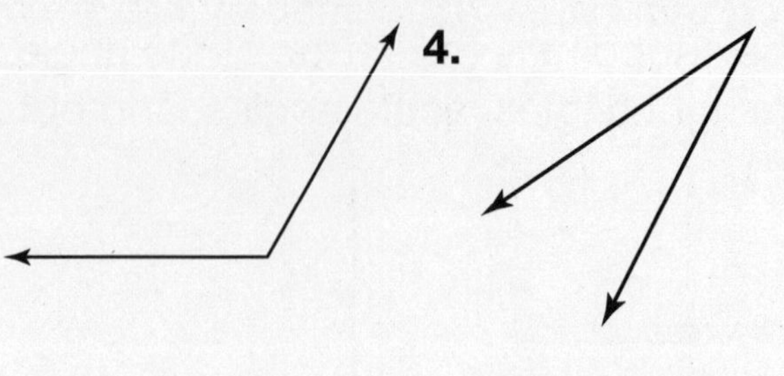

______ ______ ______ ______

Draw a picture of each.

5. Acute angle

6. Ray

7. Right angle

8. Obtuse angle

9. How are perpendicular lines and intersecting lines alike? How are they different?

____

____

10. **Reasoning** Jill said that an angle is made of any two rays. Is she correct? Explain.

____

____

11. At what time do the hands of a clock form an acute angle?

A 2:00 **B** 4:00 **C** 6:00 **D** 8:00

Name ______________________________

Polygons

Polygons are closed shapes that are made up of line segments.

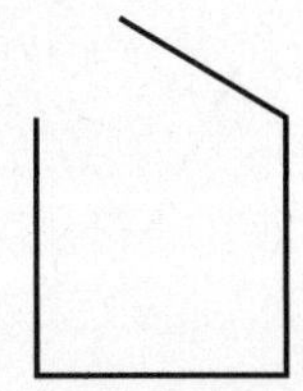
Not a polygon
Not a closed shape

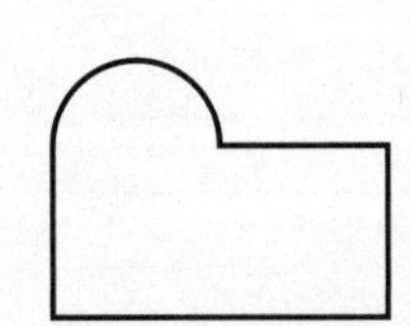
Not a polygon
Not all line segments

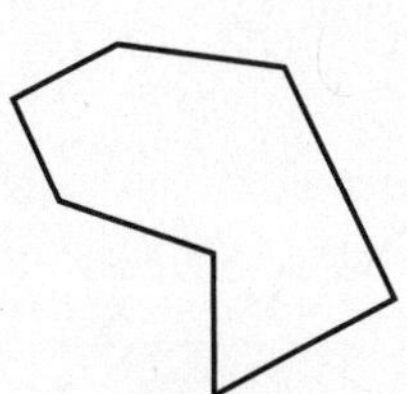
Polygon
Closed shape
All line segments

A polygon is named by the number of sides it has.

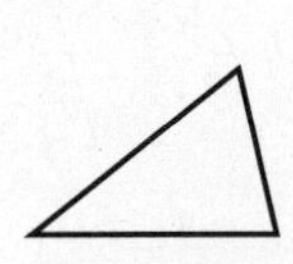
Triangle
3 sides

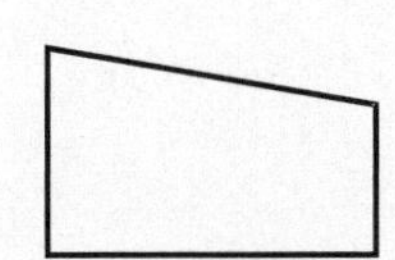
Quadrilateral
4 sides

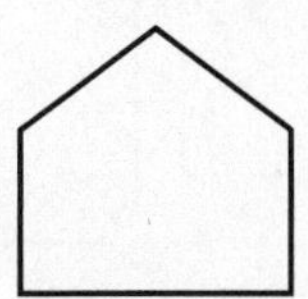
Pentagon
5 sides

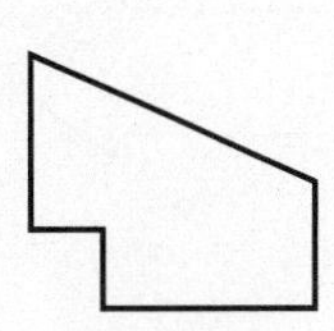
Hexagon
6 sides

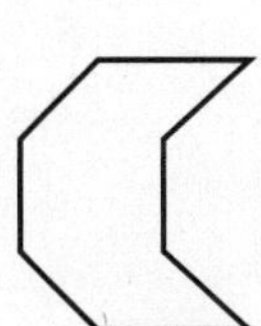
Octagon
8 sides

Is each shape a polygon? If so, give its name. If not, explain why.

1. 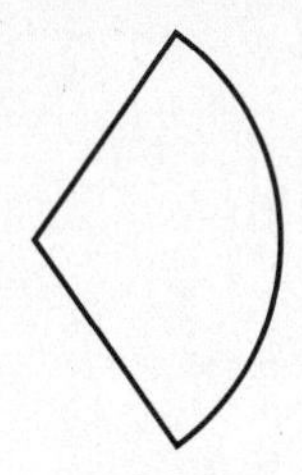

____

____

2. 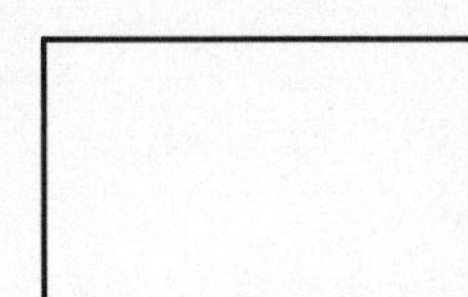

____

____

3. 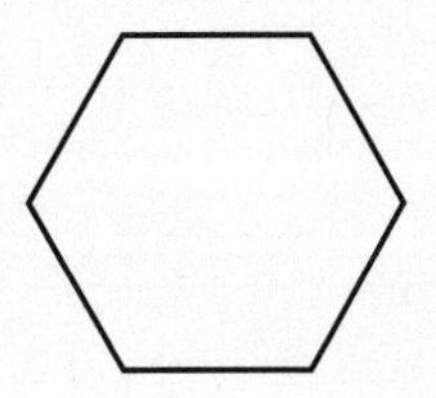

____

____

4. 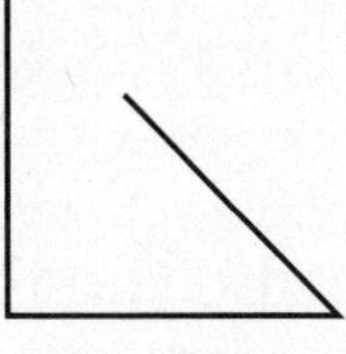

____

____

Name ______________________

Practice 11-3

Polygons

Name the polygon. Write if it is convex or concave.

1. 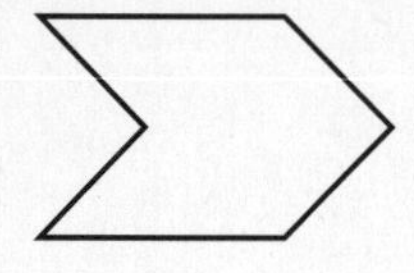
2. 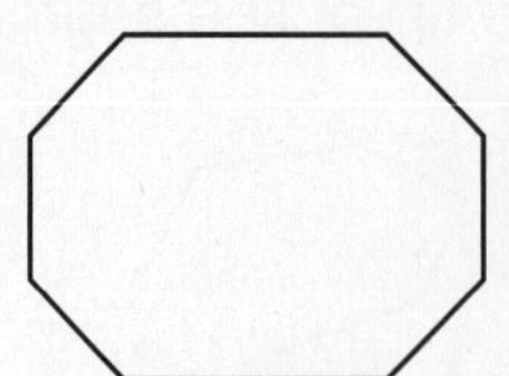
3. 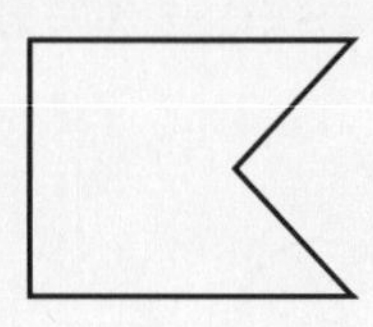
4. 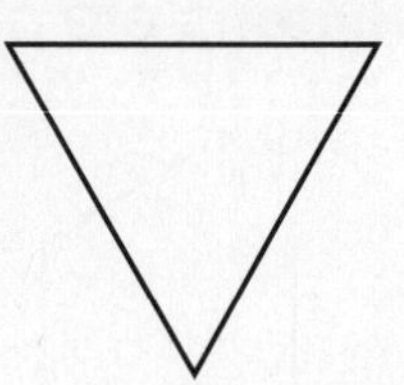

Is each shape a polygon? If it is not, explain why.

5. 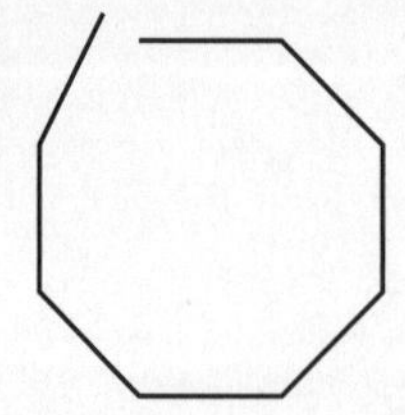
6. 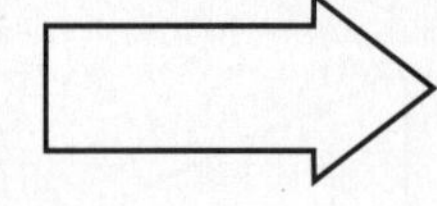
7. 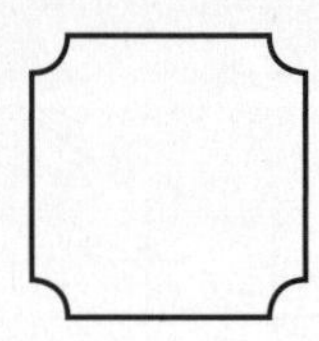
8. 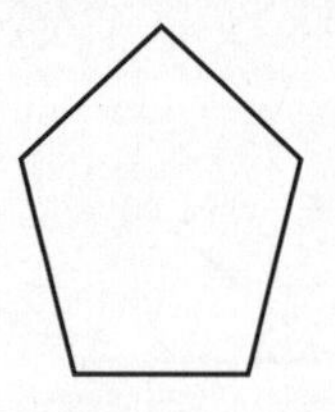

9. Draw one diagonal in the shape for Exercise 8.

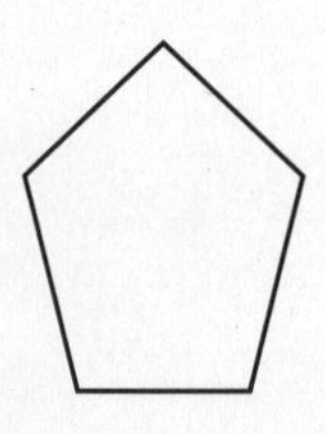

10. Juan said that the two shapes below are quadrilaterals. Is he correct? Explain.

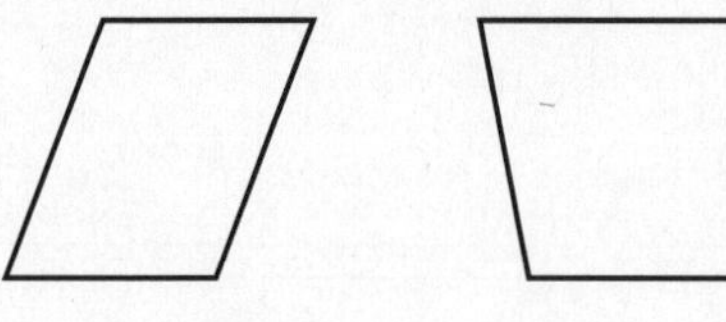

11. **Reason** Two sides of a polygon are parallel line segments. What is the least number of sides the polygon could have?

12. How many more sides does an octagon have than a pentagon?

A 1 **B** 2 **C** 3 **D** 4

Name ______________________________

Triangles

Triangles are polygons with three sides.

Triangles can be named by the lengths of their sides.

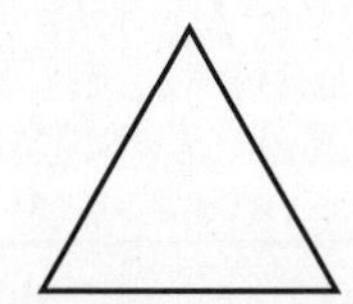

Equilateral Triangle
All sides are the same length.

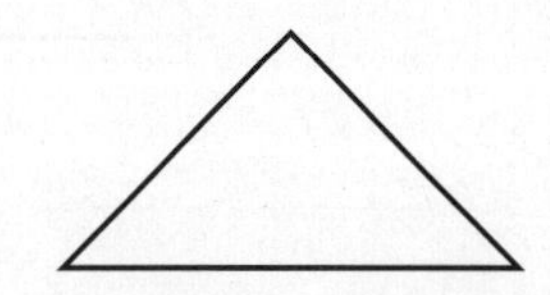

Isosceles Triangle
At least two sides are the same length.

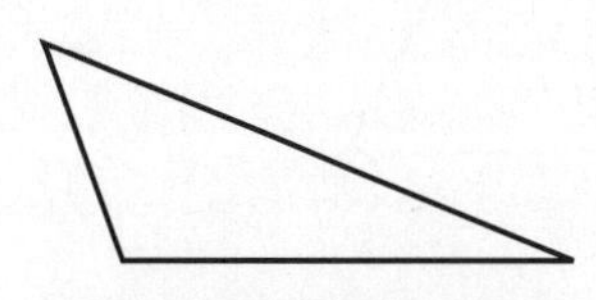

Scalene Triangle
No sides are the same length.

Triangles can also be named by their angles.

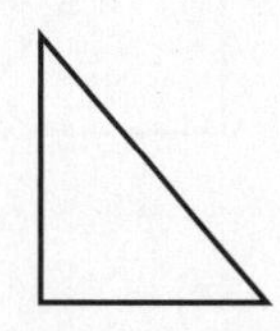

Right Triangle
One angle is a right angle.

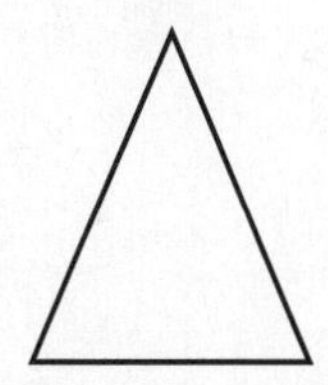

Acute Triangle
All three angles are acute.

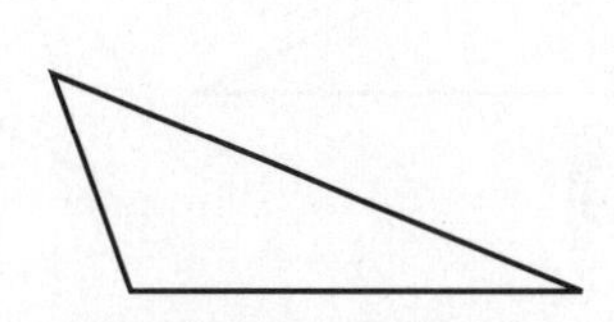

Obtuse Triangle
One angle is obtuse.

1. Tell if the triangle is equilateral, isosceles, or scalene.

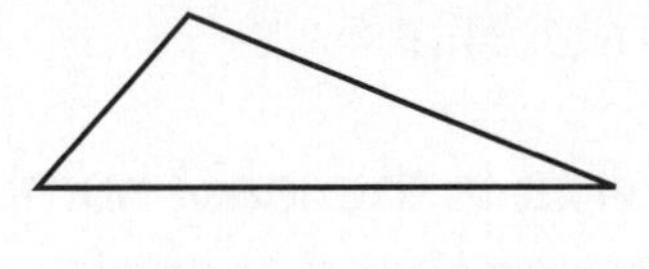

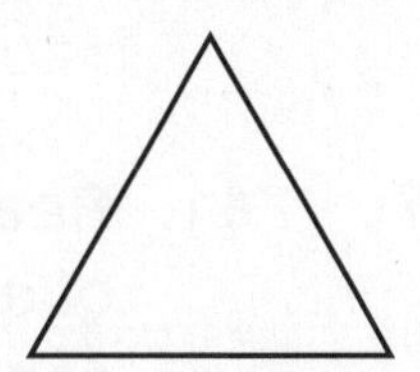

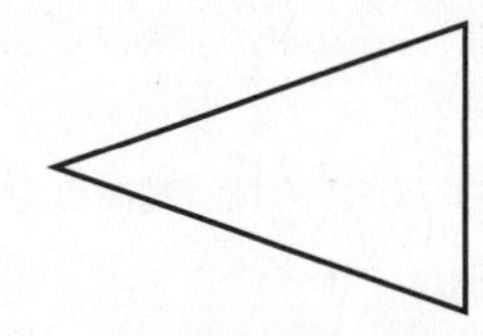

______________ ______________ ______________

2. Tell if the triangle is right, acute, or obtuse.

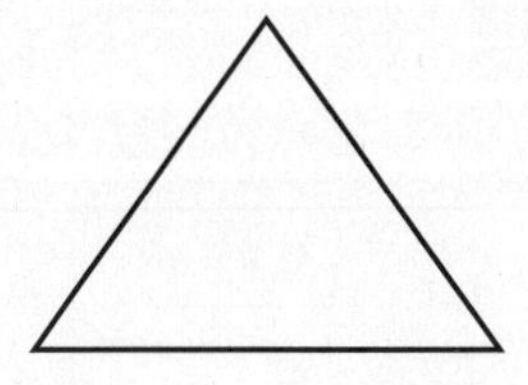

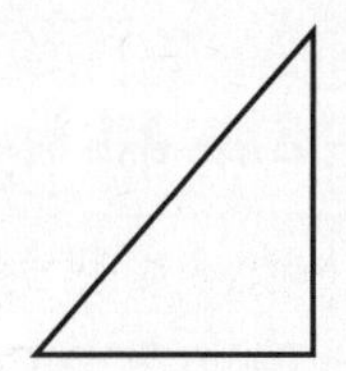

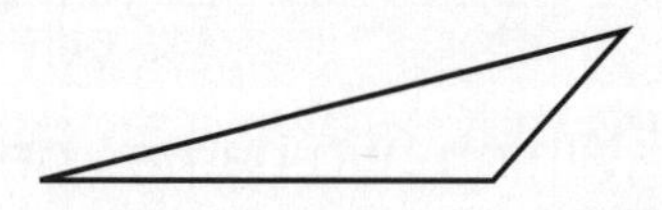

______________ ______________ ______________

Name ______________________

Triangles

Tell if each triangle is equilateral, isosceles, or scalene.

1. 
______

2. 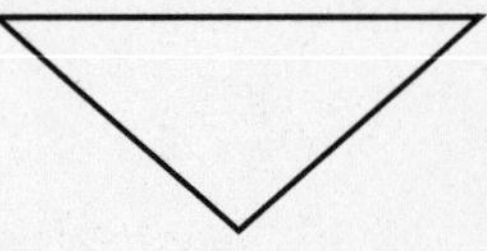
______

3. 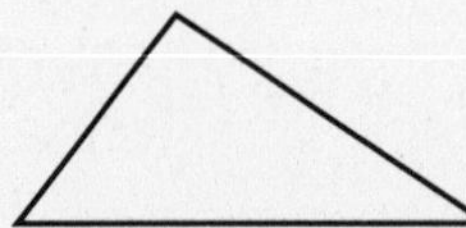
______

4. 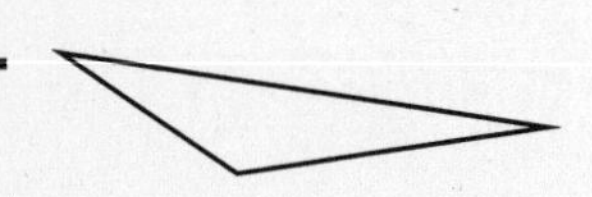
______

Tell if each triangle is right, acute, or obtuse.

5. 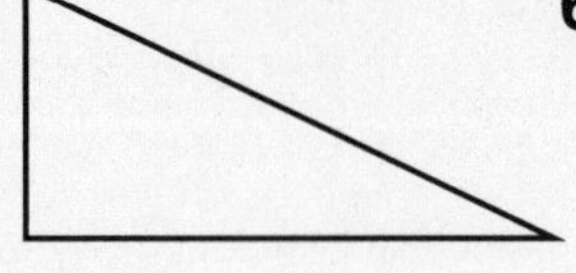
______

6. 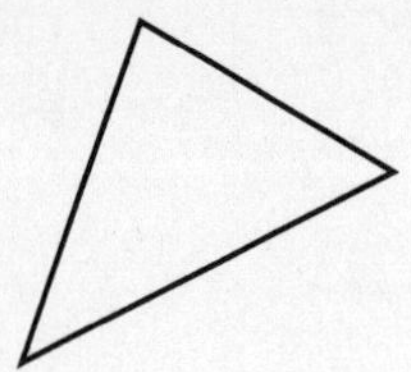
______

7. 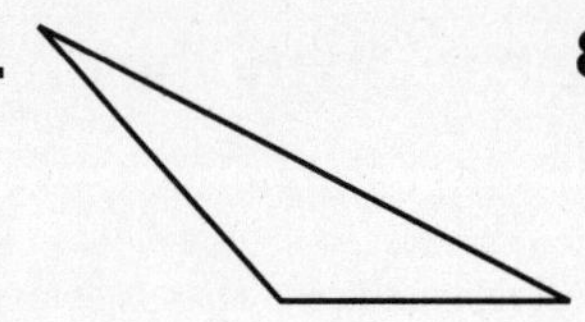
______

8. 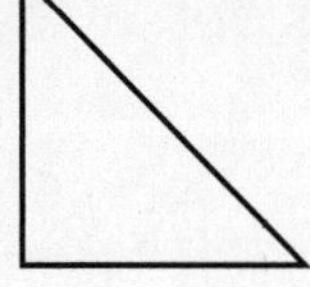
______

9. Write two names that describe the triangle shown at the right.

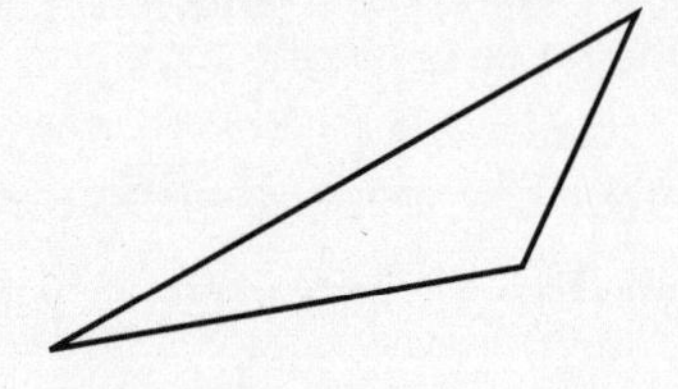

____

10. Can a triangle have 2 right angles? Explain.

____

____

____

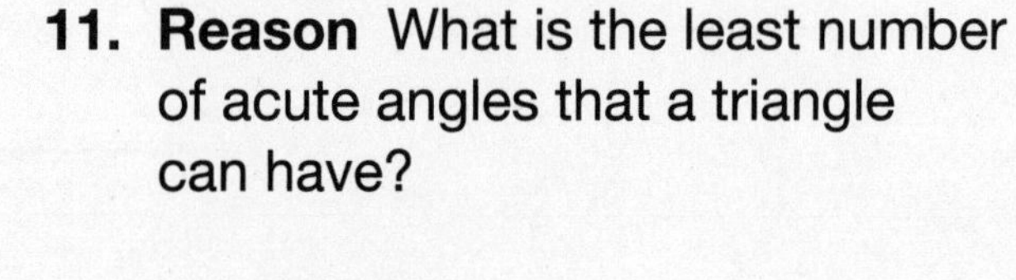

11. **Reason** What is the least number of acute angles that a triangle can have?

______

12. Which two names describe the triangle at the right?

A Equilateral, acute

B Equilateral, right

C Scalene, acute

D Isosceles, obtuse

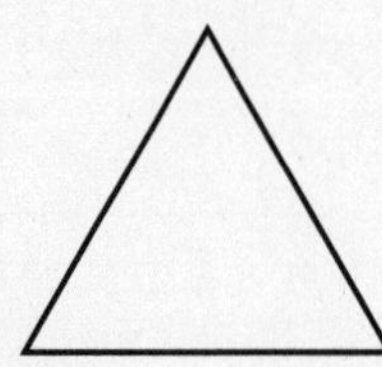

Name ______________________

Reteaching
11-5

Quadrilaterals

Quadrilaterals are polygons with four sides. Some quadrilaterals have special names because of their sides. Some have special names because of their angles. Here are some examples.

	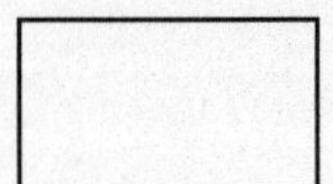	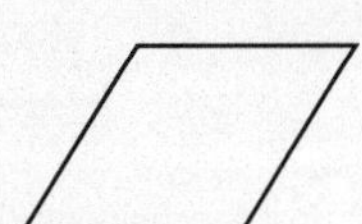	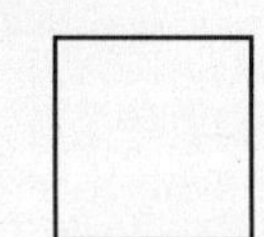	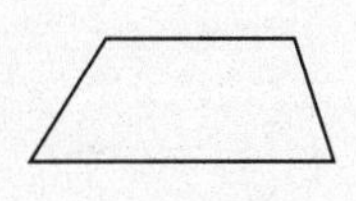
Parallelogram	**Rectangle**	**Rhombus**	**Square**	**Trapezoid**
Opposite sides are equal and parallel.	Parallelogram with four right angles	Parallelogram with four equal sides	A rhombus with four right angles	Exactly one pair of parallel sides

Write as many names as possible for each quadrilateral.

1. 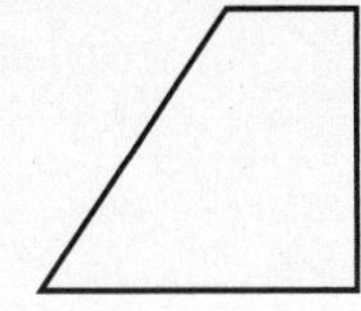

____

____

2. 

____

____

3. 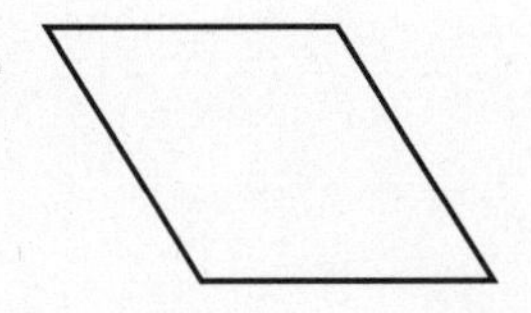

____

____

4. 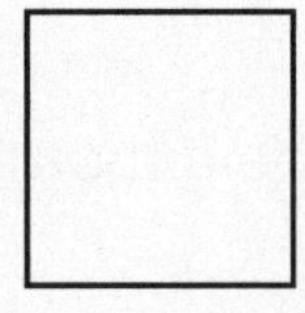

____

____

5. Reason Is a trapezoid also a parallelogram? Explain why or why not.

____

____

Name ______________________

Practice 11-5

Quadrilaterals

Write as many names as possible for each quadrilateral.

1. 2. 3. 4.

In **5–8**, write the name that best describes the quadrilateral.

5. A parallelogram with four equal sides, but no right angles

6. A rectangle with four right angles and all sides the same length

7. A quadrilateral that has exactly one pair of parallel sides

8. A parallelogram with four right angles

9. Can a rectangle also be a rhombus? Explain.

10. Which is the correct name for this shape?

A Rhombus

B Trapezoid

C Parallelogram

D Rectangle

Name ______________________________

Combining and Separating Shapes

You can combine or separate shapes to make new shapes.

What shape can you make by putting together these two squares?

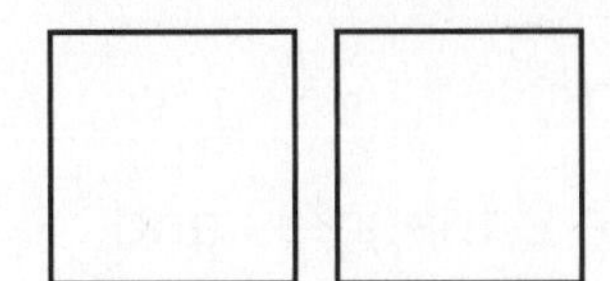

You can make a rectangle.

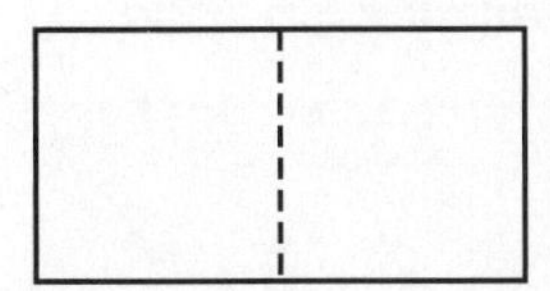

What shapes can you make by cutting this rhombus on a diagonal?

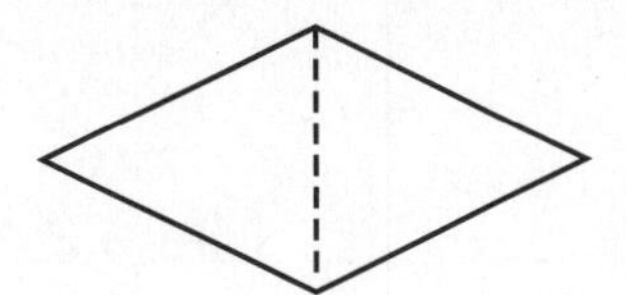

You can make 2 triangles.

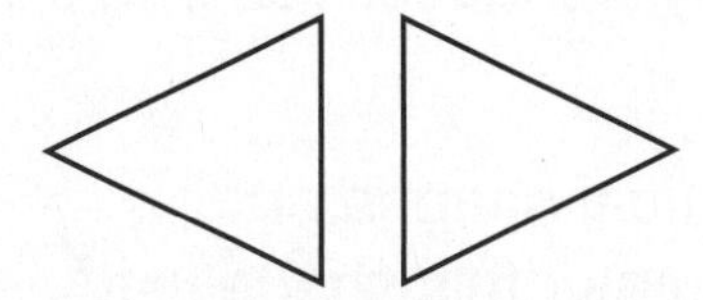

In **1** and **2**, write the name of a polygon that can be made by putting the shapes together.

1. 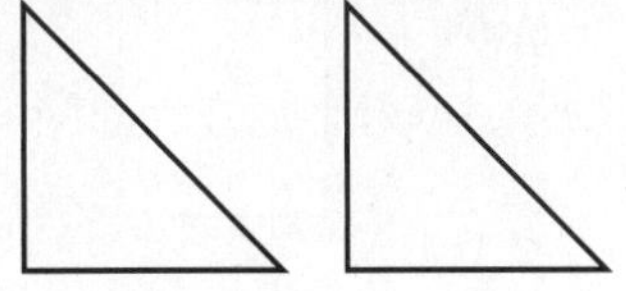

____

2. 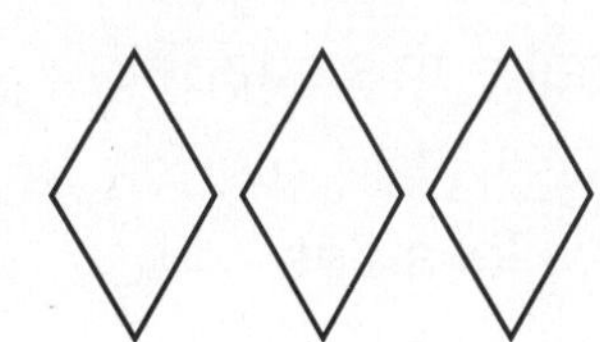

____

In **3–5**, draw one or more diagonals. Write the names of the new shapes you make.

3. 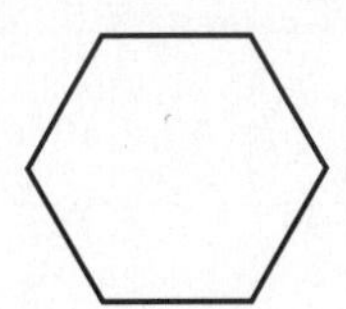

____

4. 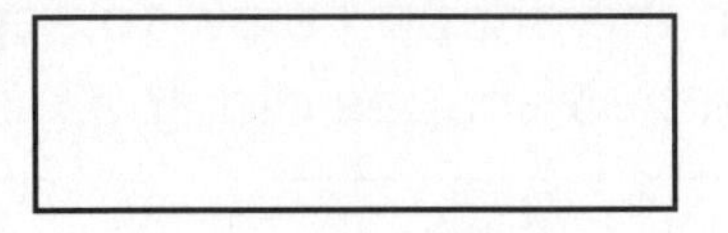

____

5. 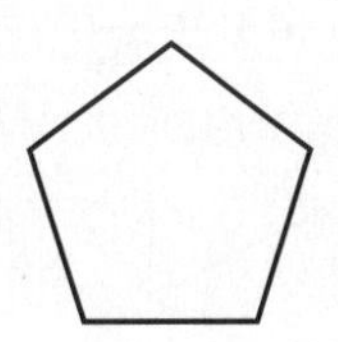

____

6. Two shapes can be put together in different ways. Using the triangles in Exercise 1, draw pictures to show an example.

____

____

Name ______________________

Combining and Separating Shapes

In **1–3**, draw one or more diagonals to make the new shapes named.

1. 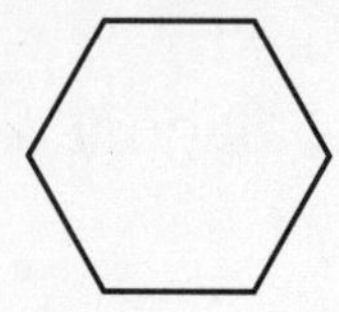

Make 2 triangles and 1 trapezoid.

2. 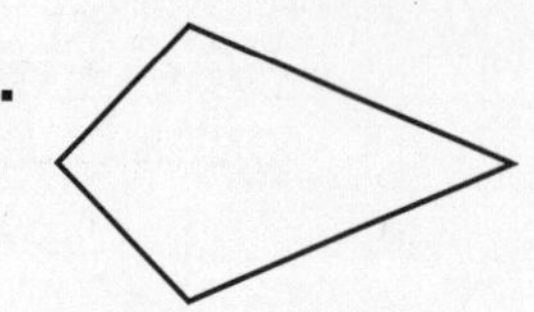

Make 2 different sized triangles.

3. 

Make 2 triangles and 1 rhombus.

For **4–6**, use Lenny's shapes. You can trace and cut them out if you need to.

Lenny's Shapes

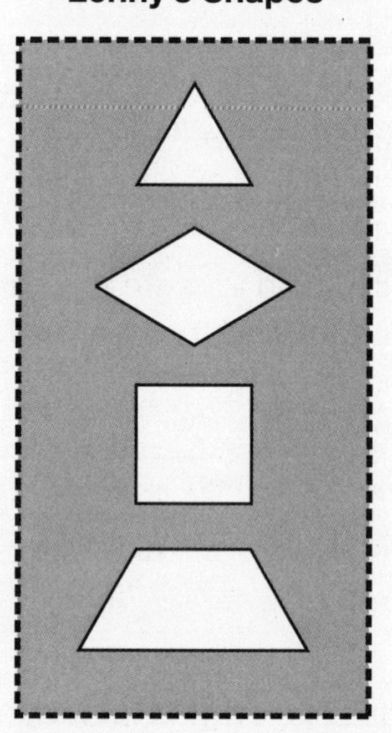

4. Which 3 identical shapes put together will make this shape?

____

5. Which 4 identical shapes put together will make this shape?

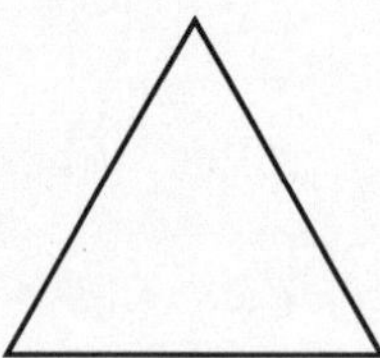

____

6. Which 4 identical shapes put together will make this shape?

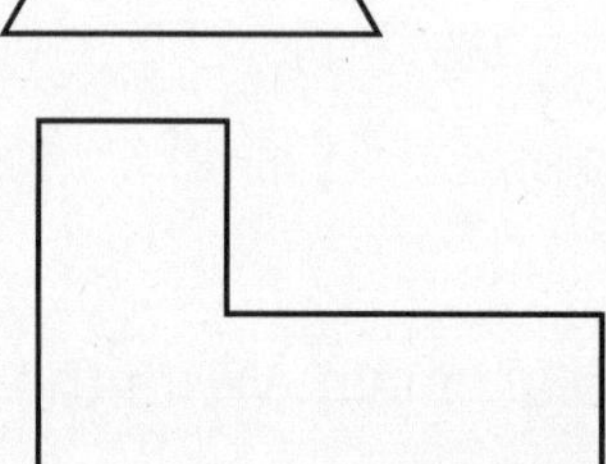

____

7. Maria drew a diagonal on the shape below to separate it into two shapes. Which two shapes did she make?

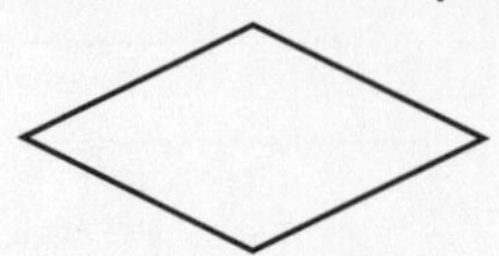

A 2 rhombuses **B** 2 trapezoids **C** 2 triangles **D** 2 parallelograms

8. What different shapes can you make by cutting a hexagon on one or more of its diagonals? Give at least two examples.

____

____

Name ______________________________

Reteaching
11-7

Making New Shapes

You can cut apart a shape and rearrange the pieces to make a new shape.

Cut a hexagon along a middle diagonal to make 2 trapezoids.

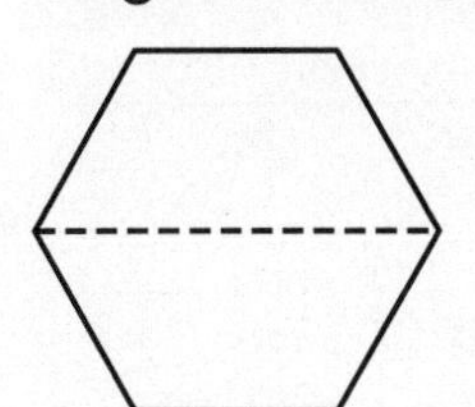

Rearrange the trapezoids to make a parallelogram.

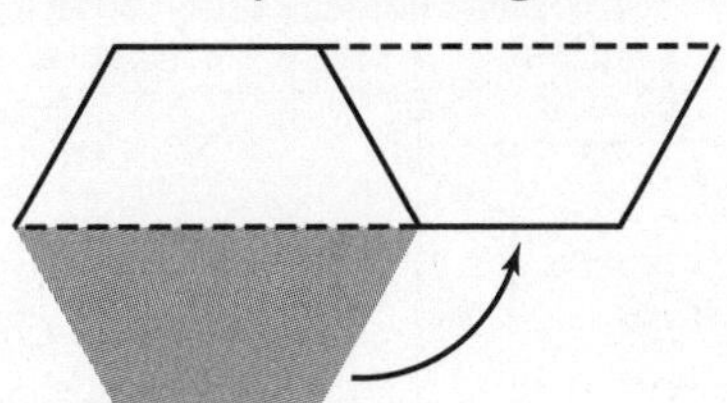

In **1** and **2**, trace and cut out the triangles. Cut along the dashed lines. Rearrange the pieces to make a new shape. Draw the new shape. What shape did you make?

1. 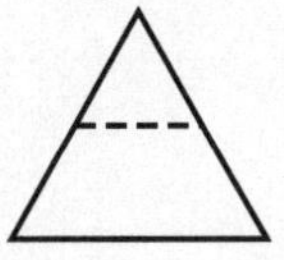

____

2. 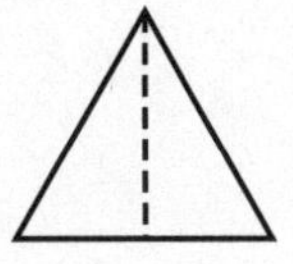

____

In **3–5**, think about cutting each polygon on the dashed lines. Can you rearrange the pieces to make the new shape?

3. A rectangle?

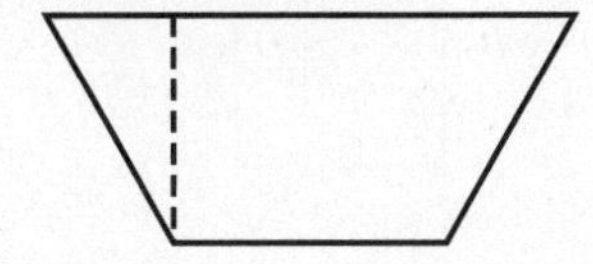

____

4. A triangle?

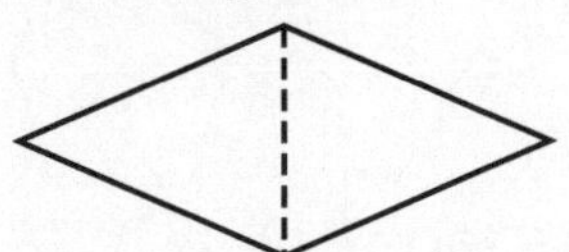

____

5. A square?

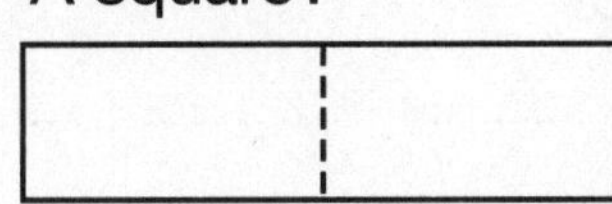

____

6. How many different shapes can you make with the 4 triangles cut from this rectangle? How do you know?

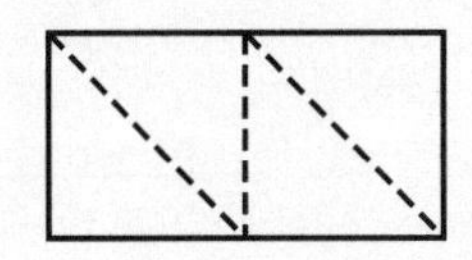

Name ______________________________

Making New Shapes

In **1–4**, trace and carefully cut out each shape. Then cut along the dashed lines. Rearrange the pieces to make a new shape. Name the new shape.

1.

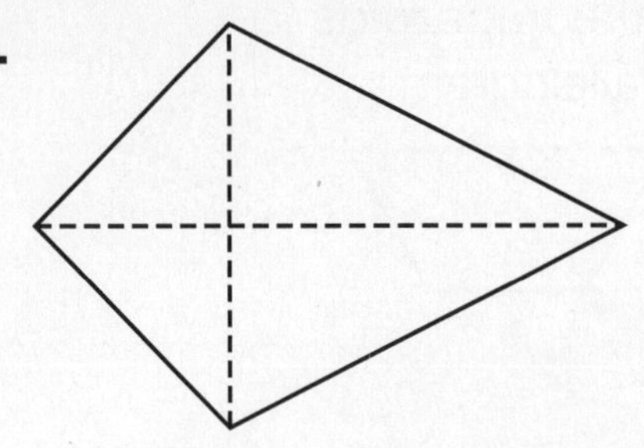

2.

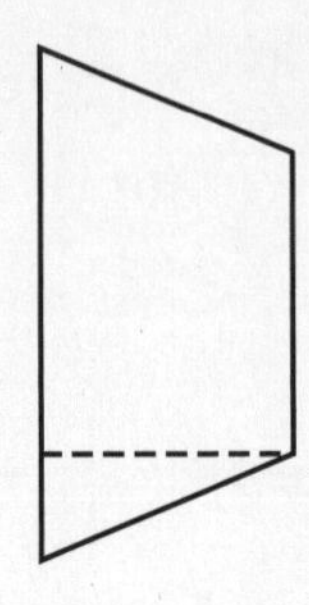

3.

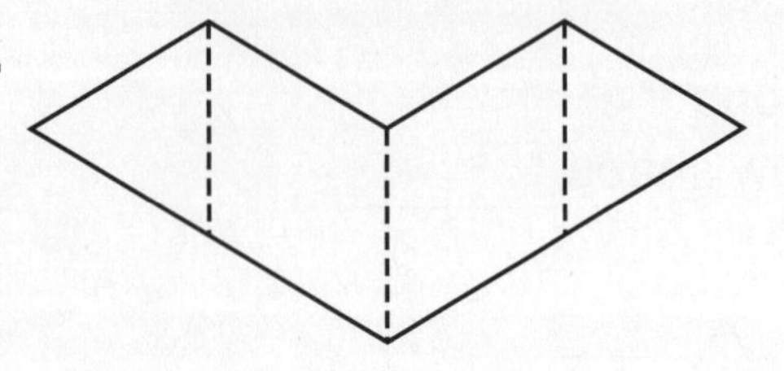

4.

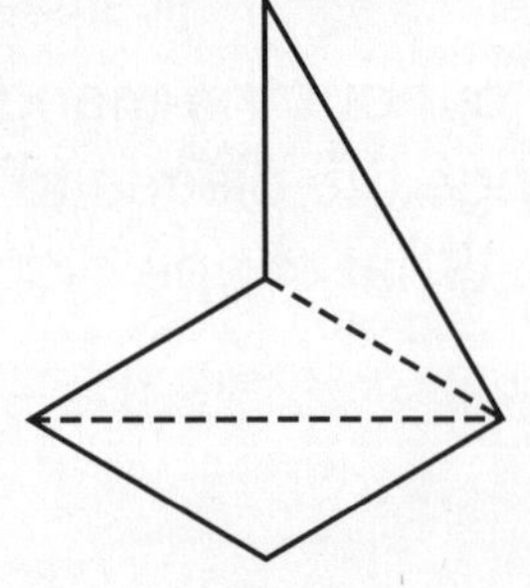

5. **Reason** Lena is making a puzzle. She cuts a shape into two pieces and rearranges them to make the shape below.

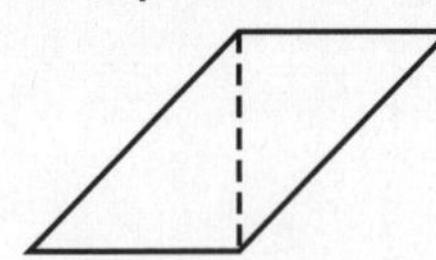

Which shape did she start with?

A 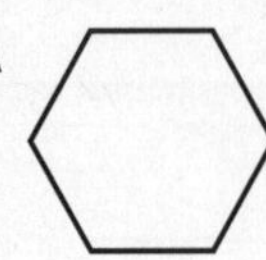

B 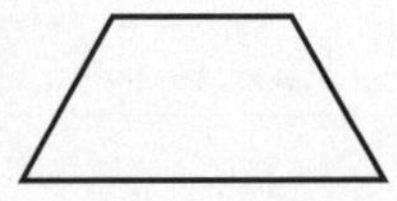

C 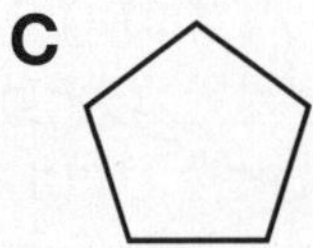

D 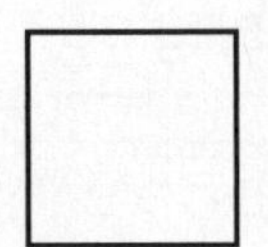

6. Draw a picture to show how you can rearrange the four triangles cut from a rectangle to make a concave hexagon.

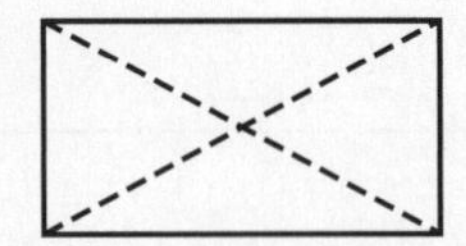

Name ______________________________

Problem Solving: Solve a Simpler Problem

Lou sees rectangles and squares in this tile design. How many large and small rectangles and squares are there in all?

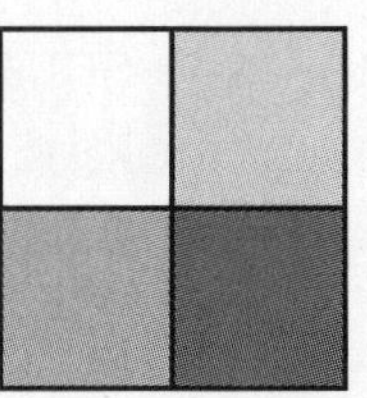

Find and count each size of square or rectangle

How many 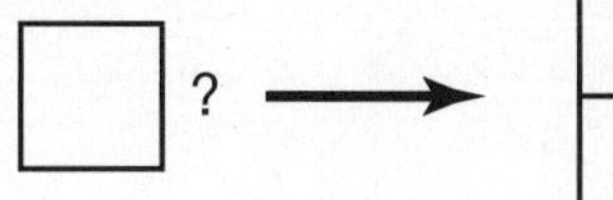 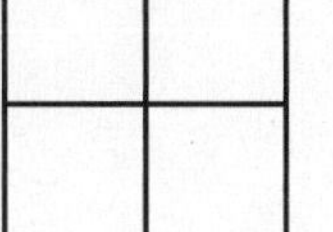 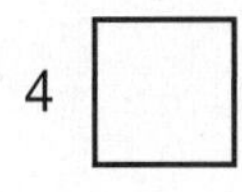

How many 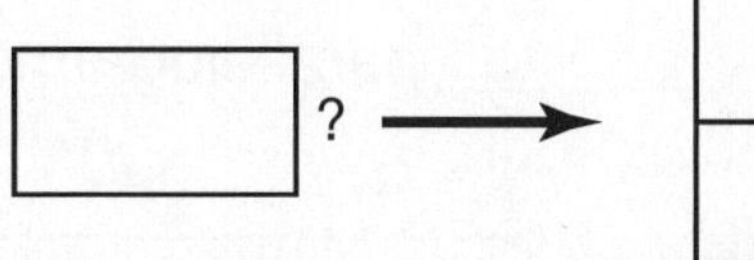 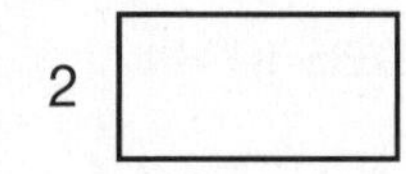

How many 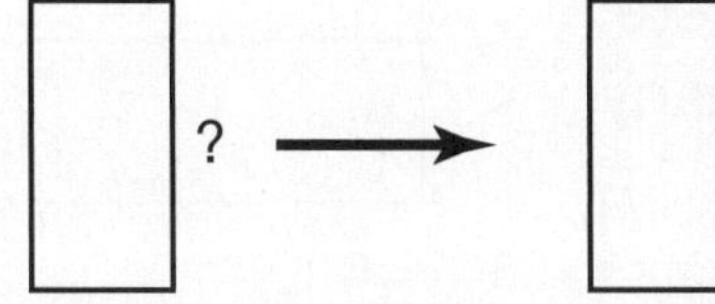 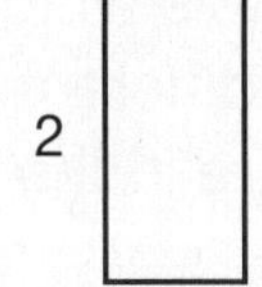

How many 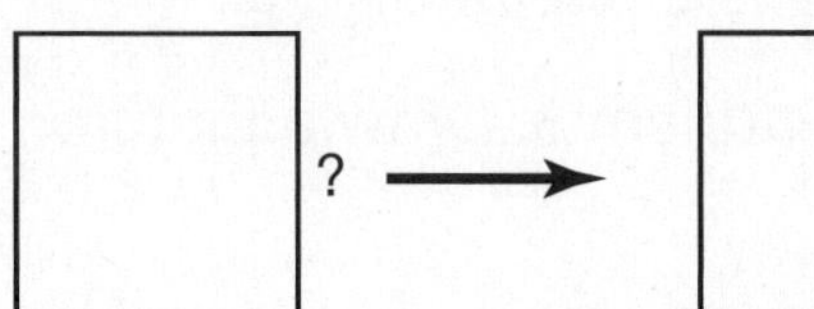 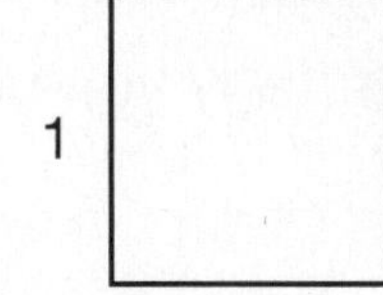

Add: $4 + 2 + 2 + 1 = 9$ There are 9 squares and rectangles in the design.

Break the problem into simpler problems to help you solve.

1. How many rectangles in all are in the design?

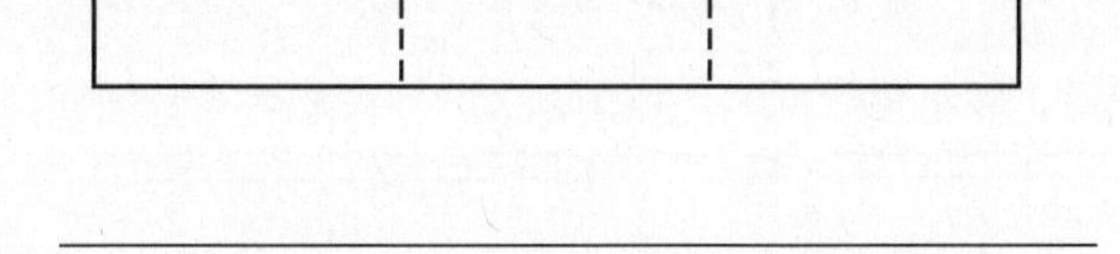

____

____

____

_______ rectangles in all

2. How many rhombuses in all are in the design?

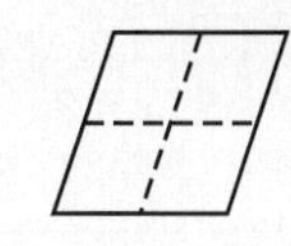

____

____

_______ rhombuses in all

Name ____________________

Problem Solving: Solve a Simpler Problem

1. Jorge sees that there are small and large squares in the tile design below. How many squares are there in all in the design?

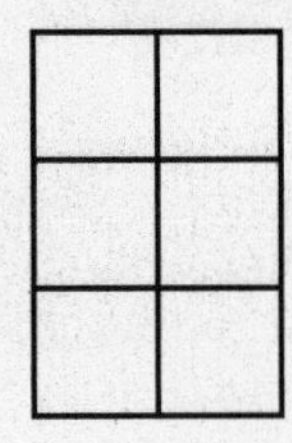

_______ squares in all

2. Sandi counted all the parallelograms of any size she could find in the design below. How many parallelograms are there in all?

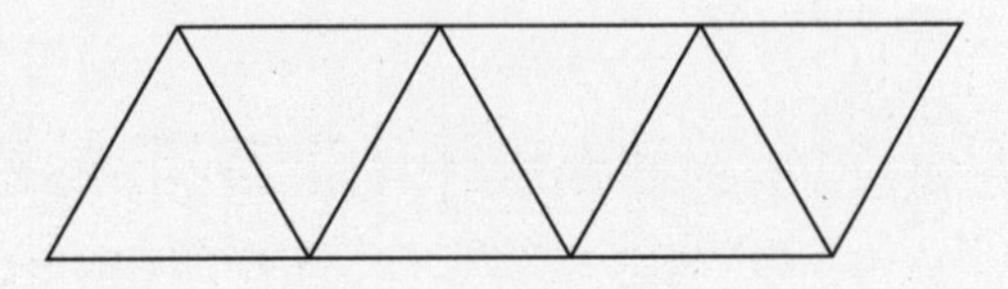

_______ parallelograms in all

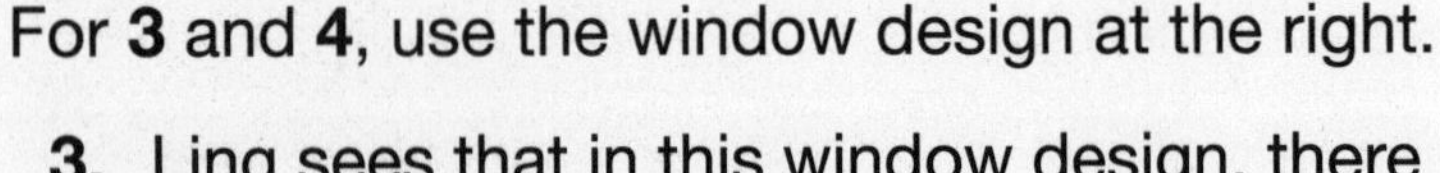

For **3** and **4**, use the window design at the right.

3. Ling sees that in this window design, there are rectangles of different sizes. How many rectangles in all are in the design?

_______ rectangles in all

4. Explain the strategy you used to solve Problem 3. Draw a picture.

____

____

5. Eric's notebook has 30 pages. He wants to write a number on each page. How many digits will he write when he numbers all the pages in the notebook?

A 9 **B** 29 **C** 49 **D** 51

Name ______________________________

Problem Solving: Make and Test Generalizations

A generalization is a statement that makes a conclusion about all of the things in a group. For example, look at these three shapes.

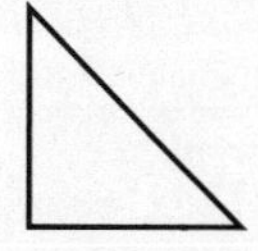 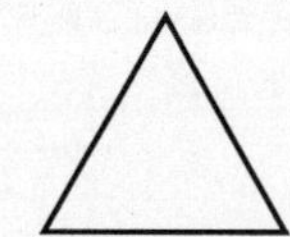 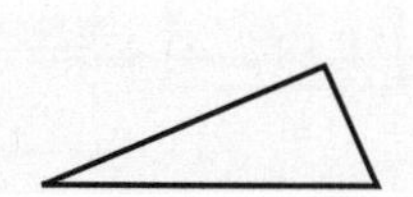

Make a generalization: The shapes are all acute triangles.
Test your generalization. The shape on the left has a right angle.
It is a right triangle. This generalization is not true.

Try another generalization: The shapes are all triangles.
Each of the shapes is a polygon with 3 sides. This generalization is correct.

Make and test a generalization for each set of polygons.

1. 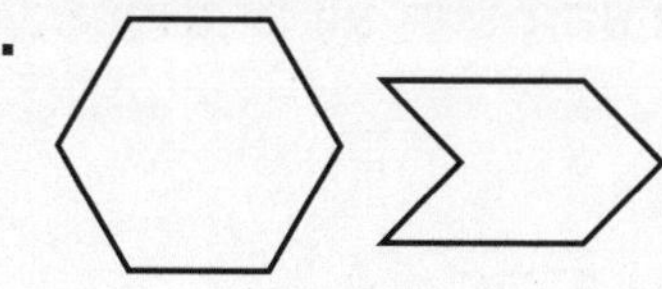

____

____

2. 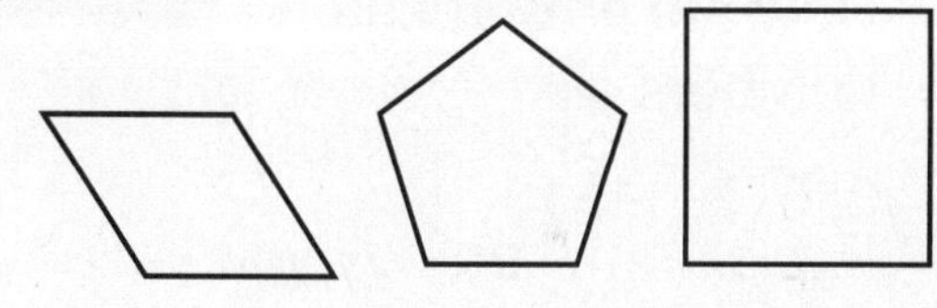

____

____

3. 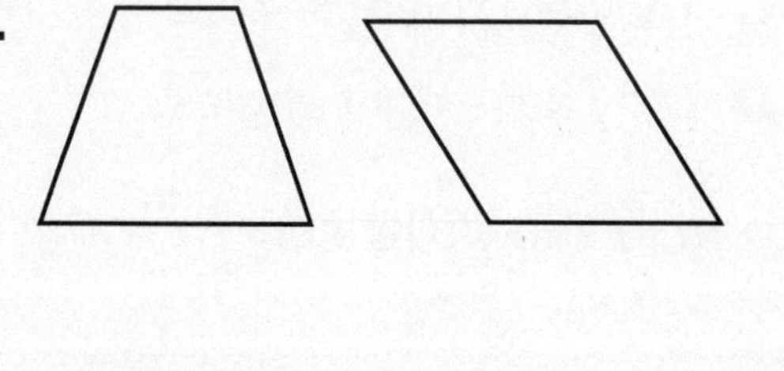

____

____

4. 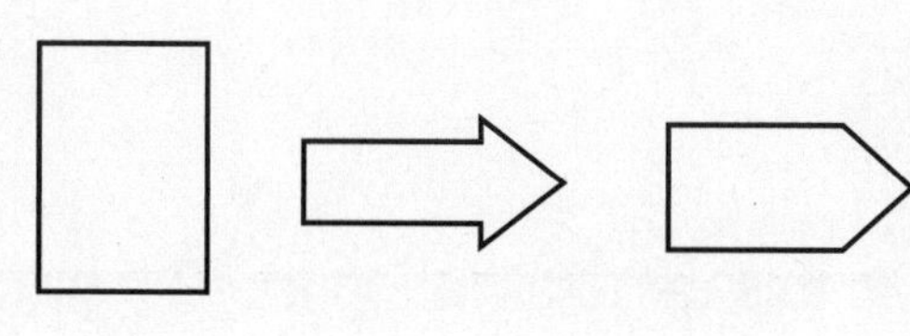

____

____

Name ____________________

Problem Solving: Make and Test Generalizations

In **1–4**, make a generalization for each set of polygons.

1. 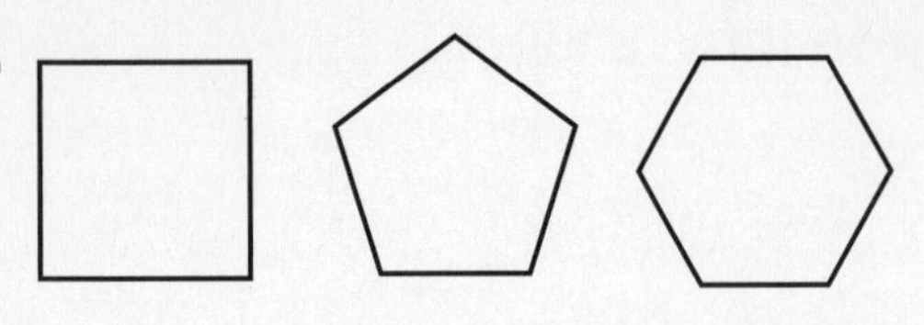

2. 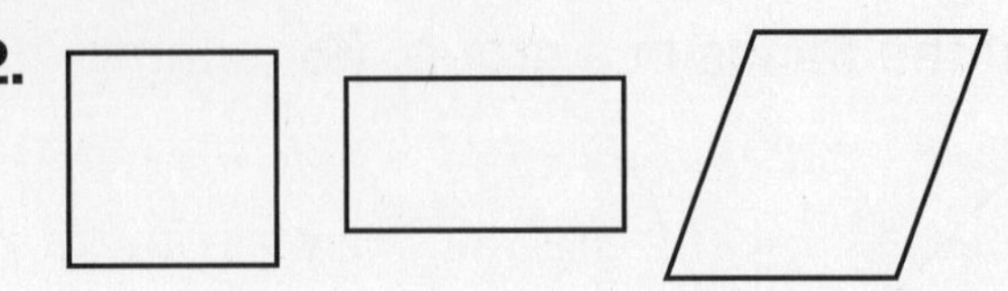

____

3. 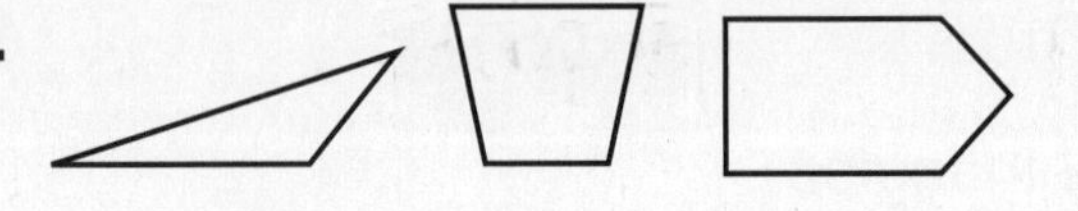

4. 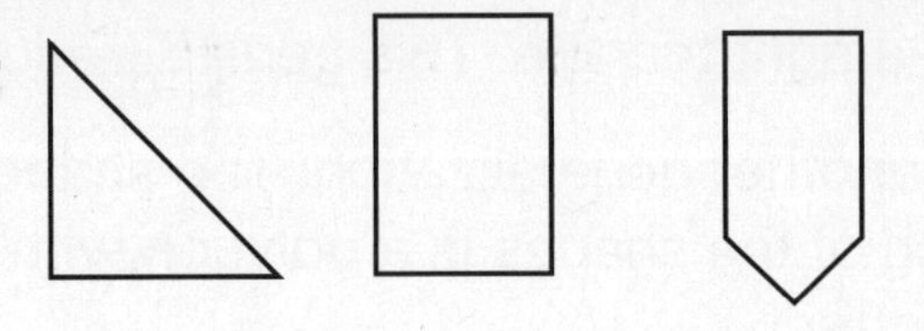

____

5. How are all of these numbers alike?

3, 5, 7, 11, 13

____

6. What is the same in all of these polygons?

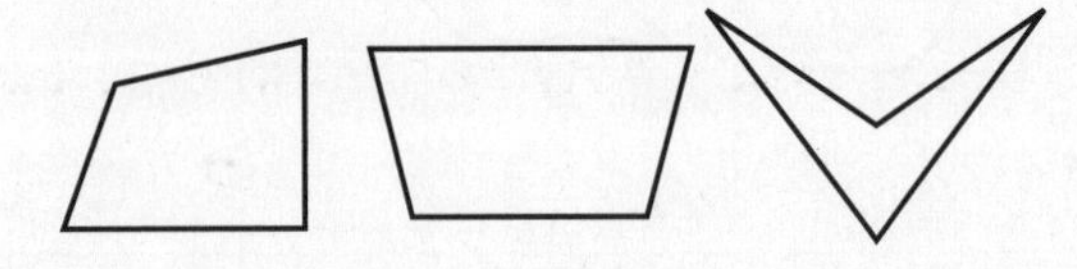

A They are convex.

B They are rhombuses.

C They are quadrilaterals.

D They have right angles.

7. Is this generalization true? If not, draw a picture to show why not.
All triangles have at least 2 acute angles.

____

Name ______________________

Time to the Half Hour and Quarter Hour

An hour is 60 minutes long. A half hour is 30 minutes long.
A quarter hour is 15 minutes long.

The A.M. hours are the hours from 12 midnight to 12 noon.
The P.M. hours are the hours from 12 noon to 12 midnight.

The clocks show three different times.

9:30
nine thirty
half past nine

12:15
twelve fifteen
15 minutes after 12
quarter after 12

1:45
one forty-five
45 minutes after 1
15 minutes to 2
quarter to 2

Write the time shown on each clock in two ways.

1.

____

____

2.

____

____

3.

____

____

4. How many minutes are there in three quarters of an hour? Explain your answer.

____

____

____

Name ______________________

Practice
12-1

Time to the Half Hour and Quarter Hour

Write the time shown on each clock in two ways.

1.

Quarter to 7

____

2.

Quarter past 4

____

3.

Half hour past 7

____

4.

Half hour past 10

____

5.

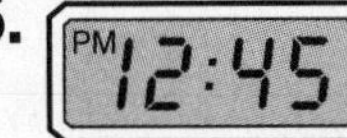

Quarter to 1

____

6.

Quarter past 11

____

7. The school bus stops at Randy's stop at 8:15 A.M. Randy arrived at the bus stop at quarter after 8. Did he miss the bus? Explain.

No because, it is the Same, Because 1 Quarter equalls to 15 mins

____

8. Which does **NOT** describe the time shown on the clock?

A five forty-five

B five fifteen

C quarter after five

D fifteen minutes after five

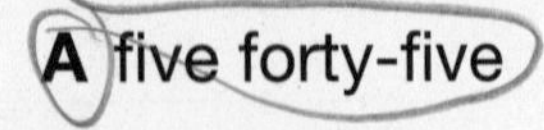

Name ______________________

Reteaching
12-2

Time to the Minute

You can skip count by fives and then count on to tell time when the minute hand is between numbers.

The minute hand is between 7 and 8.

Count by 5s from 12 to 7. That is 35 minutes.

Count 3 more minutes. There are 38 minutes.

The hour hand is between 11 and 12. The time is 11:38, or 22 minutes to 12.

Write the time shown on each clock two ways.

1.

3:41

41 mins past 3

2. ______________________

____

3.

____

____

Name ____________________

Practice
12-2

Time to the Minute

Write the time shown on each clock in two ways.

1.

6:47

47 mins past 6

2.

9:47

47 mins past 9

3.

____

____

4.

4:51

51 mins past 4

5.

____

____

6.  PM 6:23

6:23

23 mins past 6

7. What type of angle is formed by a clock's hands when it is 3:00? ____________________

8. The movie Mike watched lasted 1 hour 26 minutes. How many minutes did the movie last? 86 mins

9. Jan's alarm clock rang at the time shown on the clock below. At what time did the alarm clock ring?

A six ten

B six twenty-two

C six thirty-eight

D seven twenty-two

Name ______________________________

Units of Time

Reteaching

12-3

There are 60 minutes (min) in an hour (h).
There are 24 hours in a day (d).
There are 7 days in a week (wk).

To change from a larger unit to a smaller unit, multiply.

To find the number of hours in 2 days, multiply: $2 \times 24 = 48$.
So, there are 48 hours in 2 days.

Complete to change the units.

1. 6 weeks = ■■ days

____

2. 3 days = ■■ hours

____

3. How many days are there in 7 weeks?

____

4. How many minutes are there in 9 hours?

____

5. How many days are there in 3 weeks, 4 days?

____

6. How many minutes are there in 4 hours, 30 minutes?

____

7. **Writing to Explain** Nikki's school day lasts 7 hours, 20 minutes. How many minutes does Nikki's school day last? Explain how you found your answer.

____

____

____

____

Name ______________________

Units of Time

Change the units. Complete.

1. 5 hours = ■■■ minutes

2. 3 weeks = ■■ days

3. 8 weeks = ■■ days

4. 6 hours = ■■■ minutes

5. How many minutes are in 3 hours, 30 minutes?

6. How many days are there in 4 weeks, 3 days?

7. Kendra watched two movies. The first lasted 100 minutes. The second lasted 1 hour, 55 minutes. Which movie was longer? By how many minutes?

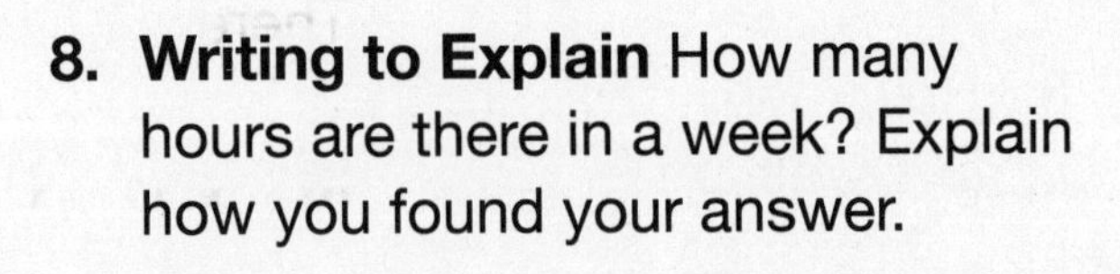

8. **Writing to Explain** How many hours are there in a week? Explain how you found your answer.

9. The Wilson family is going on a 5-week vacation through Australia and New Zealand this summer. How many days will the Wilson's be on vacation?

10. Lacy slept 8 hours last night. How many minutes did Lacy sleep?

A 400 **C** 640

B 480 **D** 800

Name ______________________

Reteaching
12-4

Elapsed Time

A children's museum is open from 1:00 P.M. to 6:35 P.M. every day. How long is the museum open?

Step 1

Start at the starting time.

The museum is open 5 hours, 35 minutes.

Step 2

Count the hours.

There are 5 hours.

Step 3

Count the minutes.

There are 35 minutes.

Find the elapsed time.

1. Start Time: 3:30 P.M.
End Time: 7:00 P.M.

____

2. Start Time: 8:10 A.M.
End Time: 10:55 A.M.

____

3. Start Time: 1:20 P.M.
End Time: 2:00 P.M.

____

4. Start Time: 8:00 A.M.
End Time: 1:15 P.M.

____

5. Write a Problem Write the start time and the ending time of an activity that you did during the weekend. Then find the elapsed time. Write your answer in hours and minutes.

____

____

____

Name ______________________

Practice
12-4

Elapsed Time

Find the elapsed time.

1. Start Time: 6:00 P.M.
   End Time: 7:15 P.M.
   ____

2. Start Time: 9:30 A.M.
   End Time: 1:45 P.M.
   ____

3. Start Time: 3:10 P.M.
   End Time: 4:00 P.M.
   ____

4. Start Time: 11:30 A.M.
   End Time: 5:30 P.M.
   ____

5. Start Time: 7:30 A.M.
   End Time: 10:50 A.M.
   3h and 20mins

6. Start Time: 9:00 P.M.
   End Time: 4:30 A.M.
   ____

7. Edie is 1 year old. She naps from 12:45 P.M. to 2:30 P.M. each day. How long is Edie's nap?
   ____

8. Mr. Wellborn arrives at work at 8:40 A.M. He leaves for work 50 minutes before he arrives. At what times does Mr. Wellborn leave for work?
   7:50 AM

9. **Writing to Explain** How long is your school day? Explain how you found your answer.
   ____
   ____
   ____
   ____

10. Gary's father dropped him off at soccer practice at 2:45 P.M. His mother picked him up at 5:00 P.M. How long did soccer practice last?
    A 2 hours, 15 minutes
    B 2 hours, 25 minutes
    C 3 hours, 15 minutes
    D 3 hours, 25 minutes

Name ______________________________

Problem Solving: Work Backward

Natalie finished listening to music at 4:30 P.M. She had listened to a CD that lasted 40 minutes. She spent 15 minutes listening to radio music after the CD finished. Then she listened to another CD for 45 minutes. At what time did Natalie start listening to music?

You can work backward to solve problems. Use each piece of information to find the starting time.

Natalie finished listening to music at 4:30 P.M.

She listened to the second CD for 45 minutes.	45 minutes before 4:30 P.M. is 3:45 P.M.	
She spent 15 minutes listening to radio music.	15 minutes from 3:45 P.M. is 3:30 P.M.	
She listened to the first CD for 40 minutes.	40 minutes before 3:30 P.M. is 2:50 P.M.	

Natalie started listening to music at 2:50 P.M.

Solve the problem by drawing a picture and working backward.

1. The temperature at 6 P.M. was 72°F. This temperature was 8°F less than at 4 P.M. The temperature at 10 A.M. was 5°F greater than the 4 P.M. temperature. What was the temperature at 10 A.M.?

____

Name ____________________

Practice
12-5

Problem Solving: Work Backward

Solve the problem by drawing a picture or a number line and working backward.

1. Will arrived at his mother's office at 3 P.M. It took him 30 minutes to walk from his home to the mall. He was in the mall for 45 minutes. It then took him 15 minutes to walk to his mother's office. At what time did Will leave home?

   1:30 pm

2. At 12 noon, Leslie recorded the temperature as 56°F. The temperature had increased by 8°F from 10 A.M. The temperature at 8 A.M. was 2°F warmer than it was at 10 A.M. What was the temperature at 8 A.M.?

   56° F

3. The test that Keyshawn's class took finished at 10:30 A.M. The first part of the test took 30 minutes. There was a 15-minute break. The second part of the test also took 30 minutes. At what time did the test start?

   9:15 AM

4. The temperature was 16°C when Becky returned home at 6 P.M. The temperature was 4°C warmer at 3 P.M. than it was at 6 P.M. It was 3°C warmer at 12 noon than it was at 3 P.M. What was the temperature at 12 noon?

   ____

5. Elliot finished studying at 4:45 P.M. He spent 30 minutes reading a social studies chapter. He spent 45 minutes on his math homework. In between studying, Elliot took a 20-minute break. At what time did Elliot begin studying?

   A 3:00 P.M. **B** 3:10 P.M. **C** 3:30 P.M. **D** 6:20 P.M.

Name ___________________________

Reteaching
13-1

Understanding Perimeter

The **perimeter** of a figure is the distance around it.

The perimeter is found by adding the lengths of the sides.

4 in. + 6 in. + 7 in. + 5 in. + 11 in. + 11 in. = 44 in.

The perimeter of the figure is 44 inches.

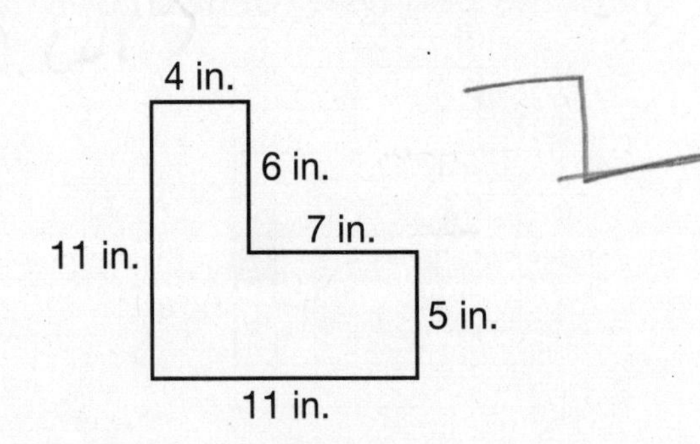

1.

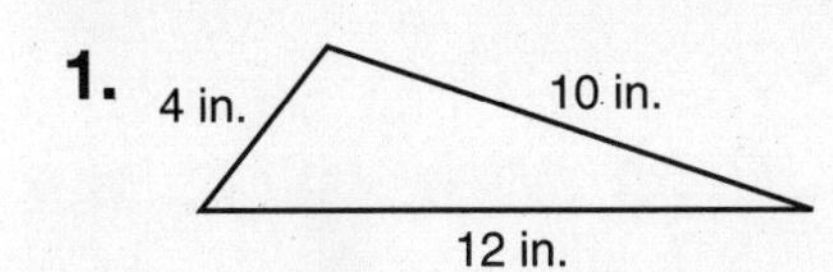

____

2.

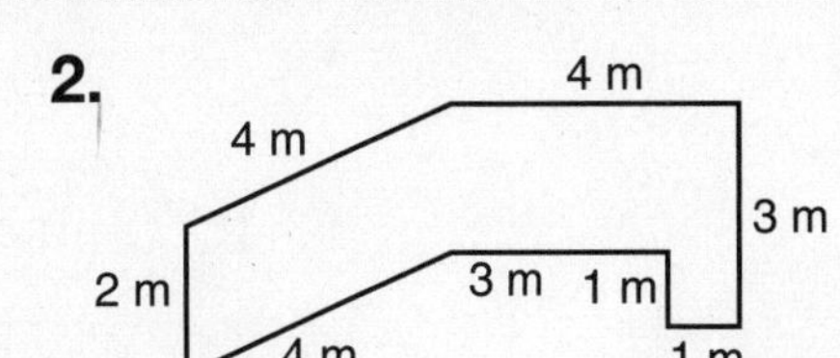

____

3.

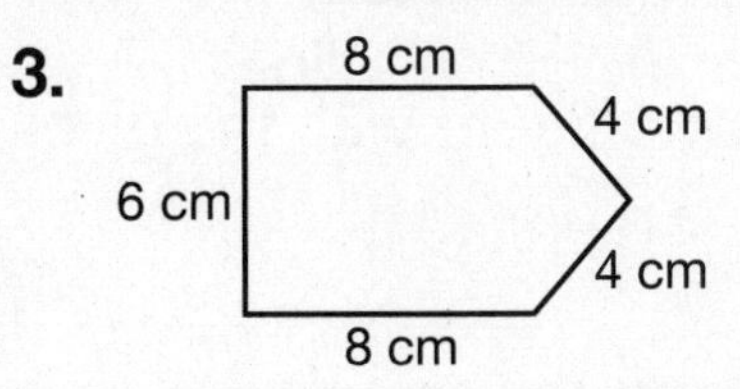

____

Draw a figure with the given perimeter.

4. 6 units

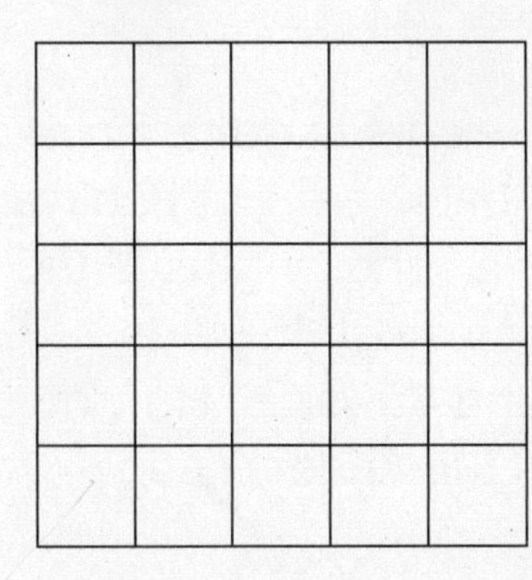

5. 10 units

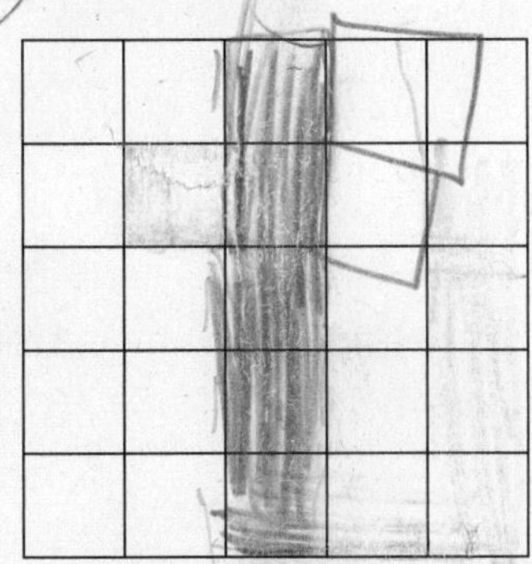

6. 12 units

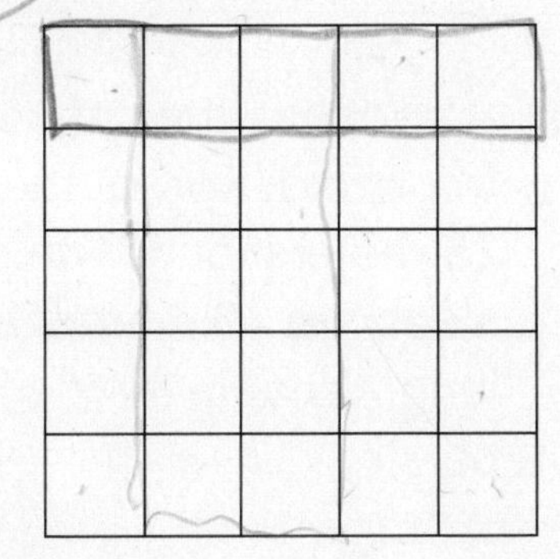

7. A rectangle has a length of 5 yards and a width of 3 yards. What is its perimeter? Explain your answer.

____

____

Name ________________________________

Practice
13-1

Understanding Perimeter

Find the perimeter of each polygon.

1.

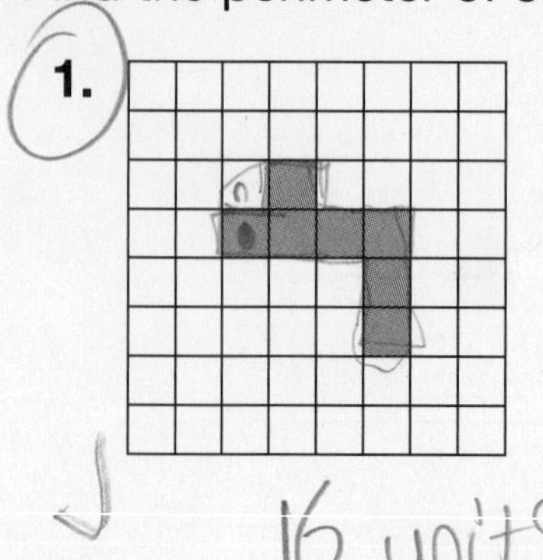

2.

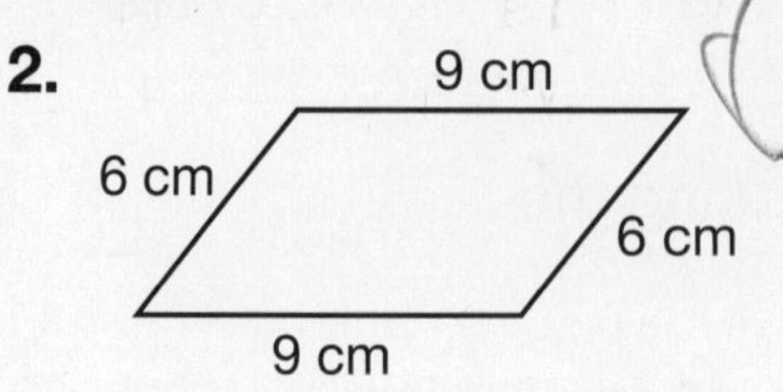

3.

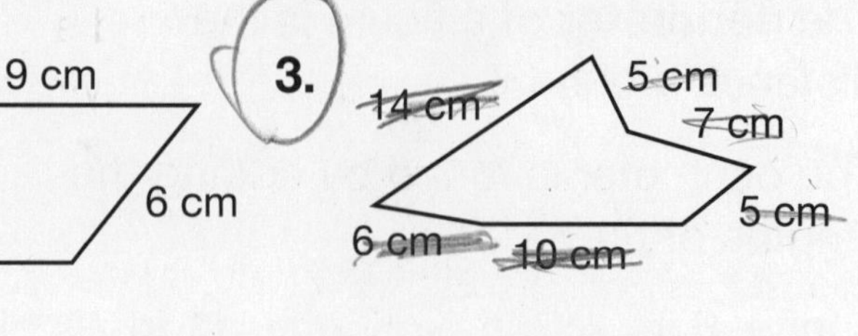

Draw a figure with the given perimeter.

4. 10 units

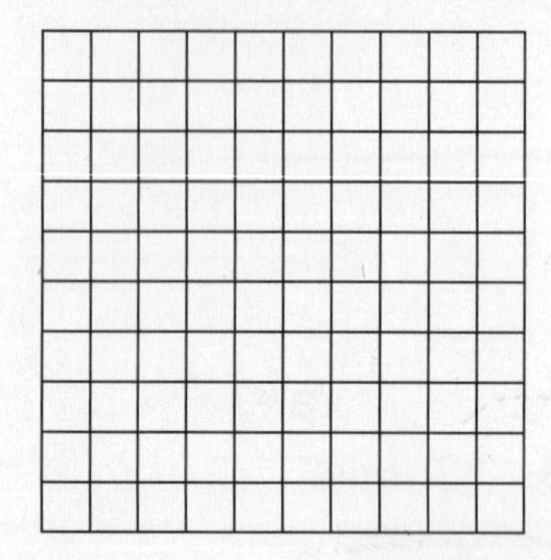

5. 22 units

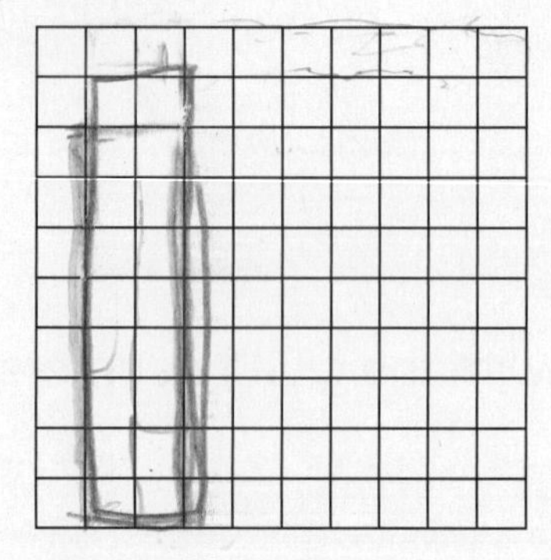

6. A park has the shape of a trapezoid. Two of the sides are 25 meters long. The other two sides are 40 meters and 20 meters long. What is the perimeter of the park?

____

7. Mr. Anders wants to put a fence around his backyard. His backyard is rectangular. The lengths of the sides are 75 yards, 45 yards, 75 yards, and 45 yards. How much fencing will Mr. Anders need?

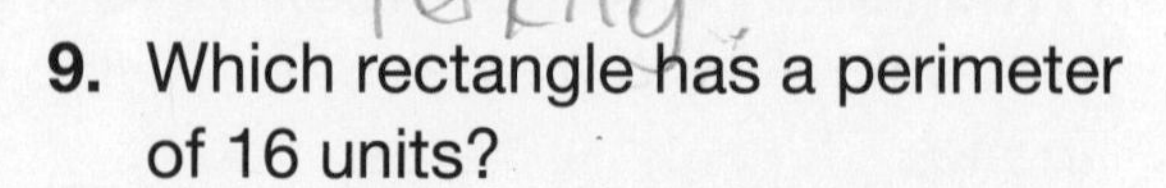

8. Communicate When finding the perimeter of a figure on a grid, why do you not count the spaces inside the grid?

____

____

9. Which rectangle has a perimeter of 16 units?

A Length 5 units, width 3 units

B Length 10 units, width 6 units

C Length 8 units, width 1 unit

D Length 6 units, width 3 units

Name ___________________________

Reteaching
13-2

Tools and Units for Perimeter

Mrs. Ramirez is putting tape around a section of the playground that will be used for playing basketball. She needs to measure the perimeter.

Basketball

Swings and Slides

Which tool should she use?

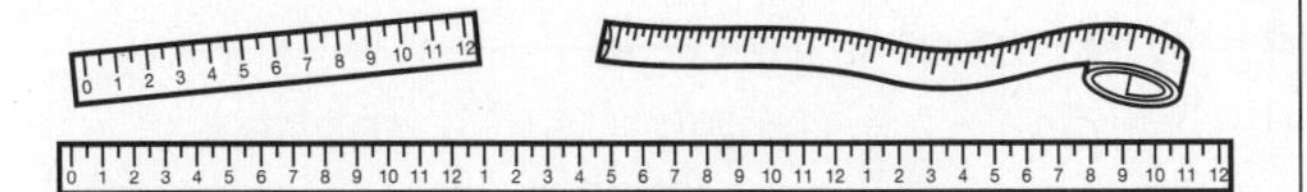

Mrs. Ramirez could use a ruler, a yardstick, or a measuring tape.

The part of the playground that Mrs. Ramirez is measuring is large, so she should use a yardstick or a measuring tape.

Which unit should she use?

Mrs. Ramirez could use inches, feet, yards, or miles.

The perimeter is not long enough to use miles. Yards and feet are longer than inches. Since the playground is big, yards or feet would be the best choice.

In **1** and **2**, circle the better tool for measuring the perimeter of each.

1. A room
Yardstick   Ruler

2. A curved window
Measuring tape   Yardstick

In **3** and **4**, circle the better unit for measuring the perimeter of each.

3. A photograph
Feet   Inches

4. A football field
Yards   Inches

In **5** and **6**, use the diagram. Circle the best answer.

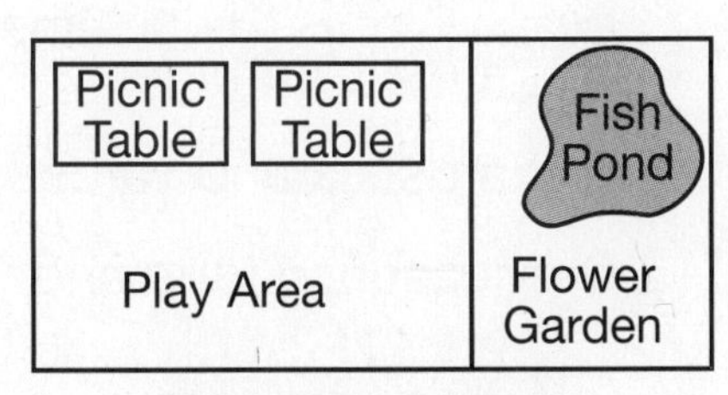

Main Street Park

5. Which is the better tool for measuring the distance around the edge of the fish pond?
Ruler   Measuring tape

6. Which is the better unit for measuring the perimeter of the play area?
Inches   Yards

7. Writing to Explain Why might you need to measure a perimeter with a measuring tape instead of a ruler?

____

____

Name ____________________

Practice 13-2

Tools and Units for Perimeter

In **1** and **2**, circle the better tool for measuring the perimeter of each.

1. A round clock
Yardstick   Measuring tape

2. A square classroom
Ruler   Yardstick

In **3** and **4**, circle the best unit for measuring the perimeter of each.

3. A parking lot
Yards   Inches   Miles

4. The top of your desk
Yards   Miles   Inches

In **5** and **6**, choose the best tool and unit from the list.

Tools
Measuring tape
Ruler
Yardstick

Units
Miles
Yards
Feet
Inches

5. Mrs. Lenz wants to put ribbon around the edge of a pillow. Which tool and unit should she use to measure the perimeter of the pillow?

____

6. Mr. Paz wants to put a fence around a baseball field. Which tool and unit should he use to measure the perimeter of the baseball field?

____

7. Which tool and unit is the best choice for measuring the perimeter of a picture on the wall?

A Ruler and inches
B Yardstick and feet
C Yardstick and yards
D Measuring tape and yards

8. Which of these units could NOT be used to measure the perimeter of a gymnasium?

A Feet
B Inches
C Miles
D Yards

9. How are a ruler, a yardstick, and a measuring tape the same? How are they different?

____

____

____

Name ___________________

Reteaching 13-3

Perimeter of Common Shapes

Use the properties of these common shapes to find the missing side lengths. Then find the perimeter.

Rectangle

Two pairs of sides have the same length.

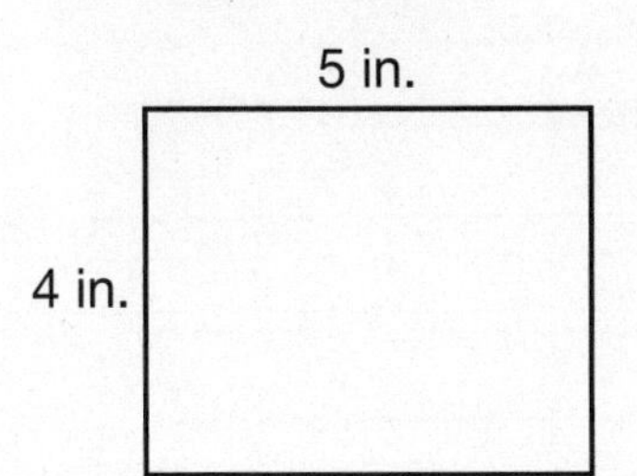

4 in. + 5 in. + 4 in. + 5 in. = 18 in.

Square

All 4 sides have the same length.

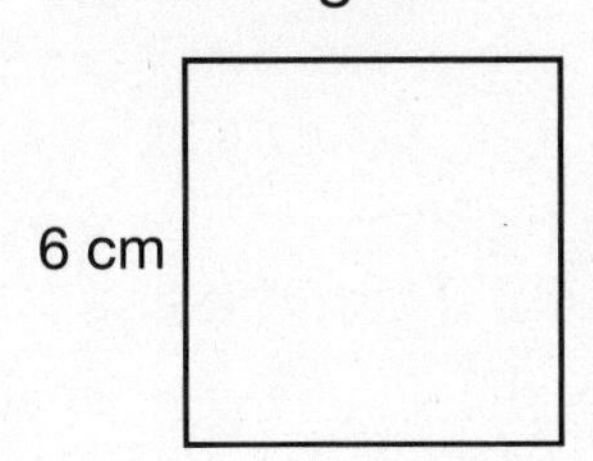

6 cm + 6 cm + 6 cm + 6 cm = 24 cm

Equilateral Triangle

All 3 sides have the same length.

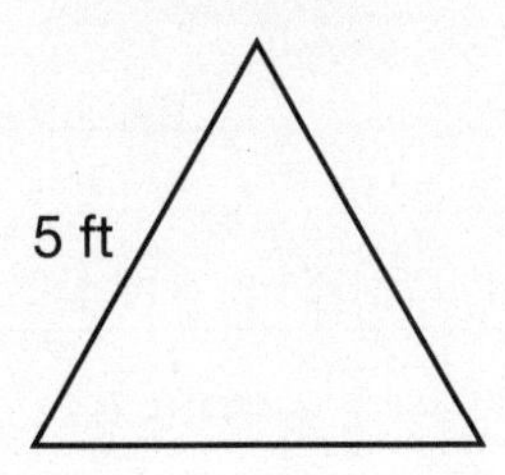

5 ft + 5 ft + 5 ft = 15 ft

Find the perimeter of each polygon.

1. 

3x4=12cm.

2. 4 cm, 2 cm

____

3. 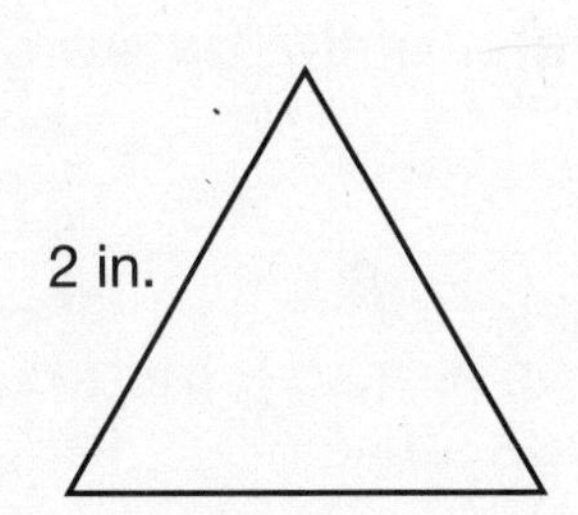

____

4. 6 ft, 5 ft

____

5. **Reason** Can two squares of different sizes have the same perimeter? Explain.

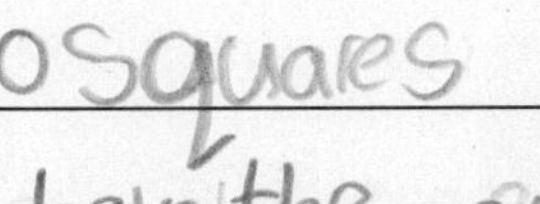
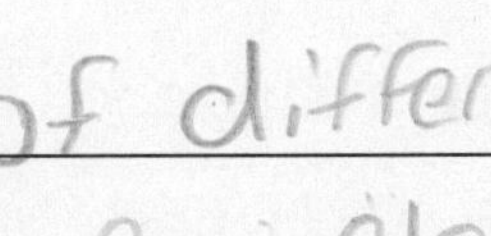
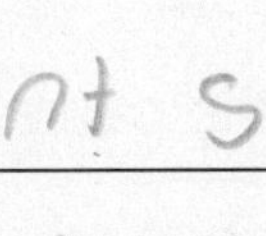
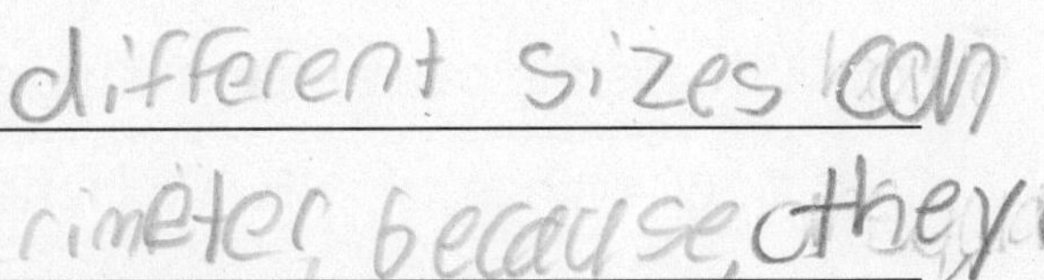

Yes, Two squares of different sizes can have not have the same perimeter, because they are different sizes.

Name ______________________

Perimeter of Common Shapes

Use an inch ruler to measure the length of the sides of each polygon. Find the perimeter.

1.

____

2.

____

Find the perimeter of each shape.

3.

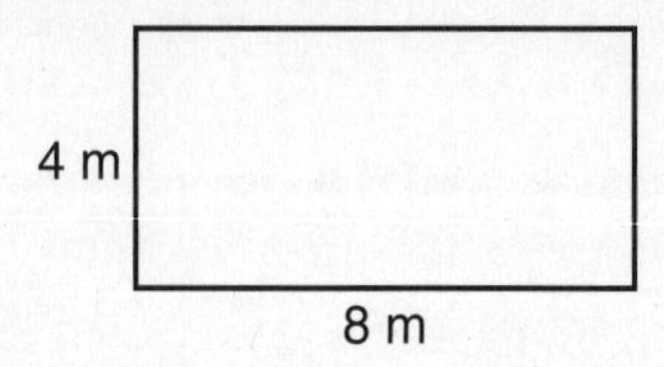

____

4.

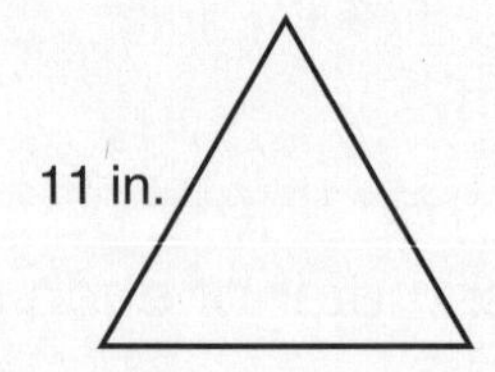

33 in.

5. The largest room in Lauren's house is shaped like a square with sides of 6 yards. What is the perimeter of that room?

____

6. The basketball court at Johnson Elementary School is in the shape of a rectangle. It is 92 feet long and 46 feet wide. What is the perimeter of the basketball court?

____

7. A square has 9-inch sides. Every side of a pentagon is also 9 inches long. Are their perimeters the same? Explain your answer.

No, because, a pentagon has more sides than a square.

8. What is the perimeter of a hexagon that has equal sides of 12 inches?

A 60 inches **B** 66 inches **C** 72 inches **D** 84 inches

Name ______________________________

Different Shapes with the Same Perimeter

Different shapes can have the same perimeter.

These shapes have the same perimeter.

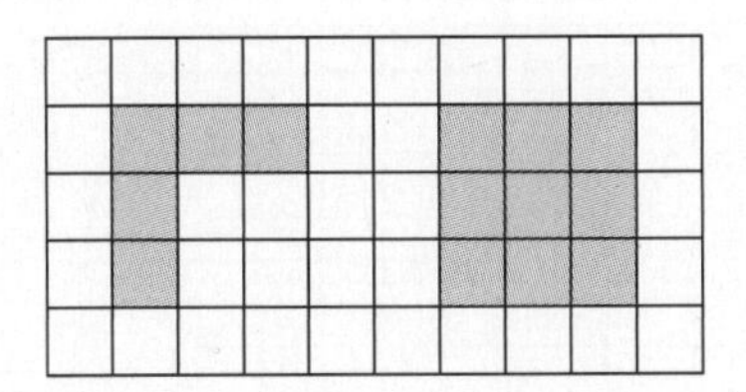

Both of these shapes have perimeters of 12 units.

Rectangles with different shapes can also have the same perimeter.

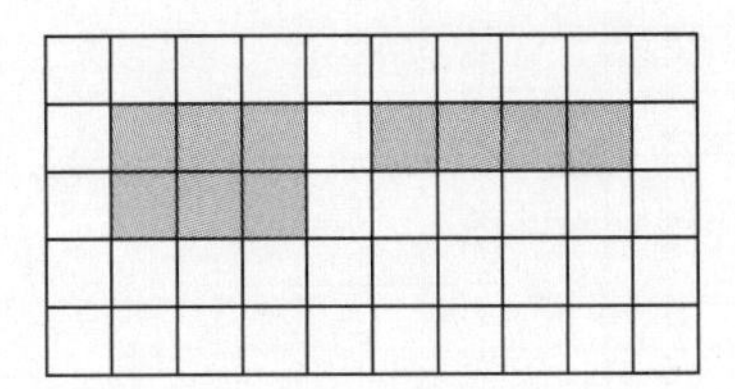

Both of these rectangles have perimeters of 10 units.

Draw a figure with each perimeter.

1. 8 units

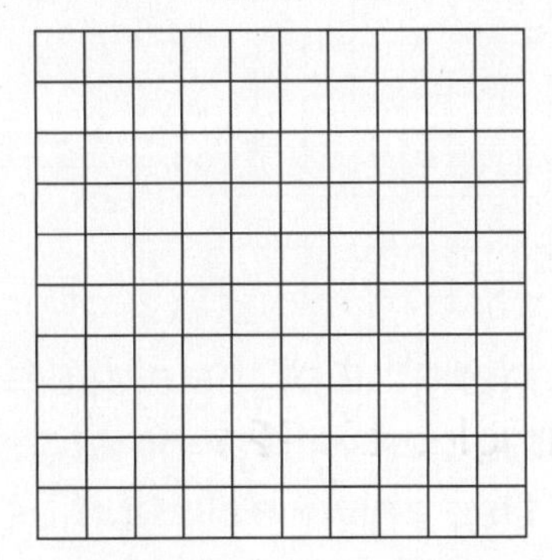

2. 12 units

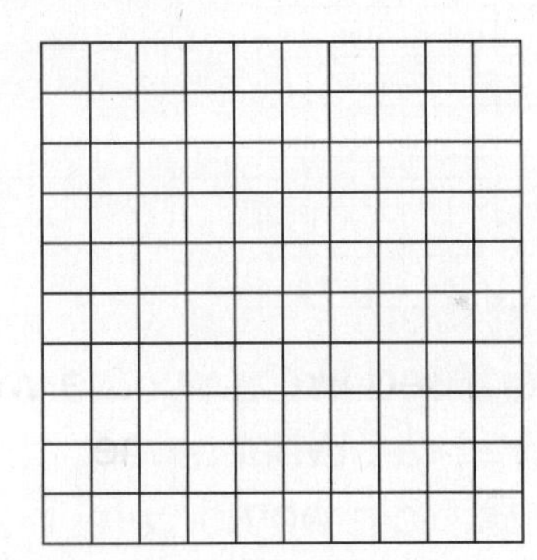

3. 10 units

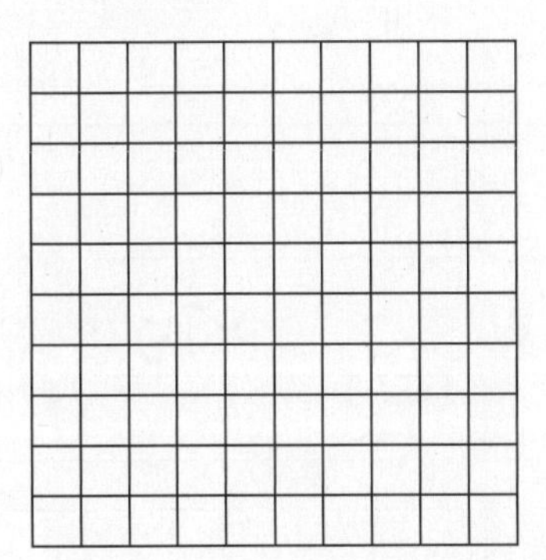

4. 14 units

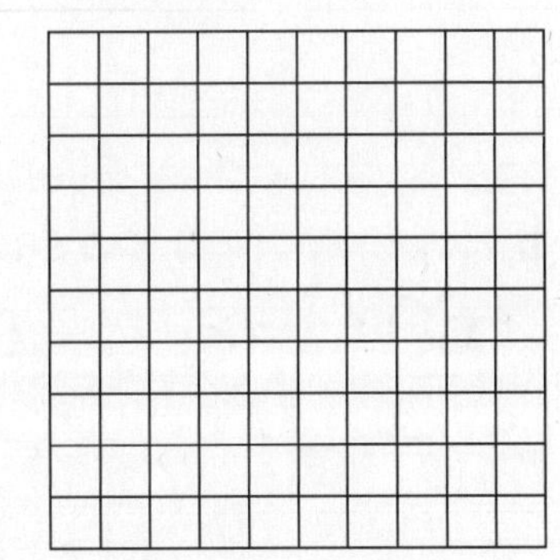

5. Name the lengths of the sides of three rectangles that have perimeters of 14 units. Use only whole numbers.

____

Name ______________________

Practice **13-4**

Different Shapes with the Same Perimeter

Draw a figure with the given perimeter on the grid paper.

1. 10 units

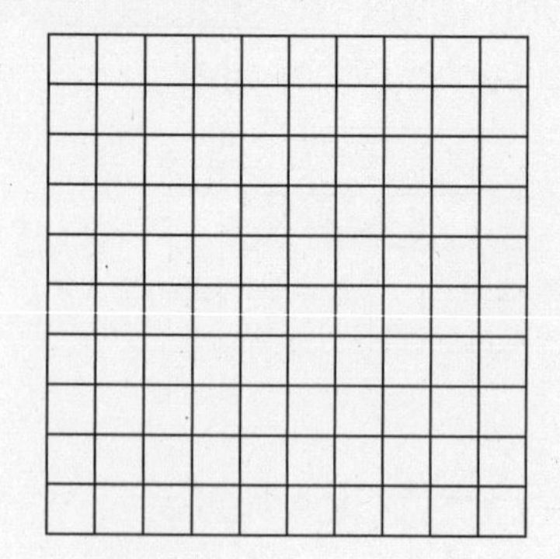

2. 16 units

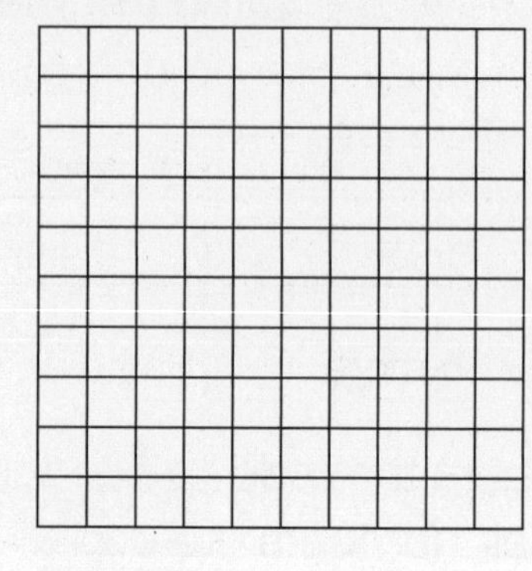

3. 14 units

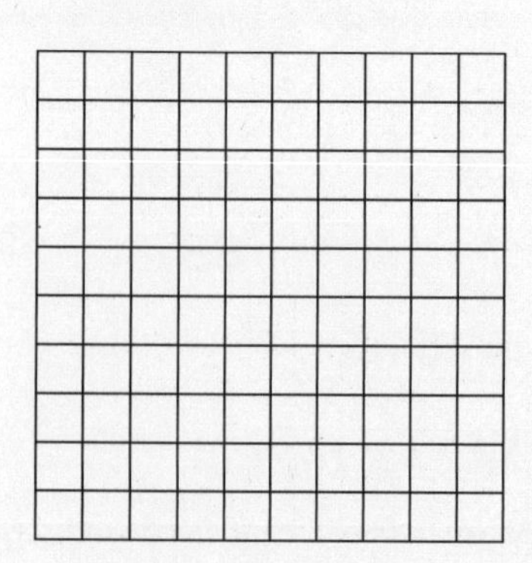

4. 18 units

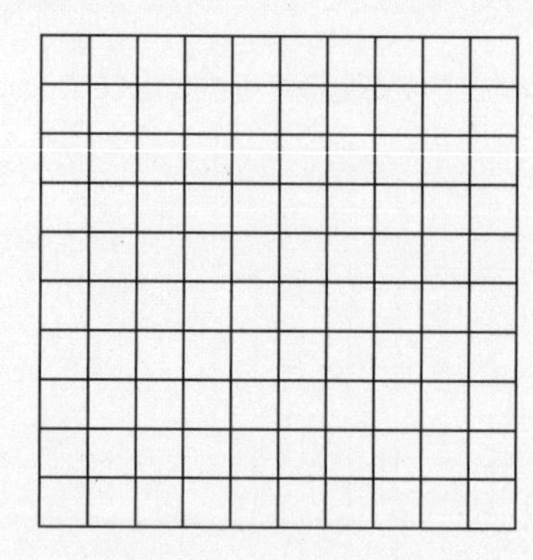

5. Writing to Explain Can you draw a square with a perimeter of 20 units? Explain why or why not.

____

____

____

6. Name the lengths of the sides of three rectangles with perimeters of 12 units. Use only whole numbers.

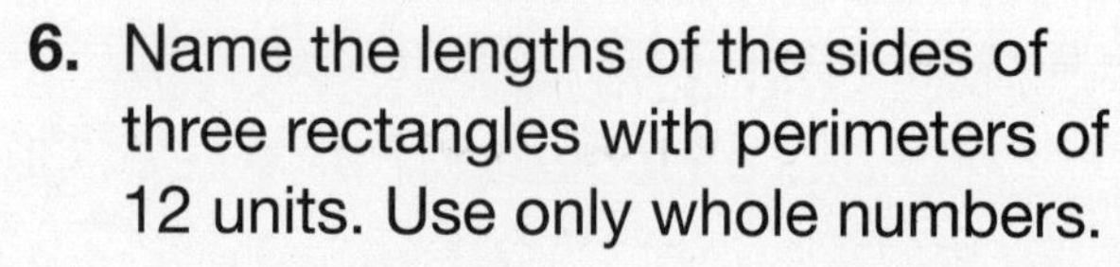

____

____

____

7. Which figures have the same perimeter?

A

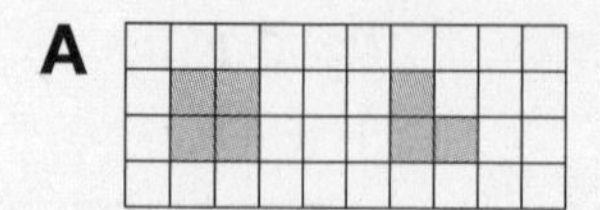

C

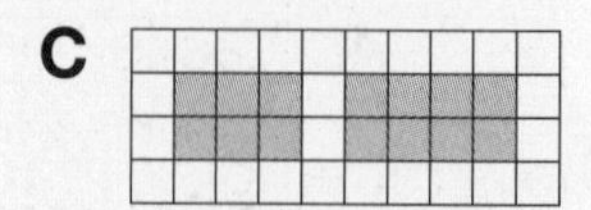

B

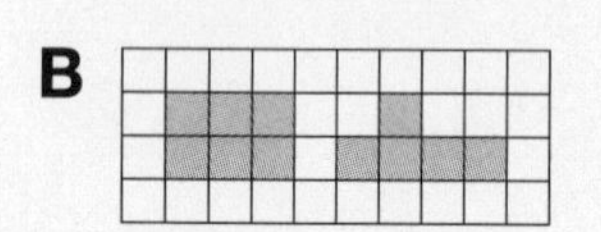

D

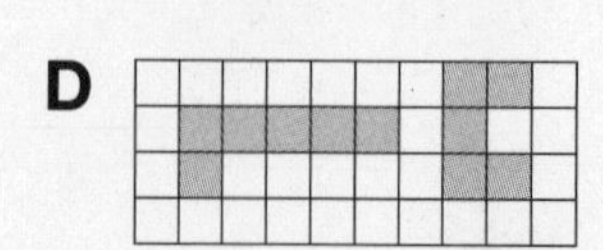

Name ____________________

Problem Solving: Try, Check, and Revise

Bryce, Julie, and Katie saved a total of $50 to buy a gift for their mother. Julie and Katie saved the same amount of money. Bryce saved $5 more. How much money did Bryce save?

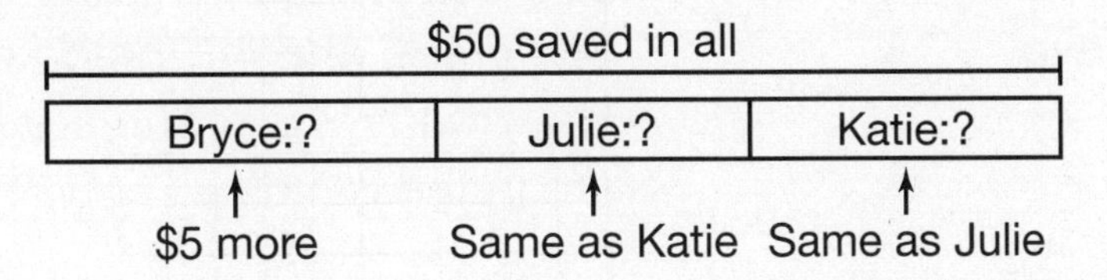

Try three numbers that add to 50. Julie and Katie saved the same amount, so their numbers are equal. Bryce's amount is $5 more.

Try #1

Try: $15 + $10 + $10 = $35

Check: $35 is too low.

You need $15 more.

Try #2

Revise by adding $5 more for each person.

Try: $20 + $15 + $15 = $50

Check: This is correct.

Bryce saved $20 for the gift.

1. Ben and Cole have 36 airplane models all together. Ben has 8 more than Cole. How many airplane models does Ben have?

   ____

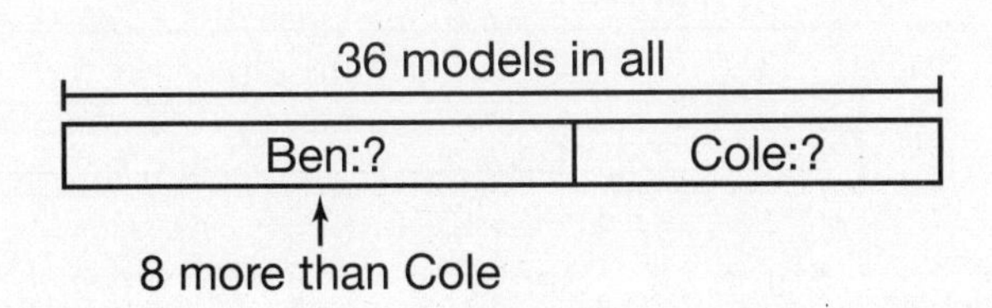

2. Jan, Mya, and Sara ran a total of 64 miles last week. Jan and Mya ran the same number of miles. Sara ran 8 less miles than Mya. How many miles did Sara run?

   ____

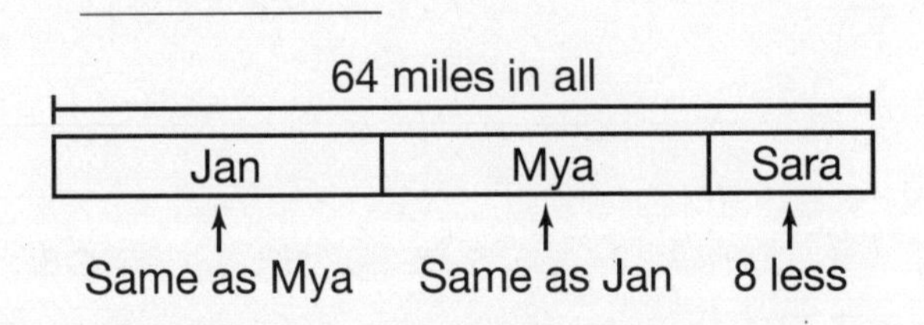

3. Sven is thinking of two numbers. The sum is 12. The difference is 4. What are the two numbers?

   ____

4. Lee is thinking of two numbers. The product is 18. The quotient is 2. What are the two numbers?

   ____

Name ______________________

Practice
13-5

Problem Solving: Try, Check, and Revise

1. Carly and Rob combined their DVD collections. Now they have 42 DVDs all together. Carly had 4 more DVDs than Rob. How many DVDs did Carly have?

____

42 DVDs in all

Carly:?	Rob:?

↑ 4 more than Rob

2. There are 33 students in the band. There are 6 more 5th-grade students than 3rd-grade students. There is an equal number of 3rd-grade and 4th-grade students. How many 3rd-grade students are in the band?

____

33 students in all

3rd:?	4th:?	5th:?
↑ Same as Grade 4	↑ Same as Grade 3	↑ 6 more than Grade 3

3. Dave delivered 52 newspapers in all on Saturday and Sunday. He delivered 8 more newspapers on Sunday than on Saturday. How many newspapers did Dave deliver on Sunday? Explain how you solved.

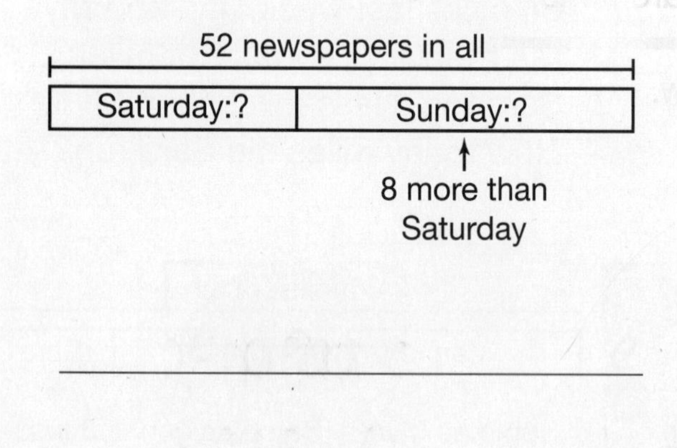

____

____

____

4. There are 24 students in Ms. Messing's class. Six more students walk to school than ride their bikes. The number of students who ride their bikes is the same as the number of students who are driven to school. How many students walk to school?

____

24 students in all

Driven:?	Bike:?	Walk:?
↑ Same as Bike	↑ Same as Driven	↑ 6 more than Bike

5. Jill is thinking of two numbers. They have a sum of 27 and a difference of 7. What are the two numbers?

A 27 and 7 **B** 20 and 7 **C** 15 and 12 **D** 17 and 10

Name ______________________

Covering Regions

Area is the number of square units used to cover a region.

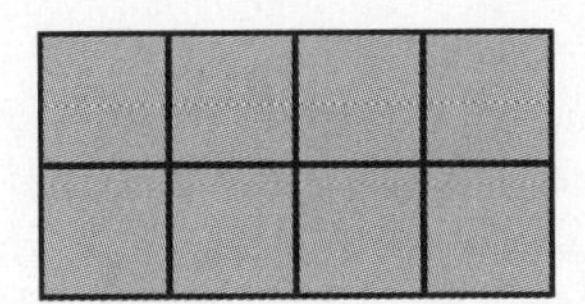

In the shape above, you can find the exact area by counting the number of square units that make up the rectangle.

There are 8 squares in the shape.

So, the area of the shape is 8 square units.

Sometimes you can estimate the area.

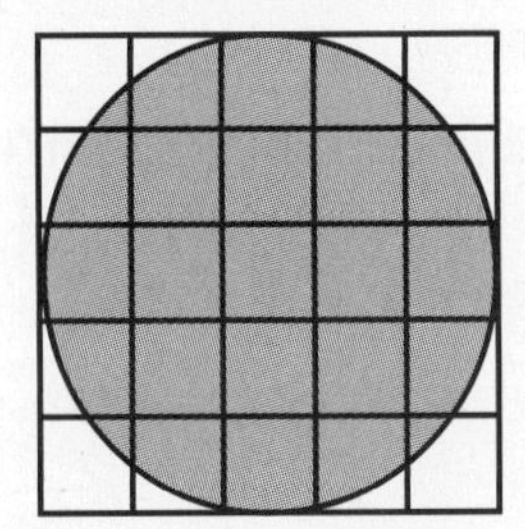

There are about 20 squares in the shape.

So, the area of the shape is about 20 square units.

Count to find the area of the shapes below.
Tell if the area is exact or an estimate.

1.

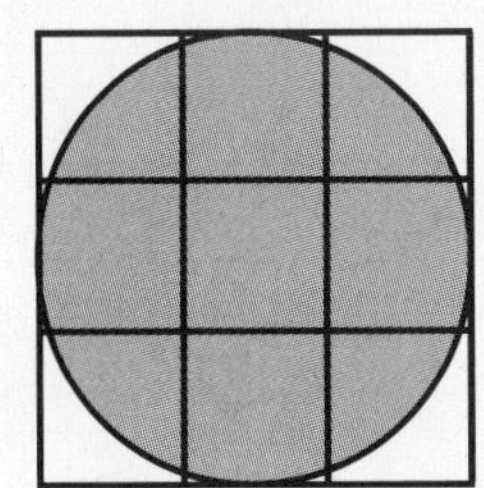

____

____

2.

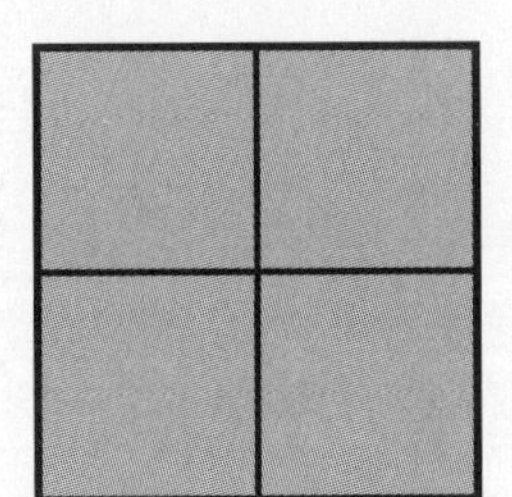

____

____

3.

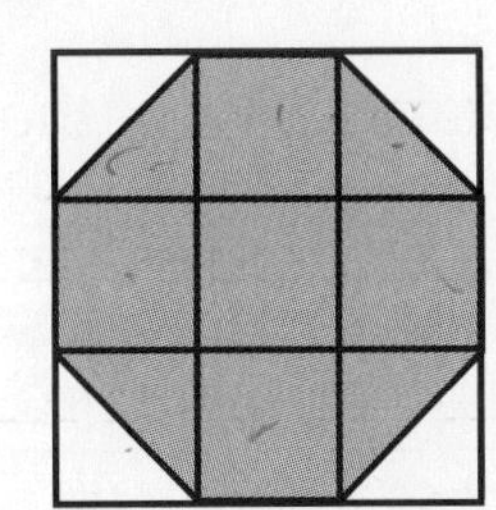

7 squareunits.
estimate

Name ____________________

Covering Regions

For **1** through **4**, use the diagram below.

Athletic Field

Soccer
Baseball
Tennis
Empty

1. What is the area of the soccer section of the field? ____________________

2. What is the area of the field that is NOT being used? ____________________

3. How many square units of the field are being used? ____________________

4. If the school used the soccer and baseball fields to build a football stadium, how large could the area of the stadium be?

____

5. What is the area of the shaded section?

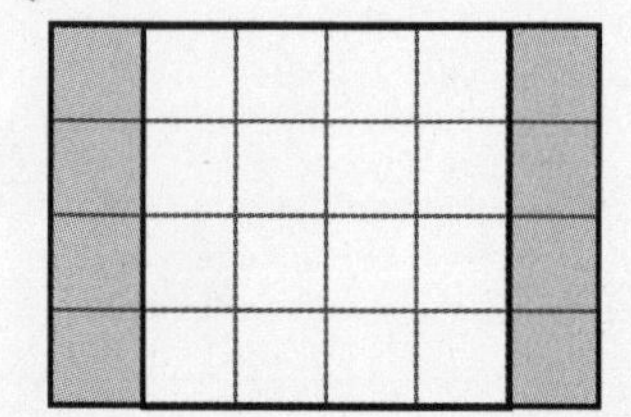

A 16 square units **B** 12 square units **C** 8 square units **D** 4 square units

6. What is the area of the hexagon shown below? Explain.

The area of the hexagon is 4 square units, because there are 2 full squares and 4 half squares and, if you add 2 halves it equals 1 full square so since 4 ÷ 2 = 2 the half squares equal 2. So 2+2=4 square units.

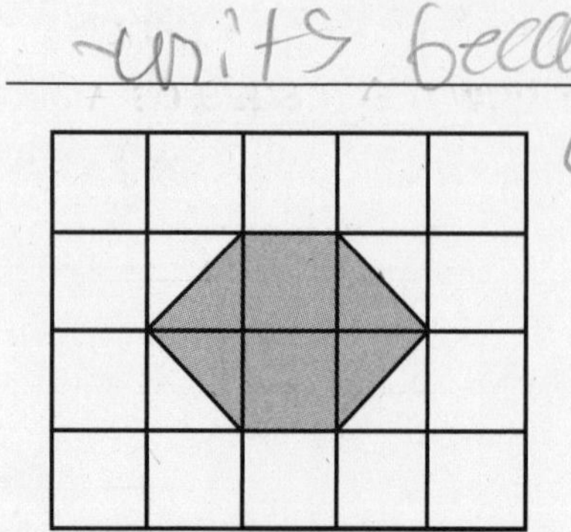

Name ____________________

Area and Units

A square unit is a square with sides that are each 1 unit long.

□ = 1 square unit

The number of square units needed to cover the region inside a figure is its area.

Pam wants to make flash cards for her study group. She wants each flash card to have an area of 15 square units. Should she use square centimeters or square inches as a unit?

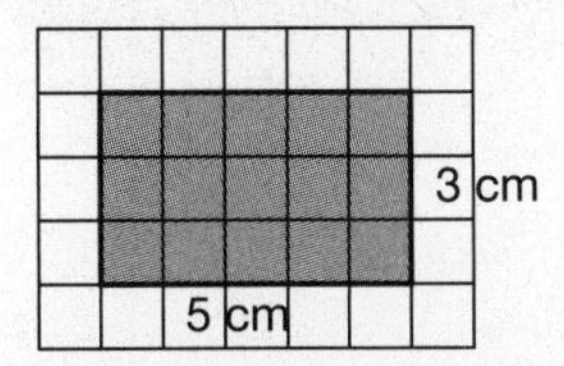

□ = 1 square centimeter

A square centimeter is a square that has a length of 1 cm on each side. If Pam uses square centimeters the area would be 15 square centimeters. That seems too small for a flash card.

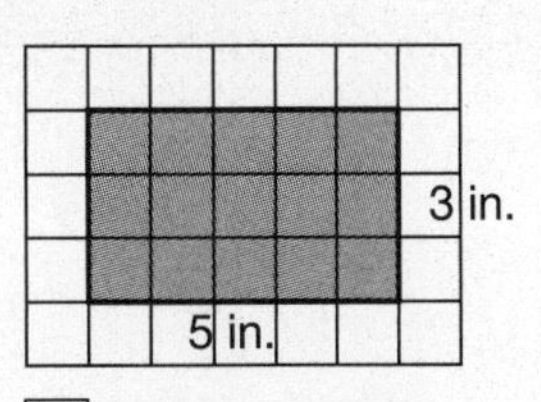

□ = 1 square inch

A square inch is a square that has a length of 1 inch on each side. If Pam uses square inches the area would be 15 square inches. That seems a reasonable size for a flash card.

Pam should use square inches as the unit.

What is the area of each figure shown below?

1.

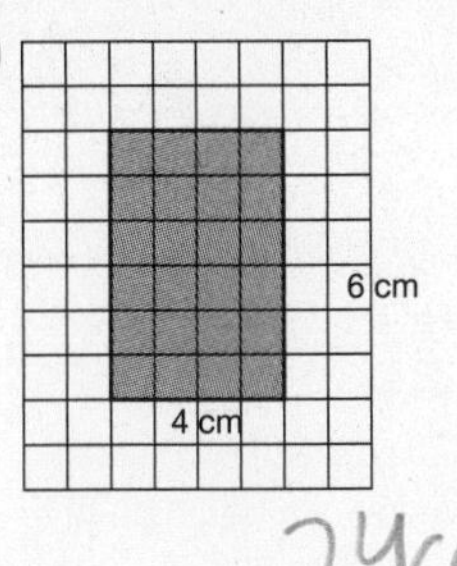

24cm

2.

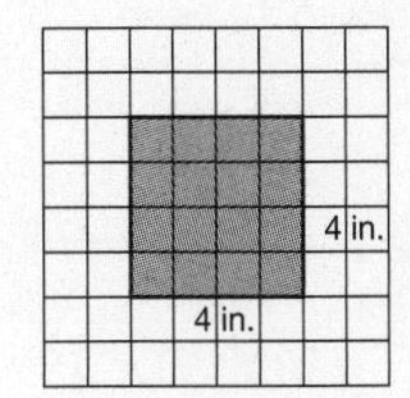

____

3. Is the area of a paperback book cover closer to 28 square inches or 28 square centimeters? Tell how you decided.

A paper back book cover is closer to 28 square inches I decided that because inches in bigger than cm.

4. Maria wants to draw a painting with an area of 40 square inches. If she drew her painting on 1-inch grid paper how many squares would the painting cover? Tell how you know.

____

____

Name ______________________________

Area and Units

1. Use a ruler to draw a figure with an area of 3 square centimeters.

2. Which of these figures has an area of 16 square inches?

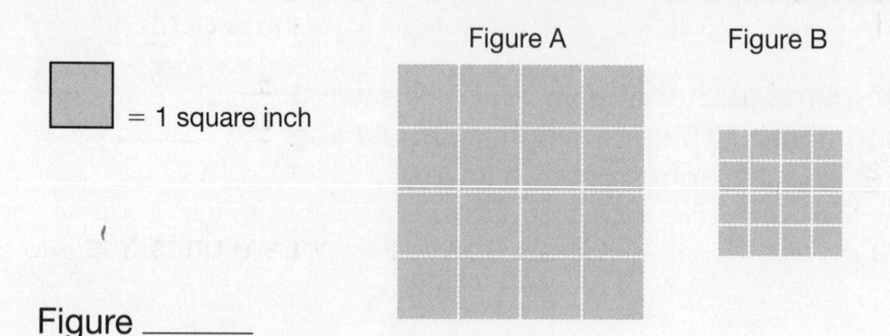

Figure ______

3. **Draw a Picture** Maya made a sign with an area of 48 square centimeters. Use centimeter grid paper to draw a shape that shows what her sign could look like.

4. Suppose Maya made another sign with an area of 48 square inches. Would this sign be larger or smaller than the sign with an area of 48 square centimeters? Explain how you know.

____

____

____

5. What is the area of this figure in square centimeters?

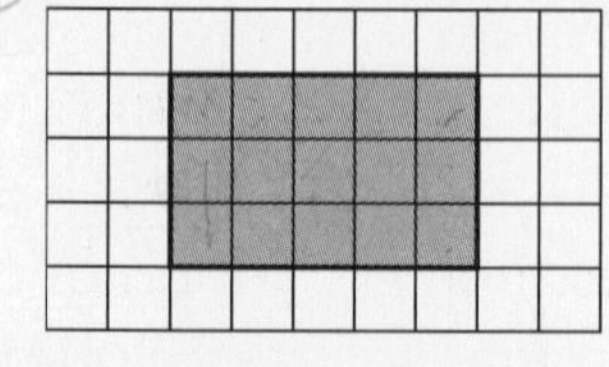

☐ = 1 square centimeter

A 12 **B** 14 **C** 15 **D** 17

Name ___ 6 ✓

Standard Units

You can use the standard units of length shown below to measure area.

Customary Units of Length

Unit	Square Unit
inch (in.)	square inch
foot (ft)	square foot
yard (yd)	square yard
mile (mi)	square mile

Metric Units of Length

Unit	Square Unit
centimeter (cm)	square centimeter
meter (m)	square meter
kilometer (km)	square kilometer

Count how many square units this figure covers.

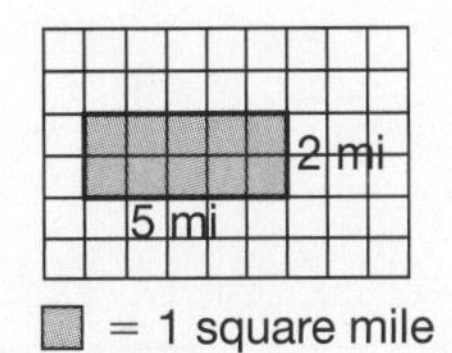

■ = 1 square mile

- The figure covers 10 square units.
- Each unit equals 1 square mile.

The area of the figure is 10 square miles.

Count how many square units this figure covers.

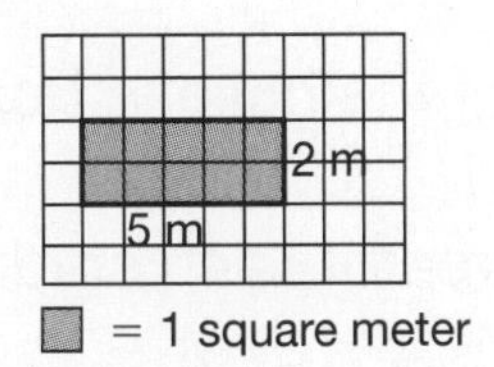

■ = 1 square meter

- The figure covers 10 square units.
- Each unit equals 1 square meter.

The area of the figure is 10 square meters.

For **1** through **3**, count the square units. Then write the area.

1.

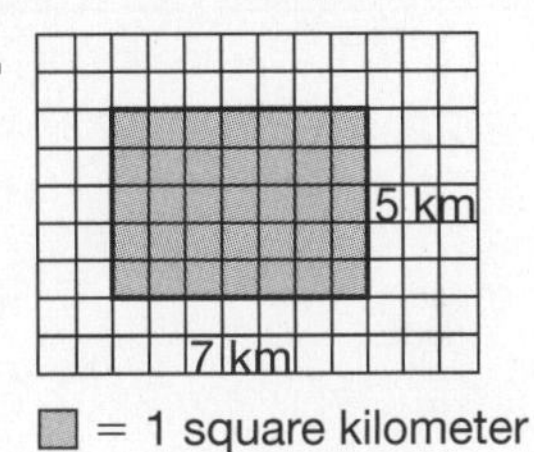

■ = 1 square kilometer

2.

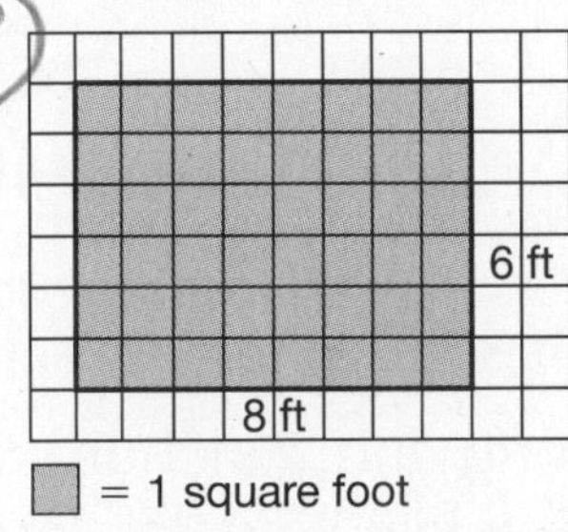

■ = 1 square foot

3.

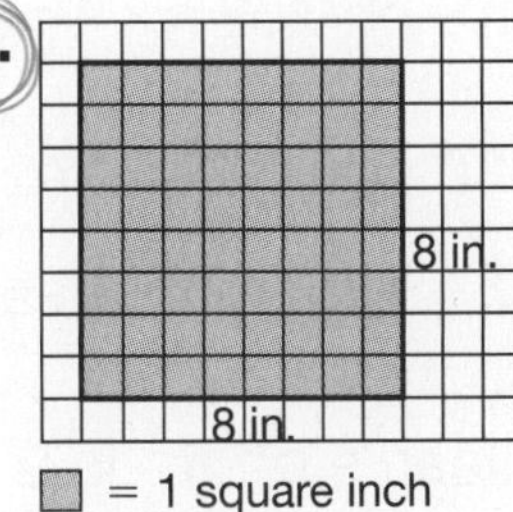

■ = 1 square inch

___ 48 Ft. ___ 68 In.

___ ___ ___

4. Use Tools Use grid paper to show how to find the area of a garden that measures 6 feet by 4 feet.

6X4=24Ft.

Name ____________________

Practice
14-3

Standard Units

For **1** through **3**, count the square units. Then write the area.

1.

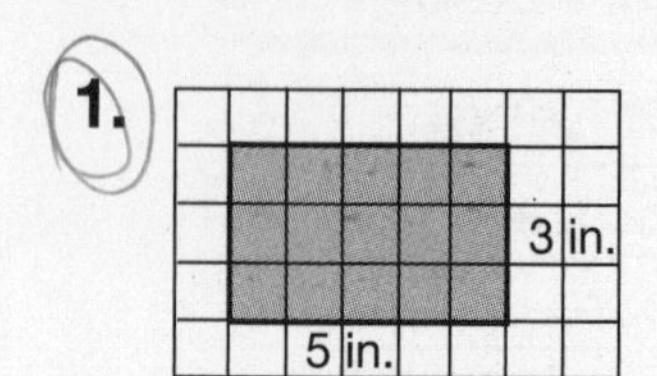

15 in.

2.

5 mi
5 mi

25 mi

3.

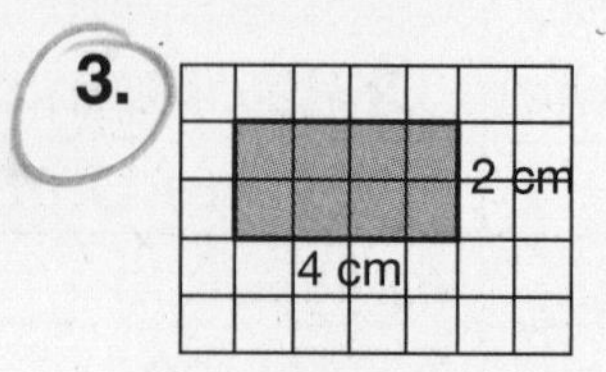

8 Square cm

Use the diagram of the bulletin board for **4** through **6**.

4. What is the area of each student's photo?

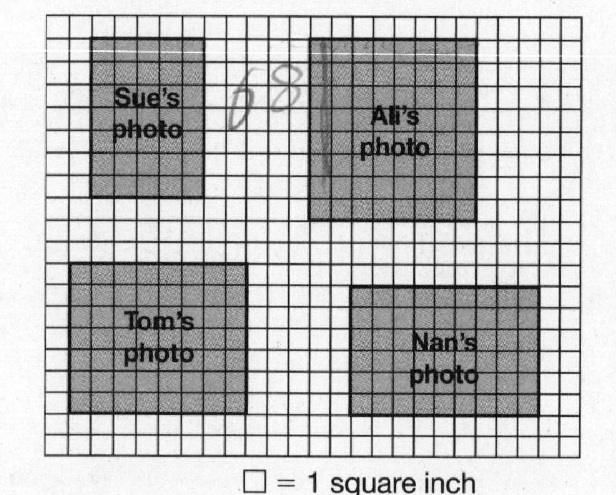

☐ = 1 square inch

5. What is the area of Sue's photo and Tom's photo?

A 80 square inches

B 81 square inches

C 90 square inches

D 91 square inches

6. Colleen's photo is 9 inches long and 7 inches wide. Is it larger or smaller than Ali's photo? Explain how you know.

Colleen's photo is smaller than Ali's photo because 9x7=63 and 8x8=68 and 68 is bigger than 63.

Name ______________________

Area of Squares and Rectangles

What is the area of this rectangle?

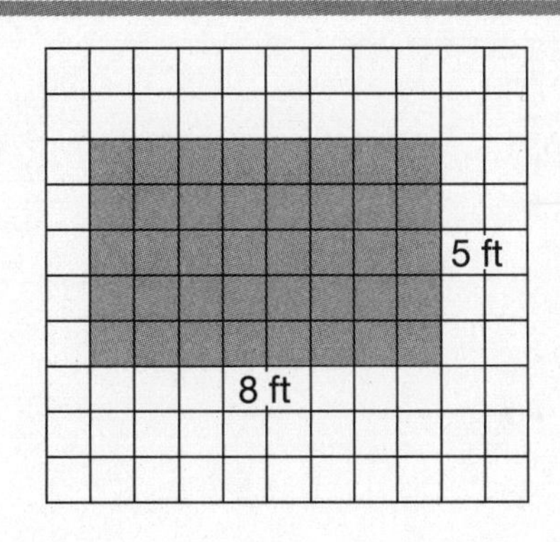

Use the formula $A = \ell \times w$:

$A = 8 \times 5$

$A = 40$

The area is 40 square feet.

What is the area of this figure?

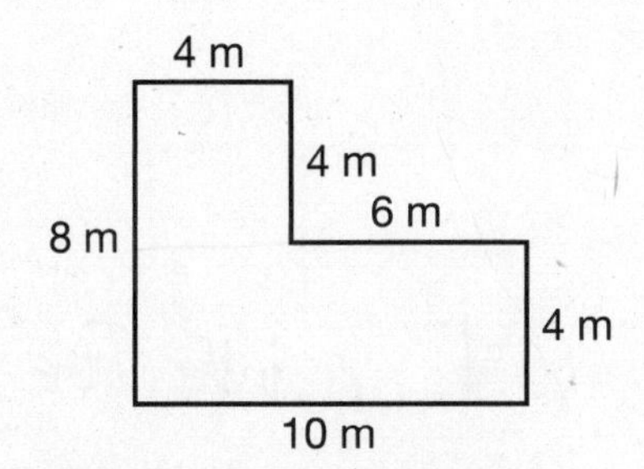

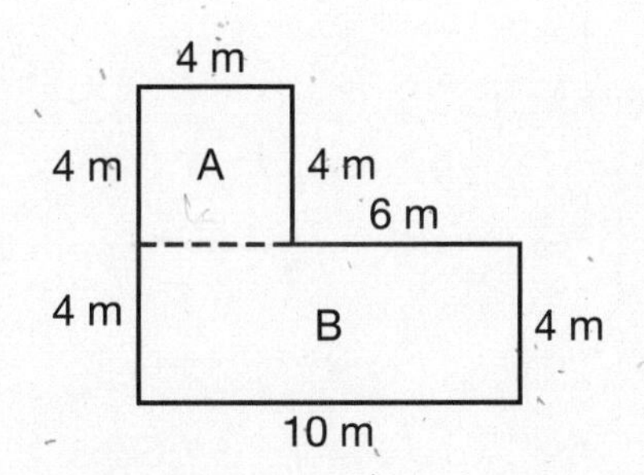

You can draw segments to divide the figure into rectangles. Then find the area of each rectangle and add.

Rectangle A	Rectangle B
$A = \ell \times w$	$A = \ell \times w$
$A = 4 \times 4$	$A = 4 \times 10$
$= 16$	$= 40$

$16 + 40 = 56$, so the area of the original figure is 56 square meters.

Find the area of each figure.

1.

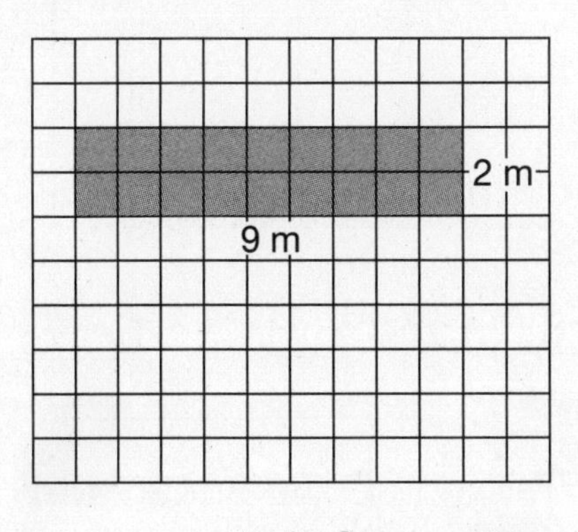

____

2.

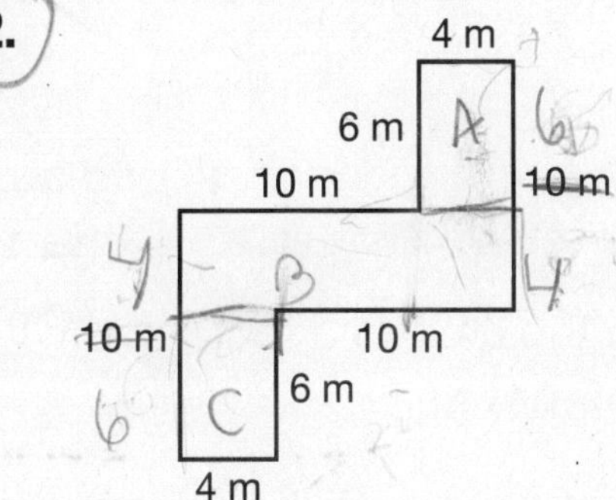

____

3. Reason The area of a rectangle is 56 square inches. The width of the rectangle is 7 in. What is the length? ______________________

Name ____________________

Practice 14-4

Area of Squares and Rectangles

Find the area of each figure.

1.

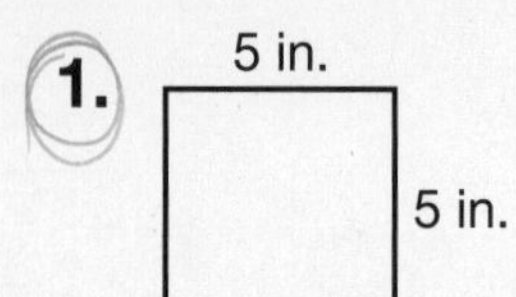

25 in.

2.

5 ft

9 ft

3.

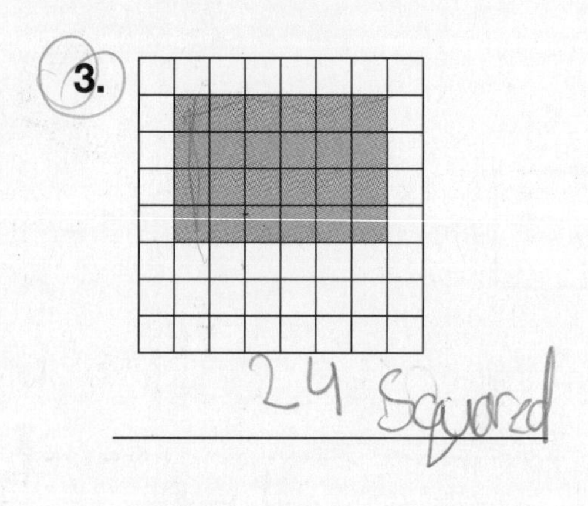

24 Squared

4.

8 cm

2 cm

5. What is the area of one bedroom?

____

6. What is the area of the garage?

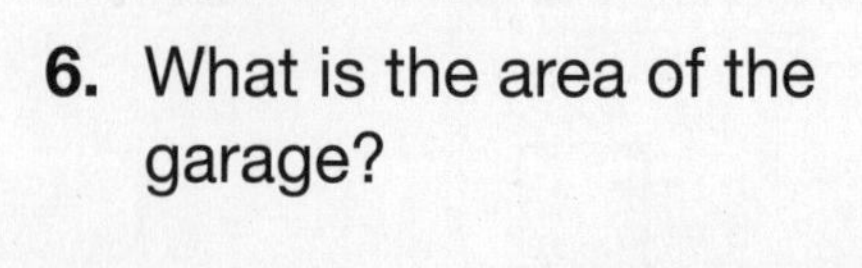

____

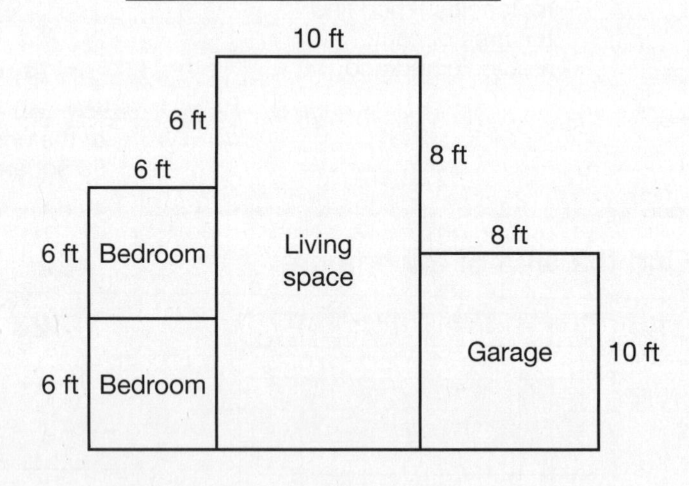

7. Which is the area of a rectangle with a length of 6 cm and a width of 9 cm?

A 63 square cm **B** 54 square cm **C** 45 square cm **D** 36 square cm

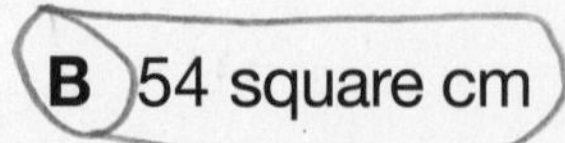

8. Writing to Explain Explain how you would find the length of one side of a square if the area is 16 square units.

Find the half of 16.

Name ______________________________

Area and the Distributive Property

Suppose you separate a rectangle into two smaller rectangles. The area of the large rectangle is equal to the sum of the areas of the two small rectangles. You can use the Distributive Property to break apart facts to find the product.

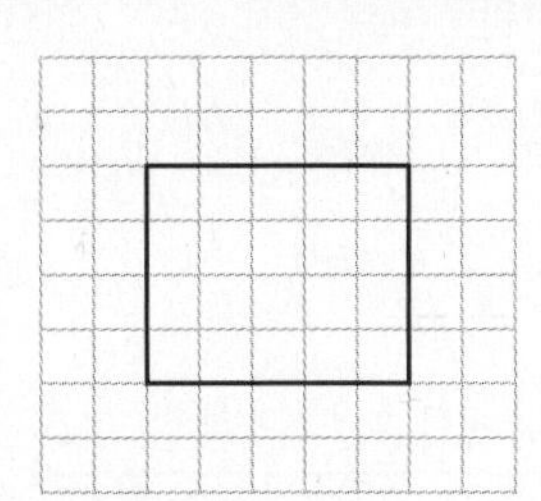 Write the multiplication fact that represents the area of the large rectangle. $4 \times 5 = 20$	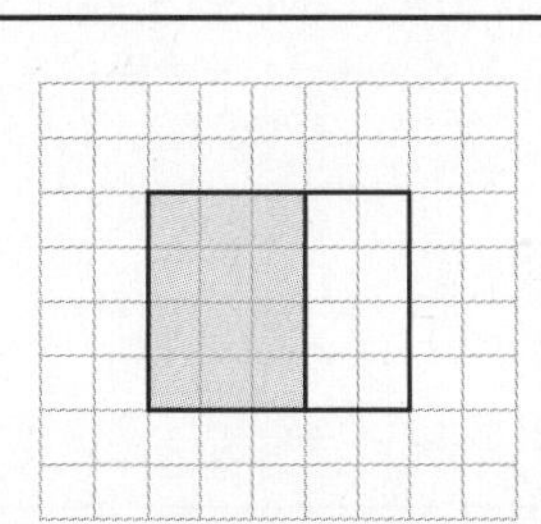 Write multiplication facts that represent the areas of each of the smaller rectangles. $4 \times 3 = 12$ $4 \times 2 = 8$ $12 + 8 = 20$

You can write an equation to show that the area of the large rectangle is equal to the sum of the areas of the two small rectangles.

$4 \times 5 = 4 \times (3 + 2) = (4 \times 3) + (4 \times 2)$

Write the equation that represents the picture.

1. 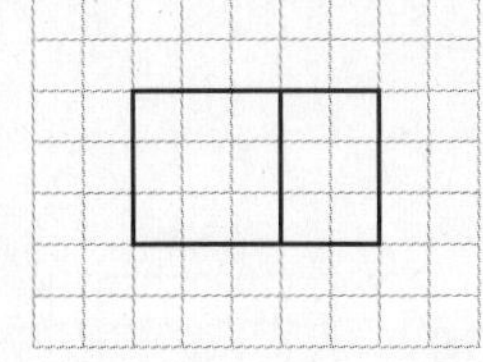

$\underline{\ 3\ } \times \underline{\quad} = \underline{\quad} \times (\underline{\ 2\ } + \underline{\quad}) =$

$(\underline{\ 3\ } \times \underline{\quad}) + (\underline{\quad} \times \underline{\ 3\ })$

2. 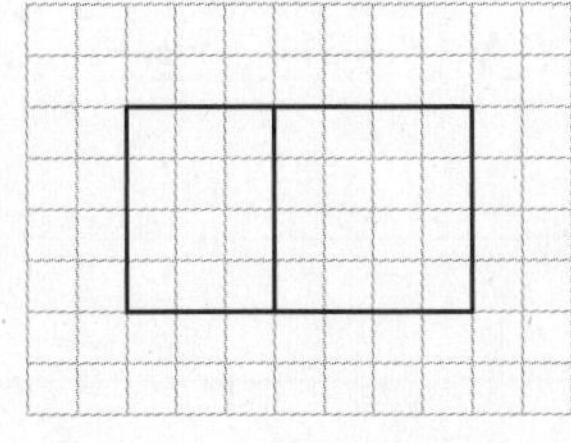

$\underline{\quad} \times \underline{\ 7\ } = \underline{\quad} \times (\underline{\quad} + \underline{\ 4\ }) =$

$(\underline{\quad} \times \underline{\ 3\ }) + (\underline{\ 4\ } \times \underline{\quad})$

Name ______________________________

Practice
14-5

Area and the Distributive Property

Write the equation that represents the picture.

1.

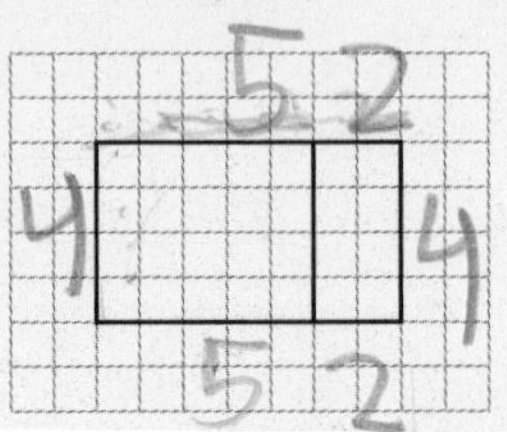

____

____

2.

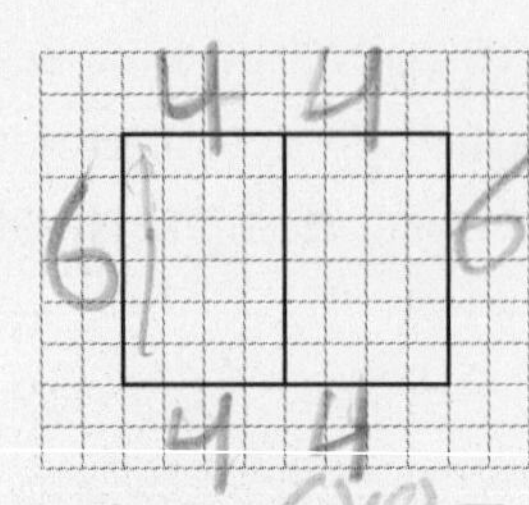

____

____

3.

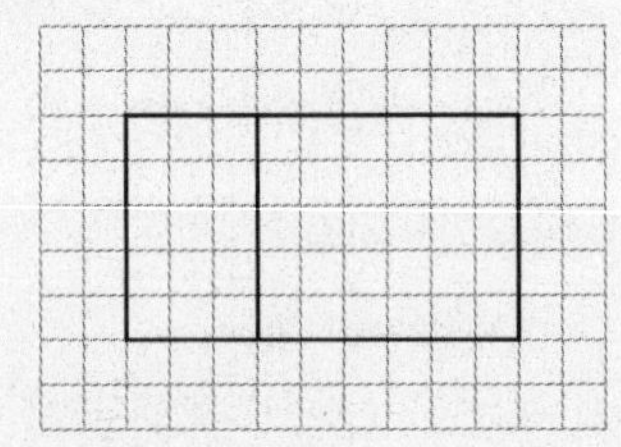

____

____

Choose the picture the equation represents.

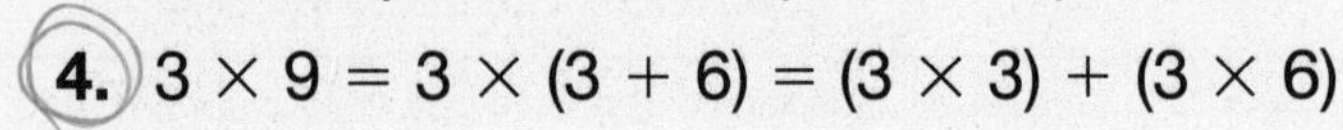

4. $3 \times 9 = 3 \times (3 + 6) = (3 \times 3) + (3 \times 6)$

A

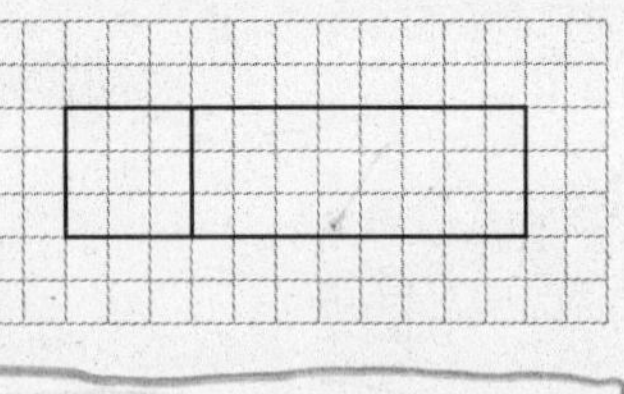

C

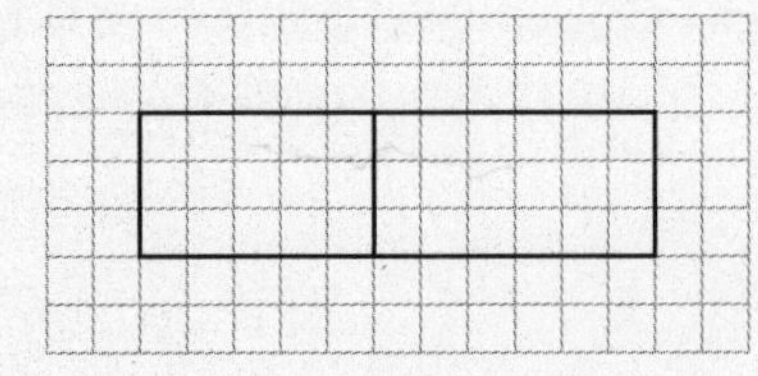

B

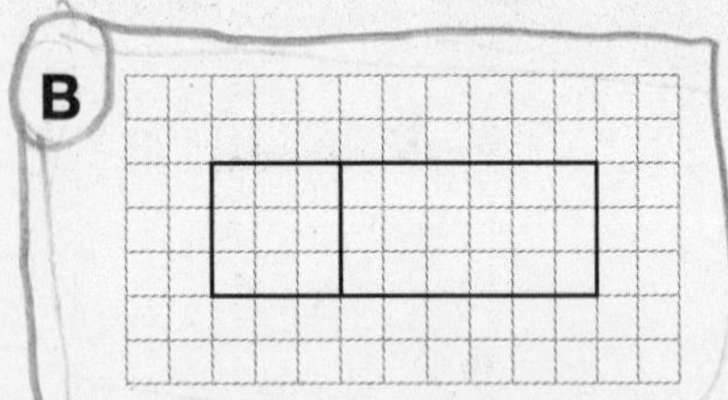

D

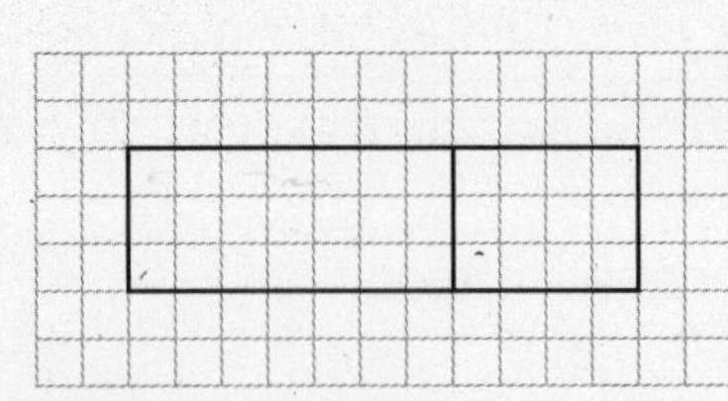

5. Reason Lee wants to cut this piece of canvas into two rectangles that are 3×2 and 3×5. He wants the sum of the areas of the two small rectangles to be the same as the area of the large rectangle. Can he do this? Explain.

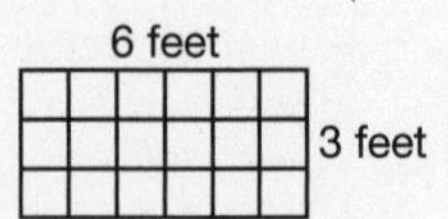

____

____

____

Name ______________________

Problem Solving: Solve a Simpler Problem

How can you find the area of the shaded figure to the right?

Think of a simpler problem to solve that will help you find the answer.

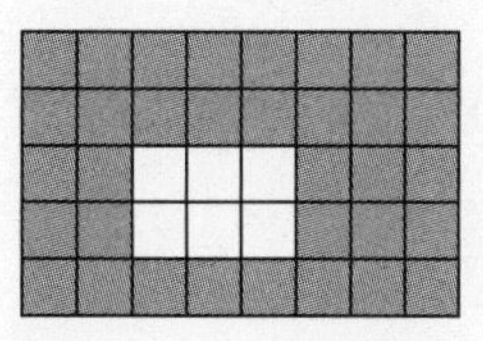

= 1 square inch

Find the area of the whole rectangle. $5 \times 8 = 40$

Find the area of the small rectangle. $2 \times 3 = 6$

Subtract to find the area of the shaded part. 40 sq in. − 6 sq in. = 34 sq in.

The area of the shaded figure is 34 square inches.

Solve. Use simpler problems.

1. Tyler High School has a T painted on the football field. The shaded part of the figure is the part that needs to be painted. What is the area of the painted part?

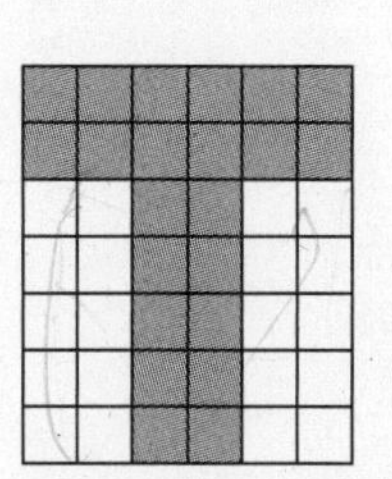

= 1 square meter

2. Maria is tiling one of the walls in her kitchen. The shaded part of the figure is the part that needs to be tiled. What is the area of the part that needs tiling?

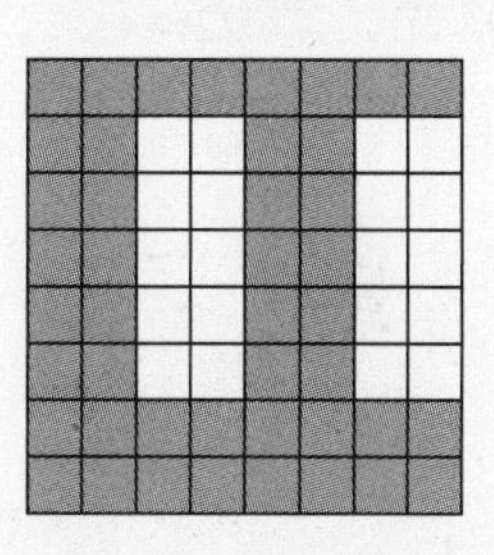

= 1 square yard

____

3. **Communicate** Explain how you found your answer for Exercise 2.

____

____

Name ______________________________

Practice
14-6

Problem Solving: Solve a Simpler Problem

Solve. Use simpler problems.

1. Ms. Finn is going to tile her kitchen floor. The shaded part of the figure is the part that needs to be tiled. What is the area of the shaded part?

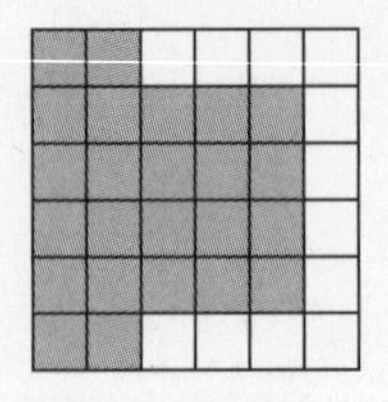

□ = 1 square yard

____

2. Alice is going to paint one of the walls in her bedroom. The shaded part of the figure is the part that needs to be painted. What is the area of the shaded part?

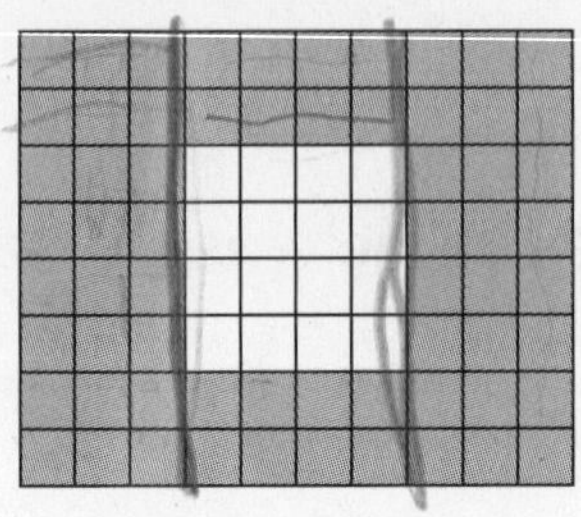

□ = 1 square foot

64 Square Feet X

3. Harrison High School has an H painted on the football field. The shaded part of the figure is the part that needs to be painted. What is the area of the shaded part?

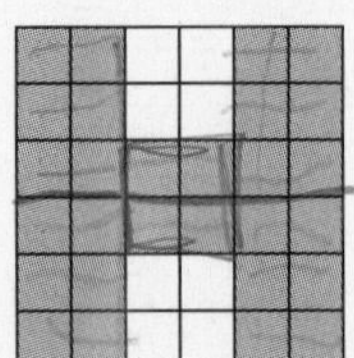

□ = 1 square meter

✓ 28 Square meters

4. Mr. Rosen is going to repair the tiles in a shower. The shaded part of the figure is the part that needs to be tiled. What is the area of the shaded part?

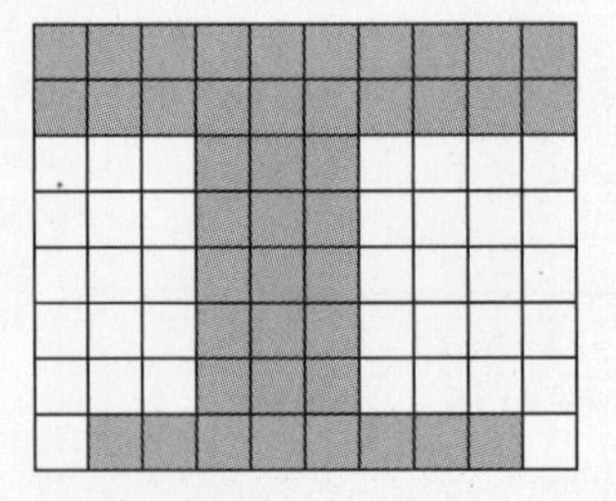

□ = 1 square foot

____

5. Luann is going to paint an L on her fence. The shaded part of the figure is the part that needs to be painted. What is the area of the shaded part?

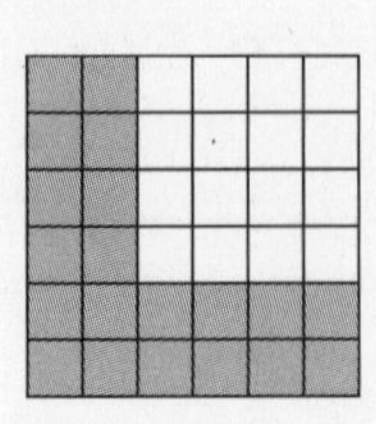

□ = 1 square inch

____

Name ____________________

Area of Irregular Shapes

To estimate the area of an irregular shape, you can add squares on a grid, or you can subtract squares from a larger area.

Adding Squares

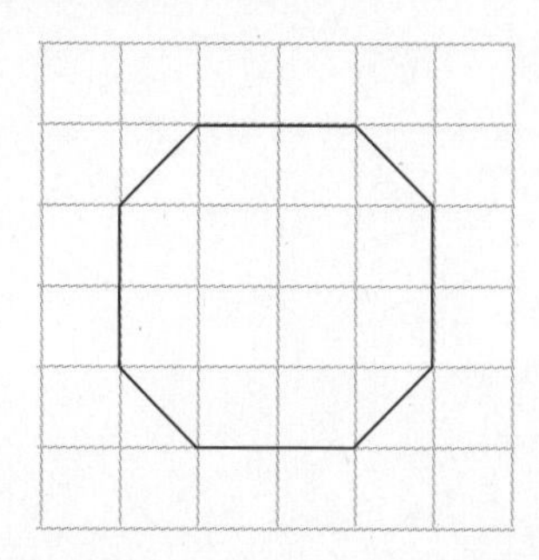

First, count the number of whole squares. There are 12 whole squares.

Then count the partial squares. There are 4 partial squares.

Estimate how many whole squares the partial squares would equal. They equal about 2 whole squares.

Finally, add the whole squares and the estimate for the partial squares to find the total estimated area.

$12 + 2 = 14$. The area is about 14 square units.

Subtract from a Larger Area

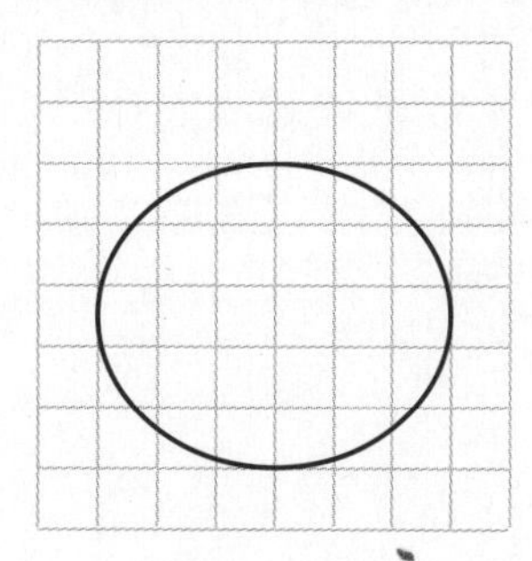

First, find the area of a regular shape that is larger than the irregular shape.

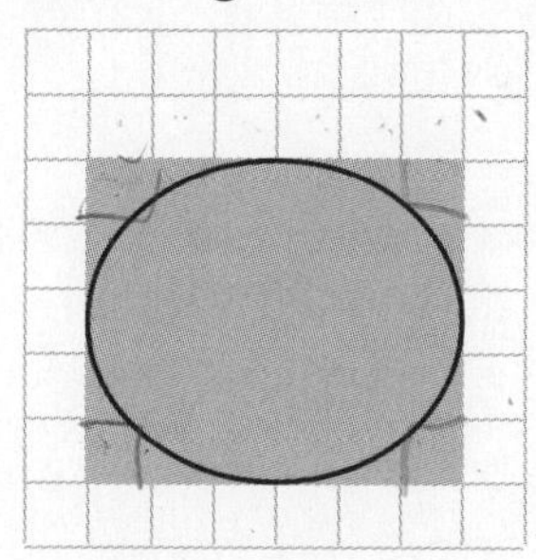

The gray rectangle has an area of 30 square units.

Subtract the squares that are not part of the irregular shape. There is about 1 square subtracted at each corner, so subtract 4 squares.

$30 - 4 = 26$. The area is about 26 square units.

Find the area of each shape.

1.

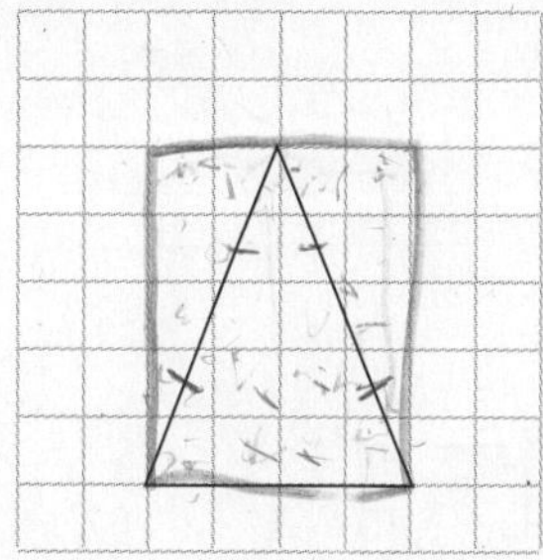

~ 10 square units.

2.

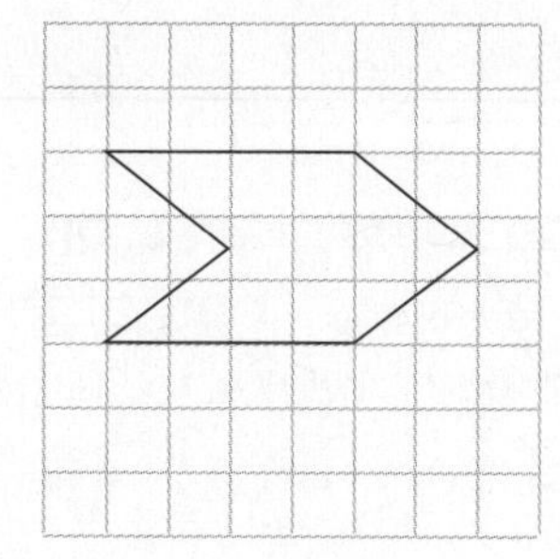

____

Name ______________________

Practice
14-7

Area of Irregular Shapes

Find the area of each shape.

1\. 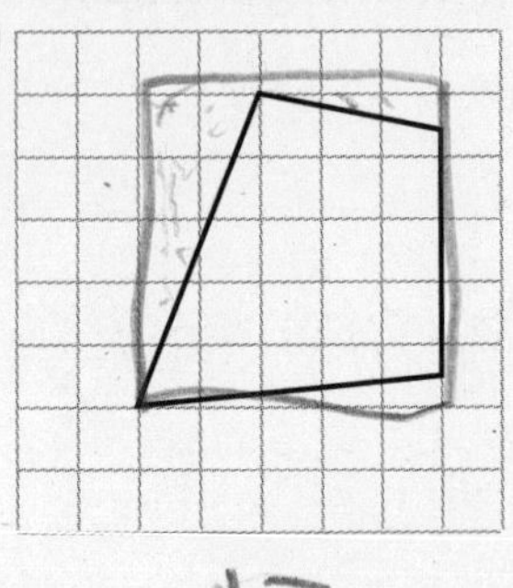

17

2\. 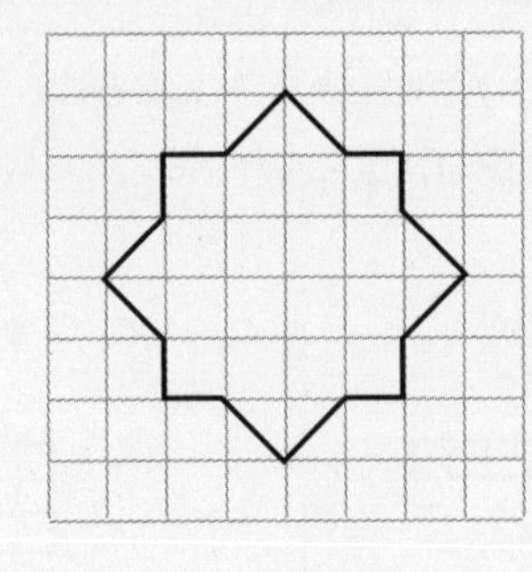

______

3\. 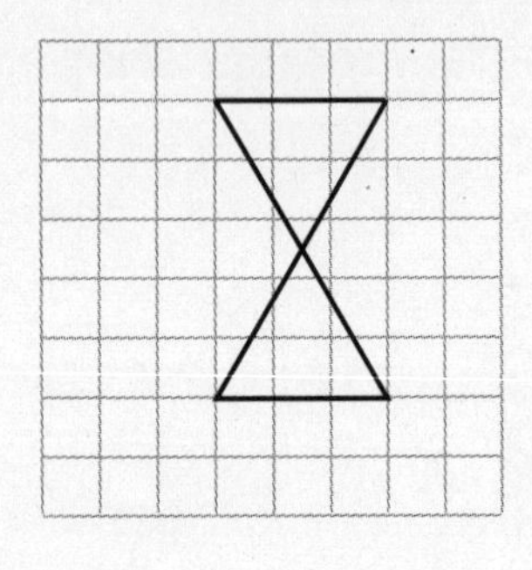

______

4\. 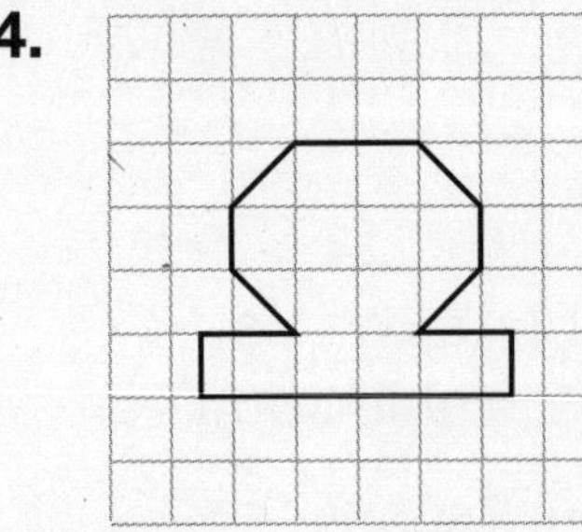

______

5\. 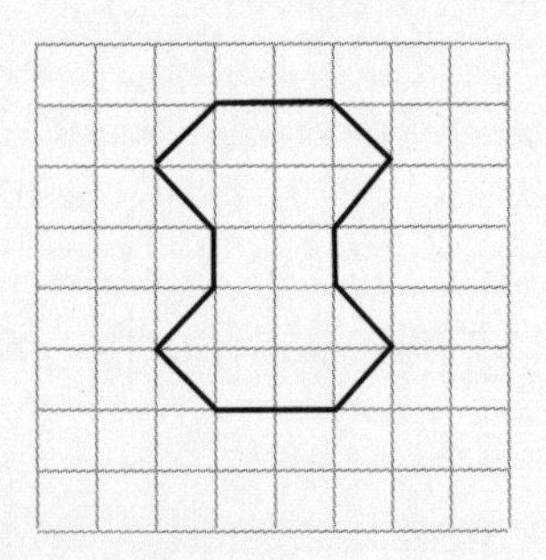

______

6\. 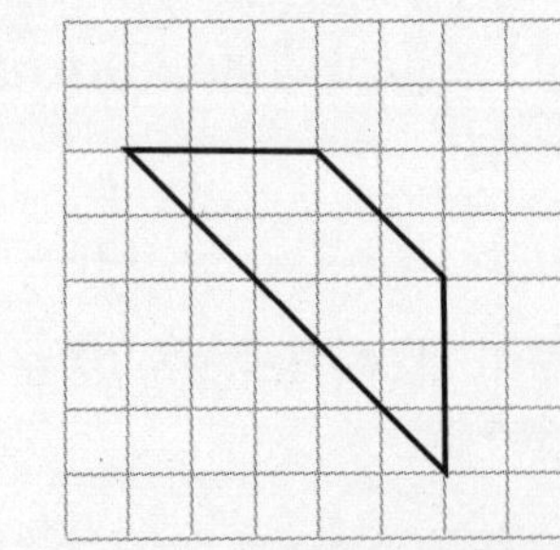

______

7\. 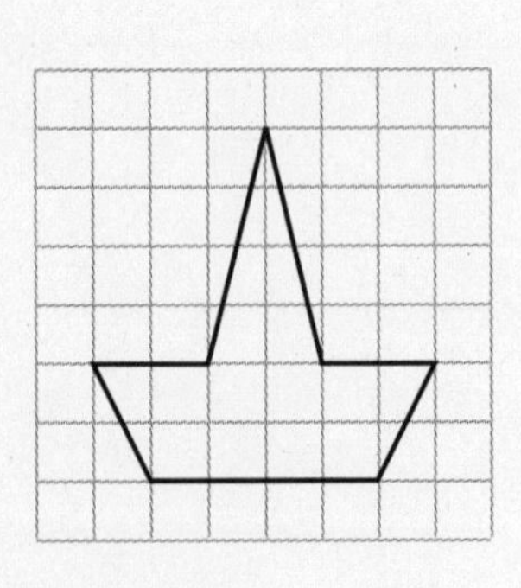

______

8\. 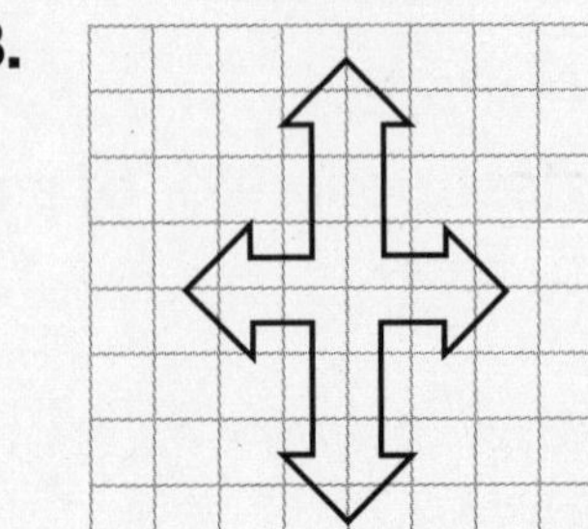

______

Name ______________________________

Reteaching
14-8

Same Area, Different Perimeter

Make three rectangles with an area of 18 square feet that have a different perimeter. Use grid paper or color tiles to help you.

1st Rectangle

Find the area:
$A = \ell \times w$
$= 18 \times 1$
$= 18$ square feet

Find the perimeter:
$P = (2 \times \ell) + (2 \times w)$
$= (2 \times 18) + (2 \times 1)$
$= 36 + 2 = 38$ feet

2nd Rectangle

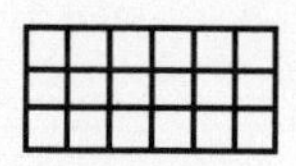

Find the area:
$A = \ell \times w$
$= 6 \times 3$
$= 18$ square feet

Find the perimeter:
$P = (2 \times \ell) + (2 \times w)$
$= (2 \times 6) + (2 \times 3)$
$= 12 + 6 = 18$ feet

3rd Rectangle

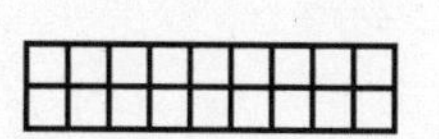

Find the area:
$A = \ell \times w$
$= 9 \times 2$
$= 18$ square feet

Find the perimeter:
$P = (2 \times \ell) + (2 \times w)$
$= (2 \times 9) + (2 \times 2)$
$= 18 + 4 = 22$ feet

Solve.

1. Draw two different perimeters of a rectangle with an area of 14 units. Name their dimensions.

2. What is the greatest perimeter of a rectangle with an area of 39 square feet? ____________

3. What is the least perimeter of a rectangle with an area of 32 square feet? ____________

4. **Reason** A rectangle has an area of 42 square inches. Which has a greater perimeter, the rectangle with the dimensions 21×2 or the dimensions 6×7? ____________

Name ______________________

Practice
14-8

Same Area, Different Perimeter

For **1** through **9,** write “yes” if the 2 rectangles have the same area and “no” if they do not. If they have the same area, tell which one has the smaller perimeter.

1.
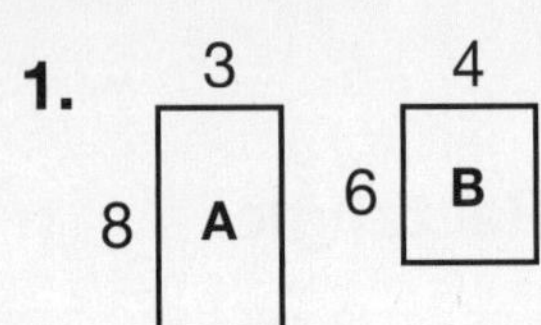

____

2. 6, 5, C; 10, 3, D

____

3.
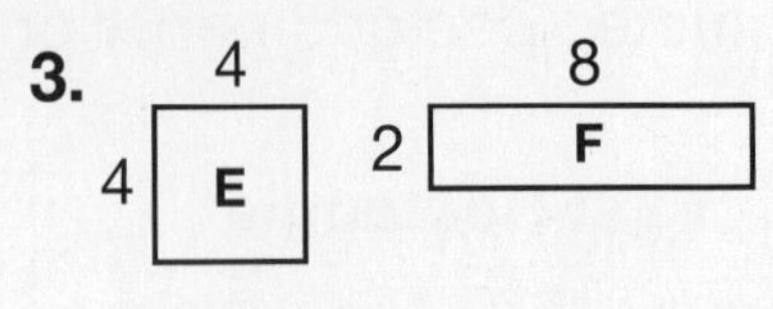

____

4. 5, 8, G; 20, 2, H

____

5. 6, 8, I; 12, 4, J

____

6. 2, 6, K; 3, 4, L

____

7. 10, 10, M; 30, 3, N

____

8. 4, 9, O; 13, 2, P

____

9.
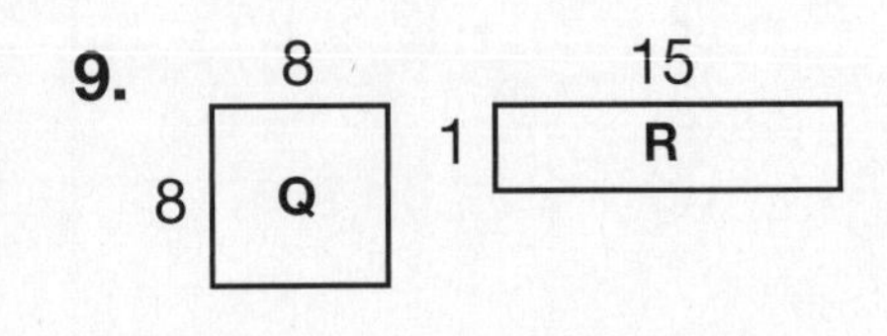

____

10. Two rectangles have an area of 36 square inches. Name two possible perimeters for the rectangles. ______________________

11. The length of a rectangle is 6 inches and the width is 5 inches. Which rectangle has the same area?

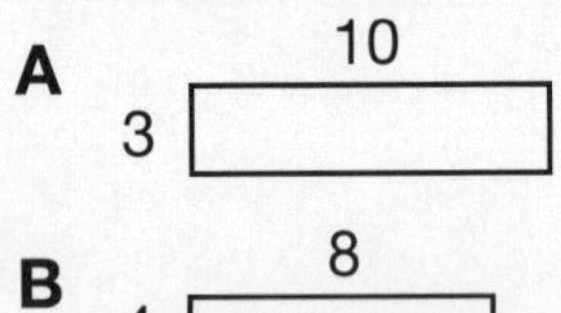

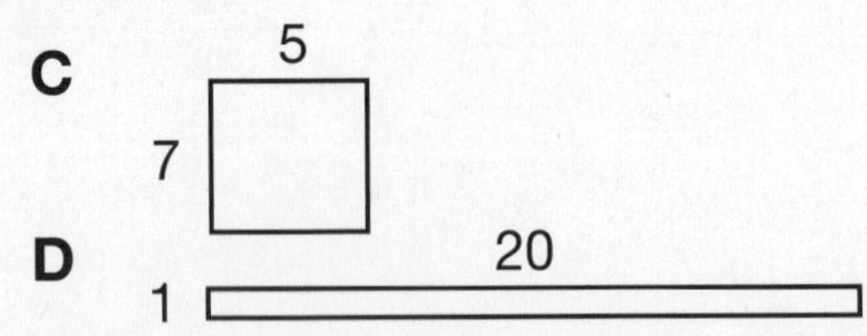

12. Writing to Explain The area of a rectangle is 100 square inches. The perimeter of the rectangle is 40 inches. A second rectangle has the same area but a different perimeter. Is the second rectangle a square? Explain why or why not.

____

____

Name ______________________________

Equal Areas and Fractions

You can use equal areas to model unit fractions. Divide this square into two equal parts.

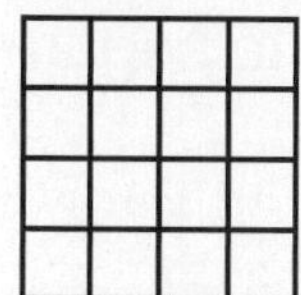

Here's one way.
Draw a line to separate the rectangle into 2 equal parts. Since each part has the same area it is $\frac{1}{2}$ of the whole.

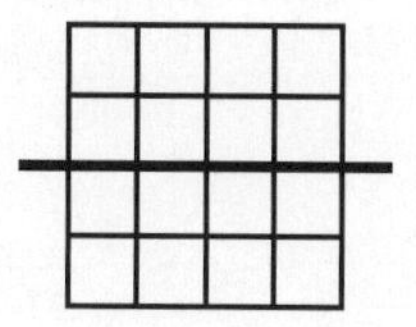

Here's another way
Draw a line to separate the rectangle into 2 equal parts. Since each part has the same area it is $\frac{1}{2}$ of the whole.

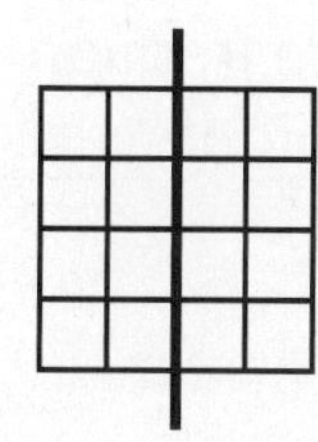

For **1–2**, show two ways to separate the rectangle into equal parts.

1. 4 equal parts

In each rectangle, what is the fraction that shows the area of one of the parts? What is the area of each part?

____

2. 6 equal parts

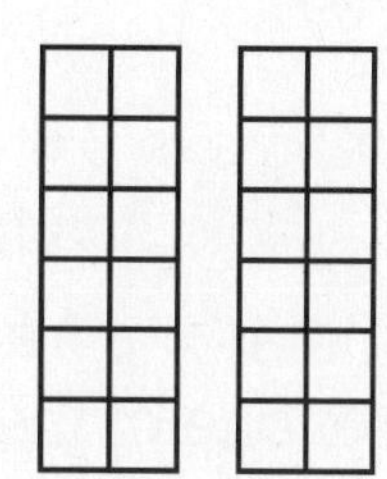

In each rectangle, what is the fraction that shows the area of one of the parts? What is the area of each part?

____

Name ______________________

Equal Areas and Fractions

For **1** through **3**, show two ways to separate the rectangle into equal parts.

1. 4 equal parts

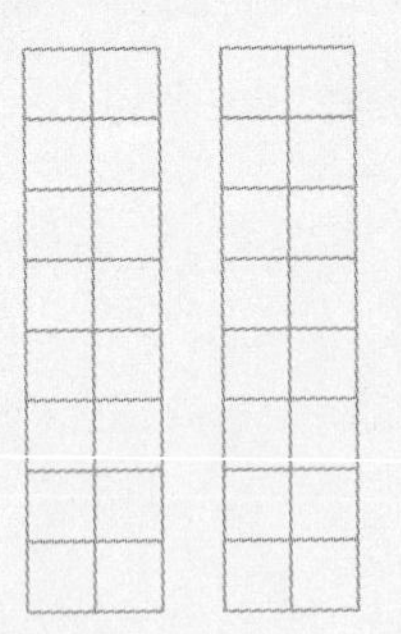

In each rectangle, what is the fraction that shows the area of one of the parts?

____

2. 3 equal parts

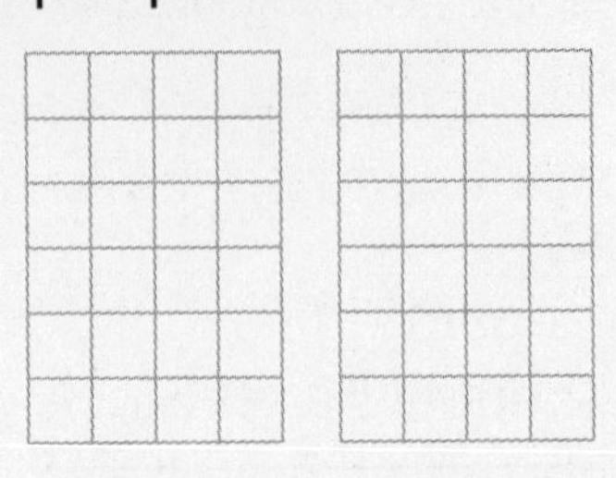

In each rectangle, what is the fraction that shows the area of one of the parts?

____

3. 6 equal parts

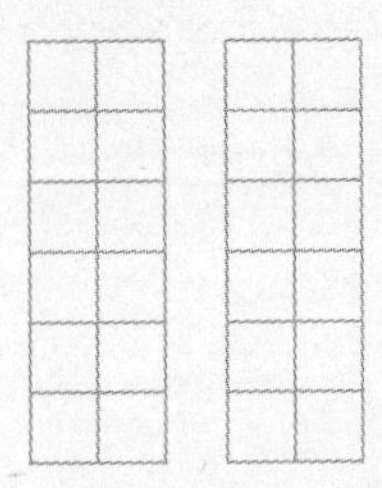

In each rectangle, what is the fraction that shows the area of one of the parts?

____

4. Tom separated the rectangle shown below into 8 equal parts. What fraction shows the area of one of the parts?

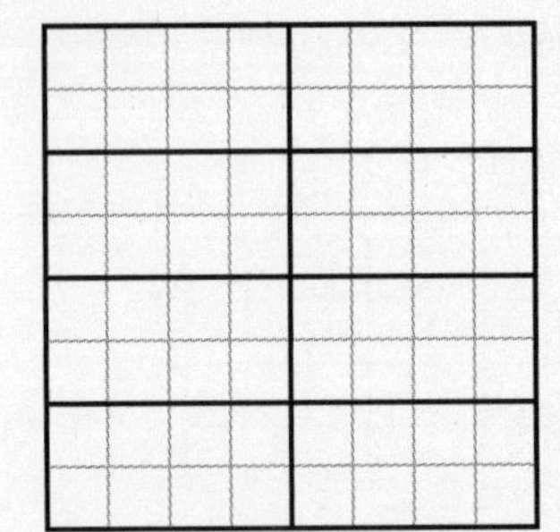

____

5. Mai drew the design shown below. Each square in the design has the same area. Which fraction shows the area of one of the squares?

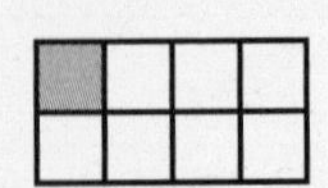

A $\frac{1}{4}$ **B** $\frac{1}{3}$ **C** $\frac{1}{6}$ **D** $\frac{1}{8}$

Name ______________________________

Reteaching
14-10

Problem Solving: Selecting Appropriate Measurement Units and Tools

When you measure the area of an object, you need to choose the best measurement unit and the best measurement tool.

Here are some measurement units that you can use to measure area.

square inches square feet square yards square miles	square centimeters square meters square kilometers

Here are some measurement tools that you can use to measure length to find area.

inch ruler
or
centimeter ruler

yardstick
or
meter stick

For **1** through **3,** circle the measurement unit that you would use to measure the area of each item.

1. the city of Miami

square feet
or
square miles

2. an index card

square centimeters
or
square meters

3. a TV screen

square inches
or
square miles

For **4** through **6,** circle the measurement tool that you would use to find the area of each item.

4. a postcard

inch ruler
or
yard stick

5. a classroom wall

centimeter ruler
or
meter stick

6. an ice skating rink

inch ruler
or
yardstick

7. Writing to Explain Tell which measurement tool you would use to measure the area of a student desk. Explain your thinking.

____

____

____

Name ______________________________

Problem Solving: Selecting Appropriate Measurement Units and Tools

For **1** through **4,** name the measurement unit you would use to measure the area of each item.

1. blanket ____________

2. New York City ____________

3. table tennis table ____________

4. vegetable garden ____________

For **5** through **8,** name the measurement tool you would use to measure the area of each item.

5. roof of a building ____________ ____________

6. pizza pie ____________ ____________

7. movie screen ____________ ____________

8. crayon box ____________ ____________

9. Carl wants to measure the area of his kitchen floor. Which unit of measurement should he use?

A Inches

B Feet

C Square inches

D Square feet

10. Inez wants to find the area of a small photo. Which measurement tool should she use?

A Inch ruler

B Meter stick

C Scale

D Yardstick

11. Give an example of an area that you would measure in square miles.

____

12. Jeremiah wants to use a meter stick to measure the dimensions of a magazine cover to find its area. Is that an appropriate measurement tool? Explain why or why not.

____

____

Name ________________________________

Reteaching
15-1

Customary Units of Capacity

Capacity is the amount of liquid a container can hold. The containers show the different units of customary capacity.

cup (c)

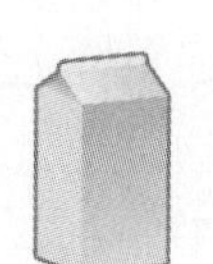
pint (pt)
1 pt = 2 c

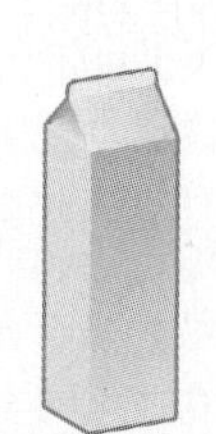
quart (qt)
1 qt = 2 pt

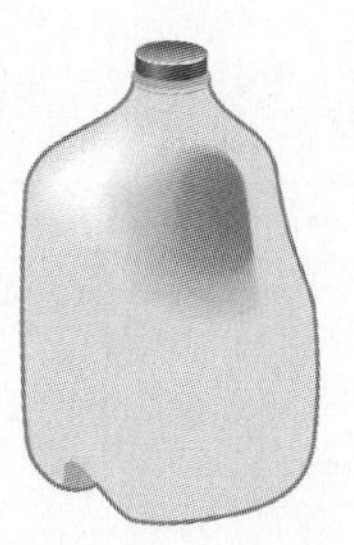
gallon (gal)
1 gal = 4 qt

Choose the better estimate for each.

1. 

1 c or 1 gal ________

2. 

1 qt or 1 gal ________

3. 

1 c or 1 qt ________

4. small water bottle

1 pt or 1 gal ________

5. bucket

1 c or 1 gal ________

6. bathroom sink

2 c or 2 gal ________

7. **Reason** Suppose you want to fill a pot with 1 gallon of water. You can use a measuring cup the size of a cup or a quart. Which would be best to use? Explain your reasoning.

____

____

____

Name ____________________

Practice
15-1

Customary Units of Capacity

Choose the better estimate for each.

1.  

1 c or 1 gal

____

2. 

3 qt or 3 gal

____

3. 

1 pt or 1 gal

____

4. 

10 qt or 10 gal

____

5. coffee pot
1 c or 1 gal

____

6. bowl of soup
1 pt or 1 gal

____

7. tea kettle
1 qt or 1 gal

____

8. small milk carton
1 c or 1 gal

____

Choose the better unit to measure the capacity of each.

9. hot tub
qt or gal

____

10. shampoo bottle
pt or gal

____

11. bucket
c or gal

____

12. sports cooler
qt or gal

____

13. Reasonableness John has 4 cups filled with fruit juice. He said that he has a gallon of fruit juice. Is his statement reasonable? Explain why or why not.

____

____

____

14. Reason Which measurement best describes the capacity of a kitchen sink?

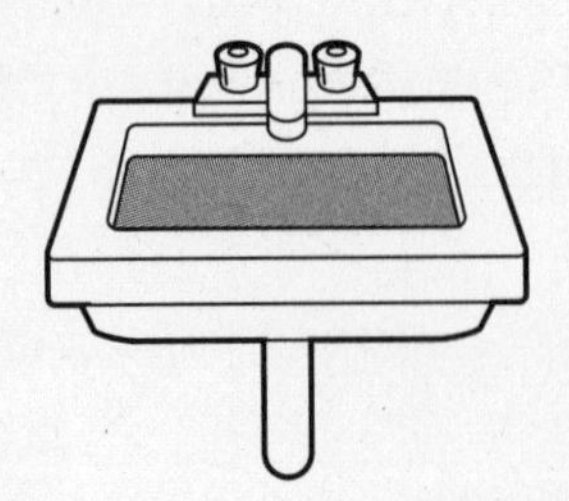

A 5 quarts **B** 5 pints **C** 5 cups **D** 5 gallons

Name ______________________________

Metric Units of Capacity

Two units of capacity in the metric system are milliliters (mL) and liters (L).

1 liter = 1,000 milliliters

Milliliters are used to measure very small amounts of liquid.

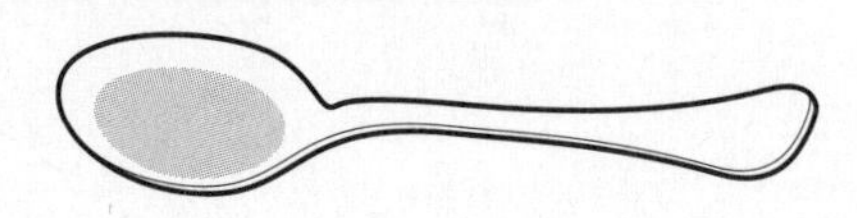

1 teaspoon = 5 milliliters

A liter is slightly larger than a quart. Many beverages are sold in 1-liter and 2-liter bottles.

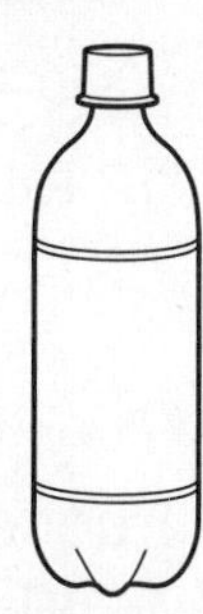

Choose the better estimate for each.

1.

350 mL or 35 L

____

2.

100 mL or 10 L

____

3.

30 mL or 3 L

____

4. small milk carton

250 mL or 25 L

____

5. soup can

500 mL or 5 L

____

6. sports cooler

4 L or 40 L

____

7. Reasonableness Which is the better unit to use to measure the capacity of a bathtub: milliliters or liters? Explain your choice.

____

____

____

Name ______________________

Metric Units of Capacity

Choose the better estimate for each.

1. 

2 mL or 2 L

______

2. 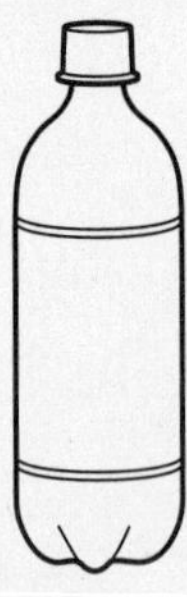

2 mL or 2 L

______

3. 

5 mL or 5 L

______

4. 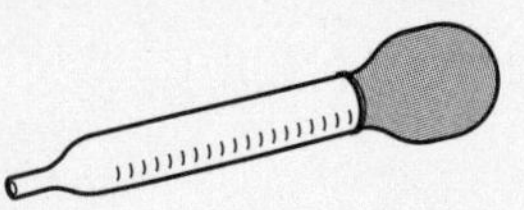

1 mL or 1 L

______

5. kitchen sink
2 L or 20 L

______

6. coffee cup
250 mL or 25 L

______

7. thermos
2 L or 20 L

______

8. pitcher
40 mL or 4 L

______

Choose the better unit to measure the capacity of each.

9. tea cup
mL or L

______

10. bath tub
mL or L

______

11. glass of juice
mL or L

______

12. washing machine
mL or L

______

13. Reason A liter is equal to 100 centiliters. Is a centiliter a greater measure than a milliliter? Explain.

____

____

____

14. Reason Which is the best estimate for the capacity of a large bottle of water?

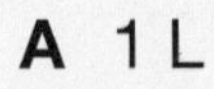

A 1 L   **C** 4 L

B 400 mL   **D** 40 mL

Name ______________________

Reteaching
15-3

Units of Mass

Mass is the measure of how much matter is in an object. Units of mass include grams (g) and kilograms (kg).

1 kilogram = 1,000 grams

A paper clip has a mass of about 1 gram.

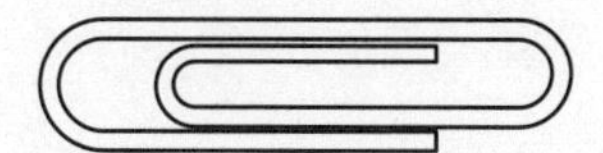

A large baseball bat has a mass of about 1 kilogram.

Choose the better estimate for each.

1. 

150 g or 3 kg

______

2. 

1 g or 100 g

______

3. 

300 g or 3 kg

______

4. soccer ball
10 g or 1 kg

______

5. tiger
30 kg or 300 kg

______

6. dime
2 g or 2 kg

______

7. **Reason** Julie has a box of paper clips that have a mass of 1 gram each. The entire box has a mass of 1 kilogram. How many paper clips are in the box? Explain your answer.

____

____

____

Name ______________________________

Units of Mass

Choose the better estimate for each.

1. 

3 g or 3 kg

______

2. 

40 g or 40 kg

______

3. 

250 g or 25 kg

______

4. 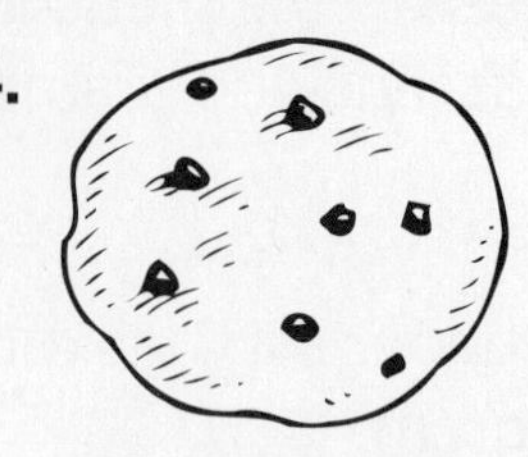

30 g or 300 g

______

5. crayon
20 g or 200 g

______

6. large dog
5 kg or 50 kg

______

7. quarter
5 g or 500 g

______

8. adult male
7 kg or 70 kg

______

Choose the best tool to measure each.

9. the mass of a phone ______

10. the length of a crayon ______

11. the temperature ______

12. the time for dinner ______

13. the capacity of a bowl ______

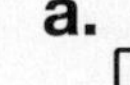

a. 

b. 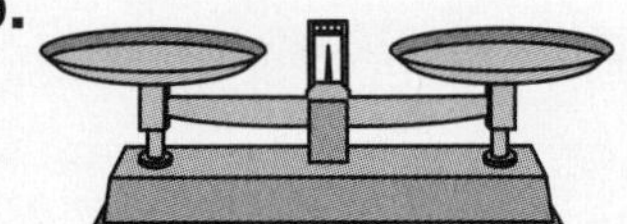

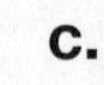

c. 

d. 

e. 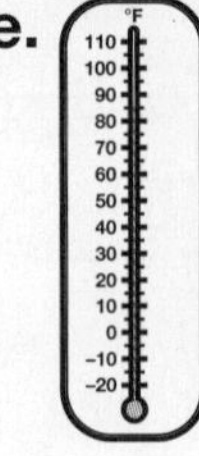

14. Writing to Explain Would you use grams or kilograms to find the mass of a letter? Explain.

____

____

____

15. Reason Which is the best estimate for the mass of a pair of sneakers?

A 1 kg **B** 1 g **C** 10 kg **D** 10 g

Name ____________________

Units of Weight

Weight is the measure of how heavy an object is.
The units of weight are listed below.

1 pound (lb) = 16 ounces (oz)
1 ton (T) = 2,000 pounds

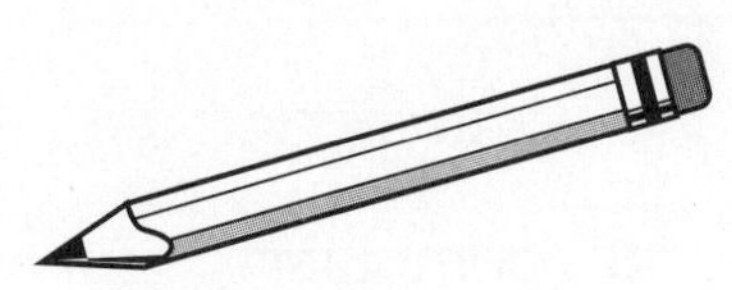

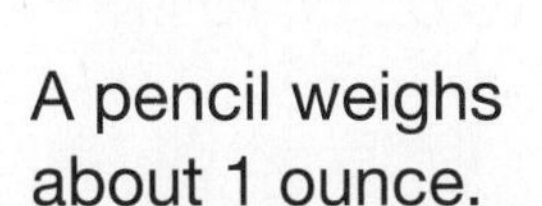

A pencil weighs about 1 ounce.

A telephone weighs about 1 pound.

A small car weighs about 1 ton.

Choose the better estimate for each.

1. 

1 oz or 1 lb

____

2. 

10 oz or 10 lb

____

3. 

50 lb or 500 lb

____

4. paperback book
1 oz or 1 lb

____

5. baseball
5 oz or 5 lb

____

6. radio
2 oz or 2 lb

____

7. **Reason** Mrs. Robertson wants to buy as big a package of chopped meat as possible. There is a 20-ounce package and a 1-pound package. She only wants to buy one package. Which should she buy?

____

____

____

Name ______________________________

Units of Weight

Practice
15-4

Choose the better estimate for each.

1. 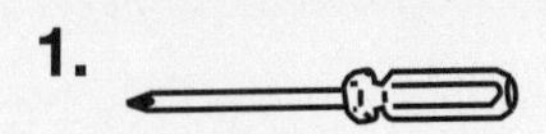

3 oz or 3 lb

____

2. 

30 oz or 30 lb

____

3. 

2 oz or 2 lb

____

4. 

500 lb or 5 T

____

5. DVD
1 oz or 1 lb

____

6. chair
20 oz or 20 lb

____

7. cell phone
6 oz or 6 lb

____

8. computer
10 oz or 10 lb

____

Choose the better unit to measure the weight of each.

9. car
lb or T

____

10. strawberry
oz or lb

____

11. baseball
oz or lb

____

12. book
lb or T

____

13. Critique Reasoning Emily said the larger an object is, the more it weighs. Is Emily correct? Explain why or why not.

____

____

____

14. Reason Which of the following objects can best be measured in ounces?

A pencil **B** couch **C** desk **D** doghouse

Name ______________________________

Problem Solving: Draw a Picture

Mrs. Jones bought 45 liters of juice for the school picnic. At the picnic teachers and students drank 32 liters of juice. How many liters of juice were left?

You can draw a picture of the information given in the problem to solve it.

45 liters	
32 liters	?

To find the number of liters that were left, you can subtract 45 − 32.

$$\begin{array}{r} 45 \\ -\ 32 \\ \hline 13 \end{array}$$

So, 13 liters of juice were left.

For **1-2**, draw a picture to solve.

1. At the doctor's office Frank and Dino were each weighed on the scale. Frank weighed 93 pounds and Dino weighed 86 pounds. What is their total weight?

2. A small bicycle has a mass of 7 kilograms. The total mass of all the small bicycles at Mike's Bike Shop is 21 kilograms. How many small bicycles does Mike's Bike Shop have?

3. **Writing to Explain** How did you know which operation to use to solve Problem 2?

____

____

____

Name ____________________

Practice
15-5

Problem Solving: Draw a Picture

The table to the right shows the mass of fat in grams per serving for certain foods. Use the table for **1–2**. Draw a picture to solve.

Total Fat (per serving)

Food	Amount of Fat (g)
Cheddar Cheese	9
Honey Ham	2
Mixed Nuts	15

1. What is the sum of the number of grams of total fat per serving for cheddar cheese and mixed nuts.

2. A package of cheddar cheese has 8 servings. How many total grams of fat are in a package of cheese?

3. The capacity of a bottle of juice is 30 fluid ounces. Maggie wants to put the juice into 6 smaller containers. She wants each container to have the same amount of juice. How many ounces of juice should she put in each container? Draw a picture to solve.

4. **Write a Problem** Write a real-world problem that involves weight, mass, or capacity and can be solved by drawing a picture.

____

____

____

Name ___________________

Line Plots

A line plot is used in the same way as a tally chart. It is used to show numerical data. A line plot uses an X to show an outcome.

The data show the numbers spun in 30 spins.

Spinner Results

1	2	4	3	6	5	1	7	4	3
2	6	3	5	4	7	1	2	6	1
1	3	6	2	5	1	4	2	7	3

Sections

The line plot at the right can be used to show the data.

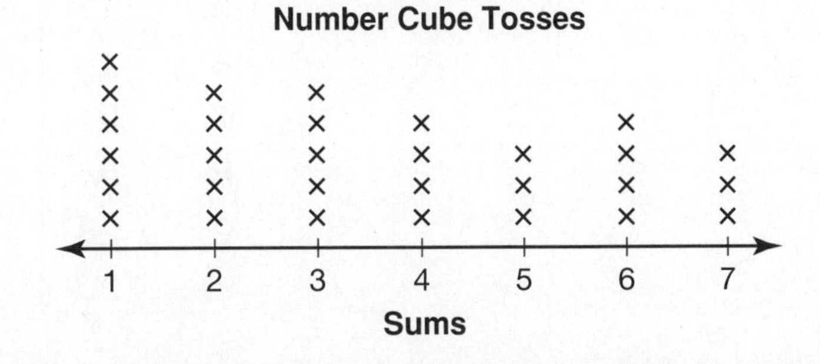

Mark played a game with two number cubes. He found the sum of the number cubes. The results are shown in the table.

1. Make a line plot to show the data.

Number Cube Tosses

Toss	Sum	Toss	Sum	Toss	Sum
1	7	11	6	21	7
2	4	12	9	22	10
3	6	13	9	23	9
4	8	14	10	24	7
5	5	15	10	25	5
6	5	16	5	26	12
7	6	17	8	27	7
8	2	18	5	28	9
9	10	19	3	29	8
10	8	20	8	30	12

2. How many Xs do you show for 8?

____

3. Which sum from 2–12 did Mark not toss at all?

____

Name ______________________________

Line Plots

For **1** through **4**, use the data at the right.

1. Make a line plot to show the data.

Number of Points Katie Scored

Game	Pts	Game	Pts	Game	Pts
1	23	11	25	21	24
2	25	12	30	22	26
3	30	13	27	23	25
4	25	14	22	24	28
5	21	15	26	25	27
6	26	16	21	26	26
7	21	17	29	27	29
8	24	18	25	28	30
9	28	19	21	29	22
10	20	20	23	30	24

2. How many Xs do you show for 24 points?

____

3. Which number of points did Katie only score once?

____

4. Which number of points did Katie score the most?

____

5. Which two point totals did Katie score exactly four times each?

____

For **6** and **7**, use the line plot at the right.

6. How many fewer students read 5 books than 8 books?

____

7. How many students read fewer than 7 books?

A 11 **C** 17

B 14 **D** 22

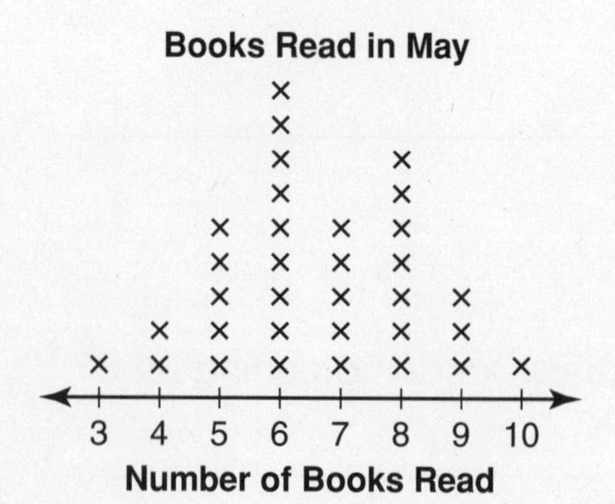

Name ______________________________

Length and Line Plots

Dorothy measured the lengths of the fingers on her left hand. She also measured the length of her thumb.

Dorothy wants to make a line plot to show the measurements. The line plot can organize the data of her finger and thumb measurements.

Remember the steps for making a line plot.

Draw a number line and choose a scale based on the data collected. The scale should show data values from the least to greatest.

Write a title for the line plot.

Mark an X for each length.

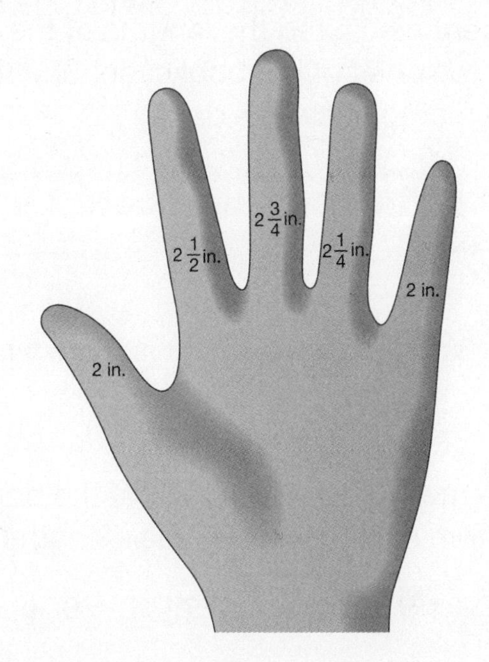

1. What numbers should Dorothy use as the scale of the line plot?

____

2. How many Xs, or data points, should Dorothy have on the line plot?

____

3. Complete this line plot to show Dorothy's data.

The Lengths of Dorothy's Fingers in Inches

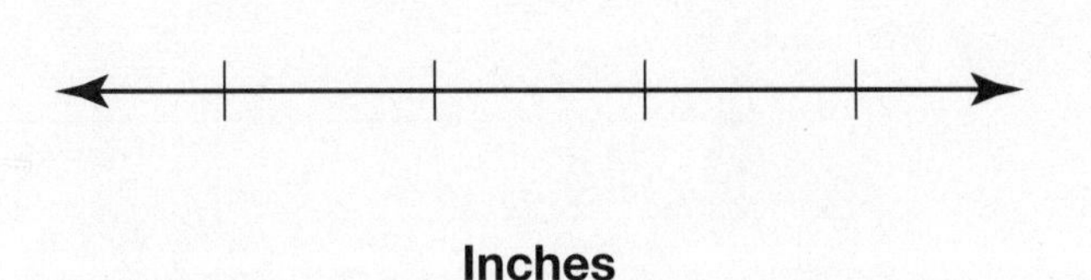

Inches

4. How long is Dorothy's shortest finger?

____

5. How long is her longest finger?

____

6. **Use Tools** Which length is used more than once?

____

Name ______________________

Length and Line Plots

Practice
16-2

Japera measured the lengths of the books in the top shelf of her bookcase. She made a line plot to show the data.

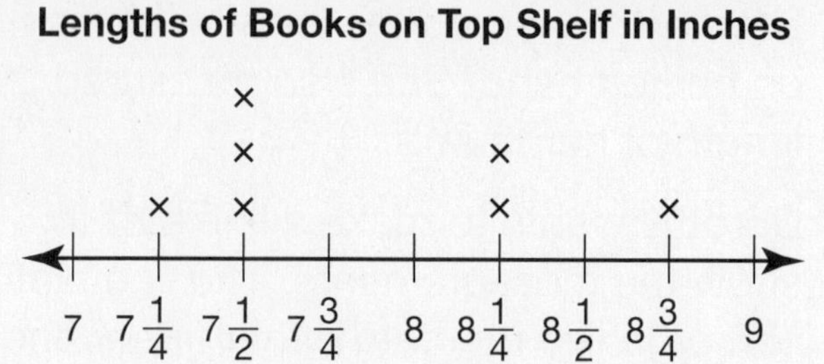

1. How many books are on the top shelf?

____

2. What length of book is shown most often?

____

She measured the lengths of the books on the bottom shelf and listed their lengths.

$8\frac{3}{4}$ in., $9\frac{1}{2}$ in., $8\frac{1}{4}$ in., $9\frac{1}{4}$ in., 10 in., $9\frac{1}{4}$ in., $8\frac{1}{2}$ in.

3. Make a line plot that displays the lengths of the books on the bottom shelf.

____

4. Use Tools Which shelf has the most books that are the same size?

____

5. How many different lengths of books are on the bottom shelf?

____

6. Writing to Explain Does Japera keep the longer books on the top or the bottom shelf? How do you know?

____

____

____

7. Which length of book is most common on the bottom shelf?

A 2 inches

B $8\frac{3}{4}$ inches

C $9\frac{1}{4}$ inches

D 10 inches

Name ______________________________

Reading Pictographs and Bar Graphs

Pictographs use pictures or parts of pictures to represent data.

Gold Medals Won at 1998 Winter Olympics

Japan	
Italy	
Canada	
Korea	

Each = 1 gold medal.

Look at the key to see what each symbol represents. Count the symbols next to a country to see how many medals were won.

Which country has the fewest symbols? Italy.
How many gold medals did Italy win? 2 gold medals.

Bar graphs use bars set along a scale to represent data.

Silver Medals Won at 2000 Summer Olympics

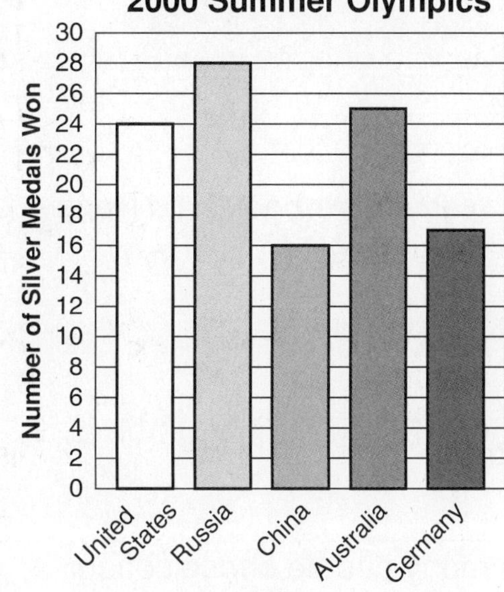

Country

Choose a country and use the scale to find how high the bar reaches. That number represents how many medals were won.

Which country has the tallest bar? Russia.
How many silver medals did Russia win? 28 silver medals.

Use the pictograph to answer **1** and **2**.

1. How many houses were built in City B in 2002?

____

2. How many houses were built in City A in 2002?

____

Number of Houses Built in 2002

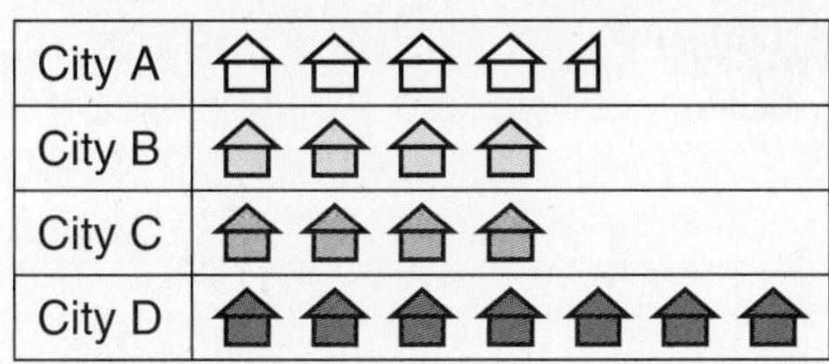

Each = 10 houses.
Each = 5 houses.

Name ______________________

Reading Pictographs and Bar Graphs

For **1** through **4**, use the pictograph at the right.

Books Read

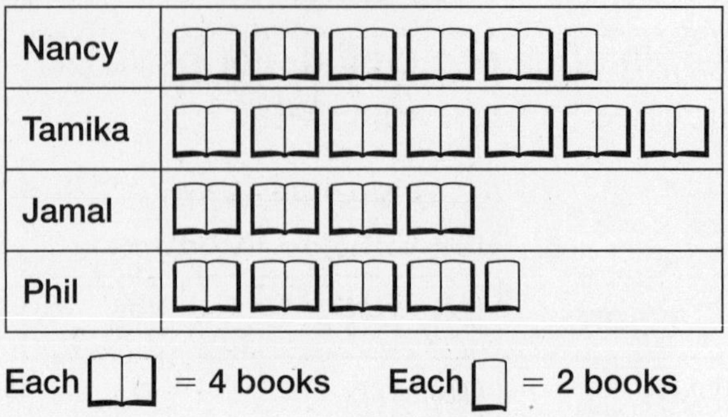

Nancy	
Tamika	
Jamal	
Phil	

Each = 4 books   Each = 2 books

1. Who read the most books?

   ____

2. Who read exactly 18 books?

   ____

3. How many more books did Nancy read than Jamal?

   ____

4. Who read the fewest books?

   ____

For **5** through **8**, use the bar graph at the right.

Favorite Sport

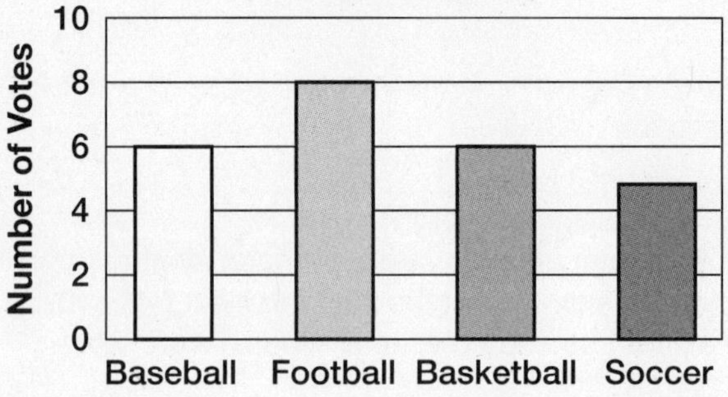

Number of Votes

10
8
6
4
2
0

Baseball Football Basketball Soccer

5. How many people chose soccer as their favorite sport?

   ____

6. Which sport was voted as a favorite the most?

   ____

7. **Reasonableness** Casey said that 40 people were surveyed. Is his answer reasonable? Explain.

   ____

   ____

   ____

8. Which sentence is true?

   A Baseball and basketball received the same number of votes.

   B More people chose soccer than baseball.

   C More people chose football than basketball and soccer combined.

   D More people chose baseball than football.

Name ______________________

Making Pictographs

The tally table shows food items that were ordered for lunch.
Follow the steps below to make the pictograph.

Food	Tally	Number
Pasta	𝍸 I	6
Salad	IIII	4
Casserole	𝍸 𝍸	10
Fish	𝍸 III	8

Items Ordered

Pasta	3 forks
Salad	2 forks
Casserole	5 forks
Fish	4 forks

Each fork = 2 meals

Step 1

Write a title that explains what the pictograph shows.

Step 2

Choose a symbol. For this pictograph, use a fork. Decide how many meals each fork will represent.

Step 3

Draw the number of symbols that are needed for each food.

The tally table shows how Ms. Hashimoto's class voted for their favorite types of movies to rent.

1. Complete the table.

Favorite Video	Tally	Number
Action	𝍸 III	
Comedy	III	
Drama	𝍸 I	
Animated	𝍸 𝍸	

2. Complete the pictograph.

____

Action	
Comedy	
Drama	
Animated	

Each [video symbol] = ___ votes.

3. Writing to Explain How did you choose the number that each symbol represents?

____

____

Name ______________________________

Making Pictographs

For **1** and **2**, use the chart.

1. Make a pictograph to show the data in the chart. Write a title. Choose the key.

Color of Cars

Color	Tally	Number
Red	卌 卌 卌 I	16
Green	卌 卌 卌 卌	20
Silver	卌 卌 卌 卌 IIII	24
Black	卌 卌 IIII	14

2. Reasonableness Why did you choose the number for each symbol that you chose?

____

____

____

3. Fred is going to make a pictograph showing the number of tomatoes that he picked each day. He picked 30 Monday, 25 Tuesday, 35 Wednesday, and 40 Thursday. Which would be the best number to use for each symbol?

A 1 **C** 5

B 2 **D** 20

4. Explain It Pamela made a pictograph showing students' favorite drinks. Pamela drew 3 glasses to represent the 6 students who chose chocolate milk. Is her pictograph correct? Explain.

Favorite Drinks

Drink	Number of Students
Chocolate milk	
Fruit juice	

Key Each = 2 students.

____

____

____

Name ______________________

Making Bar Graphs

Reteaching
16-5

The table shows the number of birds that visited a bird feeder.

Day	Number of Birds
Monday	6
Tuesday	4
Wednesday	7
Thursday	5
Friday	3

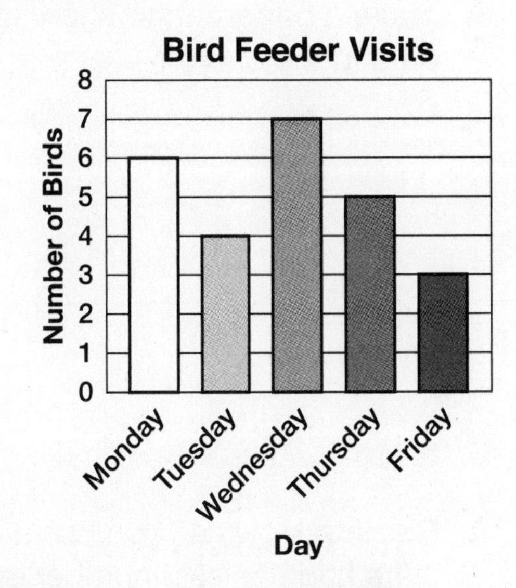

Follow the steps below to make the bar graph at the right.

Step 1

Write each of the days and label the bottom of the graph "Day."

Step 2

Number the scale. Label the scale "Number of Birds."

Step 3

Make the bars for each day.

Step 4

Give the graph a title.

Use the table below for **1** and **2**.

Field Day Results

Team	Points
Bulls	45
Colts	30
Pigs	25
Rams	40

1. Make a bar graph. Remember to label your graph and add a title.

2. Writing to Explain Why did you choose the scale you did?

____

____

Name ______________________________

Practice
16-5

Making Bar Graphs

For **1** and **2**, use the chart at the right.

Favorite States to Visit

State	Number of Votes
New York	25
Florida	35
California	30
Hawaii	20

1. Make a bar graph to show the data in the chart.

2. Reason How can you use a bar graph to determine which state had the least number of votes?

____

____

3. Explain It Describe your process for determining the scale for a bar graph.

____

____

____

4. The table at the right shows the number of phone calls Mrs. Walker made during 5 days of fundraising. Which is the scale you would use to make a bar graph of the data?

Fundraising Calls

Day	Phone Calls
Saturday	26
Sunday	19
Monday	20
Tuesday	24
Wednesday	16

A by 1s

B by 2s

C by 7s

D by 10s

Name ______________________________

Problem Solving: Use Tables and Graphs to Draw Conclusions

Students were asked to name their favorite type of dog. The pictograph shows the results of the survey.

Students' Favorite Dogs

Dog	Number Counted
Beagle	🐕 🐕 🐕
Collie	🐕 🐕 🐕 🐕 🐕
Shepherd	🐕 🐕 ½🐕
Poodle	🐕
Dalmatian	🐕 🐕

Each 🐕 = 2 votes.

Which dog was chosen by *exactly* 5 students? Shepherd

Which dog was chosen by 2 more students than a Dalmatian? Beagle

For **1** through **3**, use the chart below.

Quarter	Points Scored
1st	7
2nd	3
3rd	10
4th	6

1. The chart shows how many points a football team scored. How many points were scored altogether?

____

2. Write a Problem Write a word problem that is different from Exercise 1 that can be solved by reading the chart.

____

____

3. Make a graph to represent the data in the chart. Choose a bar graph or a pictograph.

Name ______________________________

Practice
16-6

Problem Solving: Use Tables and Graphs to Draw Conclusions

Use the pictographs for **1 through 4**.

Girls Shoes Sold at Just Shoes

Sneakers	
Sandals	
Pumps	
Boots	

Each [shoe] = 10 shoes.

Girls Shoes Sold at All Shoes

Sneakers	
Sandals	
Pumps	
Boots	

Each [shoe] = 5 shoes.

1. Which type of shoe was sold the most at Just Shoes?

____

2. Which two types of shoes were sold equally at All Shoes?

____

3. Which store sold the most pumps?

____

4. How many sneakers were sold in all?

____

For **5** and **6**, use the bar graph at the right.

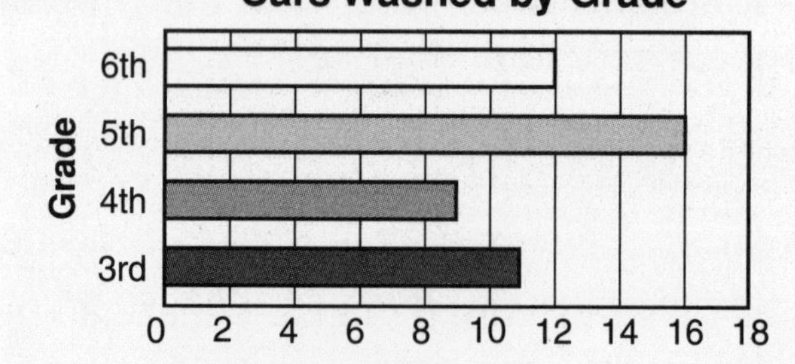

5. How many cars were washed altogether?

____

6. **Write a Problem** Write a word problem different from Exercise 5 that can be solved by reading the graph.

____

____

Students Receiving an A or a B

Test	Tally
1	卌 卌 ||
2	卌 卌 卌 |
3	卌 卌 卌
4	卌 |||

7. According to the tally chart, how many more students received an A or a B in Test 2 than in Test 4?

____

Name ______________________

Step-Up 1
Reteaching

Arrays and Multiplying by 10 and 100

You can use addition to help you multiply.

Find 2 × 10.

There are two groups of 10.

Add 10 two times.
$10 + 10 = 20$
or
Multiply 2 groups of 10.
$2 \times 10 = 20$

Find 2 × 100.

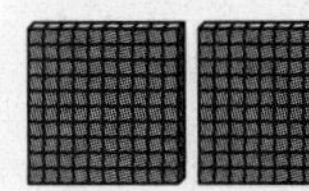

There are two groups of 100.

Add 100 two times.
$100 + 100 = 200$
or
Multiply 2 groups of 100.
$2 \times 100 = 200$

Find each product.

1. Find 4×10.

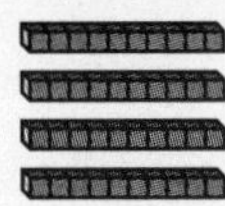

Add: $10 + 10 + 10 + 10 =$ _____

So, $4 \times 10 =$ _____.

2. Find 3×100.

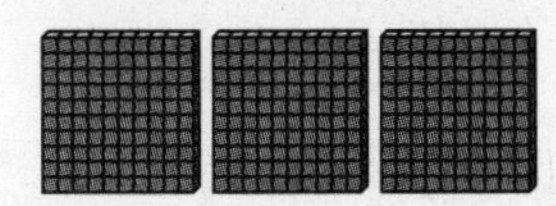

Add: $100 + 100 + 100 =$ _____

So, $3 \times 100 =$ _____.

3. **Reasonableness** Michael used addition to find 8×100 and he said the product is 80. What did he do wrong?

____

4. Draw two sets of arrays to represent 6×10 and 5×100. Then show how to use addition and multiplication to find each product.

Name ____________________

Step-Up 1
Practice

Arrays and Multiplying by 10 and 100

Find each product.

1. $4 \times 10 =$ ______

2. $2 \times 100 =$ ______

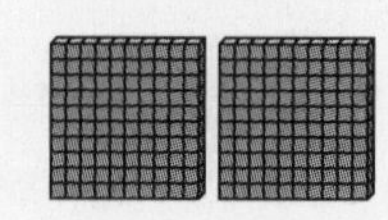

3. $2 \times 10 =$ ______

4. $6 \times 10 =$ ______

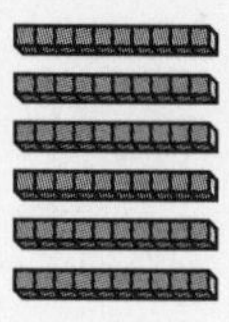

5. $3 \times 100 =$ ______

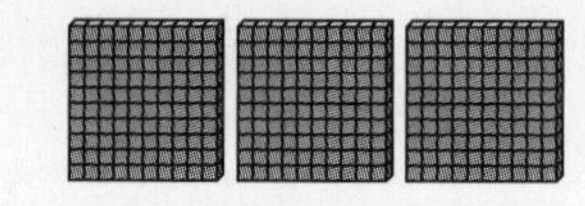

6. $4 \times 100 =$ ______

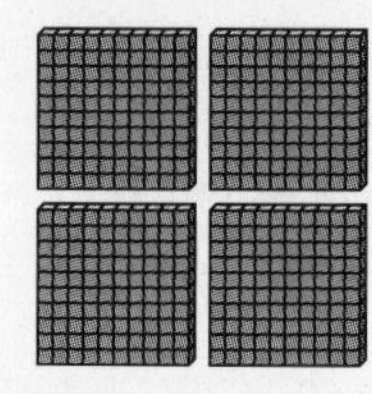

7. **Reason** What whole number could you use to complete $\square \times 100 = \square 00$ so that $\square 00$ is greater than 500 but less than 700?

____

8. Mr. Mitchell does 100 sit-ups every morning. How many sit-ups will he do in 9 days?

A 90 **B** 100 **C** 109 **D** 900

9. Jackie has 10 groups of pennies with 3 pennies in each group. Carlos has 5 groups of pennies with 100 pennies in each group. Who has more pennies? Explain how you know.

____

____

____

____

Name ______________________________

Step-Up 2
Reteaching

Breaking Apart Arrays

You can use arrays of place-value blocks to multiply.

Find the product for 4×16.

What You Show

$4 \times 10 = 40$ $4 \times 6 = 24$

$40 + 24 = 64$

Use the array to find the partial products and the product.

1. $\begin{array}{r} 12 \\ \times \ \ 3 \\ \hline \end{array}$

2.

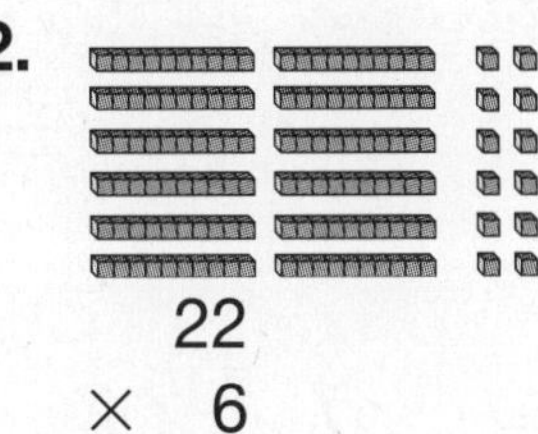

$\begin{array}{r} 22 \\ \times \ \ 6 \\ \hline \end{array}$

Complete the calculation.

3. $\begin{array}{r} 15 \\ \times \ \ 4 \\ \hline \end{array}$

4. $\begin{array}{r} 22 \\ \times \ \ 4 \\ \hline \end{array}$

5. $\begin{array}{r} 14 \\ \times \ \ 6 \\ \hline \end{array}$

6. $\begin{array}{r} 16 \\ \times \ \ 6 \\ \hline \end{array}$

7. $\begin{array}{r} 12 \\ \times \ \ 5 \\ \hline \end{array}$

8. $\begin{array}{r} 13 \\ \times \ \ 4 \\ \hline \end{array}$

9. $\begin{array}{r} 15 \\ \times \ \ 5 \\ \hline \end{array}$

10. $\begin{array}{r} 16 \\ \times \ \ 7 \\ \hline \end{array}$

11. Reason What two simpler problems can you use to find 4×22? (Hint: Think about tens and ones.)

____

____

Name ______________________________

Breaking Apart Arrays

Use the array to find the partial products and the product.

Complete the calculation.

1.
$$\begin{array}{r} 14 \\ \times\ 4 \\ \hline \square\square \\ +\ \square\square \\ \hline \square\square \end{array}$$

2.
$$\begin{array}{r} 12 \\ \times\ 5 \\ \hline \square\square \\ +\ \square\square \\ \hline \square\square \end{array}$$

3.
$$\begin{array}{r} 17 \\ \times\ 4 \\ \hline \end{array}$$

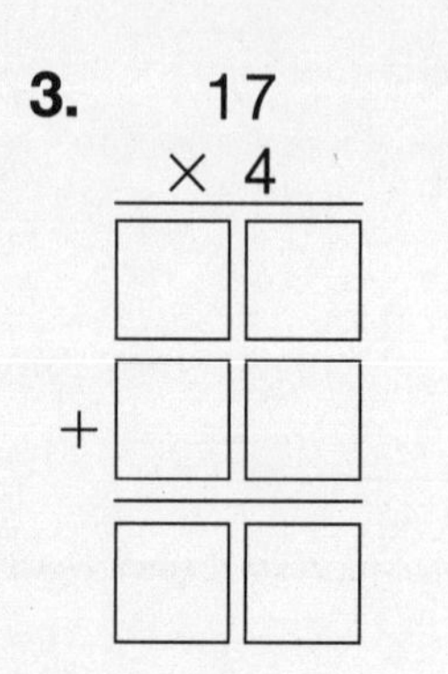

4.
$$\begin{array}{r} 25 \\ \times\ 3 \\ \hline \square\square \\ +\ \square\square \\ \hline \square\square \end{array}$$

5.
$$\begin{array}{r} 21 \\ \times\ 4 \\ \hline \end{array}$$

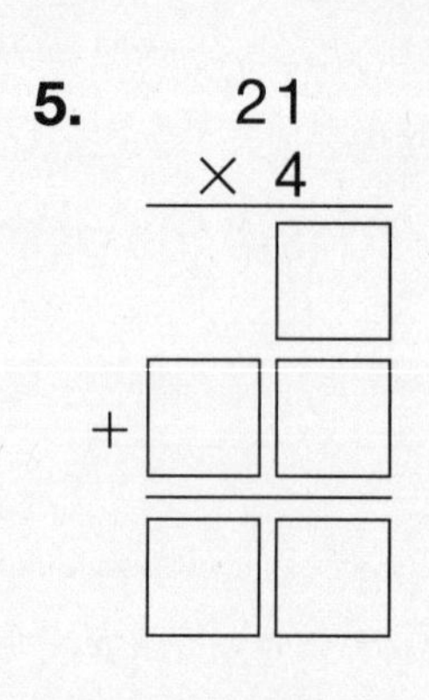

6. $4 \times 17 =$ ______ **7.** $5 \times 24 =$ ______ **8.** $3 \times 18 =$ ______

9. $5 \times 29 =$ ______ **10.** $23 \times 3 =$ ______ **11.** $21 \times 6 =$ ______

12. Clyde planted 4 rows of tomato seeds. Each row has 12 seeds. How many tomato seeds did Clyde plant? ______________

13. Find 7×22.

A 54 **B** 144 **C** 152 **D** 154

14. Write a description of an array of stickers using the product of 3×15.

____

____

____

____

Name ______________________________

Step-Up 3
Reteaching

Using an Expanded Algorithm

You can use arrays of place-value blocks to multiply.

Find the product for 4×14.

What You Show	What You Write
$4 \times 10 = 40$ $4 \times 4 = 16$ $40 + 16 = 56$	$\begin{array}{rl} 14 & \\ \times\ 4 & \\ \hline 16 & 4 \times 4 \text{ ones} \\ +40 & 4 \times 1 \text{ ten} \\ \hline 56 & \end{array}$

Draw an array for each problem to find the partial products and the product. Complete the calculation.

1. $\begin{array}{r} 16 \\ \times\ 4 \\ \hline \end{array}$

2. $\begin{array}{r} 21 \\ \times\ 6 \\ \hline \end{array}$

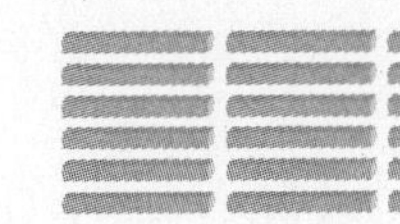

3. $\begin{array}{r} 17 \\ \times\ 6 \\ \hline \end{array}$

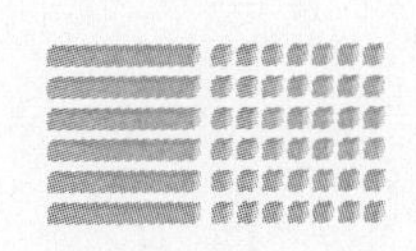

4. $\begin{array}{r} 13 \\ \times\ 2 \\ \hline \end{array}$

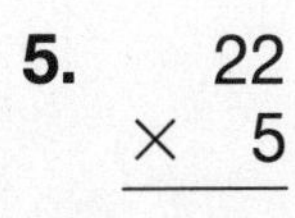

5. $\begin{array}{r} 22 \\ \times\ 5 \\ \hline \end{array}$

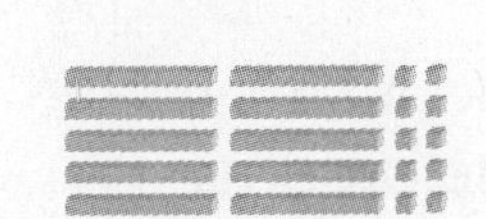

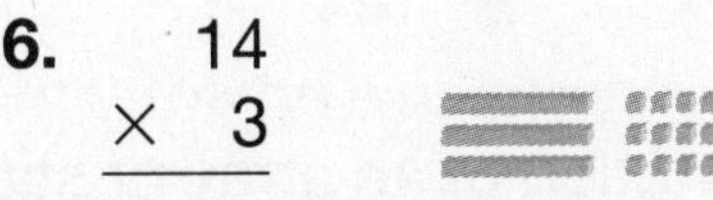

6. $\begin{array}{r} 14 \\ \times\ 3 \\ \hline \end{array}$

7. **Reason** What two simpler problems can you use to find 7×38? (Hint: Think about the tens and ones.)

____

Name ____________________

Using an Expanded Algorithm

Use the array to find the partial products. Add the partial products to find the product.

1. $\begin{array}{r} 42 \\ \times \ 6 \\ \hline \end{array}$

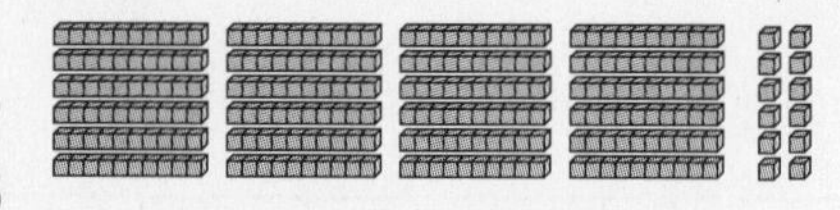

2. $\begin{array}{r} 37 \\ \times \ 7 \\ \hline \end{array}$

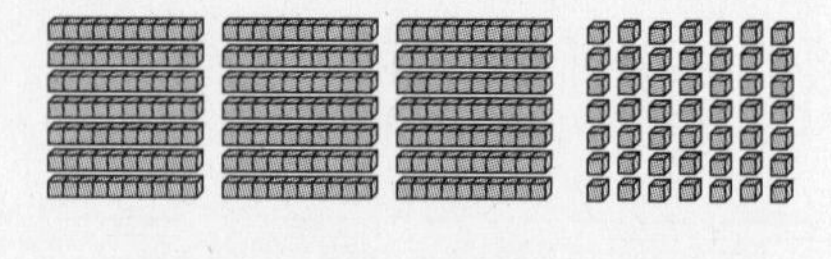

3. $\begin{array}{r} 21 \\ \times \ 4 \\ \hline \end{array}$

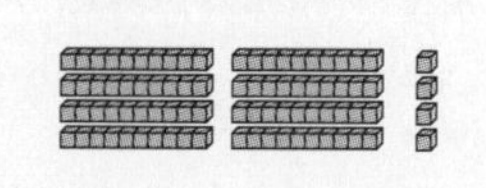

4. $\begin{array}{r} 35 \\ \times \ 4 \\ \hline \end{array}$

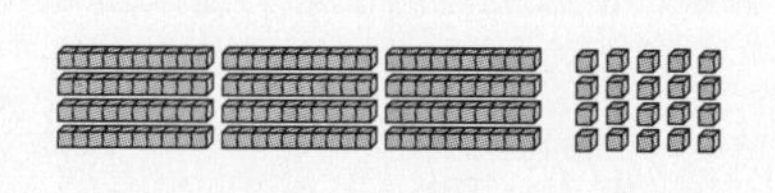

5. $8 \times 14 =$ ____________

6. $5 \times 52 =$ ____________

7. $8 \times 42 =$ ____________

8. $7 \times 26 =$ ____________

9. $4 \times 62 =$ ____________

10. $9 \times 76 =$ ____________

11. Rodney can type 62 words per minute. How many words can Rodney type in 5 minutes? ____________

12. Find 8×34.

A 172 **B** 262 **C** 272 **D** 372

13. Explain how you can use an array to find partial products and the product for 6×36.

____

____

____

Name ______________________

Step-Up 4
Reteaching

Multiplying 2-Digit by 1-Digit Numbers

Here is how to multiply a 2-digit number by a 1-digit number using paper and pencil.

Find 3 × 24.	What You **Think**	What You **Write**
Step 1 Multiply the ones. Regroup if necessary.	3 × 4 = 12 ones Regroup 12 ones as 1 ten 2 ones.	1 24 x 3 2
Step 2 Multiply the tens. Add any extra tens.	3 × 2 tens = 6 tens 6 tens + 1 ten = 7 tens	1 24 x 3 72

Is your answer reasonable?

Exact: 3 × 24 = 72

Round 24 to 20.

Estimate: 3 × 20 = 60 Since 72 is close to 60, the answer is reasonable.

Find each product. Decide if your answer is reasonable.

1. 33 × 3

2. 17 × 5

3. 24 × 7

4. 48 × 6

5. 62 × 8

6. 36 × 6

7. 88 × 5

8. 52 × 9

9. **Estimation** Use estimation to decide which has the greater product: 813 × 5 or 907 × 4. ______________

Name ______________________

Step-Up 4

Practice

Multiplying 2-Digit by 1-Digit Numbers

Find each product. Decide if your answer is reasonable.

1.
```
   1 8
×    4
   7 [ ]
```

2.
```
    2 4
×     7
[ ] 6 [ ]
```

3.
```
    5 1
×     4
[ ] 0 [ ]
```

4. 49×7

5. 48×5

6. 53×9

7. 29×6

8. $81 \times 6 =$ ______

9. $89 \times 8 =$ ______

10. $77 \times 8 =$ ______

11. $94 \times 5 =$ ______

12. Reason Kendra says that $6 \times 65 = 390$. Estimate to check Kendra's answer. Is she right? Explain.

____

____

13. A large truck uses about 18 gallons of fuel in 1 hour of work. How many gallons of fuel are needed for 7 hours of work? ______

14. Which of the following is a reasonable estimate for 8×62?

A 48 **B** 480 **C** 540 **D** 660

15. Tyrone has 6 times as many marbles as his sister Pam. Pam has 34 marbles. Louis has 202 marbles. Who has more marbles, Tyrone or Louis? Explain how you found your answer.

____

____

Name ______________________________

Step-Up 5
Reteaching

Using Models to Divide

You can use models to help you solve division problems.
The models below can help you find 59 ÷ 4.
Find 59 ÷ 4.
Estimate 60 ÷ 4 = 15.

First divide the tens.

```
    1
4 )59
  -4        4 tens
```

There is one tens block in each of 4 groups.

Now, change the tens into ones.

```
    1
4 )59
  -4        4 tens
   19       19 ones
```

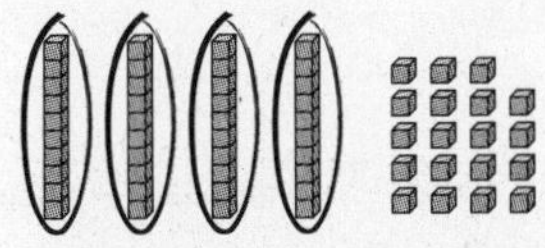

1 tens block and 9 ones blocks are equal to 19 ones blocks.

Next, divide the ones.

```
   14
4 )59
  -4        4 tens
   19       19 ones
  -16
    3
```

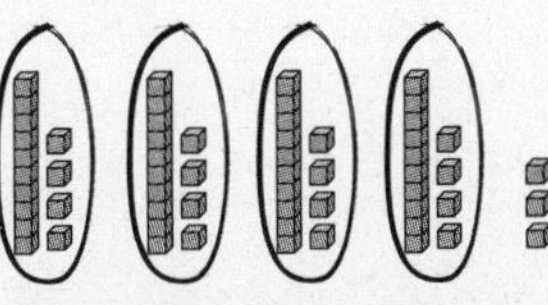

Each of the 4 groups has 1 tens block and 4 ones blocks.

Write the remainder.

```
   14 R3
4 )59
  -4        4 tens
   19       19 ones
  -16
    3  <--  remainder
```

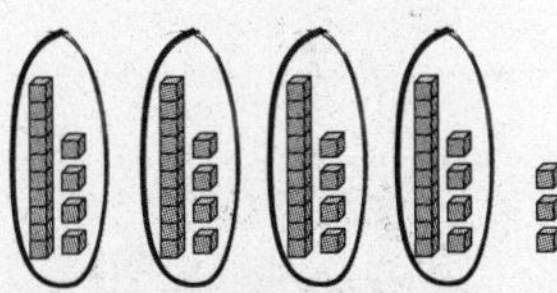

There are 3 ones blocks left.
59 ÷ 4 = 14 R3

Use the models below to help you fill in the boxes.

1. 67 ÷ ☐ = ☐ R2

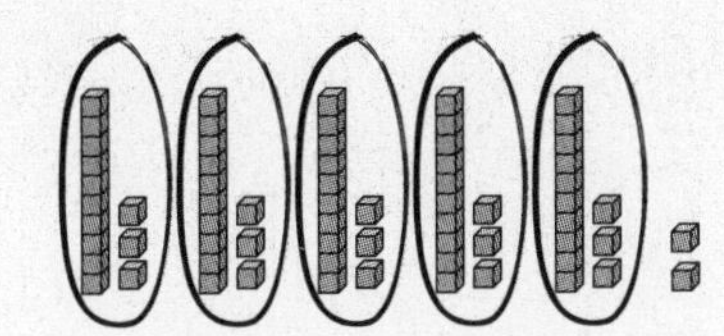

2. 85 ÷ 4 = ☐ R ☐

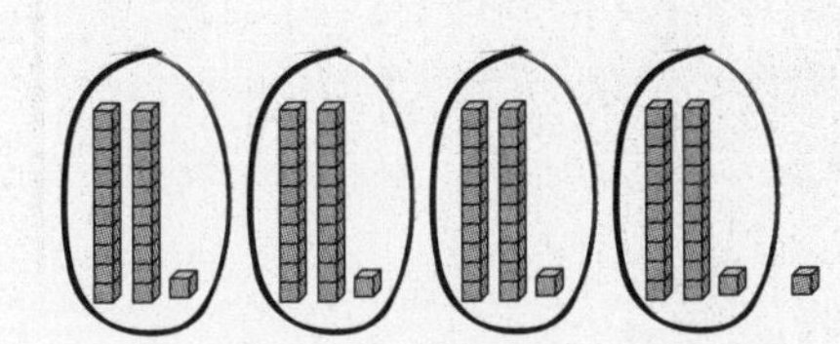

3. ☐ ÷ 6 = ☐ R5

4. 97 ÷ ☐ = ☐ R ☐

Name ______________________

Using Models to Divide

Find how many are in each group and how many are left over.

1. 72 CDs in 5 organizers

____

2. 54 stickers on 9 rolls

____

3. 62 plants in 7 rows

____

4. 98 chairs for 6 tables

____

In **5** through **8**, use the model to complete each division sentence.

5. 23 ÷ ☐ = ☐ R3

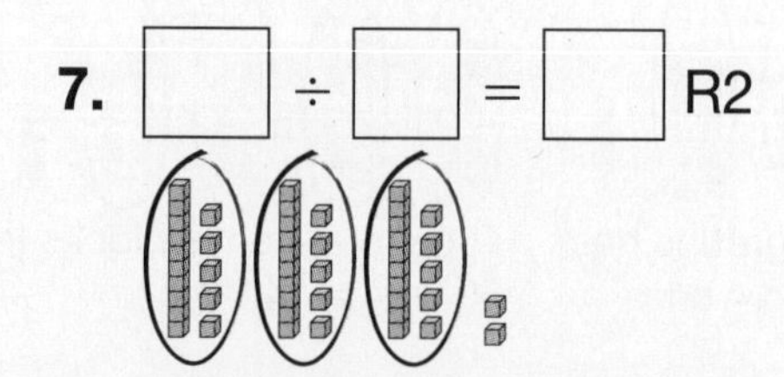

6. ☐ ÷ 7 = ☐

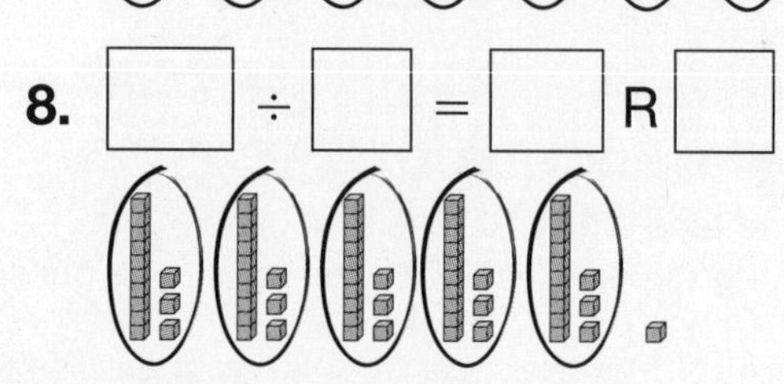

7. ☐ ÷ ☐ = ☐ R2

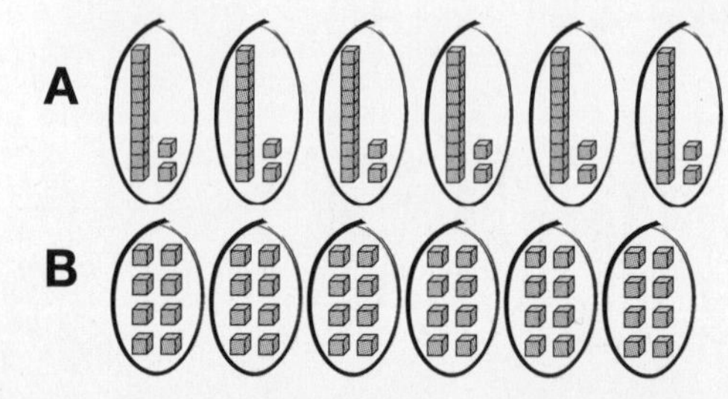

8. ☐ ÷ ☐ = ☐ R ☐

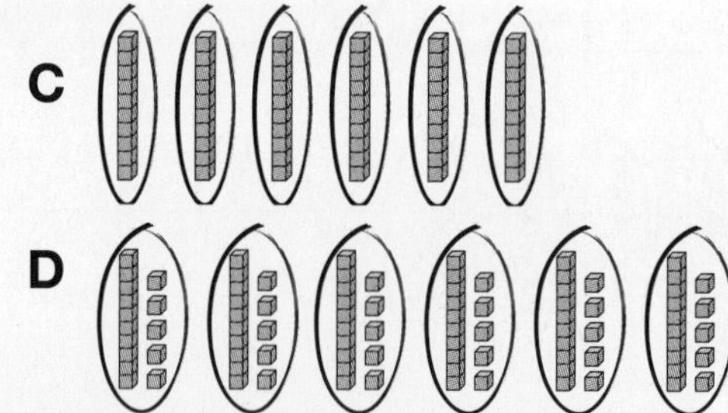

9. Corey has 90 marbles. He decides to share them with his 6 friends so they can play a game. Which of the following models shows Corey sharing his marbles?

A

C

B

D

10. At Mr. Avery's farm there are 47 cows. There are 3 people who milk the cows each day. Does each person milk the same number of cows? Use a model to help you.

____

____

Name ______________________________

Dividing 2-Digit by 1-Digit Numbers

Step-Up 6
Reteaching

Find 92 ÷ 6.

Step 1:
To decide where to place the first digit in the quotient, compare the first digit of the dividend with the divisor.

6)92

9 > 6, so the first digit in the quotient will go in the tens place.

Step 2:
Divide the tens. Use multiplication facts and compatible numbers.

Think: 6 × ? = 6
Multiply. 6 × 1 = 6
Write 1 in the tens place of the quotient.

```
  1
6)92
 -6↓
  32
```

Subtract. 9 − 6 = 3
Compare. 3 < 6
Bring down the ones.

Step 3:
Divide the ones. Use multiplication facts and compatible numbers.

Think: 6 × ? is about 32
Multiply. 6 × 5 = 30
Write 5 in the ones place of the quotient.

```
  15 R2
6)92
 -6↓
  32
 -30
   2
```

Subtract. 32 − 30 = 2
Compare. 2 < 6
There are no more digits to bring down, so 2 is the remainder.

Step 4:
Check by multiplying and then adding the remainder.

6 × 15 = 90
90 + 2 = 92

In **1** and **2** complete each division problem.

1.

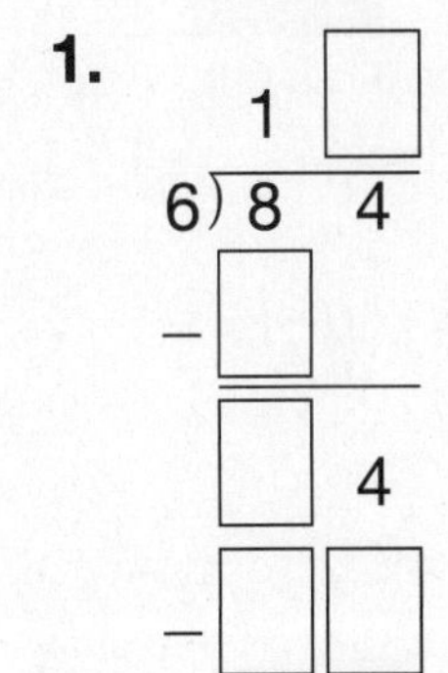

2.

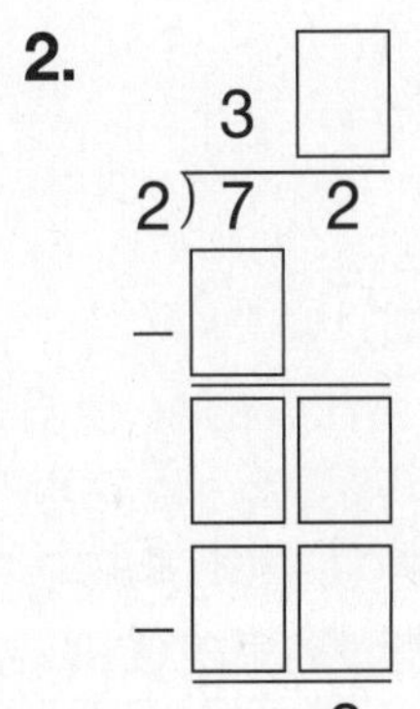

Find each quotient. Check your answers.

3. 4)86 **4.** 5)91 **5.** 3)76

Name ______________________

Step-Up 6
Practice

Dividing 2-Digit by 1-Digit Numbers

In **1** through **3**, complete each division problem.

1.

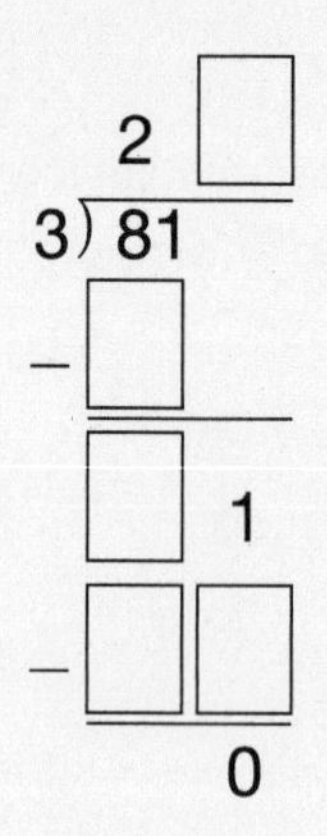

2.

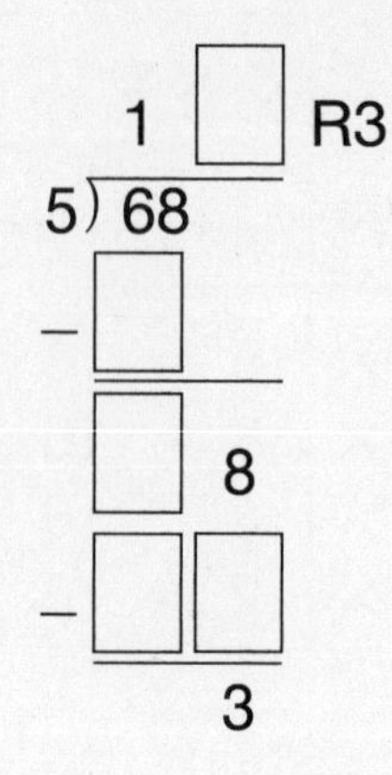

3.

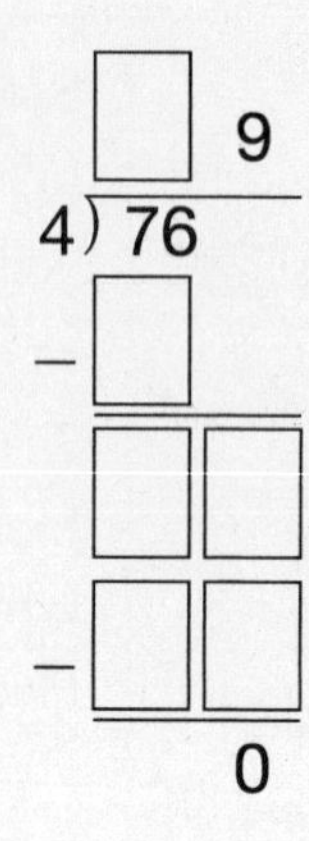

For **4** through **11**, find each quotient. Check your answers.

4. $2\overline{)89}$ **5.** $5\overline{)68}$ **6.** $4\overline{)92}$ **7.** $3\overline{)63}$

8. $6\overline{)96}$ **9.** $7\overline{)86}$ **10.** $2\overline{)92}$ **11.** $8\overline{)95}$

Mrs. Allen is planning to provide snacks for 72 fifth graders when they go on a field trip to the aquarium. Each student will receive 1 of each snack. Using the bar graph to the right, how many packages of each snack does Mrs. Allen need?

Field Trip Snacks

Snacks per Package: 0, 2, 4, 6, 8, 10, 12

Snacks: Applesauce, Fruit cup

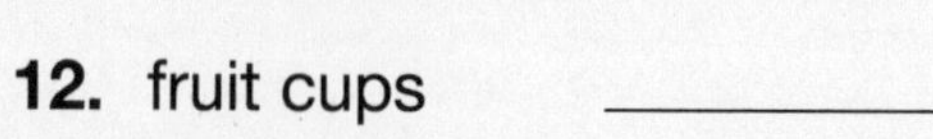

12. fruit cups ________

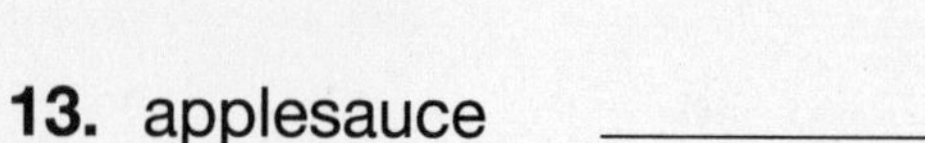

13. applesauce ________

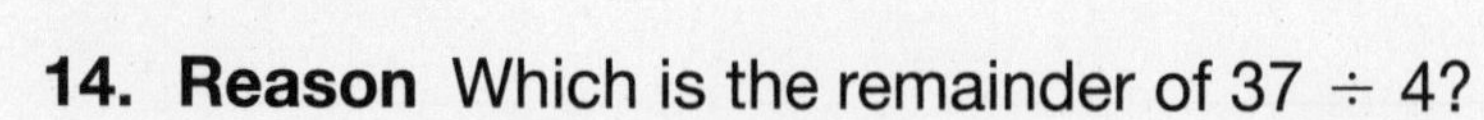

14. Reason Which is the remainder of 37 ÷ 4?

A 1 **B** 2 **C** 3 **D** 4

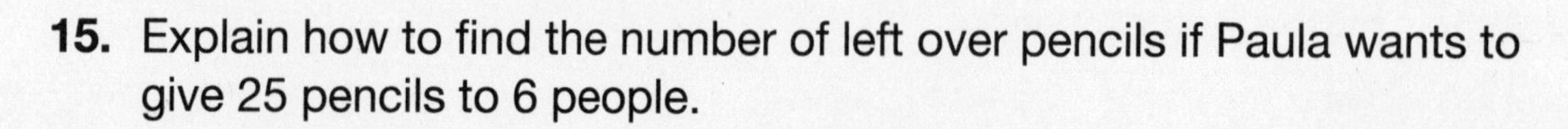

15. Explain how to find the number of left over pencils if Paula wants to give 25 pencils to 6 people.

____

____

____

Name ____________________

Factors

When multiplying two numbers, you know that both numbers are factors of the product.

Example 1

Find the factors of 24.

Factors ↓ ↓ Product ↓

$1 \times 24 = 24$
$2 \times 12 = 24$
$3 \times 8 = 24$
$4 \times 6 = 24$
$6 \times 4 = 24$
$8 \times 3 = 24$
$12 \times 2 = 24$
$24 \times 1 = 24$

Factors of 24:
1, 2, 3, 4, 6, 8, 12, and 24

Example 2

Find the factors of 16.

$1 \times 16 = 16$
$2 \times 8 = 16$
$4 \times 4 = 16$
$8 \times 2 = 16$
$16 \times 1 = 16$

Factors of 16:
1, 2, 4, 8, and 16

List all the factors of each number. Use counters to help.

1. 16 ____________

2. 21 ____________

3. 13 ____________

4. 25 ____________

5. 3 ____________

6. 18 ____________

7. Reason Look at 2×7 and 3×6. Are these numbers all factors of 18? Explain your answer.

____

____

Name ______________________________

Step-Up 7
Practice

Factors

For **1** through **12**, find all the factors of each number.

1. 28 **2.** 19 **3.** 8 **4.** 37

5. 25 **6.** 11 **7.** 36 **8.** 73

9. 15 **10.** 17 **11.** 7 **12.** 21

13. Tina buys 36 party favors to give out at a picnic. Which number will NOT let her divide the party favors evenly among the guests?

A 4 **B** 6 **C** 8 **D** 9

14. Mrs. Quinn wants to arrange her students' artwork in an array on the wall. If Mrs. Quinn has 21 pictures to hang, describe the arrays she can make.

15. Mrs. Barry has 27 watches on display at her store. Mr. Barry says that she can make only 1 row with all 27 watches. Is Mr. Barry right? Explain.

Name ______________________

Modeling Addition of Fractions

Eight friends want to see a movie. Four of them want to see a comedy. Two want to see an action movie and two want to see a science-fiction movie. What fraction of the group wants to see either a comedy or a science-fiction movie?

You can use a model to add fractions.

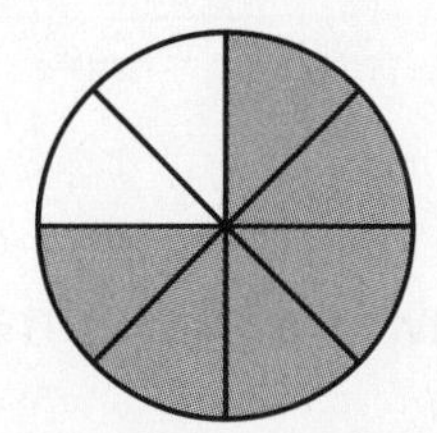

Look at the circle. It is divided into eighths, because there are eight people in the group. Each person represents $\frac{1}{8}$ of the group. Four people want to see a comedy. Shade in four of the sections to represent $\frac{4}{8}$. Two people want to see a science-fiction movie. Shade in two more sections to represent $\frac{2}{8}$. Count the number of shaded sections. There are six. So, $\frac{6}{8}$ of the group wants to see either a comedy or a science fiction movie.

$\frac{4}{8} + \frac{2}{8} = \frac{6}{8}$ Write the sum in simplest form. $\frac{6 \div 2}{8 \div 2} = \frac{3}{4}$

Find each sum. Simplify, if possible.

1. $\frac{3}{5} + \frac{1}{5}$ ______ **2.** $\frac{4}{6} + \frac{2}{6}$ ______ **3.** $\frac{3}{8} + \frac{3}{8}$ ______

4. $\frac{2}{6} + \frac{1}{6}$ ______ **5.** $\frac{2}{5} + \frac{2}{5}$ ______ **6.** $\frac{4}{10} + \frac{6}{10}$ ______

7. $\frac{5}{8} + \frac{3}{8}$ ______ **8.** $\frac{4}{10} + \frac{1}{10}$ ______ **9.** $\frac{3}{4} + \frac{1}{4}$ ______

10. $\frac{3}{10} + \frac{6}{10}$ ______ **11.** $\frac{2}{6} + \frac{1}{6} + \frac{2}{6}$ ______ **12.** $\frac{1}{12} + \frac{4}{12} + \frac{3}{12}$ ______

13. Reason We can express time as a fraction of an hour. For example, 15 minutes is $\frac{1}{4}$ hour. 30 minutes is $\frac{1}{2}$ hour. What fraction of an hour is 45 minutes? ______

Name ______________________________

Step-Up 8
Practice

Modeling Addition of Fractions

Find each sum. Simplify if possible. You may use fraction strips.

1. $\frac{2}{4} + \frac{1}{4}$ ____________ **2.** $\frac{1}{5} + \frac{1}{5}$ ____________ **3.** $\frac{3}{12} + \frac{8}{12}$ ____________

4. $\frac{2}{6} + \frac{2}{6}$ ____________ **5.** $\frac{1}{2} + \frac{1}{2}$ ____________ **6.** $\frac{3}{8} + \frac{2}{8}$ ____________

7. $\frac{3}{8} + \frac{4}{8}$ ____________ **8.** $\frac{4}{10} + \frac{1}{10}$ ____________ **9.** $\frac{1}{6} + \frac{4}{6}$ ____________

10. Model A rectangular garden is divided into 8 equal parts. Draw a picture that shows $\frac{3}{8} + \frac{3}{8} = \frac{6}{8}$, or $\frac{3}{4}$.

11. Each day, Steven walked $\frac{1}{12}$ mile more than the previous day. The first day he walked $\frac{1}{12}$, the second day he walked $\frac{2}{12}$ mile, the third day he walked $\frac{3}{12}$ mile. On which day did the sum of his walks total at least 1 complete mile?

____

12. Find the missing value in the equation.

$\frac{2}{12} + \frac{2}{12} + \frac{?}{12} = \frac{1}{2}$

A 1 **B** 2 **C** 3 **D** 4

13. There are five people sitting around the dinner table. Each person has $\frac{2}{10}$ of a pie on their plate. How much pie is left? Explain.

____

____

____

Name ______________________________

Modeling Subtraction of Fractions

Karla made a pizza and cut it into 10 slices. She ate four slices. What fraction of the pizza is left?

You can use a model to subtract fractions.

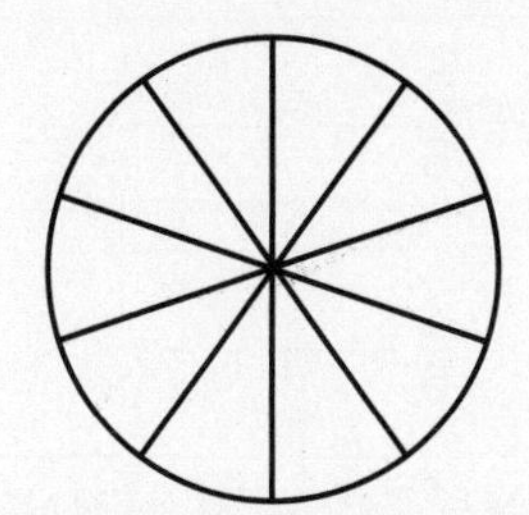

Karla's pizza is divided into 10 slices. One way to show this is $\frac{10}{10} = 1$ whole pizza. Karla ate four slices of the pizza. Cross out four of the slices. Count the number of slices left. There are 6 slices or $\frac{6}{10}$ of the pizza left.

$\frac{10}{10} - \frac{4}{10} = \frac{6}{10}$

Write the answer in simplest form, if possible.

$\frac{6 \div 2}{10 \div 2} = \frac{3}{5}$

Use fraction strips or models to subtract. Simplify if possible.

1. $\frac{4}{5} - \frac{1}{5} =$ __________ **2.** $\frac{8}{10} - \frac{3}{10} =$ __________ **3.** $\frac{4}{4} - \frac{3}{4} =$ __________

4. $\frac{6}{10} - \frac{2}{10} =$ __________ **5.** $\frac{3}{6} - \frac{2}{6} =$ __________ **6.** $\frac{11}{12} - \frac{9}{12} =$ __________

7. $\frac{6}{6} - \frac{3}{6} =$ __________ **8.** $\frac{8}{8} - \frac{6}{8} =$ __________ **9.** $\frac{15}{16} - \frac{7}{16} =$ __________

10. $\frac{9}{12} - \frac{7}{12} =$ __________ **11.** $\frac{9}{10} - \frac{7}{10} =$ __________ **12.** $\frac{10}{12} - \frac{7}{12} =$ __________

13. Find *n*.

$n - \frac{2}{6} = \frac{2}{6}$ __________

Name ____________________

Modeling Subtraction of Fractions

Use fraction strips to subtract. Simplify if possible.

1. $\frac{9}{12} - \frac{5}{12}$ ____________

2. $\frac{8}{12} - \frac{6}{12}$ ____________

3. $\frac{2}{2} - \frac{2}{2}$ ____________

4. $\frac{5}{6} - \frac{2}{6}$ ____________

5. $\frac{6}{6} - \frac{5}{6}$ ____________

6. $\frac{10}{10} - \frac{4}{10}$ ____________

7. $\frac{7}{8} - \frac{4}{8}$ ____________

8. $\frac{7}{8} - \frac{2}{8}$ ____________

9. $\frac{4}{4} - \frac{3}{4}$ ____________

10. $\frac{3}{5} - \frac{1}{5}$ ____________

11. $\frac{3}{5} - \frac{2}{5}$ ____________

12. $\frac{9}{12} - \frac{2}{12}$ ____________

13. Find $\frac{13}{16} - n$ if $n = \frac{8}{16}$. ____________

14. **Model** Harriet has $\frac{4}{5}$ tank of gas left in her car. If she needs $\frac{2}{5}$ tank to go to her friend's house and another $\frac{1}{5}$ tank to get back home, does she have enough gas? Draw a diagram and explain your answer.

____

____

15. Alicia had $\frac{9}{12}$ yard of fabric. She used $\frac{6}{12}$ for a pillow. How much fabric does she have left? Explain how you found your answer.

____

____

Name ______________________________

Fractions and Decimals

Fractions with a denominator of 10, 100, or 1,000 can be written as a decimal. Tenths, hundredths, and thousandths are written as digits to the right of the decimal point.

The shaded part is $\frac{2}{10}$.

Write it as a decimal: 0.2

Word form: two tenths

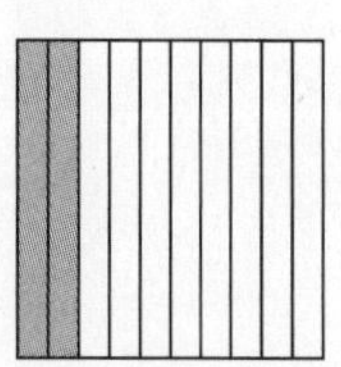

The shaded part is $\frac{13}{100}$.

Write it as a decimal: 0.13

Word form: thirteen hundredths

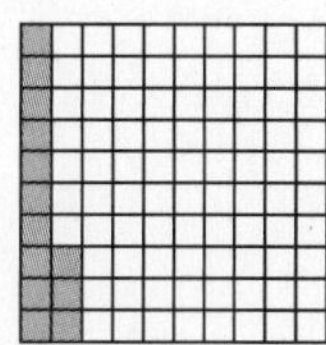

Write a fraction and a decimal to tell how much is shaded.

1. 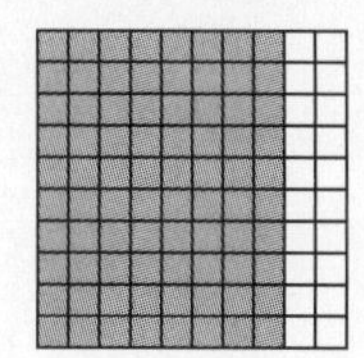

____

2. 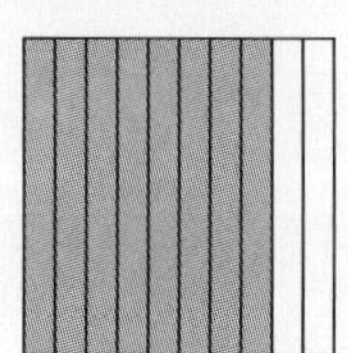

____

3. How are the two shaded grids alike? How are they different?

____

____

____

____

Write each fraction as a decimal.

4. $\frac{9}{100}$ ______________

5. $\frac{275}{1{,}000}$ ______________

6. $\frac{3}{10}$ ______________

7. $\frac{9}{10}$ ______________

Write each decimal as a fraction.

8. 0.148 ______________

9. 0.07 ______________

10. 0.40 ______________

11. 0.76 ______________

Name ______________________

Fractions and Decimals

Write a fraction and a decimal to show how much is shaded.

1. 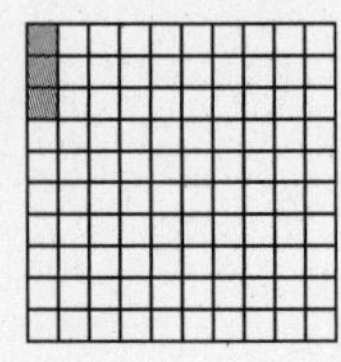

____

2. 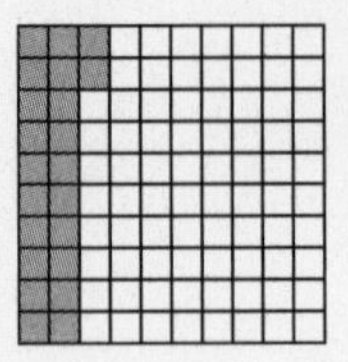

____

3. 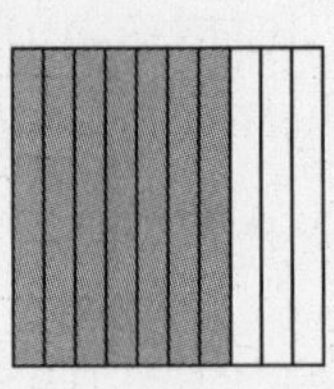

____

Draw a model that shows each decimal.

4. 0.78 **5.** 0.16 **6.** 0.3

Write each fraction as a decimal.

7. $\frac{165}{1,000}$ ________ **8.** $\frac{17}{100}$ ________ **9.** $\frac{1}{100}$ ________ **10.** $\frac{4}{10}$ ________

Write each decimal as a fraction.

11. 0.03 ________ **12.** 0.036 ________ **13.** 0.5 ________ **14.** 0.78 ________

15. In the decimal models, how many strips equal 10 small squares?

A 7 **B** 1 **C** 70 **D** 10

16. Explain the steps you would take to write $\frac{19}{100}$ as a decimal.

____

____

____